D1179644

KING ALFRED'S COLLEGE
WINCHESTER

01962 82730

WITHDRAWN
THE LIBRARY
UNIVERSITY OF
WINCHESTER

KA 0216804 9

OXFORD HISTORICAL MONOGRAPHS

EDITORS

M. H. KEEN

H. C. G. MATTHEW

A. J. NICHOLLS

P. LANGFORD

H. M. MAYR-HARTING

SIR KEITH THOMAS

VIOLENCE AND SOCIAL ORDER

East Anglia
1422–1442

PHILIPPA C. MADDERN

CLARENDON PRESS · OXFORD
1992

Oxford University Press, Walton Street, Oxford OX2 6DP

Oxford New York Toronto
Delhi Bombay Calcutta Madras Karachi
Petaling Jaya Singapore Hong Kong Tokyo
Nairobi Dar es Salaam Cape Town
Melbourne Auckland

and associated companies in
Berlin Ibadan

Oxford is a trade mark of Oxford University Press

Published in the United States
by Oxford University Press, New York

© Philippa C. Maddern 1992

All rights reserved. No part of this publication may be reproduced,
stored in a retrieval system, or transmitted, in any form or by any means,
electronic, mechanical, photocopying, recording or otherwise, without
the prior permission of Oxford University Press

British Library Cataloguing in Publication Data
Data available

Library of Congress Cataloging in Publication Data
Data available
ISBN 0–19–820235–0

Typeset by Cambridge Composing (UK) Ltd
Printed and bound in
Great Britain by Biddles Ltd,
Guildford and King's Lynn

KING ALFRED'S COLLEGE
WINCHESTER

942·
043   02/680 9

MAD

ACKNOWLEDGEMENTS

I would like to thank Dr G. L. Harriss, whose criticisms have always been enjoyable as well as illuminating. Andrew King advised me on maps of Norwich; Diana Spelman gave me hospitality as well as invaluable information on Common Pleas cases. Amanda Bevan, Laurie Kaufman, Dr E. Powell, Dr J. Retallack, Dr D. Garrioch, and Professor F. W. Kent all read parts of the first, and subsequent drafts. Dr Paul Kelly, Dr R. Kerr, Clive Payne, and Dr J. Rowett gave me good advice on the treatment of statistics. I have tried to do justice to the very constructive criticisms of all these scholars; the remaining shortcomings of the work are my own fault.

Lastly, I want to thank all the fifteen people with whom, at various times, I have shared houses in Oxford and Melbourne. I could not have finished the book without their friendship.

P.M.

CONTENTS

LIST OF FIGURES

LIST OF MAPS

LIST OF TABLES

ABBREVIATIONS

BIHR	*Bulletin of the Institute of Historical Research*
Brut	*The Brut*, p.2, ed. F. W. Brie (EETS, 136; 1908)
CCLR	*Calender of Close Rolls*
CPR	*Calender of Patent Rolls*
Dives 1	*Dives and Pauper*, i/1, ed. P. H. Barnum (EETS, 275; 1976)
Dives 2	*Dives and Pauper*, i/2, ed. P. H. Barnum (EETS, 280; 1980)
DNB	*Dictionary of National Biogaphy*
EETS	Early English Text Society
English Chronicle	*An English Chronicle of the Reigns of Richard II, Henry IV, Henry V, and Henry VI, (1377–1461)*, ed. J. S. Davies (Camden Society, OS 64; 1855)
Feudal Aids	*Feudal Aids* (6 vols.; HMSO, 1899–1920)
Gregory's Chronicle	*The Historical Collections of a Citizen of London*, ed. J. Gairdner, (Camden Society, NS 17; 1876)
Holdsworth	W. Holdsworth, *A History of English Law* (16 vols.; London, 1903–66)
IPM	*Calendarium Inquisitionum post mortem sive excaetarum*, iii and iv (London, 1821 and 1828)
N & NRO	Norwich and Norfolk Record Office
PL	*Paston Letters and Papers of the Fifteenth Century*, ed. N. Davis (2 vols.; Oxford, 1971 and 1976)
POPC	*Proceedings and Ordinances of the Privy Council of England (1386-1542)*, ed. Sir N. H. Nicholas (7 vols.; Record Commission: London, 1834–7)
Rot. Parl.	*Rotuli Parliamentorum: ut et petitiones et placita in parliamento* (6 vols.; n. p., 1832)
VCH	*The Victoria History of the Counties of England*

Note: All manuscripts quoted in the book are from the Public Record Office, unless otherwise stated. With King's Bench manuscripts, the letter 'R' before a membrane number denotes the Rex section of the roll.

I

A QUESTION OF VIOLENCE

The consideration of public order or disorder has pervaded the field of fifteenth-century English history ever since Kingsford set himself, in 1923, to rebut Denton's gloomy picture of the age.[1] The question has ramifications beyond the direct problem of whether English society in the fifteenth century disintegrated into lawlessness and chaos, and if so, why (though many writers have offered suggestions on this matter alone).[2] For example, it has been taken as axiomatic that the nature and success of late-medieval government must be measured by how far it maintained public order and in particular eliminated violent crime. Thus, J. G. Bellamy wrote that 'in the England of the later middle ages, the preservation of public order was very often the biggest problem the king had to face'; 'at heart were the crucial issues of royal authority and the structure of the state'. R. A. Griffiths concurred, 'crime was endemic, and a regime's success in controlling it may be gauged by the ability to curb its violent forms.'[3] S. J. Payling, examining 'the problem of disorder' in Nottinghamshire, 1399–1461, finds that 'the starting point must be to ask how effective was the crown in the punishment of crime, particularly among the local aristocracies.'[4] The question of the control of violent crime is thus seen as central to the study of politics in fifteenth-century England.

The views of contemporaries lend some authority to this approach.

[1] C. L. Kingsford, *Prejudice and Promise in Fifteenth-Century England* (1st edn. 1925, from the Ford Lectures of 1923; English reprints: London, 1962), 68–9.

[2] See e.g. E. F. Jacob, *The Fifteenth Century 1399–1485* (Oxford, 1961), esp. 127–8 and 490–2; J. R. Lander, *Government and Community: England 1450–1509* (London, 1980), 40–2; R. A. Griffiths, *The Reign of King Henry VI* (London 1981), chs. 7 and 20, which all emphasize the violent character of the period. A contrasting view is argued in A. Goodman, *A History of England from Edward II to James I* (London, 1977), 151–3.

[3] J. G. Bellamy, *Crime and Public Order in England in the Later Middle Ages* (London, 1973), 1; and Griffiths, *Henry VI*, 129.

[4] Simon J. Payling, 'Law and Arbitration in Nottinghamshire 1399–1461', in J. Rosenthal and C. Richmond (eds.), *People, Politics and Community in the Later Middle Ages* (Gloucester, 1987), 140–60.

They clearly felt that the repression of disorder and the establishing of peace was one measure of a good king. Rulers were bidden remember

> Howe kynges kepte neyther lawe ne peace
> Went sone awaye in many dyuerse wyse
> Without thanke of God at theyr decese.[5]

Unfortunately, however, neither contemporaries nor historians provide reliable figures of violent crime at different periods in fifteenth-century England. Nor can historians agree on which years in the century excelled in producing mayhem and disorder. E. F. Jacob associated violence and dislocation with the early years of Henry V's reign and the early 1450s. Griffiths, however, argues that the climax in aristocratic feuding came in the 1420s, while Bellamy suggests that though the period 1450–64 was particularly savage and unregenerate, it was perhaps only an exaggerated version of the whole century—the sterling reign of Henry V always excepted.[6] Partly because of this uncertainty, arguments as to the comparative success of fifteenth-century monarchs in suppressing violence and disorder have for the most part been based on their reputation for so doing, rather than on assessments of crime rates, or of numbers of convictions achieved. Thus, Powell argues that the 'measured and authoritative' tone of Henry V's superior eyre in Shropshire and Staffordshire in 1414, with its timely blend of firmness and conciliation, helped to restore public order and boost royal prestige, even though it produced few criminal convictions.[7] Conversely, on the unsatisfactory reign of Henry VI, Griffiths remarks that though the state of the evidence leads one to doubt 'whether the changing nature of crime can ever be assessed from surviving judicial records alone or with the precision that would satisfy the statistically-minded', some of Henry VI's

---

[5] *The Chronicle of John Hardyng*, ed. H. Ellis (London, 1812), 413. See also the 'Tractatus de Regimine Principum ad Regem Henricum Sextum' and 'The III Consideracions Right Necesserye to the Good Governaunce of a Prince', in *Four English Political Tracts of the Later Middle Ages*, ed. J.-P. Genet (Camden Society, 4th series, 18; 1977), 70–4 and 197; and the survey of expressions of this feeling in G. L. Harriss (ed.), *Henry V: The Practice of Kingship* (Oxford, 1985), 2, 4–6, and 11–13.

[6] Jacob, *Fifteenth Century*, 127–8 and 491; Griffiths, *Henry VI*, 129–38; Bellamy, *Crime and Public Order*, 7 and 10.

[7] E. Powell, 'The King's Bench in Shropshire and Staffordshire in 1414', in E. W. Ives and A. H. Manchester (eds.), *Law, Litigants and the Legal Profession* (London, 1983), 94–103, esp. 101–2. As G. L. Harriss put it, Henry V's 'reputation for justice became a byword and its effect was preventative' (*Henry V*, 202).

own actions and decisions, particularly his passion for pardoning and his incautious and short-sighted indulgence of courtiers, servants, and friends, had the effect of stimulating, rather than pacifying, quarrels and rivalries.[8]

Keen quotes the anxious petitions of the House of Commons for 'restful government' during Henry VI's minority, and cites as evidence of the justice of their case the 'serious rioting' and threat of 'civil war' caused by magnate quarrels. Nevertheless, as he notes acutely, 'we are talking about fears rather than facts, about a decline in public confidence and not a breakdown of government.'[9] It seems that the subject of violence is at once essential and intractable to historians of fifteenth-century English politics.

It is equally so to students of the social structures of the period. Most importantly, it has coloured the whole debate on the nature of bastard feudalism as a social force. Plummer, who coined the term, clearly felt that the system led to the widespread overturning of justice by armed magnate retainers, and that this provided incontrovertible proof of social decline and turpitude. It is no surprise to find McFarlane, in one of his brilliant defences of bastard feudalism, contradicting this view. He felt that while manipulation of justice by the powerful was common

it is difficult, at least until after 1422, to find many actual examples of simple maintenance, by which I mean attempts to overawe the court by the presence of armed men. Even during the times of worst disorder under . . . Henry VI it seems to have been unusual.[10]

Where others alleged that bastard feudalism produced 'overmighty' (and thus factious and violent) subjects, McFarlane maintained that the problem of polity was rather one of 'undermighty' kings, such as Henry VI, who could neither lead nor control the magnate community.[11] McFarlane's contribution to the debate thus involved two not entirely consistent views of the effects of violence in late-medieval English society—first, that there was less violence than had been supposed, and secondly that if violence were present, it was the mark

[8] Griffiths, *Henry VI*, 562.

[9] M. H. Keen, *England in the Later Middle Ages* (London, 1975), 420–2.

[10] C. Plummer, in his intro. to J. Fortescue, *The Governance of England* (Oxford, 1885), 15–16; K. B. McFarlane, *The Nobility of Later Medieval England* (Oxford, 1973), 114–15 (from the Ford Lectures of 1953).

[11] K. B. McFarlane, *England in the Fifteenth Century: Collected Essays* (London, 1981), esp. 41–2 and 238–9.

of an incapable king, not a flawed social system. He thus indirectly but strongly supported the notion that violence is significant mainly as a measure of the success or failure of fifteenth-century kingship. ✲

McFarlane's first contention—that violence was in fact not wide-spread in fifteenth-century England—has gained only limited accept-ance. In this period, according to Lander, the forms of legal procedure 'very often spilled over into actual violence'. Griffiths writes of the 'endemic' crime of the era. Virgoe describes the murder of Edmund Clippesby (1392) as 'an example of the violence endemic in late medieval East Anglia'.[12] Stone argues that the rate of violent crime in medieval England was around 20 per 100,000 of population per annum as opposed to 2 per 100,000 in the nineteenth century.[13] Even a critic of his position concedes that 'the trend . . . seems to be broadly correct.'[14] Recent studies of late-medieval counties remark on 'the gentry and magnate crime which constituted the greatest threat to public order', the 'competition for the limited resources of local society [which] was insistent and often violent', and the 'high level of gentry-related crime and violence'.[15] A country community which regulated its affairs largely without violence is assumed to be the exception to this rule; Saul writes of Sussex, 'It may or may not be a tribute to the effectiveness of magnate management in the county that Sussex saw so little, if any, of the violent feuding . . . that disturbed the peace of other counties in the late middle ages.'[16] It is almost as if faith in a high level of violence has become necessary to historians, to support their interpretations both of the state of government and of the nature of social structure in fifteenth-century England.

This faith survives in the face of a grave lack of evidence. Unassailable proof of a high rate of violence at any time in fifteenth-

---

[12] Lander, *Government and Community*, 40; Griffiths, *Henry VI*, 129; R. Virgoe, 'The Murder of Edmund Clippesby', *Norfolk Archaeology*, 35 (1972), 302.

[13] L. Stone, 'Interpersonal Violence in English Society 1300–1980', *Past and Present*, 101 (1983), 22–33. His source for these figures (p. 26) rather confusingly estimates these rates 'for periods ranging from several years to several decades'.

[14] J. A. Sharpe, 'The History of Violence in England; Some Observations', *Past and Present*, 108 (1985), 206.

[15] Payling, 'Law and Arbitration in Nottinghamshire', 140; P. Morgan, *War and Society in Medieval Cheshire 1277–1403* (Manchester, for the Chetham Society, 1987), 86; and S. Wright, *The Derbyshire Gentry in the Fifteenth Century* (Derbyshire Record Society, 8; 1983), 140.

[16] N. Saul, *Scenes from Provincial Life: Knightly Families in Sussex 1280–1400* (Oxford, 1986), 73.

century England is difficult to find. McFarlane was right to point out that

> If history is written from the preambles to statutes, the denunciations of moralists and reformers, and the *ex parte* statements of those engaged in litigation, there is every chance that it will be a record of bloodshed and injustice.[17]

Yet this is precisely the sort of basis on which many historians perforce rely.[18] Even these records may be less redolent of bloodthirsty deeds than is sometimes supposed. A search through that reputed repository of tales of terrible violence, the Paston Letters, yields (from the 1,288 pages of the Davis edition, spanning the years 1424 to 1518) a grand total of thirty-six references to violence involving the Pastons or their East Anglian neighbours, even including such trivialities as the injured hand sustained by John Paston II in a friendly tourney at Eltham.[19] If we add the reports of battles, executions, and piracy which reached the Pastons from the rest of Britain and France, the total rises to seventy instances; but even this is surely not unduly alarming.

Worse still, in the legal records—the very places where one would hope to find evidence of violence—the rate of allegations of violent crime is at best variable, and often very low. The records of King's Bench contain many cases which, though listed as occurring with violence, may not actually have involved force.[20] The only instances we can be cautiously certain about are the comparatively small numbers of assault, murder, mayhem, and riot; and even this figure may be inflated by false allegations.[21] Kimball's edition of the Shropshire peace rolls for 1400–1414 shows only eighty-five allegations of violence out of 240, plus eight doubtful cases (of rape and breaking and entering).[22] This must, however, be compared with the proceedings of the superior eyre in Shropshire and Staffordshire in 1414, where indictments of homicides from coroners' juries, peace sessions, and *coram rege* totalled 500 for each county, or more than half the

[17] McFarlane, *Nobility*, 115.
[18] See e.g. Bellamy, *Crime and Public Order*, 4–6; Griffiths, *Henry VI*, 144–54 and 567; Keen, *England in the Later Middle Ages*, 420–1.
[19] *Paston Letters and Papers of the Fifteenth Century*, ed. N. Davis (2 vols.; Oxford, 1971 and 1976), i. 396 (hereinafter referred to as *PL*).
[20] See Table 2.1 and Ch. 2.
[21] Compare Tables 2.1 and 2.3, and see Ch. 2.
[22] E. Kimball (ed.), *The Shropshire Peace Roll, 1400–1414* (Shrewsbury, 1959), 35–9. See Ch. 3 for a discussion of the doubtful nature of the charge of rape in the 15th cent.

indictments for all offences.[23] On the other hand, cases on the East Anglian gaol delivery files, are almost overwhelmingly concerned with non-violent crime.[24] Similarly, Putnam set herself to classify the cases recorded in peace sessions of the fourteenth and fifteenth centuries. The resulting table categorizes cases into felonies, trespasses, and economic offences. Making the cautious assumption that most cases of serious violence would fall among the felonies, and allowing that economic offences were non-violent, it is obvious that there is no consistent proportion of violent to non-violent crimes. One Norfolk roll has 256 economic offences to seventy-one felonies; on the other hand, a Somerset record gives sixty-two felonies and no economic offences. In between these two extremes fall an incredible range of ratios of felony to economic offences. All that can be deduced from this evidence is that either there was an infinite variety of crime and violence rates within England in the late Middle Ages, or that there was an infinite variety in the ways in which peace sessions recorded, and dealt with, local crime.[25]

Yet evidence of violence in the community is important to other major debates in the field; for instance, the origins of the Wars of the Roses. Storey's thesis that the wars were an outcome of baronial factionalism deriving from 'the corruption of the legal system in Henry VI's reign, and the growing scale and intensity of private feuds' has become a classic, duly echoed in succeeding texts.[26] 'The origin of the wars themselves', declares Goodman, 'lay in Henry VI's inability in the 1440's to contain the spread of local faction and violence.'[27] This argument reinforces the notion that Henry VI's reign can be tried and proved wanting by the evidence of a rise in violence and disorder. Furthermore, it implies, as Storey himself pointed out in 1970, that historians should examine more closely the motives and machinations

---

[23] Powell, 'The King's Bench', 97; however, these indictments covered at least a 15-year period, and many of the indictments at peace sessions or *coram rege* were duplicates of those on coroners' rolls.

[24] See Table 2.6.

[25] B. H. Putnam (ed.), *Proceedings before the Justices of the Peace in the Fourteenth and Fifteenth Centuries* (London, 1938), intro., p. cxiii.

[26] R. L. Storey, *The End of the House of Lancaster* (London, 1966; paperback edn. Gloucester, 1986) esp. 191–3. My arguments, of course, relate only to the earlier period covered in Storey's work.

[27] A. Goodman, *The Wars of the Roses* (London, 1981), 220; cf. also D. R. Cook *Lancastrians and Yorkists: The Wars of the Roses* (Seminar Studies in History; London, 1984), 8.

of the provincial élites (whose violent feuds spawned the wars) rather than the policies and ambitions of the rulers at the centre.[28] This view is surely responsible in part for the rise of provincial history as a genre in late-medieval English historiography. Studies of the local communities of late-medieval England which have appeared over the last decade often include an examination of the contribution of bastard feudalism to maintenance, lawlessness, and disorder.[29]

Why, then, is evidence for this vital element in such plausible arguments so hard to find? I suggest it is because two erroneous assumptions have been made about violence and disorder.

The first is that violence—in any society—is clearly definable. The second is that it is unquestionably disruptive and destabilizing. The first view apparently underpins Bellamy's belief that contemporary commentators can be taken at face value when they describe the effects of riots, robberies, maintenance, and disorder in the kingdom.[30] It is also evident in the choice of metaphors historians employ in dsscribing late-medieval violence. To speak of violence as 'endemic', for instance, is to portray it as a disease, as unmistakable and deadly as an outbreak of plague.[31]

These views of violence in turn sustain three assumptions; that theoretically (if the sources existed and were rigorously analysed) we could know for certain whether rates of violence were going up or down at any one point in the century; that even where the sources are scanty or opaque, an estimate of the violence or crime rate may be made; and that either calculation will show whether fifteenth-century England was a characteristically violent, disordered, and badly governed society.

Clearly, however, there are both practical and theoretical difficulties

---

[28] R. Storey, 'Lincolnshire and the Wars of the Roses', *Nottingham Medieval Studies*, 14 (1970), 82.

[29] See esp. M. C. Carpenter, 'Political Society in Warwickshire, c.1401–1472', Ph.D. thesis (Cambridge, 1976) 107–58; and A. Herbert, 'Herefordshire, 1413–1461: Some Aspects of Society and Public Order' and M. Cherry, 'The Struggle for Power in Mid-Fifteenth-Century Devonshire', both in the significantly titled *Patronage, the Crown and the Provinces in Later Medieval England*, ed. R. A. Griffiths (Gloucester, 1981). Also N. Saul, *Knights and Esquires: The Gloucestershire Gentry in the Fourteenth Century* (Oxford, 1981), esp. ch. 5, and id., *Scenes from Provincial Life*, Ch. 3; Morgan, *War and Society in Medieval Cheshire*; and Wright, *Derbyshire Gentry*, ch. 9. However it is noteworthy that M. Bennett's *Community, Class and Careerism*, (Cambridge, 1983) largely divorces the issues of provincial history and public order.

[30] Bellamy, *Crime and Public Order*, 4–9.

[31] See above, n. 12.

in quantifying violence. The evident imperfections of the source materials tend to focus our attention first on the practical problems. Historians find that records of crime have disappeared, that cases must be traced through a plethora of different courts and jurisdictions, that demographic evidence is so scanty and unreliable that population estimates (and hence crime rates) are rarely convincing.[32] This is painfully obvious even when, as in Hammer's study of Oxford homicides for 1342–8, the situation seems to favour the historian. Here, by good fortune, a run of coroners' rolls has survived; and Hammer's estimate of the sample population—about 5,500—is rendered more convincing by the happy chance that the cases are confined to one city, and the dates allow the use of Russell's calculations of population on the 1377 poll-tax returns.[33] But these advantages do not outweigh the difficulties of the exercise. As soon as Hammer, for comparative purposes, sets about constructing a crime rate, the problems emerge. Modern homicide rates are calculated as n per 100,000 of population per anum. Put into these terms, Hammer's figures, precisely because they are so small, are gravely imprecise; one death more or less per year would send the homicide rate up or down by 18 per 100,000 (about the equivalent of the highest incidences he quotes of homicide in the modern USA). This undermines the whole purpose of comparing quantities of violence in medieval and modern times.[34] Furthermore, the number of homicides per year in Oxford varied between two and nine, with the smaller numbers at each end of the time span. Hammer concludes that the 1342 and 1348 records may be incomplete; but it is equally possible that 1342–8 saw a miniature crime wave, and that the figures are untypical of homicide rates in Oxford over the century. It is impossible to assess from these figures the level of crime normal to fourteenth-century Oxford, let

[32] See B. A. Hanawalt, *Crime and Conflict in English Communities, 1300–1348* (Cambridge, Mass., 1979), 12–18 for a survey of these problems; also the comments, still very pertinent, of M. Postan in his *Medieval Economy and Society*, Pelican edn. (Harmondsworth, 1975), 31–4. Even the figures on which to base an estimate of the population of individual communities are rare in the medieval period, see L. R. Poos, 'Population Turnover in Medieval Essex: The Evidence of some Early-Fourteenth-Century Tithing Lists', in L. Bonfield, R. M. Smith, and K. Wrightson (eds.), *The World We Have Gained* (Oxford, 1986), 3–10.

[33] C. I. Hammer, 'Patterns of Homicide in a Medieval University Town: Fourteenth-Century Oxford', *Past and Present*, 78 (1978), 3–23.

[34] It also reflects on Stone's argument (see above, n. 13); one of Stone's points of reference is Hammer's calculation.

alone to the late-medieval period as a whole; particularly in view of the wildly varying crime rates from other sources, dates, and places.[35] These difficulties are typical of those facing historians of crime in the late-medieval period.

Yet the practical problems of quantifying violence and deducing its effects pale into insignificance beside the theoretical pitfalls. These affect the very nature of the surviving evidence. As Hanawalt rightly points out, the apparent level of crime may fluctuate because of local and temporal variations in the enthusiasm, skill, and probity of law-enforcers; or may be misleading because the records show indictments rather than convictions; and worst of all, is almost certainly too small because

Many cases are never reported because they are settled out of court, because they are never detected, because they are concealed through personal concern for the culprit or through failure of witnesses to report a felony, or because the suspect has disappeared.[36]

All these problems arise directly because violence and crime are slippery customers to find and identify. A brief glance at the standard dictionary definitions of violence—the use of (mainly physical) power to destructive ends, or the intensity, severity, excess, or vehemence of influence, feeling, or action—shows that the categorization of any individual event as violent is ultimately dependent on the judgement of observers. They must determine according to their own ethical and cultural standards whether the ends of the power used in any case were actually destructive, and exactly how intense, severe, or excessive an action must be before it is violent.[37] Violence, in other words, is in the eye of the beholder. Moreover, the description of an act as violent is not a neutral one; it involves the ascription of meaning and purpose, ethical and otherwise, to the act. Thus, when, let us say, an assault occurred in late-medieval England, those who knew of it had to decide

---

[35] See above, nn. 20–5.

[36] Hanawalt, *Crime and Conflict*, 13–17. Hanawalt claims to have circumvented most of these problems; I doubt whether some of her assumptions (such as that policies of reform of law-keeping invariably acted within 1 or 2 years of implementation, or that the discrepancy between allegation and crime was statistically insignificant—pp. 281 and 14) are justifiable. In connection with the problem of unreported crime, Sharpe has discovered petitions on domestic violence, made to justices of the peace in 17th-cent. England, which never reached the lawcourts; even this disquieting evidence is lacking for the 15th cent. See J. A. Sharpe, 'Domestic Homicide in Early Modern England', *Historical Journal*, 24 (1981), 31.

[37] These definitions summarize those in the *OED*.

whether it did, or did not, fall into their categories of culpable violence (wife- and servant-beating often did not);[38] and whether it was, or was not, an affair for the courts to deal with.[39] The officers of the courts might or might not treat the matter as one requiring the utmost vigilance and devotion to duty; and jurors might hesitate to rate the offence (if it existed) as punishable.[40] At each of these stages, the decisions of contemporaries as to the violence or criminality of the event affected the record that survives, leading perhaps to suppression of significant material, to indictments which only vaguely represent the events, to inconclusive allegations, or to misleading verdicts. All this affects the definition of crime in legal records whose formality and official standing might seem to promise some standardization and objectivity. Clearly, in the case of less institutionalized accounts of general violence (chronicles, letters, petitions) the definitions might be even more idiosyncratic.

The definition of violence being by nature subjective, it is no surprise to find that different cultures define and describe violence in different ways. What one society classifies as violent, another may not. Thus, in late-medieval England, a priest's neglect of his parishioners' souls, by faulty teaching or bad example, could be regarded as spiritual murder and reprobated—along with literal physical slaughter—under the commandment 'Thou shalt not kill'.[41] This identification of corporeal and spiritual violence is alien to modern Western thought. Again, two cultures may agree in defining an act as violent, but put a widely differing moral construction on it. Thus Foxe, writing in sixteenth-century Protestant mode of a martyr whose 'speech was taken away by violence of the flame', evidently considered this execution by fire to be wickedly unjust.[42] Yet medieval executioners of

---

[38] See Ch. 3. It is worth noting that even 'crime' is not a neutral and invariable term; Elton and Post both point out that it was not a category favoured by pre-modern people, who tended instead to classify actions as felony, trespass, or sin. See Elton's intro. to J. S. Cockburn (ed.), *Crime in England 1550–1800* (London, 1977), esp. 2–6; and J. B. Post, 'Criminals and the Law in the Reign of Richard II with Special Reference to Hampshire', D. Phil. thesis (Oxford, 1976), 12–13.

[39] Sharpe quotes evidence to suggest that in the 18th cent. the question of whether to report a possible homicide to the coroner could be decided on a purely local level ('History of Violence', 210–11).

[40] See e.g. the work of T. A. Green on the discrepancies between juries' accounts of homicides before coroners and before the courts ('Societal Concepts of Criminal Liability for Homicide in Medieval England', *Speculum*, 47 (1972), 675–82); and Ch. 4.

[41] See Ch. 3, n. 1.

[42] John Foxe, *The Acts and Monuments*, ed. J. Pratt (8 vols.; London, 1877), vii. 115.

heretics, though they might recognize the fire as violent, presumably thought of it as a cleansing and legitimate flame.[43]

This should lead us, as historians, to be cautious both about categorizing acts in the Middle Ages as violent or non-violent, and about assigning meaning to them. Instead of trying to establish a violence or crime rate for the Middle Ages according to our own alien categories, it is probably more useful to attempt to reconstruct medieval notions of violence and its role in medieval society. It is, after all, possible to find some common ground between medieval and modern definitions of violence. In this study, for instance, I have confined my attention largely to actions against persons—cases of assault, murder, and mayhem, for example—which apparently fall into both medieval and modern categories of violence.

These acts do not, however, necessarily have the same meaning for medieval and modern people. One anachronistic viewpoint to which twentieth-century commentators are particularly prone is the assumption that violence can be confined to illegal, disruptive, and destabilizing actions.[44] President Johnson, for instance, was trying to appeal to a mass recognition of violence as irregular, disruptive, and intolerable when he proclaimed in a speech of 1968, 'My fellow citizens, we cannot . . . tolerate the sway of violent men among us . . . We cannot sanction the appeal to violence—no matter what its cause, no matter what the grievance from which it springs.'[45] According to his own categories, Johnson could properly exclude from consideration the actions of his army chiefs, then engaged in dropping napalm on Vietnam—legal warfare, in his terms, was not violent. Similarly, N. Z. Davis, in her analysis of sixteenth-century religious riots in France, was concerned to distinguish riot from the other forms of violent action so prevalent in early-modern Europe:

By religious riot I mean as a preliminary definition, any violent action, . . . undertaken against religious targets by people who are not acting *officially and formally* as agents of political and ecclesiastical authority.[46]

This leads her to propose that

---

[43] See Ch. 4.

[44] The *OED* gives this distinction as obsolete (see under 'violent' (3) and 'violently' (1)); but I doubt that it was applied in the late-medieval period (see below, n. 48).

[45] Quoted in J. H. Skolnick 'Interpreting Violence', *Journal of Interdisciplinary History*, 3: 1 (1972), 177.

[46] N. Z. Davis, 'The Rites of Violence: Religious Riot in Sixteenth-Century France', *Past and Present*, 59 (1973), 52.

The violence of the religious riot is distinguished, at least in principle, from the action of political authorities, who can legally silenc :, humiliate, demolish, punish, torture and execute; and also from the action of soldiers, who at certain times and places can legally kill and destroy.[47]

The separation of historical acts into the categories of legal force and illegal violence enables her to focus on the significance of the behaviour of the crowd rather than the authorities; but it involves some anachronistic thinking. Not all medieval violence was seen as illegal or destabilizing. The author of the official account of Edward IV's return to his kingdom in 1471 had no other apparent object towards the king than to praise him. Yet he includes the following description of the king in battle:

the Kynge, trusting verely in God's helpe, owr blessyd ladyes, and Seynt George, toke to hym great hardies and corage ... wherethrwghe ... he mannly, vigorowsly, and valliantly assayled them; [and] with great violence, bett and bare down afore hym all that stode in hys way.[48]

For this medieval writer, 'great violence' was on the side of the angels; peace, justice, and order were restored, not destroyed, by it. As Kaeuper points out, it is a misleading modern trend to associate violence with a criminal underworld. He shows that medieval English kings were consistently ambivalent about chivalric violence. Though kings might attempt to license, control, or ban some forms of knightly behaviour, 'a fourteenth-century ruler could love tournaments, and fight in them himself'.[49]

It is too simple, then, to compare violence to a virus, whose presence in a society invariably indicates social or political malaise and disorder. Violence appears, rather, in purposive and culturally determined actions; even in a society's commitment (conscious or unconscious) to a certain way of life. The purposes of such actions may range from the revolutionary to the pacificatory. Their effects may be (among others) to destabilize society, provide an outlet for tension, liberate the oppressed, or maintain the powerful. Violence is ambiguous. All its

[47] Ibid.; cf. also J. Ellul, *Violence: Reflections from a Christian Perspective*, tr. C. G. Kings (London, 1970), 3–5 and 84–5.

[48] *Historie of the Arrivall of Edward IV*, ed. J. Bruce (Camden Society, OS 1; 1838), 19–20. For the aims and distribution of the text, see J. A. F. Thomson, '"The Arrival of Edward IV"—the Development of the Text', *Speculum*, 46 (1971), 84–93.

[49] R. W. Kaeuper, *War, Justice and Public Order: England and France in the Later Middle Ages* (Oxford, 1988), 184–208 (quote from p. 192).

significance depends on the motives of the actors, and the context within which they act.

Some historians are now beginning to elucidate these aspects of medieval violence. Keen, for instance, evokes the ethic of chivalric violence which simultaneously sustained the perfect knight (the efficient and compassionate arm of the just prince) and gave rise to the banditry and oppression of errant mercenaries. Two forms of violence sprang from one set of social circumstances, with opposite effects. Contemporaries, though they deplored the unfortunate side-effect, sustained 'no real loss of confidence in chivalrous values'.[50] The values of chivalry, which stressed physical force and individualistic prowess in war were, Keen considers, integral to the social and political structures and processes of the late Middle Ages—but subtly, ambiguously, involving an unavoidable internal dialectic between order and disorder. Ruggiero, in his study of violence in early Renaissance Venice, emphasizes the necessity of examining not only crimes, but also the rituals of legal violence (for example public executions), which sustained Venice's particular cultural system.[51] Davis, examining religious riots in sixteenth-century France, concludes that the crowds might themselves take on clerical or magisterial roles—sometimes running mock trials that led to real executions.[52] The value of such studies lies less in their production of universal proofs (bad government causes violence, which destabilizes society), than in their power to clarify and make comprehensible the motives of medieval people, the systems and structures within which they acted, and the complex and multifarious functions of violence within those structures.[53]

This understanding of the ambiguities and complexities of wilful violence has important implications for analysing the relationship between violence, law, society, and politics in late-medieval England. Rosenthal, for instance, speaks of late-medieval violence in England as 'not necessarily either inchoate or irrational' and 'likely to be regulated and controlled' by social pressure. This leads him to modify the orthodox view of the links between bad government, bastard feudalism, and violence:

[50] M. Keen, *Chivalry* (New Haven, Conn., 1984), 224–37.
[51] Guido Ruggiero, *Violence in Early Renaissance Venice* (New Brunswick, NJ, 1980), esp. 1–2, 48–9, and 180–2.
[52] Davis, 'Rites of Violence', 90–1 and 61–5.
[53] See R. Harré and P. Secord, *The Explanation of Social Behaviour* (Oxford, 1972), Ch. 2. for a theoretical exposition of this type of understanding of social behaviour.

The breakdown of public order and of royal government in the fifteenth century is an arresting phenomenon, but it had two concomitants; the resort to private violence, *and* the resort to private peace-making.[54]

In a recent illuminating study, Kaeuper has shown that in both England and France in the later Middle Ages, the extension of royal power may be linked as much to increasing royal patronage and control of such semi-legitimate forms of violence as tournaments and private wars, as to royal suppression of violent crime.[55] Increasingly, too, historians are examining the status of violence as a form of litigation by other means.[56] This tends to break down the distinctions between orderly law and disorderly violence.

Nevertheless, as the references cited at the start of this chapter show, the mode of explanation which sees violence as a monolithic and unambiguously destabilizing phenomenon arising from some adventitious factor in the social or political system is still flourishing in English history.[57] There is scope for many more refined and extended studies on the role of violence in late-medieval English society.

Indeed, modifications of the old orthodoxy on law, order, and violence, have so far come about largely through new understandings of the legal, rather than the violent, aspect of the question. Recent studies of fifteenth-century law seem to show that its role in the control of violence and crime is by no means as simple as has often been assumed. The theory that the success of a royal government can be judged by its control of violent crime rests on the assumptions that royal law was the principal agent of public order in late-medieval England, and that it almost invariably functioned to repress, rather than give rise to, violent crime. Writers working from a number of viewpoints have produced evidence to suggest that these assumptions need revision.

It is now clear that royal justice was not the only means of

---

[54] J. Rosenthal, 'Feuds and Private Peace-making: A Fifteenth-Century Example', *Nottingham Medieval Studies*, 14 (1970), 84.

[55] Kaeuper, *War, Justice and Public Order*, esp. Chs. 2 and 3.

[56] See e.g. Bennett, *Community, Class and Careerism*, 220–3; and B. McLane, 'A Case Study of Violence and Litigation in the Early Fourteenth Century: The Disputes of Robert Godsfield of Sutton-Le-Marsh', *Nottingham Medieval Studies*, 28 (1984), 22–44. The writer cautiously refuses to speculate on how typical were these disputes, 'with their combined use of violent self-help and litigation' (p. 43).

[57] See above, nn. 12–15; also Hanawalt, *Crime and Conflict*, 265.

controlling disorder in late-medieval England. Indeed, as Harriss remarks, it was partly because the crown relied on the nobility and gentry in the provinces to enforce the law, that the king's justice had to be exemplary and conciliatory.[58] Furthermore, arbitration was often used to defuse potentially violent and disruptive disputes.[59] Arbitrements produced settlements apparently aimed at pacifying all parties rather than punishing one, and in this sense differed radically from the law. Yet law and arbitrement also worked harmoniously together. Arbitrements could be pleaded in the common-law courts as a bar to further legal action; and legal remedies could enforce the provisions of arbitration.[60] Litigants recognized the benefits of using both law and arbitration; unwilling antagonists might be persuaded to the negotiating table by threats of expensive lawsuits.[61] The Ladbroke manor dispute is an excellent example of a quarrel which made extensive use of various forums, common law and otherwise; it was heard in Common Pleas, King's Bench, assizes, and Chancery, as well as before several magnate councils and the king's council.[62]

This necessarily implies that public order was not the sole responsibility of royal courts and officials. Arbitrements were operated by the gentry and magnates—the very groups hitherto accused of fomenting violence and disorder! Indeed, Rawcliffe believes that baronial councils, with their staff of legal experts, helped to popularize arbitrations

---

[58] Harriss (ed.), *Henry V*, 202.

[59] Rosenthal, 'Feuds and Private Peace-making'; see also two valuable articles by E. Powell, 'Arbitration and the Law in England in the Late Middle Ages', *Transactions of the Royal Historical Society*, 5th series, 33 (1983), esp. 52–3, and 'Settlement of Disputes by Arbitration in Fifteenth-Century England', *Law and History Review*, 2 (1984), 21–43; J. B. Post 'Equitable Resorts before 1450', in E. W. Ives and A. H. Manchester (eds.), *Law, Litigants and the Legal Profession* (London, 1983), 68–79; and C. Rawcliffe, 'The Great Lord as Peacekeeper: Arbitration by English Noblemen and their Councils in the Later Middle Ages', in J. A. Guy and H. G. Beale (eds.), *Law and Social Change in British History* (London, 1984), 34–54.

[60] See e.g. KB 27 678 m 72^d (*Aubre* v. *Edrycche*), KB 27 658 m 35^d (*Beneregge* v. *Clerk*), KB 27 698 m 83^r (*Felowes* v. *Dewy*) and KB 27 732 m 60 and following (*Thomas Bachecroft* v. *John Bachecroft*). In the last case, the jury gave a verdict on the exact terms of the arbitrement. See also Powell, 'Arbitration and the Law', 56 and 63–6. This seems to negate Griffiths's argument that arbitrements actually contributed to public disorder by undermining confidence in the lawcourts (*Henry VI*, 137).

[61] Powell, 'Settlement of Disputes by Arbitration', 39–41; and Rawcliffe, 'The Great Lord as Peacekeeper', 35.

[62] J. B. Post (ed.) 'Courts, Councils and Arbitrators in the Ladbroke Manor Dispute, 1382–1400', in R. F. Hunnisett and J. B. Post (eds.), *Medieval Legal Records Edited in Memory of C. A. F. Meekings* (London, 1978), 289–339, esp. 290.

by the nobility.[63] Wright found that in Derbyshire, 'royal justice was superimposed' on a local system of collective dispute-settlement.[64] Carpenter notes incisively that English medieval landowners tended to hold ambivalent views about the centralized law establishment. Though they might complain righteously in parliament of the crown's weakness in failing to prevent unjust maintenance and violence, in the counties they wanted to oversee the legal affairs of their own local community, adjusting the law to its needs (or their own).[65] It seems that public order was thought to be as much a provincial as a royal responsibility.

To be sure, not all local arbitrations were successful; we shall see in Chapter 6 how the efforts of the duke of Suffolk to settle a political dispute in Norwich produced more rancour than harmony, and we know of cases where failed, or partisan, arbitrements led directly to violent reprisals.[66] But recent studies of royal justice show that it too did not invariably aim to punish violent crime; and could itself become a tool in violent local disputes. Thus, Powell argues that the apparent ineffectiveness of the 1414–15 superior eyre in punishing malefactors is misleading, since the court aimed rather to resolve quarrels and reconcile peace-breakers to one another and to the government.[67] Kaeuper, studying the effect of the king's courts in curbing violence, concludes that royal commissions of oyer and terminer could actually become instruments in violent quarrels.[68]

In short, the role of law in the maintenance of public order has been shown to be infinitely more various than the old orthodoxy supposed. The law was as much a tool of local politics as an instrument of royal power; and whether in the provinces, or in the king's hand, it might either provoke or suppress violence. The whole issue of public order now transcends the questions of deciding the relative efficiency of medieval kings, or the extent of magnates' depravity. It is clear that the medieval concept of public order was in some ways very different

[63] Rawcliffe, 'The Great Lord as Peacekeeper', 37.

[64] Wright, *Derbyshire Gentry*, 119.

[65] C. Carpenter, 'Law, Justice and Landowners in Late Medieval England', *Law and History Review*, 1 (1983), 205–37, esp. 214–19.

[66] See e.g. Payling's account of the dispute between Mering and Tuxford in Nottinghamshire ('Law and Arbitration in Nottinghamshire', esp. 141–2); and Wright, *Derbyshire Gentry* 123–4.

[67] Powell, 'The King's Bench', 100–3.

[68] R. W. Kaeuper, 'Law and Order in Fourteenth-Century England: The Evidence of Special Commissions of Oyer and Terminer', *Speculum*, 54 (1979), esp. 755–66.

from our own; and medieval ways of achieving order were complex and multifarious. As a result of recent research, we now have some idea of the distinctive ways in which fifteenth-century English people used, and regarded, the law. But much work remains to be done on their use and views of violence.

Is it true, for instance, that violence indicates a society destabilized by war? Some authors would say yes, on the grounds that war put a strain on the nation's resources, habituated men to violence, and removed peace-keeping agents (such as the king) from the country.[69] Yet the answer is probably more exciting and complex. It is hard to say how greatly war affected any particular community. As Morgan points out, Cheshire was probably an exceptionally militarized county, trading expertise gained in years of border warfare for personal profits, royal favour, and county liberties.[70] Yet even so, he remarks, 'the military community in the county was never more than a significant, if complementary, minority within the ranks of landed and office-holding gentry.'[71] Just as the influence of the law on crime was not all one way, so the effects of war on society might be various. The absence of landowners at war might encourage their neighbours to attack their lands and families (violently or otherwise).[72] But if war removed law-keepers from the kingdom, it also rid the country of lawless and violent men—a process which, Griffiths suggest, accounts for the lack of violence in England in the 1430s.[73] Certainly Stones, Powell, and Bellamy have shown that military service could allow quarrelsome gentry, or even bandits such as the Folvilles, to rejoin normal society.[74]

---

[69] Morgan, *War and Society in Medieval Cheshire*, 86; J. G. Bellamy, 'The Coterel Gang: An Anatomy of a Band of Fourteenth-Century Criminals', *English Historical Review*, 79 (1964), 717; Bellamy, *Crime and Public Order*, 10; Griffiths, *Henry VI*, 136; but cf. Morgan's shrewd comment that 'the records of medieval courts cannot easily be used to demonstrate that society was non-violent and equitable in the maintenance of law and royal authority' (p. 86); and Hanawalt, *Crime and Conflict*, 223–38, who argues against the assumption that peace and governmental continuity are necessary and sufficient conditions for a rule of law and a low crime rate in the 14th cent.

[70] Morgan, *War and Society in Medieval Cheshire*, esp. 34–5, 49, 53, and 168–9.

[71] Ibid. 8. On p. 39, he discusses the proportion of Cheshire men taking part in war and concludes that the cost to the community of maintaining soldiers limited the ratio to, at most, 5% of the adult male population.

[72] Ibid. 155.

[73] Griffiths, *Henry VI*, 141.

[74] E. L. G. Stones, 'The Folvilles of Ashby-Folville, Leicestershire, and their Associates in Crime, 1326–1347', *Transactions of the Royal Historical Society*, 5th series, 7 (1957), 129–30, esp. 120–1; Powell, 'The King's Bench', 102–3; and Bellamy, 'The Coterel Gang', 712–13 and 717.

Similarly, if some soldiers, such as Sir John Talbot, gained a reputation for brutality, others, such as Sir John Fastolf and Sir Thomas Erpingham, habitually refrained from importing French battlefield manners into civilian life.[75] And probably even men like Talbot viewed their own actions as part of the legitimate—indeed praiseworthy—violence of true chivalry.[76] Presumably, then, the war cannot be seen as the simple cause of destabilizing violence. It might heighten the status of socially acceptable violence, such as the behaviour of loyal knights; or even, paradoxically, promote peace.

We need to know more of how violence fitted into the context of late-medieval English provincial society. Writers who espouse the theory of a high level of violence in the provinces sometimes suggest that it was a reflection less of the chance occurrence of bad kings or wars, than of typically medieval social conditions, such as poor policing, overmighty magnates, the predominance of community norms of group action and self-help in pursuing criminals and maintaining rights,[77] or the widespread habit of weapon-carrying.[78] These arguments acknowledge violence as an integral part of social behaviour in general, but do not sufficiently highlight the complexities of its role. Community norms may have led people to violent action, but also normatively encouraged the peaceful resolution of disputes by arbitration.[79] Though violence was one option available to county families in their constant pursuit of land, status, and power, it may not have been their most commonly used resort. Carpenter concludes from her study of Warwickshire that though a weak and dilatory legal system encouraged violence and gave 'strength to the bastard feudal bond' the right sort of overmighty subject might keep the peace (and

---

[75] For Talbot's reputation, see Griffiths, *Henry VI*, 133 and 136; and A. J. Pollard, *John Talbot and the War in France 1427–1453* (London, 1983), 125–7.

[76] Ibid. 122–8; see also Ch. 3.

[77] See above, nn. 12–15; Davis, 'Rites of Violence', 69; Hanawalt, *Crime and Conflict*, 261–3. Davis also reflects on the long tradition of folk-violence, and the use of the Bible as a model for corporate violent action (pp. 81–2). See also J. B. Given, *Society and Homicide in Thirteenth-Century England* (Stanford, Calif., 1977), esp. 160–3 and 200–2; Hanawalt, *Crime and Conflict*, 261; and M. B. Becker, 'Changing Patterns of Violence and Justice in Fourteenth- and Fifteenth-Century Florence', *Comparative Studies in Society and History*, 18 (1976), 284, for 'the communal texture of everyday living' as a factor.

[78] Storey, *End of the House of Lancaster*, 86; Bellamy, *Crime and Public Order*, 25; Hammer, 'Patterns of Homicide', 21; Given, *Society and Homicide*, 188–9.

[79] See above, n. 59.

in so doing help strengthen the monarchy).[80] Wright's Derbyshire gentry pursued their grievances, on occasion, with assault and intimidation; but Wright observes nevertheless that 'force was rarely conclusive and recourse was repeatedly made to a more pacific alternative, arbitration.'[81] Bellamy believes that in the constant prestige struggles of county gentry, 'felonies were rare but trespasses . . . and private actions numerous.' Even allowing for violence committed in the course of trespass, it seems that litigation, rather than physical warfare, was the medium of dispute.[82] Saul suggests that in late-medieval Sussex there was a 'relative absence of large-scale gentry violence', but a 'high level of litigiousness', the latter to some extent obviating the need for the former.[83] This sense that gentry violence was only part of a larger system of social relationships, which also encompassed status-seeking by litigation and arbitration, highlights the urgent need to re-examine the subtle and complex function of violence in late-medieval society.

Within this social context, the relationship of prevalent arms-carrying to a high level of violence in medieval society is necessarily intriguingly indirect. Weapon-carrying may well have been common.[84] Such weapons as daggers or staves were purchasable for prices (fourpence or less) within the economic reach of many of the population.[85] But the difficulty is to deduce how generally the presence of weapons precipitated what would otherwise have been peaceful disputes into violent fights—in other words, to assess the effects of weapons on the behaviour and aims of the people who carried them. Would weapons carried for ceremonial purposes provoke violence?

[80] Carpenter, 'Political Society in Warwickshire', 109, 123–6, and 145.

[81] Wright, *Derbyshire Gentry*, 122.

[82] J. G. Bellamy, *Bastard Feudalism and the Law* (London, 1989), 12, and for litigation in pursuit of land rights, 34–56.

[83] Saul, *Scenes from Provincial Life*, 77–8. Saul thinks, however, that Sussex was unusual in this respect, and attributes its relative peacefulness to 'the absence of rival and overlapping spheres of magnate influence', and consequent social cohesion (p. 77).

[84] See the inventory of goods of Paston servants in 1473, showing that 8 out of 20 male servants owned some form of weapon (counting knives as weapons) (*PL* ii. 360–5); will of Clement Rassh, alderman and fishmonger of Norwich, 1447, bequeathing 'al þe . . . harneys wheche longyth to a man armyd', Norfolk and Norwich Record Office (hereinafter referred to as N & NRO), Wills, Aleyn, fos. 51–2; armour allegedly stolen from Sir John Curson (1439) KB 27 718 m 101ᵈ; and survey of men in the half-hundred of Ewelme able to do the king service (59 out of 84—not counting constables—practised archery or owned harness) (*The Stonor Letters and Papers, 1290–1483*, ed. C. L. Kingsford (2 vols.; Camden Society, 3rd series, 29 and 30; 1919), ii. 96–7).

[85] *PL* ii. 362–3; and JUST 3 220/1 m (15) S6 (value of a deceased man's dagger).

Might not the weapons of law-enforcers have acted as a deterrent to crime? Was weapon-carrying perhaps a form of display, intended to reinforce the public status of a gentleman in the sight of his rivals and dependants? The problem is complicated by the apparent fact that a sizeable proportion of serious crimes of violence were allegedly carried out not with the swords and armour so commonly seen among the gentry, but with commoner implements—knives, bows and arrows, farm tools—which normally had more peaceful purposes.[86] If, as the figures suggest, cheap knives and farm implements were widely used by medieval thugs and murderers, then to say that fifteenth-century England was an unusually violent society because of the availability of weapons is to assume that not only swords and staves, but also potentially lethal items of daily use, were more frequently to hand in late-medieval England than in other places and periods. This can hardly be true. Fifteenth-century criminals may have found pitchforks and pruning knives more ready to their hands than do modern thugs, but they lacked such twentieth-century aids to violence as bicycle chains, broken bottles, and electric carving knives. In all societies, weapons can be found by those who choose to use them. The important questions remaining unanswered are why people so chose, and why fifteenth-century people in particular apparently often carried weapons, but less commonly used them to kill, maim, or injure. We are dealing here not with abstract and inevitable causal chains (weapon-carrying causes destabilizing violence) but with the more difficult explanation of human actions and decisions informed by a complex web of historical circumstance.

Yet as Ruggiero remarks, the fact that violence is a cultural activity, loaded with significance, and that consequently perceptions and manifestations of violence change over time, is a great bonus for historians; it enables us to use violence as 'a key for understanding the perceptual world of a particular society'.[87] And not the perceptual

---

[86] Daggers, bow and arrows, and/or farm implements were allegedly used in only 5.2% of all cases in King's Bench from East Anglia 1422–42; but appear in 10.1% of cases of assault, murder, menaces, mayhem, and riot, and in 26% of murder cases. See e.g. KB 27 664 m 79^r, 684 Rm 6^d, and 664 Rm 3^d. The 'streforke' cited in the case of *Rex* v. *John Polle* for the killing of William Aylmer in 1428, was priced at a halfpenny (KB 27 678 Rm 21^d); cf. also JUST 3 209 m 42^d, where John Wysbeche was said to have been working alongside John Colley clearing out a drain when he attacked and killed him with a 'Turf Shovele'. See Table 2.1 for an analysis of alleged weapon-use in King's Bench cases.

[87] Ruggiero, *Violence in Early Renaissance Venice*, 153.

world alone; a study of the ways in which violence is used—its place as sanction, threat, justification, and vilification—may show how a late-medieval society was really sustained, and practically organized. The work done in this area in British history has been slight; indeed, it sometimes seems that the recognition of violence as a social phenomenon has been taken by historians as licence either to generalize beyond possibility of proof or to particularize to insignificance. Given believes that medieval violence is a reflection of pre-modern education and socialization (by such sports as wrestling for the lower classes, and by corporal punishment in childhood for all classes); also of the inability of medieval people to plan peacefully for the future.[88] Not surprisingly, he cannot cite any case where an inability to think about the future contributed to a medieval crime, and it is hard to imagine what kind of evidence he could convincingly have offered. Bellamy, by contrast, explains the Coterels as simply criminal personalities, while Hammer believes that 'sharp tongues, quick temper and strong drink' often met in fatal combination, and Griffiths that 'strictly local causes' (ambition or exasperation with the legal process) had large effect.[89] These insights, though undoubtedly plausible, do not enable us to see a logic in the perceptual or material structures of England in the later Middle Ages.

I will make no attempt to construct a crime or violence rate for fifteenth-century England (or even for East Anglia from 1422 to 1442); nor to show that England in this period was or was not quantitatively a more violent society than any other.[90] But I will try, through a close examination of some cases and their contexts, to show what fifteenth-century people thought of violence, and how they classified it, how they acted it out, and why; and to suggest what significance this had for the ways in which they pursued their quarrels, treated their servants, governed their counties or neighbourhoods, wrote and read and heard their literature, punished their felons, and envisaged their God.

The sources for this study are admittedly uneven in quality and quantity. The main repository of information about criminal violence is the legal system. For East Anglia in this period the surviving legal

[88] Given, *Society and Homicide*, 194–9 and 191–2.

[89] Bellamy, 'The Coterel Gang', 716–17; Hammer, 'Patterns of Homicide', 20; Griffiths, *Henry VI*, 130.

[90] Sharpe rightly raises the question, 'how "violent" *is* a "violent society"?' ('The History of Violence in England', 215).

records are the plea rolls and some indictments from King's Bench; some assize rolls; most of the rolls and files from the gaol delivery sessions; and miscellaneous manor and borough court rolls. These may be supplemented by extra-legal material—petitions in Chancery, a couple of petitions in parliament, two examinations before the privy council, and some references in letters, town records, and literature.[91] Such an array of material is unparalleled in late-medieval England, but still leaves many records of violent crime unaccounted for.[92] Neither coroners' rolls nor peace rolls survive; nor do records from courts of liberties in the area, such as the bishop of Ely's gaol deliveries, assizes, and peace sessions.[93] The significance of the remaining material is problematical. It consists almost entirely of allegations of crime—in the case of King's Bench, mostly by one person, though sometimes in indictments by a jury before justices. Convictions are scarce.[94] The difficulties of determining whether violence was even thought to have taken place is compounded by the formality of the records. Plaintiffs bringing a suit in King's Bench used the terms *vi et armis, cum gladiis baculis &c*, and *contra pacem domini Regis* as a matter of course, apparently only to label the case as a trespass sufficiently grave to warrant appearance in that court.[95] These phrases could be used to insinuate or strengthen the allegation of violence in a case. For the supposed Norwich riots of May Day 1437, the English certification (drawn up locally, it appears, by one of the interested parties) alleges 'force and armes' but does not cite any specific weapons carried by rioters. But when John Heydon, one of the same interested group, brought a case against the rioters in King's Bench, he necessarily alleged the use of those familiar accoutrements, *gladiis baculis &c*.[96] Most of the cases in which force and arms were alleged concern trespasses which are not necessarily violent—such as

---

[91] There were two petitions in parliament in 1429, against arsonists in Cambridge (Rot. Parl. iv. 349 and 358). Both the privy council examinations concern the disturbance of the peace sessions in Bedfordshire, 1437 and 1439, see Ch. 6.2.

[92] The gaol delivery records for most other circuits in the 14th and 15th cent. are neither so full nor so numerous; and the Paston Letters are, of course, unique to East Anglia.

[93] *The Victoria History of the Counties of England* (hereinafter referred to as *VCH*), *Cambridge and the Isle of Ely*, iv (1953), 13–14, refers to the fact that the bishop had his own gaol and appointed his own justices of the peace, who sat at Ely and Wisbech in the later years of the 15th cent.

[94] See Table 2.3.

[95] J. H. Baker, *An Introduction to English Legal History* (London, 1971), 311.

[96] KB 9 229/1 m 106 and KB 27 707 Rm 4ʳ; cf. KB 27 706 m 116ʳ; and see Ch. 6.

asporting goods, breaking and entering, poaching, and the like.[97] Most involve only those misdeeds which came to the attention of someone of wealth and standing enough to pursue matters in the king's courts.[98] Presumably, violence between humbler people was recorded, if at all, in the manor court rolls, which give instances of fines for assault, and which were enjoined to enquire into 'all maner assawtes, as of frayes . . . and of blood . . . drawing'.[99] But the survival of this sort of material is so patchy that I have deliberately left it (mostly) out of consideration.

As material for the statistical study of East Anglian violent crime 1422–42, this is certainly unsuitable. It is also difficult to use in establishing the societal values surrounding force and violence without a fair knowledge of the motives for bringing any particular suit. But the records can be made to yield an understanding of the place of violence and law in late-medieval England in other ways. Analysing the legal records as a whole gives an excellent picture of the ways in which the law was commonly used to pursue quarrels or to bring them to conclusion elsewhere; to protect individuals (innocent and guilty); and to control, or promote, violence and crime. For this purpose, legal records are well suited to statistical analysis—abundantly plentiful and invariable in format. Understanding the practical uses of law in the fifteenth century enables us to distinguish more easily the significant features of individual cases, and their place in the context of fifteenth-century litigation. Often, the first hint of a promising case-study is the fact that one case stands out from the surrounding litigation, presumably because of its importance to at least one group of contemporaries. By examining in detail the background, careers, and circumstances of the participants, probing their interactions with one another, and analysing their processes of decision-making and self-justification, we may clarify the real place and use of violence and law in that society.

It is true that the background materials for case-studies often seem

[97] See Appendix I and Table 2.1.

[98] The bulk of cases in King's Bench were brought against men of lower standing by their (male) social superiors; see Table 2.5. Even if this truly reflected a lower involvement of women as victims or perpetrators of violent crime, it is highly unlikely that it reflects accurately the class distinctions in crime; cf. Ruggiero, *Violence in Early Renaissance Venice*, 74–5, 80–1, and 120–1, which suggests that the nobility were actually more likely to perpetrate violence than were other classes, despite the fact that their crimes may often have escaped examination.

[99] e.g. SC 2 194 m 1ʳ (the Thurgeyton leet of 1431, case against John Ducheman); see also L. T. Smith (ed.), *A Commonplace Book of the Fifteenth Century* (London, 1886), 161 for the manorial law of Stuston, Suffolk.

difficult and scanty. The legal accounts of violence are formal and brief, and the explicit self-justification of the actors is generally lacking. Many defendants and victims were obscure people, of whom we know little but the meagre details required to be recorded in court. But some people went often to law, were often prosecuted, or (especially if they were of gentry status) can be traced through the patent and close rolls. From such material their habits, associates, and motives can to a certain extent be deduced. Extra-legal material provides other information.[100] A judicious selection of cases, then, should enable one to find out enough of people's actions to suggest their circumstances and motives. Furthermore, since the motives of individuals were not then, any more than now, independent of the assumptions of their society, we can study fifteenth-century literary, theological, legal, and private writings to gain a sense of the norms, guidelines, and prohibitions then surrounding the concepts of violence and law. If we cannot prove in any individual case that the protagonists were influenced by any particular example of this material, we can at least understand the general conceptual context within which violence was undertaken. This is why I examine, in Chapter 3, the concept and ethic of violence as it appears in fifteenth-century English culture.

The final chapters present the case-studies from which I draw my main deductions. It is as well to be clear at this point on what case-studies can, and cannot, achieve. One common justification for examining a single case is that it is typical of many others. Rosenthal claims this for the Hastings–Pierpoint arbitration of 1458; Stones's conclusions as to the fourteenth-century government's ability to deal with disorder rest on the hope that 'the Folvilles may be regarded as typical'.[101] Martines observes that in general,

Whether or not he make an explicit acknowledgement, the historian is greatly inclined to select . . . cases that he supposes to be representative, or which seem to exemplify a trend. In this sense he assumes them to have typicality.[102]

But as Martines himself notes, there is a 'deceptive' vicious circle here—must typicality first be confirmed by examining a vast number of cases, or does one 'as if by intuition' get 'a sense of the mainstream'

---

[100] e.g. the city of Norwich's account of the supposed 'Gladman's Insurrection', ed. G. Johnson, *Norfolk and Norwich Archaeological Society*, 1 (1847), 294–9.

[101] Rosenthal, 'Feuds and Private Peace-making', 87; Stones, 'The Folvilles', 118.

[102] L. Martines (ed.), *Violence and Civil Disorder in Italian Cities, 1200–1500* (Los Angeles, 1972), 9.

through studying the case itself?[103] He answers that the historian does both simultaneously, with a feedback effect; I doubt the efficacy of either method. I suggest that the problem arises from an insufficiently precise idea of what the historian is attempting to explain in generalizing from a few case-studies. If the goal is to be able to say that something happened in a majority of cases—that is, to prove it quantitatively normal—then generalization from a single case (however brilliant the intuition on which it is based) will never suffice. Nor can the case-study be said to function as a place of 'natural experiment' for the researcher's theory. As Geertz points out, 'a laboratory where *none* of the parameters are manipulable' is a poor testing-ground. Nor does the case microcosmically represent its society; late-medieval England did not wholly resemble rioting Norwich. Geertz suggests that the researcher should study themes and processes *within* the small area, and carry the results to the wider arena in which the same themes and processes operate. (He instances 'what colonial domination does to established frames of moral expectation'.)[104] But this promising solution does not explain what sort of themes can be studied in small groups and yet extended to larger ones, nor how we pick, from the minutiae of one case, the significant elements that will extend our understanding of the whole society. The answer, I believe, lies in distinguishing what is normal (quantitatively common) from what is normative (that is, what is believed in any society to be normal, and therefore often represented as morally right and a common guide to action). The normal cannot be perceived in a single case-study; the normative can. Wherever people justify their actions, or express expectations; in the gap between what they have done and what they say they have done, whether the lie be conscious or not; in the discrepancy between the theoretical range of their options and the few actual courses of action they hesitate between; in their reactions to what other people have done; in the ways their own statements change over time; the norms of their social group, however wide or narrow it may have been, can be perceived. Green's conclusions, for instance, about late-medieval notions of self-defence and culpable manslaughter rest on a narrow range of material—the ways in which trial juries modified the description of crimes given by coroners' juries. Yet he shows conclusively that certain theories of justifiable homicide were

---

[103] Ibid. 9–10.
[104] C. Geertz, *The Interpretation of Cultures* (London, 1975), 21–2.

commonly held in late-medieval England, and affected jury practice. His valuable conclusions on community life and thought emerge from a study of relatively few cases, in which reflections on morality are never explicitly articulated.[105]

That is why I hope, in this study of selected cases of violence in East Anglia 1422–42—some large-scale and public, such as the riots in Bedford and Norwich, some concerning gentry and some not, some outside the law and some within—to illuminate not only the cases themselves, but some of the normative aspects of violence in the fifteenth century. What provoked it? What prevented it? Was it admired or feared? What sorts of violence did people most easily engage in, and what did they shrink from? How did they deal with violence once it had broken out? What effect did it have on people's lives? The answers to these questions may not settle the long debate started by Kingsford as to how much violence there was in English society of the fifteenth century; but they will show how important violence was in English society at that time. They will not provide a handy measuring stick against which to praise or blame late-medieval English kings; they may enable us to see how and why individual rulers used violence and the law as they did. They will not either condemn or justify bastard feudalism; they may illuminate the heavily entwined functions of law and violence within that system. They will not explain the Wars of the Roses, in terms of either provincial or national politics; but they may make the whole structure and working of late-medieval English society more comprehensible to us, the strangers from the twentieth century.

---

[105] Green, 'Societal Concepts of Criminal Liability for Homicide', *passim.*

2

THE LAW AND VIOLENCE

I se that neythre plee, trety, ne werre may make my peas.

(Thomas Denys to John Paston I,
1461, *PL* ii. 231)

The most extensive and valuable material on violence in late-medieval
East Anglia is contained in the legal records of two courts—King's
Bench and gaol delivery. For these courts almost complete records
survive, 1422–42, providing not only a vast bulk of allegations of
violent crime, but also valuable information on the legal use of violence
to punish criminals.[1] These records must form the basis of any
investigation of crime and violence in East Anglia at this period.

The records themselves, however, are anything but simple. Though
it is easy to extract and tabulate the crimes of violence alleged there,
(see Table 2.1) the significance of the figures is less obvious. For
instance, Table 2.1 shows that the 2,248 cases in King's Bench at this
period included a variety of charges, from asporting goods to homicide. In order to make clear how few of the allegations actually
concerned violence towards the person, I have distinguished cases of
assault and menacing from those where only asporting goods, or
general trespass (illegally entering someone else's land, depasturing,
illegally cutting timber, and so on) were at issue. Yet even this
elementary sorting introduces anachronism. In the rolls themselves,
assault, menaces, asporting goods, and all other forms of trespass
generally appeared as writs of trespass, *vi et armis*. Unless we know
the purposes and functions of this writ we have little chance of
comprehending why it was applied to such diverse offences, and how

---

[1] It should be noted that KB 27 679, the plea roll for Hilary 1431, was under repair
during my research time, and thus could not be consulted. The workings of some other
sessions (peace sessions, oyer and terminer) can to some extent be deduced from the
cases they sent to King's Bench and gaol delivery; see below, text accompanying
nn. 65–87.

TABLE 2.1.   *Cases alleging violence in King's Bench; county of origin, crimes, and weapons alleged*

	Plea side		Rex side	
	No.	%	No.	%
Cases from each county				
Norfolk	1,099	56.8	187	59.6
Suffolk	290	15.0	57	18.2
Cambridge	210	10.9	14	4.5
Huntingdon	50	2.6	11	3.5
Bedford	144	7.5	26	8.3
Buckingham	141	7.3	19	6.1
TOTAL	1,934	100.1[a]	314	100.2
Allegations				
Assault	445	16.8	66	13.7
Asporting goods	622	23.4	73	15.1
Trespass	1,024	38.6	81	16.8
Rape/abduction	113	4.3	32	6.6
Menacing	132	5.0	15	3.1
Homicide	20	0.8	41	8.5
Maintenance	67	2.5	93	19.3
Riot	4	0.2	17	3.5
Mayhem	11	0.4	2	0.4
Other	217	8.2	63	13.0
TOTAL	2,655	100.2	483	100.0
Weapons alleged				
Sword	795	28.9	86	19.5
Stave	771	28.0	56	12.7
Dagger/Knife	18	0.7	24	5.4
Bow and arrow	28	1.1	32	7.2
Farm implement	6	0.2	9	2.0
Armour	2	0.1	9	2.0
Other	12	0.4	25	5.7
None alleged	1,120	40.7	201	45.5
TOTAL	2,752	100.1	442	100.0

[a] Discrepancies in percentages (in all Tables) arise from rounding the percentages to one decimal place.

Source: For information about how the Tables were created, see Appendix I.

the figures actually reflect the role of law and violence in late-medieval East Anglian society.

Similarly, the bare numbers of weapons alleged would suggest that where any weapon was alleged at all, swords and staves were the prevailing tools of East Anglian crime. Knowledge of the fact that the phrase '*gladiis et baculis*' was a legal commonplace in the process on writs of trespass modifies this view. Perhaps instead the comparatively small numbers of daggers, bows and arrows, and farm implements more accurately reflect the place and use of weapons in late-medieval East Anglia.

Finally, it must be noted that more than half the East Anglian cases in King's Bench at this period came from Norfolk. Admittedly, Norfolk was a large and populous county, but even this cannot account for its dominance of the records. Was Norfolk an untypically violent society? Or simply more litigious than its neighbouring counties? Without a closer examination of the use of the lawcourts, we have little hope of deciding this question. This chapter, then, will be devoted to a study of the ways in which King's Bench, peace sessions, and gaol delivery were used; the cases that were brought there and the processes that ensued; and (as far as we can discover them) the motives of the participants in these cases.

In short, the records must be put into their context. Not only are they products of a system with its own diplomatic imperatives; each paragraph on the parchment freezes one moment in a long history of transactions between litigants. In turn, each transaction, whether criminal or civil, collusive or antagonistic, violent or non-violent, was more or less shaped by the institutional possibilities and limitations of the legal system. This complicated net of personal and institutional relationships underlies all understanding of the individual cases.

The range of relationships which might result in court action was immense. There were in any case many courts in which to bring a case, and in King's Bench and gaol delivery there were many ways in which a case could be brought, with different advantages and disadvantages for the parties involved. Cases of alleged violence might appear in council or Chancery, in King's Bench, before justices of the central courts in the assizes every February and July, or before the same justices acting as commissioners of gaol delivery. Peace commissioners and commissioners of general oyer and terminer could hear and determine cases of felonious or non-felonious violence. Jury indictments of felonious violence could be taken in sheriff's tourns, courts of liberties, and manor courts, though they could not be determined (taken to a verdict) there. However, such courts might punish non-felonious violence by amercement.[2] Coroners held inquisitions on deaths which occurred in suspicious circumstances. Cases of assault even appeared in Common Pleas, though apparently in a far smaller proportion of the total number of cases than in King's Bench.[3] The King's Bench and gaol delivery records, then, form by far the greatest, but by no means the only, surviving repository of lawsuits involving violence.

In King's Bench, no record normally survives of the antecedents and consequences of the cases; so with individual cases, it is hard to tell what moved the litigants (or authorities) to bring the case to such a court in such a way. But on the broad scale, the services and possibilities theoretically available from each court, the ways in which cases were brought to these courts, and their progress once they got there, provide some evidence both of the motives of the participants and the functions of the courts in helping to order the affairs of fifteenth-century East Anglians.

Cases in Chancery, for instance, appeared at the petition of the alleged victim. The court could then issue a subpoena to bring the alleged wrongdoer in person before it to submit his or her replication to the original bill. Since Chancery's role was to deal with those cases which fell outside common law, either because no common-law remedy was available, or because poverty or maintenance prevented common law from proceeding, we find many cases where the petitioners alleged that they were 'withoute remedie at the comen lawe', because of the power and influence of the alleged wrongdoer.[4] But these complaints of unfair pressure cannot be taken at face value, since they may have been no more than levers to get cases into a court

---

[2] Records from tourns at Narford (Oct. 1405) and Clacklose Hill (Oct. 1484)—SC 2 192/75 and 192/79—show that up to two-thirds of the cases might involve assault and (occasional) blood-letting.

[3] This is my impression of cases in a selection of Common Pleas rolls from the period 1422–42; but see N. Neilson (ed.), *Year Books of Edward IV: 10 Edward IV and 49 Henry VI* (Selden Society, 47; 1930), pp. xix–xxi. She calculates that about 121 out of 3,800 cases on one Common Pleas roll (3.2%) concerned assault or other alleged violence against the person.

[4] C 1 73/91; and see M. Avery, 'The History of the Equitable Jurisdiction of Chancery before 1460', *BIHR* 42 (1969), 128–31. Before 1440 only petitions survive in any quantity; answers, replications, examinations, and judgments are hardly to be found.

TABLE 2.2. *How cases came to the court of King's Bench*

	Plea side		Rex side	
	No.	%	No.	%
Writ[a]	1,829	94.6	130	41.4
From Common Pleas	8	0.4	—	—
Appeal	56	2.9	—	—
Bill	41	2.1	1	0.3
From peace sessions[b]	—	—	113	36.0
From tourn	—	—	5	1.6
From other court	—	—	65	20.7
TOTAL	1,934	100.0	314	100.0

[a] In Rex side this category denotes those cases known only by the writ of capias recorded there.

[b] This includes the four cases brought in by justices' certification.

whose record of producing adversaries to answer charges was a good one.

In King's Bench such a varied collection of procedures were used (see Table 2.2) that it is necessary to examine the different functions of each in turn. On the plea side, clearly the favourite option was to sue out a writ of trespass *vi et armis* (in common use since the fourteenth century). Nearly 95 per cent of all cases on the plea side came into court by such a writ (though other writs, such as trespass with forcible entry, are also scattered thinly through the records).[5] No doubt the flexibility of this writ helped to account for its popularity— it covered crimes of violence to the person, threats and menaces, and damage to property including depasturing, felling of timber, and asporting goods. One drawback, though, was that plaintiffs who successfully brought charges of asporting goods could recover only damages, not the disputed goods, from the defendants.

Process upon the original writ began with a writ to the sheriff of the county to attach the defendant (that is, to secure some hold over the defendant by taking goods, chattels, or pledge). If this were impossible, the sheriff was ordered to arrest him or her (capias); this failing, to call for him/her at five county courts (exigent), and finally to outlaw

[5] The statute 8 Henry VI c. 9 allowed a writ of trespass to be sued out against disseisin 'with strong hand'.

anyone who still refused to appear. A defendant who appeared at any
stage could either traverse the suit or demur (that is, show some error
in the writ to render it not good in law). If the suit was traversed, the
sheriff of the county had then to impanel and produce a jury to give
verdict on the case. The verdict might be given at *nisi prius* (that is, at
the assizes in the county).[6]

The actual relationships between the litigants in such cases could,
however, range widely. Writs of trespass concerning damage to
property, or even assault to the person, were often used in disputes
over landownership. Thus, the charge of breaking and entering,
woodcutting, depasturing, and menacing of servants, brought by
Edward Sakevyle against Sir Thomas Sakevyle, was eventually argued
out over whether Edward's descent (and hence inheritance) from the
long-dead Andrew Sakevyle was legitimate or not. Sir John Clyfton *et
al.*, and John and Beatrice Chaumpneys, ostensibly engaged in a case
of breaking and entering, asporting goods, and depasturing, were
actually deciding whether the land in question had passed to Beatrice
from her dead brother, or whether he had first enfeoffed it to Clyfton.[7]
Sometimes the alleged defendants were not the real objects of the
plaintiff's wrath. John Adam, a Buckinghamshire esquire, brought a
case in Michaelmas 1427 against five servants of John Fitzhugh,
gentleman, for depasturing. But since their defence was that the
pasture belonged to Fitzhugh, and that they had merely pastured
beasts there on his behalf, and since Adam had brought a charge of
asporting goods against Fitzhugh himself in the preceding Hilary
term, it seems certain that Fitzhugh's husbandmen and labourers were
mere lay figures in a land dispute between two gentry.[8] This kind of
writ could also lend itself to collusive actions. Payling has shown how
collusive actions in Common Pleas figured among the shady legal
methods by which Ralph Lord Cromwell gained control of the Heriz
inheritance; we know of at least one collusive suit brought to the Rex
side of King's Bench in this period, and others are no doubt buried in
the uninformative phraseology of the plea side.[9] The suit of unlawful

---

[6] M. Hale, *Historia Placitorum Coronae* (2 vols.; London, 1736; repr. London
Professional Books Ltd.: London, 1971), ii. 194–5. In cases of felony the process
started at capias.

[7] KB 27 706 m 109 and 713 m 68[r].

[8] KB 27 663 m 22[r] and 666 m 95[r].

[9] S. J. Payling, 'Inheritance and Local Politics in the Later Middle Ages: The Case
of Ralph, Lord Cromwell, and the Heriz Inheritance', *Nottingham Medieval Studies*, 30
(1986), 84–5; and see Ch. 6, n. 75.

arrest brought by Robert Ostelyn against the earl of Oxford in Trinity 1438, was probably one of these. Verdicts in King's Bench plea side were so rare (see Table 2.3), and the verdict in this case was achieved so speedily, that one must assume co-operation by the defendant. The earl's attorney claimed that Ostelyn was a bondman of the manor of Wetyng. Ostelyn pleaded that he was of free extraction, and the jury promptly swore to the truth of this claim. The point of the whole case was probably to have Ostelyn's legal status affirmed in a court of record.[10]

Obviously, the popularity of this type of suit demonstrates not the prevalence, or acceptance, of violence in late-medieval England, but the overriding importance of property and status to the gentry of fifteenth-century English society, and the sophistication of their methods of dispute. The constant competition for livelihood and prestige was worked out by subtle means in the lawcourts. So litigious was the society that Bellamy's impression is that in the later Middle Ages,

Very few indeed of the men and women of gentry status and above ... did not appear as either plaintiff or defendant in the courts of assize, common pleas, or king's bench at some time in their lives.[11]

In this sophisticated system of dispute, the aims of the litigants might be achieved in ways which bore little relationship to the formal purposes of the courts. This can be seen by analysis of the stages which these cases reached in the court, and the time they took to do so.

Table 2.3 shows clearly how few cases in King's Bench ever came to a formal verdict. In fact, 1,824 (94.3%) of pleas of trespass *vi et armis* reached no verdict because of the non-appearance of defendants or juries; and in King's Bench as a whole all but 11.2 per cent of cases either produced defendants at attachment (or later, of their own volition) or never produced them at all.[12] This apparent failure to achieve anything was due partly to the court's cumbersome procedures. At every stage a writ (attachment, capias, and so on) had to be sent out to the sheriff of the county. The actual production of the

---

[10] KB 27 709 m 43ʳ. By the following Michaelmas term, the jury had assessed damages at 100s., of which Ostelyn immediately acknowledged himself satisfied.

[11] Bellamy, *Bastard Feudalism and the Law*, 34.

[12] See Table 2.3. In cases where a jury was called, the defendant had almost always appeared at the attachment stage.

TABLE 2.3. *Stages at which process ceased in King's Bench cases and verdicts recorded*

	Plea side		Rex side	
	No.	%	No.	%
Stages Reached				
Attachment or capias	88	4.6	35	11.2
First exigent	694	35.9	21	6.7
Second exigent	111	5.7	2	0.6
Third exigent	54	2.8	3	1.0
Fourth exigent	19	1.0	4	1.3
Outlawed	4	0.2	4	1.3
Defendant ill	17	0.9	1	0.3
Appeared at attachment	126	6.5	3	1.0
Appeared later	41	2.1	2	0.6
Jury called	646	33.4	38	12.1
Verdict/end	132	6.8	201	64.0
Pleaded guilty	2	0.1	—	—
TOTAL	1,934	100.0	314	100.1
Results				
None known	1,789	92.5	112	35.7
Pleaded pardon/made fine	17	0.9	45	14.3
Demurred/plaintiff failed	36	1.9	46	14.7
Acquitted	14	0.7	100	33.1
Damages unpaid	34	1.8	1	0.3
Damages paid	40	2.1	2	0.6
To be executed	1	0.1	1	0.3
Pleaded clergy/supersedeas	3	0.2	3	1.0
TOTAL	1,934	100.2	314	100.0

defendant thus depended on the sheriff and his officers, who were not eager to pursue difficult or dangerous arrests. Furthermore, the system allowed the sheriff great leeway. At all stages, formally correct returns could be made excusing the failure of the defendant or jury to appear. To attachment, the return could be that the defendant had no property in the county; to arrest, that he could not be found; to exigent, that the writ had arrived too late, that the series of five exigents was incomplete, or that the defendant had appeared, but was too ill to

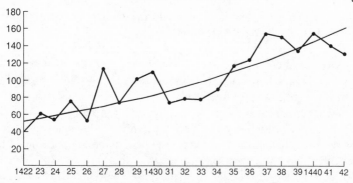

F I G. 2.1 Number of King's Bench cases per year (with trend line)

travel; to the gathering of a jury, that the men had failed to appear.[13] Thus, with no risk of being fined, a sheriff could delay verdict in a case almost interminably.[14]

The interesting point is that this did not discourage litigants. On the contrary, as Figure 2.1 shows, King's Bench was increasingly popular throughout the period 1422–42.[15] Some plaintiffs, undaunted by their apparent frustration, returned to it repeatedly. Indeed, thirty-six plaintiffs can be identified who between them brought 284 cases to court (15 per cent of all plea side cases, minus appeals). Sir Henry Inglose and Henry Sturmer, the two most enthusiastic litigants, brought, respectively, thirty-nine and thirty-seven suits into King's Bench in these twenty years. Most of the suits brought by these people were of trespass *vi et armis*; 258 out of 380 allegations were of asporting goods or property damage, rather than personal violence. Of these gentlemanly affairs, 92.3 per cent reached no verdict. Clearly,

[13] Note that a return of insufficient property for attachment was made of Henry Fraunceys, though in the same roll he appears as bailing someone for £10; he thus seems to have been both propertied and handy to the court (KB 27 718 m 79d and Rm 20d). Similarly, the Wiltshire sheriff in 1464–5 twice returned a *non est inventus* to the capias for a defendant who simultaneously appeared on a jury of the county (M. M. Condon (ed.), 'A Wiltshire Sheriff's Notebook, 1464–5', in R. F. Hunnisett and J. B. Post (eds.), *Medieval Legal Records Edited in Memory of C. A. F. Meekings* (London, 1978), 412–13.

[14] Sheriffs were fined, but only for formal errors in the return of writs, e.g. Giles Daubeney, of Bedford and Buckingham, was once fined for returning 20, rather than 24, names for a jury (KB 27 684 fines d).

[15] The trend line was drawn using the methods outlined in R. Floud, *An Introduction to Quantitative Methods for Historians*, 2nd edn. (London, 1979), 97–109.

such well-practised plaintiffs benefited from something other than the power of the court to produce verdicts.

One function of these suits was, of course, to harass the defendant to settle out of court. This is suggested by the fact that most cases on plea side King's Bench left the court at two points—the first exigent, or the calling of the jury (see Table 2.3). These two stages accounted for the disappearance from the records of 1,340 cases out of 1,934 (nearly 70 per cent). They also mark the points at which most pressure was put on defendants. At the first exigent, a defendant was forced to recognize that the sheriff had undertaken the process which might end in outlawry; at the calling of the jury, any defendant risked an unfavourable verdict. The number of cases which apparently finish at this point thus probably indicates that many defendants were persuaded to settle up quietly. In general, this process was rapid and efficient. Contrary to popular belief, King's Bench cases were not often prolonged interminably.[16] As Table 2.4 shows, the vast majority (nearly 80 per cent) stayed for less than a year on the court's records. Presumably the purposes they served were achieved in that time.

Evidence from private papers supports this picture. In 1461, John Paston I was advised to seek award rather than bring a lawsuit, on the grounds of expense. In another Paston case, a lawsuit produced a promise to pay a debt.[17] Litigation could indeed be expensive—Hugh Dalby's account as attorney for the duke of Norfolk in a single Coventry case of waste in 1426–9 ran to 114*s*.[18] Sir John Fastolf spent £1,085 in ten years on the legal defence of three manors.[19] Thomas Playter, in the year 1459–60, claimed from the Pastons £35. 0*s*. 10*d*. plus a gown, for pursuing their various legal matters, though this included reimbursement for travel, accommodation, and entertainment, which could be spent as easily on arranging an arbitration as pursuing a lawsuit.[20] Keeping a lawyer on permanent retainer, Ives

---

[16] See M. Blatcher, *The Court of King's Bench, 1450–1550* (London, 1978), 49–61.

[17] *PL* ii. 232 and i. 616.

[18] E 101 514/17.

[19] A. R. Smith, 'Aspects of the Career of Sir John Fastolf (1380–1459)' D.Phil. thesis (Oxford, 1982), 12. Smith calculates that Fastolf's legal expenses, 'including losses of revenue when his opponents occupied his possessions' totalled £1,650. He notes that Fastolf's careful purchasing policies kept expensive lawsuits to a minimum; see his 'Litigation and Politics: Sir John Fastolf's Defence of his English Property', in T. Pollard (ed.), *Property and Politics: Essays in Later Medieval English History* (Gloucester, 1984), 59–73, esp. 60.

[20] C. Richmond, 'The Expenses of Thomas Playter of Sotterley, 1459–1460', *Proceedings of the Suffolk Institute of Archaeology and History*, 35 (1981), 45–9.

TABLE 2.4. *Duration of cases in King's Bench*

Time in years	Time in court[a]		Lag: crime to court[b]		Total time[c]	
	No.	%	No.	%	No.	%
1	1,783	79.31	469	44.00	257	24.10
2	220	9.79	214	20.08	242	22.70
3	98	4.36	109	10.23	145	13.60
4	52	2.31	81	7.60	123	11.54
5	27	1.20	51	4.78	71	6.66
6	21	0.93	28	2.63	52	4.88
7	14	0.62	28	2.63	43	4.03
8	8	0.36	19	1.78	30	2.81
9	8	0.36	18	1.69	27	2.53
10	5	0.22	8	0.75	15	1.41
11	4	0.18	9	0.84	7	0.66
12–23	8	0.36	32	3.02	54	5.07
TOTAL	2,248	100.00	1,066[d]	100.03	1,066[d]	99.99

[a] Length of time between first and last appearance of cases in King's Bench.
[b] Length of time between alleged dates of crimes and first appearance of cases in King's Bench.
[c] Length of time between alleged dates of crimes and last appearance of cases in King's Bench.
[d] The total number of cases is less than 2,248 because the alleged date of the crime was recorded only in those cases where a defendant appeared.
Source: For calculation of these figures, see Appendix I.

found, might cost between £1 and £2 per year. For each case, clients paid not only to consult their lawyers and to obtain documents and settle court fees, but also to have their lawyers conduct formal stages in the process, represent them in court, and argue the case. It was thus easy to run up significant legal expenses, especially if a senior member of the legal profession was involved. In 1501 the citizens of Canterbury paid 13s. 4d. just to obtain their first consultation with the recorder of London.[21] No wonder that a fifteenth-century satirical poem summed up with cutting brevity the relationship between property, litigation, expense, and settlement:

[21] E. W. Ives, *The Common Lawyers of Pre-Reformation England; Thomas Kebell: A Case Study* (Cambridge, 1983), 288–306; though the Canterbury case was exceptional. Apparently 3s. 4d. was the more usual fee for consultation and pleading.

Pees maketh plente;
Plente maketh pride;
Pride maketh plee;
Plee maketh povert;
Povert maketh pees.[22]

Not surprisingly, then, threat of a suit could galvanize a defendant into a paroxysm of widespread negotiation. In 1464 William Jenney brought proceedings against John Paston I. Paston's steward immediately contacted a sympathetic friend, Sir William Calthorpe, to persuade him to put pressure, in turn, on the undersheriff to 'sece the callyng of the writtes and to retorne that ye [Paston] appered the furst day'.[23]

But it is clear that apparently inconclusive cases could be used for other ends besides simply persuading an opponent to settle a pre-existing argument. Again, the Paston letters give a good example. In 1440 Robert Repps delightedly reported a triumph of the duke of Norfolk's faction over the earl of Suffolk's men. Robert Lyston, a Suffolk supporter, had sued an assize of novel disseisin against Sir Robert Wyngfield, a Norfolk man, and got 700 marks in damages. But Wyngfield, a devious adversary, found a way to retaliate by law. He had Lyston 'sotylly' outlawed in Nottinghamshire—presumably by suing out a writ against him in that county without his knowledge. An outlaw's goods were forfeit to the king; in this case, the treasurer granted 700 marks from Lyston's goods to the duke of Norfolk, who promptly paid the money over to Wyngfield. 'And here is greet hevyng an shovyng be my lord of Suffolk and all his counsell for to aspye hough this mater kam aboute', concluded Repps gleefully.[24] The only point of Wyngfield's suit was to outlaw Lyston; the ostensible matter of the writ was irrelevant to the real quarrel.

The tedious procedures of King's Bench were clearly valuable to landed gentry. No wonder, then, that by far the largest group of plaintiffs whose status is known were gentry (Table 2.5). In all plea side cases, 23.5 per cent of plaintiffs are recorded as being of gentry status or above, as against 4.7 per cent of defendants. It is true that the Statute of Additions ensured that occupation or status would be

---

[22] *Medieval English Lyrics*, ed. R. T. Davies, Faber edn. (London, 1963), 240.
[23] *PL* ii. 299.
[24] *PL* ii. 22; Lyston's name is wrongly given as 'John', but KB 27 720 fines m 2[d] establishes the identity and confirms Repps's story.

more commonly recorded for defendants than for plaintiffs; 97.8 per cent of defendants had their status or occupation recorded by the court, whereas 66.8 per cent of plaintiffs remained unclassified.[25] Yet even if we assume that all the 66.8 per cent of unclassified plaintiffs were below gentry status, and all the 2.2 per cent of unclassified defendants were of gentry status or above, the proportion of plaintiffs who were gentry would still exceed that of defendants, by 23.5 to 6.9 per cent.[26] Most defendants were classed as yeomen or husbandmen; these two groups made up 51.8 per cent of plea side defendants. It seems that East Anglian gentry used King's Bench largely to further land disputes by bringing cases against their opponents' servants and tenants.

The two other ways in which cases could come to King's Bench plea side also allowed a range of options for litigants. First, a case against a plaintiff who was already in London (in custody in the Marshalsey, perhaps) could originate by bill of complaint. This was rare in the period 1422–42 (the frequent use of the Bill of Middlesex to secure a writ of *latitat* was still to come).[27] Yet the labyrinthine machinations of fifteenth-century litigants took procedures on bills into account. In Trinity 1430, John Pekker, a London vintner, brought a bill against Gilbert Debenham of Suffolk for assault and robbery. The sheriff never returned a jury panel, so the case lapsed; but in the course of it, Debenham and four mainpernors were made to give a security of peace to Pekker. Nearly five years later, it was alleged in King's Bench Rex side that Debenham had assaulted two Suffolk bailiffs and taken from them the felon they had arrested. This misdeed had, to my knowledge, not the slightest connection with Pekker's case, but it was said to be in breach of Debenham's security of peace. His mainpernors (who stood to lose £20 apiece) took this seriously; the writ ordering them to have Debenham in court in the following Easter term produced his prompt appearance. Again, the

---

[25] This statute (1 Henry V c. 5) ordered that in original writs in personal actions, appeals, and indictments 'additions [to the name of the defendant] shall be made of their Estate or Degree, or Mystery'. The statute seems to have been well observed in the East Anglian records 1422–42.

[26] In fact, some of the plaintiffs for whom no status was entered were certainly gentry; John Thurton, for instance, is given no status when he sued Sir John Curson in KB 27 727 m 38ʳ, but appears later as a 'gentleman' defendant (KB 27 734 m 8ʳ).

[27] Sir W. Holdsworth, *A History of English Law*, 4th edn. (16 vols.; London, 1936; repr. 1966), ii. 340 (hereinafter referred to as Holdsworth); cf. the central argument of Blatcher, *The Court of King's Bench*.

TABLE 2.5. *Status/occupation of plaintiffs and defendants in King's Bench*

| Status/occupation | Plaintiffs | | Defendants | | | |
| | | | Plea side | | Rex side | |
	No.	%	No.	%	No.	%
None given	1,688	66.8	101	2.2	21	2.2
Peer	26	1.0	3	0.1	—	—
Knight/Lady	250	9.9	14	0.3	7	0.7
Prioress/Prior/Abbess/Abbot/ Bishop/Archbishop	98	3.9	12	0.3	9	1.0
Esquire	214	8.5	63	1.4	22	2.3
Gentleman/Gentlewoman	5	0.2	124	2.7	66	7.0
Franklin/Freeholder	1	*	24	0.5	9	1.0
Yeoman	2	*	897	19.5	280	29.5
Husbandman	2	*	1,483	32.3	162	17.1
Labourer	—	—	299	6.5	39	4.1
Shepherd	—	—	34	0.7	2	0.2
Ploughman	1	*	15	0.3	5	0.5
Cleric	109	4.3	233	5.1	54	5.7
Merchant/Burgess	10	0.4	34	0.7	5	0.5
Draper	1	*	11	0.2	2	0.2
Tailor	2	*	70	1.5	21	2.2
Webster/(worsted) weaver	2	*	59	1.3	26	2.7
Fuller	1	*	43	0.9	4	0.4
Lytster/Dyer	4	*	17	0.4	11	1.2
Cordwainer/Souter	—	—	46	1.0	12	1.3
Tanner	—	—	3	0.1	—	—
Miller	—	—	19	0.4	1	0.1
Baker	—	—	11	0.2	—	—
Brewer	—	—	11	0.2	1	0.1
Butcher	1	*	100	2.2	13	1.4
Skinner	—	—	27	0.6	3	0.3
Carpenter	—	—	30	0.7	4	0.4
Mason	—	—	16	0.4	5	0.5
Smith	—	—	38	0.8	9	1.0
Barber	1	*	27	0.6	6	0.6
Boatman/Shipman/Fisher	2	*	86	1.9	13	1.4
Servant	2	*	54	1.2	11	1.2

TABLE 2.5. (*Cont.*)

Status/occupation	Plaintiffs		Defendants			
			Plea side		Rex side	
	No.	%	No.	%	No.	%
Singleman/Singlewoman	—	—	8	0.2	5	0.5
Widow	32	1.3	51	1.1	3	0.3
Wife	60	2.4	119	2.6	5	0.5
Spinster	—	—	2	*	—	—
Monk/Nun	2	*	3	0.1	2	0.2
Other	11	0.4	411	8.9	111	11.7
TOTAL	2,527		4,598		949	

* These percentages were too small to be useful.

Pekker case finally served a purpose far removed from its ostensible one.[28]

Secondly, plaintiffs could bring appeals to the plea side of King's Bench. These could concern four types of crime (murder, robbery in breach of the king's peace, rape and abduction, and mayhem) and various rules controlled their use. An appeal was to be made within a year of the alleged crime. An appeal of murder must come from the nearest kin of the slain, such as widow, brother, or son; but widows who remarried could not pursue appeals. Process on an appeal started with capias and ended in jury verdict or outlawry. An appellor who did not appear to prosecute the case could be fined; afterwards, the case might proceed at suit of the king, or might lapse. Fifteenth-century litigants appreciated the niceties of these rules, though appeals, like bills, were quite rare in King's Bench (see Table 2.2). For instance, in an appeal of robbery (as contrasted with a writ of trespass *vi et armis*), the plaintiff could recover the goods taken. This probably accounts for the fact that though robbery from the person technically implied violence, only two out of seven appeals for robbery actually allege violence, threatened or actual, against the person. We may assume that these appeals were more useful to plaintiffs who really wanted the return of specific goods than to those who wished to

---

[28] KB 27 677 m 60ʳ and 696 Rm 16ʳ.

punish violence.[29] That appeals could be part of long drawn-out property transactions, in which the orientation of the parties might change dramatically, is shown by the strange case of Richard Broughton's appeal of robbery of livestock against Alexander Bosoune, Joan Spicer, and Thomas Iselham, in Buckingham in 1439. The jury was called, but did not come until Michaelmas 1440, when Broughton failed to appear. The defendants were declared not guilty on his suit, and he was duly fined 6 marks for not pursuing it—for which Thomas Iselham (either the defendant himself or the defendant's father) stood surety! The case then proceeded at the king's suit; a jury appeared in the Trinity term of 1441, and gave another verdict of not guilty, with damages of 250 marks divided between Bosoune, Spicer, and Iselham. Perhaps not surprisingly in view of the preceding transactions, the jury, when asked whether Broughton was able to pay such damages replied firmly 'no'. The defendants then blamed the whole quarrel on another man altogether. It seems most likely that the original appeal helped to bring a settlement between the parties, one provision of which was that Broughton should drop the appeal, but the defendants should save him from the consequences of his default.[30]

Were other appeals—such as those for homicide—less liable to such manœuvring? Apparently not. Here too the rules of the courts provided unexpected loopholes and avenues for enterprise. The fact that an appeal could fail through non-appearance of the appellor, encouraged defendants to pursue a strategy of non-appearance, hoping to wear out the patience, or resources, of their opponents. Indeed, fourteen out of fifty-six appeals cases lapsed for this reason. Wise managers of litigation therefore attempted to ensure that their appellors remained eligible to pursue the appeal. This, combined with the provision that appeals of murder should come from the next-of-kin, led to widows being badgered to appeal, and to refrain from remarriage, for the sake of others' quarrels. In the 1470s, the opponents of the Paston brothers at the siege of Caister afterwards encouraged two women widowed by the siege to bring an appeal against the Pastons. One woman told a Paston servant in 1471 that she had been 'entretyd . . . to be my lordys [the duke of Norfolk's]

---

[29] See C. Whittick, 'The Role of the Criminal Appeal in the Fifteenth Century', in J. A. Guy and H. G. Beale (eds.), *Law and Social Change in British History* (London, 1984), 60–1 for contemporary recognition of the advantages of this system for the recovery of goods stolen from churches.

[30] KB 27 714 m 61ʳ and 718 fines m 1ᵈ.

wedowe by the space of an hole yere . . . and ther-to . . . bowne in an obligacyon'. But finding that 'she had neuer non avayle þer-of, butt it was sewyd to hyr gret labore and losse', she remarried, thus forfeiting her right to pursue the appeal. Clearly the women were pawns in the complex game of litigation and siege warfare played out between the Pastons and the duke of Norfolk. The duke's party harassed them to appeal, and the Pastons hunted them up to 'inquire whether they be maryed . . . ageyn . . . for I holde the hoorys weddyd'.[31] Cases like these bear witness to the fact that fatalities occurred; but do not prove that even the closest relatives of the slain regarded them as cases of deliberate homicide.

Appeals could also produce private negotiation. In 1456, the archbishop of Canterbury wrote to John Paston I about the plight of Robert Offord, defendant in a murder case, asking Paston to persuade the sheriff to 'surceesse of þ'execucion of any processe vppon þ'exigent . . . lating hym wite þat we haue written to the saide [appellor] for a conuenient treetie to be taken'.[32] This may mean that some appeals which lapsed through the failure of the defendant to appear were actually concluded out of court.

In King's Bench Rex side, too, cases might appear in various ways (see Table 2.2). A jury could indict a defendant directly for trial in King's Bench.[33] However, most Rex side defendants in this period were indicted at other courts—before the justices of the peace, for instance, or the seneschal of the liberty of Bury St Edmunds, or at a sheriff's tourn. The case was then removed to King's Bench by writ of *certiorari*. Of 314 Rex side cases, 179 appeared in this way. The *certiorari* may also have been used in the 130 cases of maintenance, murder, and other felonies in which only a writ of capias is recorded; for once the case reached King's Bench, the familiar processes, starting with capias and ending (theoretically) with verdict or outlawry were set in motion. In those cases where no defendant came, there is no way of telling whether the writs of capias were issued as a result of indictment into King's Bench or the issue of writ of *certiorari*.[34] Justices of the peace could also bring cases—but only cases of riot— to the court, by making a formal certification under the statutes 13

---

[31] *PL* ii. 433–4 and i. 443–4; note that this involved an unpleasant denigration of the women's honour.
[32] *PL* ii. 158–9.
[33] 6 Henry VI c. 1.
[34] See the statutes 6 Henry VI c. 1 and 10 Henry VI c. 6.

Henry IV c. 7 and 8 Henry VI c. 14. This was ra re; four cases occur in the period 1422–42, two of them in the complicated affair of the disturbed peace sessions at Bedford in 1439, which I will discuss more fully in Chapter 6.

As in the plea side, the formal, and apparently impersonal, proceedings hide a multiplicity of canny, purposeful devices for pursuing out-of-court concerns. I shall discuss the uses and procedures of indictments in the provinces later in the chapter.[35] But a survey of the writ of *certiorari* shows that litigants probably understood well the opportunities it gave them.

The writ was available to plaintiffs, defendants, or justices. One might surmise that justices of the peace would use it to remove to King's Bench cases of particular gravity or forensic complexity. But Blatcher is apparently right to remark on the paucity of cases which seem 'important or difficult enough to merit the attention of the superior court'.[36] Justices therefore may not have been the main users of the writ. Its flexibility for plaintiffs is illustrated by cases in the year books and by statute law. The year book for 1471, for example, quotes an argument about the dubious right of a defendant to secure by *certiorari* a reattachment of the plaintiff to hear the verdict in a case interrupted by the changeover of kings. The justices apparently took it for granted that a plaintiff could secure reattachment of a defendant in this way.[37] The statue 10 Henry VI c. 6 was intended to stop plaintiffs from using the writ to remove indictments to King's Bench 'unknown to the Party so indicted or appealed', thus procuring the outlawry of the hapless defendant.[38] This may account for some of the 130 writs of capias in cases where defendants never appeared; though it is admittedly hard to tell whether the makers of the statute had assessed the scope of the problem accurately, and whether the statute had the desired effect.[39]

Certiorari also had uses for defendants, as Post's examination of the writ in Hampshire in the late fourteenth century shows. Post compares the outcome of cases brought to the court by *certiorari* and by appeal. He finds that *certiorari* cases tended to end favourably to the defend-

[35] See nn. 52–61.
[36] Blatcher, *The Court of King's Bench*, 48
[37] Neilson (ed.), *Year Books of Edward IV*, 114–15 and 128.
[38] Cf., for instance, Sir Robert Wyngfield's manœuvre against Lyston (above, n. 24).
[39] Certainly there is no noticeable drop in the number of cases coming in from East Anglia by *certiorari* after 1432.

ants, who generally gained either an acquittal or a pardon, while appeals more often resulted in a verdict favourable to the appellor. He notes the comparatively high proportion of defendants who appeared in cases brought by *certiorari*, and deduces that they probably sued out the writ in order to display pardons already bought, or register acquittals of which they were certain beforehand.[40] This manœuvre was apparently undertaken in East Anglia in the fifteenth century, though much less often than in Post's sample of cases. The contrast between the outcomes of appeals, and of those cases brought in by *certiorari* is hardly observable. True, of 309 cases perhaps brought by *certiorari*, only three reached a verdict favourable to the plaintiff. But of fifty-six appeals brought in King's Bench, only one resulted in a hanging verdict; in another damages were awarded, but we have no evidence that they were paid. Clearly the rate of verdicts favourable to the plaintiffs was very low, both for appeals and for *certiorari* cases (see Table 2.3). It is also true that a greater proportion of Rex side cases ended in pardons or acquittals than did cases of appeals—45.5 as opposed to 23.2 per cent. But the difference disappears if one counts, in appeals, the 25 per cent of cases where the defendant was discharged because the plaintiff failed to appear, a happy outcome unavailable to defendants in *certiorari* cases. (Perhaps they purchased pardons or arranged acquittals because they had no chance of evading punishment by persuading or forcing an appellor to give up an appeal?) Finally, an examination of the thirty-six Rex side cases ending in pardons or fines suggests that little more than half were in fact brought by the defendant. For if defendants sued out the writ to display pardons already granted, we would expect them to plead pardon or make fine in the same term that the case was brought to King's Bench. But in seventeen cases, no pardon was pleaded nor fine made until at least a term after the case appeared; in thirteen of these the delay between the case's appearance and the defendant's ran into years. We must presume that in these cases, the *certiorari* was sued out for the purposes of the plaintiffs. However, in nineteen cases, pardons or fines appeared promptly enough to suggest defendants triumphantly vindicating themselves. In three instances the defendants had previously been outlawed in inferior courts, yet were immediately on

---

[40] J. B. Post, 'Criminals and the Law in the Reign of Richard II with Special Reference to Hampshire', D.Phil. thesis (Oxford, 1976), 274–78.

hand to plead their pardons, thus presumably checkmating their adversaries.[41]

Whether defendants or plaintiffs brought cases into the Rex side of King's Bench, the motives seem to differ from those of litigants on the plea side. It was clearly important to these people to have a verdict recorded—of the 310 cases, 119 (38.4 per cent) reached an end of some sort.[42] However, verdicts against defendants were very few; in three cases of alleged violence against the person, damages were awarded, and there was one sentence of execution—for a woman's complicity in the murder of her husband.[43] Two cases where no actual violence was alleged ended in the defendants pleading clergy. Presumably the aim of the litigants was not to achieve the formal punishments available to the courts. But possibly the nuisance to the defendant of having to appear in court and await a jury verdict, was used as a kind of informal sanction against unacceptable behaviour.

Clearly, too, the Rex side of King's Bench could become a place to test disputed property and legal rights, as the collusive action between the priory and the citizens of Norwich shows.[44] One must suspect that the many cases of maintenance and embracery (known only by the capias which appears in the records) were in fact moves in more long drawn-out quarrels. It is at least clear that these do not necessarily represent an upsurge in the intimidation of juries by the violent retainers of bastard feudalism. There were ninety-two of these cases (nearly 30 per cent of all Rex side cases minus certifications); but

[41] It seems that the writ of *certiorari* was used by 17th-cent. defendants in Chancery and King's Bench to delay the progress of cases in lower courts, sometimes indefinitely; see J. S. Cockburn, *A History of English Assizes 1558–1714* (Cambridge, 1972), 130–1. Lambard includes the writ of *certiorari* among the impediments to a case being determined at the peace sessions (W. Lambard, *Eirenarcha or of the Office of the Justices of the Peace* (London 1581; repr. Theatrum Orbis Terrarum Ltd.: Amsterdam, 1970), 409–14). It is tempting, but untenable, to read this ploy back into the 15th cent. Cockburn's evidence implies that the defendants were trying to avoid appearance altogether. This was not common practice in East Anglia 1422–42. In 171 of the 179 cases we know to have been brought to the Rex side by *certiorari*, the defendants appeared, and either traversed or demurred. Even counting all the writs on the Rex side as issued after a *certiorari* (excluding the 4 cases of certification by justices of the peace), most cases (55.2%) produced a defendant.

[42] This figure of 310 cases excludes the 4 justices' certifications.

[43] KB 27 690 Rm 3ʳ—Margery Tatenell, widow of Walter, was condemned to be burned. One other death sentence was recorded in King's Bench—in a plea side bill against the murderer of Thomas Cutte of Buckinghamshire (KB 27 666 m 38ʳ).

[44] See Ch. 6, n. 75.

none show any proof that violence was used. Indeed, in the instances where a detailed account is given, the offence was bribery rather than violence. In 1440–1, Henry Sturmer argued that the jurors in an assize of novel disseisin between himself, Sir John Fastolf, and others on one hand, and Sir John Curson *et al.* on the other, had taken 'gifts' of up to 5 marks, plus food and travelling expenses from the opposing camp.[45] Whatever the status of the allegation, it was clearly one issue in a continuing (non-violent) property dispute. Similarly, in 1426 Walter Aslak and Richard Killyngworth were engaged in a complicated dispute with William Paston over alleged defamation of Paston.[46] Presumably as an aid to his cause, Aslak brought a suit to the plea side of King's Bench in Michaelmas 1427, which alleged that the jurors in Paston's action against him and Killyngworth in the Norwich guild-hall had been bribed with sums of up to 22 shillings each.[47] The evidence of these cases suggests either that juries could earn some pleasant bonuses from the litigiousness of their neighbours, or that the renowned Norfolk legal establishment (of which Sturmer was a busy member) had realized the nuisance value of alleging maintenance in the pursuit of other quarrels.

So much for the possibilities and uses of the central court of King's Bench. It is at least clear that though the cases I have dealt with alleged violence, it is difficult to prove that the disputes which spawned them actually involved serious force. By far the majority of cases in Table 2.1 dealt with charges of asporting goods and damage to property, which need never have involved personal violence; and it seems that even allegations of assault, and other violence against the person, might be used simply to further the litigants' pursuit of property rights, rather than to signify the occurrence of actual violence. But what of the courts in the provinces—the sessions of oyer and terminer, assizes, gaol deliveries, peace sessions, sheriff's tourns, coroners' inquiries, and manor courts?

The depressing scarcity of evidence from these sessions must be emphasized here. From East Anglia 1422–42, neither peace rolls, coroners' rolls, nor sheriffs' tourns records survive. There are docu-

---

[45] KB 27 716 Rm 69ʳ and 718 Rm 31ᵈ. Bellamy implies that the practice of ensuring the attendance of jurors by providing them with travelling expenses and lodging was fairly common in the 15th and 16th cent. (*Bastard Feudalism and the Law*, 28).

[46] See Aslak's petition to the duke of Bedford, *PL* ii. 505–7.

[47] KB 27 666 m 118ʳ.

ments from only two of four known sessions of oyer and terminer.[48] I have found no relevant evidence from church courts. Records from manor courts and courts of liberties and towns exist in quantity, but they are too fragmentary and unevenly distributed geographically and chronologically to be used in this study.[49] Deductions about the work of justices of the peace, coroners, and commissioners of oyer and terminer must therefore be made from the surviving records of the cases they sent to King's Bench and gaol delivery.

Twice yearly, in late February and late July, the justices of gaol delivery set out to tour the six East Anglian counties—Norfolk, Suffolk, Cambridge, Huntingdon, Bedford, and Buckingham. We are lucky to have records of 199 out of the 252 sessions which must have been held, plus evidence from twenty-five town gaol deliveries. The justices' object was, ostensibly, to hear and determine the cases of prisoners held in the county (and town) gaols. The whole complexion of gaol delivery sessions was thus very different from King's Bench. The problem of getting defendants in court was forestalled. The sheriff and his officers had already arrested and imprisoned the suspects, juries had been impanelled, and the sheriff had seen to the compilation of a calendar of cases for the judges' guidance. As can be seen from Table 2.6, all cases came to a verdict, except for those few referred to another court, those where the suspect escaped, or where some unfortunate had died in prison before the justices arrived. In other words (though contemporaries would never have put it this way) King's Bench was largely a court for civil suits; whereas gaol delivery was a court where the punishment of crime notionally took place. This is not to say that the court was mainly concerned with violent crime— an overwhelming proportion of charges (86 per cent) were of non-violent offences, mainly larceny. But it is fair to assume that a suspect

---

[48] Two were general commissions; one sat in East Anglia in June 1427 under Humphrey of Gloucester (*CPR, 1422–9*, 404); the other at Henhowe in May 1431 (*CPR, 1429–36*, 132). Cases from these are represented only by indictments transferred to King's Bench. A damaged manuscript containing cases from a Cambridge oyer and terminer of 1430 (apparently issued in response to a parliamentary petition against Cambridge arsonists—*Rot. Parl.* iv. 349 and 358) survives in JUST 3 8/4; and see Ch. 6 for an account of a Norfolk oyer and terminer of 1441. Other commissions were issued, but produced no evidence that sessions actually took place; for a Cambridge example, see *CPR, 1422–9*, 173–4 and Ch 5.3.

[49] See the Court Rolls (General) series in the Public Record Office; also N & NRO YC/4 for some Yarmouth court records. Such sources are potentially very valuable for future study, but to include them in my statistics would be to mislead the reader.

brought to gaol delivery had been treated as a criminal, rather than as an honourable anatagonist is a property dispute. In view of this, it is not surprising that a survey of gaol delivery records gives the impression that even fewer of the defendants were gentry than in King's Bench. Labourers, servants, yeomen, husbandmen, tailors, weavers, shepherds, carpenters, 'common thieves', and the like fill the lists of defendants; gentlemen are almost never encountered answering to offences at gaol delivery.[50]

Table 2.6 shows that the sessions were well used; a total of about 2,508 cases appeared over twenty years, more than in King's Bench. Most were for crimes which involved no necessary violence against the person. By far the majority of cases in the category of non-violent crimes were of larceny, though there were some instances of trespass and (occasionally) lollardry. Rape/ravishment has been included in this category since, as the analysis of these cases in Chapter 3 makes clear, they were often brought by fathers or husbands wishing to recover the value of goods taken by their eloping daughters and wives. Alongside these instances of non-violent crime occur 210 cases of homicide, robbery (which technically implied assault), other forms of assault, and other crimes which may have involved violence, such as arson.

In general a case at gaol delivery followed one of three procedures. First, any prisoner appearing on indictment or appeal had either to traverse or demur the case. If the case was traversed, a jury gave the verdict. Secondly, prisoners might have been arrested on suspicion of felony or trespass (mainly larceny), probably by warrant of a justice of peace.[51] They were brought before the court, and proclamation was made that indictments could be taken against them. If any appeared, the case proceeded as above. Thirdly, such a suspect might appear, but have no indictment or appeal made against him or her. The suspect was then held to be acquitted. Justices of gaol delivery could

[50] I have not carried out a strict statistical survey of the status of defendants in gaol delivery, but see e.g. the 50-odd pages of JUST 3 209, JUST 3 8/4, JUST 3 8/11, and JUST 3 8/13.

[51] *The Boke of Justices of the Peas* (n.p., 1506; repr. London Professional Books Ltd.: London, 1972) gives examples of warrants to arrest rioters and to send suspected felons arrested by the constables to gaol. Gaol delivery records show cases where the suspects were arrested on suspicion of felony, or to give security of the peace, by order of justices of the peace, see e.g. JUST 3 220/3 m 7 (Bedford 1441 by John Broughton), JUST 3 219/3 m 55ʳ (Bedford 1427 by Hugh Hasilden), and JUST 3 206 m 21ᵈ (Huntingdon 1427 by Roger Hunte).

TABLE 2.6.   *Cases at gaol deliveries in East Anglia, 1422–1442*

	No.	%
How cases came to court		
Indictments before justices of the peace	1,240	49.4
Indictments before seneschal of Bury St Edmunds	146	5.8
Indictments before coroners	39	1.6
Indictments before sheriff's tourns	8	0.3
Indictments at views of frankpledge	10	0.4
Indictments before other courts	7	0.3
Appeals	71	2.8
Arrests on suspicion	987	39.3
TOTAL	2,508	99.9[a]
Crimes alleged		
Non-violent crimes (including rape/ravishment)	1,315	86.2
Homicide	104	6.8
Assault and robbery	51	3.3
Assault and rape	14	0.9
Assault	12	0.8
Other	29	1.9
TOTAL	1,525[b]	99.9[a]
Verdicts		
Acquitted	1,137	45.9
Acquitted for lack of indictment	888	35.9
Acquitted for mistake in the indictment	64	2.6
Acquitted because of insanity	1	—
Delivered for examination for heresy	9	0.4
Delivered to other courts	32	1.3
Pardoned	7	0.3
Escaped	23	0.9
Executed	248	10.0
Pleaded clergy	47	1.9
Turned approver	6	0.2
Abjured the realm	2	0.1
Died in gaol	12	0.5
TOTAL	2,476[c]	100.0

[a] This discrepancy arises from rounding the percentages to one decimal place.

[b] This does not exactly equal the total number of cases less arrests on suspicion of unspecified crime because some arrests on suspicion later produced indictments and some cases involved more than one charge.

[c] This does not exactly equal the total number of 2,508 because some arrests on suspicion led to an indictment, and thus appear twice in the records, but with only one verdict.

remand cases to the next gaol delivery for lack of time to take or try an indictment.

Indictments were made by a hundred jury before sessions such as the peace sessions; and the usual procedures of capias, exigent, and so on applied to the suspect.[52] But considerable detective work might take place before the charge was compiled, presumably by such figures of the local legal establishment as justices of the peace, undersheriffs, and constables. For example, the indictment of Richard Fayrcok and Martin Budde for the murder of Richer Lound alleged that the crime took place in Lound's own hall at night when the three were alone. Yet the charge describes in painstaking detail where Lound was in the hall, what he was wearing, what Fayrcok said as he struck the fatal blow. According to the indictment, to bury the body the killers dug a hole among the trees in the garden, cutting through the roots of trees—'amputand. radicis arbor.' This suggests that someone had verified the existence of the newly dug grave. Since it was also alleged that the area had been replanted to deceive searchers, it seems that someone (presumably a local legal official) organized an inquiry into Lound's disappearance which succeeded in discovering the grave.[53] Possibly this, and other details of the crime, were discovered by examination of the suspects. Sixteenth-century justices certainly took depositions and made examinations; this practice may have started, however informally, in the fifteenth century.[54] In arrests on suspicion of felony, local legal officers must have played even more prominent parts. Walter Cholestre/Margery, for instance, was originally arrested on suspicion of felony. When he was later hanged for horse-stealing, his only chattel was an 'instrumentum ferreum pro seris equinis frangendis', presumably found on him at the time of his arrest. He

[52] See e.g. writs to the sheriff to produce William Compton before several Norfolk peace sessions, 1424–5 and 1427 (KB 9 224 m 184).

[53] JUST 3 220/1 pt. ii (77) S7; and see Ch. 4.

[54] J. G. Gleason, *The Justices of the Peace in England 1558–1640* (Oxford, 1969), 9 and 12 (excerpts from Lambard's diary). As Bellamy points out, Sir Thomas More, writing in 1533, claimed that examination was often necessary to bring to light cases of treason and felony—without 'dyligent politike serche & examinacio[n]s' by 'the kinges honorable cou[n]saile, and the iudges & iustices of peace', 'many such mischiefes [would] passe bi, & by indightment neuer would be founden' (*The Workes of Sir Thomas More* (2 vols., 1557; repr. Scholar Press: London, 1978), ii. 990; cf. J. G. Bellamy, *Criminal Law and Society in Late Medieval and Tudor England* (Gloucester, 1984), 40). However, the work in question—'The Debellacyon of Salem and Bizance'—comprises an extended justification of the suit ex officio. More thus had incentives to stress that examination, as compared to jury indictment, was a normal process of law.

was thus left with little option but to turn approver, confess his crimes and those of his associates, and explain that another man had ordered him to have the picklock made.[55]

However, this does not imply that personal quarrels never entered the proceedings of gaol delivery. Jury indictments could be directed or modified by interested parties. In the Bateman murder case, six separate juries presented indictments to the justices of the peace at Cambridge on 18 March 1423.[56] But their accounts were formalized into two allegations—one of murder *modo guerrino* and *ex malicia praecogitata*, the other that the Batemans were common *insidiatores viarum*. Someone, if only the clerk of the sessions at which the indictments were taken, had organized these reports. Justices of the peace could intervene—Thomas Derham, a Norfolk justice, was presented at the 1427 oyer and terminer for refusing to take an indictment of murder against William Compton, instructing the jury to indict another man instead.[57] Though his interference was subject to inquiry, remarks in the Paston letters suggest that his behaviour was common, and to a certain extent accepted, among the gentry community. Margaret Paston, in 1465, resigned herself to the fact that 'as for any jndytementes that we schuld labor a-yenst them [the duke of Suffolk's men], it is but wast werk, for the scheryf ner the jurrours wol no thyng do a-yenst them.'[58] In 1456 William Worcester censured Thomas Higham, a justice who took an indictment unfavourable to Worcester's master, Sir John Fastolf, because he had not 'letted the presentment or . . . moderated othyrwyse'.[59] Indeed, Whittick suggests that the popularity of the appeal in the fifteenth century, despite the paucity of convictions, leads to

the inescapable conclusion . . . that the object of an appeal was not vengeance exacted by the defendant's death, but the return of a chattel or a financial settlement after the greatest possible harassment of the other party.[60]

Also, many instances occur in the gaol delivery records of a defendant being accused of the same crime by both appeal and indictment.

---

[55] JUST 3 212 m 17[r.d.]
[56] See Ch. 5.3.
[57] KB 27 666 Rm 28[r] (Compton was indicted before William Babington and John Cottesmore, however—KB 9 224 m 184).
[58] *PL* i. 314.
[59] *PL* ii. 156.
[60] Whittick, 'Role of the Criminal Appeal', 63.

These may indicate the recognition, by juries as well as individuals, of a dangerous criminal in the community. But it is equally likely that they show appellors pursuing quarrels with all means at their disposal. As Whittick points out, for instance, it was in the interests of plaintiffs to have appeals backed by indictments, since the central courts at least held that the existence of an indictment was evidence that the accompanying appeal was not simply malicious.[61]

What could the users of gaol deliveries hope to achieve? Their aims can hardly have resembled those of plaintiffs in King's Bench, since the outcomes of cases in the two courts were so different. A suit in King's Bench might constitute a warning ('settle up or else'); or might be used to disadvantage or dishonour an opponent by outlawry. At gaol delivery, the time for warnings was past; the suspect had already been arrested and imprisoned. Similarly, outlawry was out of the question. Once at gaol delivery the suspect faced the most unpleasant prospects of punishment. The law allowed only two sentences—fines for those judged guilty of a trespass, and execution for convicted felons.[62] We know of 248 cases (about 10 per cent) where sentence of execution was given, compared to the nugatory figure of two defendants (0.09 per cent) sentenced to death in King's Bench.

Of course, as Table 2.6 shows, 84 per cent of those tried were acquitted. But even these had been forced to spend some time in prison. Post has suggested that justices of gaol delivery in Hampshire in the fourteenth century used remands from one session to the next as a means of imposing short gaol sentences on prisoners whose crimes were felt to merit a punishment somewhere between fine and hanging.[63] East Anglian justices of the peace probably followed a similar plan. In Suffolk (the only county for which sufficiently detailed records were kept) most indictments heard at gaol delivery had actually been taken more than three months before. This allows the possibility that cases were not simply remanded from peace sessions to an imminent gaol delivery, but that some policy dictated the imprisoning of suspects for these stretches of time. Certainly, cases are known where men 'of bad fame', or those whom the justices suspected of being indictable in another county, were remanded to a later gaol

---

[61] Ibid. 66–7.

[62] I shall deal with the ways of avoiding these punishments below. There were, of course, various methods of execution prescribed by law.

[63] Post, 'Criminals and the Law', 86–95.

delivery despite the fact that no crime was proved, or even specifically alleged, against them.[64] In short, whatever the relationship between defendants and those who secured their appearance (whether that of opponents in outside quarrels, or criminals versus law-keepers) the interactions between the parties were punitive, in a way that interactions in King's Bench were not.

The main function of the gaol deliveries within the legal system of the county was clearly to co-operate with the peace sessions. About half the gaol delivery cases (1,240 of 2,508, or 49.4 per cent) originated there by indictment, and justices of the peace were also responsible for the appearance of some of the defendants arrested on suspicion. The personnel of gaol deliveries and peace sessions also overlapped considerably in practice. Commissioners of gaol delivery were generally also commissioners of the peace, so indictments could be taken at gaol delivery sessions as before justices of the peace. Peace commissioners probably sat with justices of gaol delivery at the sessions, and not merely as interested onlookers.[65] The records of King's Bench and gaol delivery give dates for 230 peace sessions in the period 1422–42 (see Table 2.7), of which thirty-six were held at times when the assizes and gaol delivery would also have been sitting. Twelve of these thirty-six we know to have been simultaneous with either a gaol delivery or an assize session. A comparison of known dates of peace sessions, gaol delivery, and assizes shows that on at least five occasions (24 July 1427, 22 July 1437, 24 July 1439, and 22 February 1440 in Suffolk, and 25 July 1431 in Cambridge) all three were held on one day.[66] On such occasions, apparently, all justices—of gaol delivery, of assize, and of the peace—might in effect operate together. Justices of gaol delivery, either with peace commissioners or separately, took indictments as justices of the peace.[67] The Cambridge assize roll (1422) shows justices of assize and gaol delivery taking securities as justices of the peace; while in July 1422 John Burgoyne,

---

[64] See JUST 3 207 m 23[d], 206 m 25[d], and 209 m 36[d], for examples.

[65] The gaol delivery files for most counties include a membrane which lists the names of coroners, escheator, justices, and other functionaries. Since the justices named are only a selection of those on the relevant peace commission, and since we know that in the 16th cent. justices of the peace always sat with the commissioners of gaol delivery (A. Harding, *The Law Courts of Medieval England* (London, 1973), 96) we can assume that they are lists of those justices who attended the gaol delivery sessions.

[66] Better records for counties other than Suffolk would probably show more instances.

[67] See e.g. KB 27 677 Rm 7[r], 689 Rm 9[r], 704 Rm 17[r], and 682 Rm 8[r].

TABLE 2.7. *Known dates of peace sessions in East Anglia, 1422–1442*

Date	Norfolk	Suffolk	Cambs.	Hunts.	Beds.	Bucks.	Total
1422		25 June					6
		27 June					
		29 June					
		1 July					
		24 July					
		5 Nov.					
1423	9 Apr.*	9 Apr.*	18 Mar.				7
	16 Dec.	*24 July*					
		25 Sept.					
		28 Sept.					
1424	18 July	23 Feb.					8
	26 Sept.	5 Apr.					
		22 July					
		4 Nov.					
		19 Dec.					
		21 Dec.					
1425	28 May	13 Jan.*			9 Jan.*		9
	18 July	15 Jan.					
		17 Apr.					
		18 Apr.					
		19 Sept.					
		20 Sept.					
1426	18 Jan.	21 Feb.					7
	20 July	25 May					
		3 June					
		30 July					
		6 Oct.*					
1427	11 Apr.	9 Jan.*	13 Jan.*	30 June	15 Sept.		17
	4 June	13 Jan.*					
	22 July	13 Feb.					
		22 Feb.					
		28 Apr.					
		30 Apr.					
		1 May					
		2 May					
		5 May					
		24 July					
		4 Oct.*					

TABLE 2.7. (*Cont.*)

Date	Norfolk	Suffolk	Cambs.	Hunts.	Beds.	Bucks.	Total
1428	5 June	12 Jan.*	12 Jan.*	24 July	22 Jan.		16
	12 June	15 Jan.*	20 July				
	19 July	26 Feb.					
		27 Feb.					
		31 May					
		4 June					
		21 Oct.					
		14 Dec.					
		16 Dec.					
1429		4 Apr.	12 Jan.*	12 Apr.	3 Oct.*		12
		6 Apr.	11 Apr.				
		7 Apr.					
		24 May					
		25 May					
		28 May					
		15 Sept.					
		16 Sept.					
1430	19 Jan.	20 Feb.	4 Apr.		13 Jan.*		9
	20 Feb.	16 Sept.					
	6 June	19 Sept.					
	6 July						
1431	9 Jan.*	15 Jan.	*25 July*		16 Apr.	24 May	12
	20 Jan.	7 Apr.*				28 May	
	12 Apr.	9 June					
	26 July	22 Oct.					
1432	29 Apr.	26 Apr.*	11 Jan.*			26 Apr.*	8
	22 Sept.	30 Apr.*	13 Oct.*			1 May	
1433		19 Feb.					3
		17 Sept.					
		21 Sept.					
1434	11 Jan.*	10 Apr.		2 Oct.	18 Jan.		5
	22 Feb.						
1435	22 Apr.*	8 Jan.*		23 July	4 Oct.		9
		21 Feb.					
		23 Feb.					
		23 Apr.*					
		25 Apr.*					
		22 July					

TABLE 2.7.   *(Cont.)*

Date	Norfolk	Suffolk	Cambs.	Hunts.	Beds.	Bucks.	Total
1436	12 Apr.*	10 Jan.*		6 Oct.*		12 Jan.*	17
	23 July	15 Jan.				20 Aug.	
	27 July	19 Jan.					
	25 Sept.	20 Jan.					
	20 Nov.	12 Apr.*					
		22 Sept.					
		26 Sept.					
		29 Sept.*					
		1 Oct.*					
1437	3 Oct.*	12 Jan.*	1 May			10 Jan.*	12
	23 Dec.	18 Jan.					
	31 Dec.	25 Feb.					
		11 Apr.					
		22 May					
		22 July					
		24 July					
1438	22 Dec.	10 Jan.*		21 Apr.	15 July	24 Apr.	19
	30 Dec.	14 Jan.			6 Oct.	23 June	
		22 Feb.					
		25 Feb.					
		18 Apr.*					
		19 Apr.*					
		23 Apr.					
		28 July					
		30 July					
		22 Sept.					
		26 Sept.					
		27 Sept.					
1439	2 June	12 Jan.	19 Feb.			1 June	14
	29 Sept.*	13 Jan.					
	1 Oct.*	18 Feb.					
		20 Feb.					
		26 Feb.					
		2 Mar.					
		3 Mar.					
		26 Mar.					
		24 July					

TABLE 2.7. (*Cont.*)

Date	Norfolk	Suffolk	Cambs.	Hunts.	Beds.	Bucks.	Total
1440	27 Sept.	9 Jan.	25 June		11 Jan.*		20
	3 Oct.*	17 Feb.	10 Oct.		12 Jan.*		
		22 *Feb.*			26 July		
		1 Mar.					
		6 Apr.					
		18 Apr.					
		23 July					
		25 *July*					
		16 Sept.					
		14 Oct.					
		12 Dec.					
		13 Dec.					
		14 Dec.					
1441	31 July	6 Jan.*	19 July	28 Apr.	10 Jan.*		11
	26 Sept.	12 Jan.*					
		14 Jan.*					
		2 Mar.					
		21 Apr.*					
		8 June					
1442	5 Jan.	12 Jan.*			9 Jan.*		9
	19 Feb.	25 May			29 May		
	9 Apr.				1 Oct.*		
	27 Sept.						
TOTAL	48	132	15	8	17	10	230

Note: Dates marked with an asterisk are within the limits laid down for quarterly sessions. Dates on which we know a gaol delivery or assize to have been held are italicized.

a Cambridge justice, sat with the assize judges, William Babyngton and John Cottesmore.[68]

To fit the work-loads of three judicial bodies into one session must have been difficult, since justices of assize and gaol delivery spent the shortest possible time in each county. They generally sat one day in each place on the circuit, and commonly completed the tour of six

[68] JUST 1 1533.

counties in twelve days.[69] Analysis of the surviving assize roll, and gaol delivery roll and files, for one of these multi-purpose sessions on 24 July 1427 at Henhowe, confirms the impression that little of the courts' supposed work was completed, and that very hastily. The assize roll and gaol delivery files show that at least twenty procedures were to be gone through—two cases of novel disseisin, two essoins taken, three indictments made before Robert Caundyssh and William Goderede, and thirteen prisoners awaiting delivery from gaol.[70] From the gaol delivery roll it seems that prisoners were swept through in batches; Thomas Smert, John Meyr, John Flenton, and Andrew Warner were all acquitted of varying charges by one jury, though they appeared separately on the files, and only three of them came from the same hundred. Of nine prisoners arrested on suspicion, three were speedily acquitted for lack of indictment, another by jury, and five were remanded to appear at the next gaol delivery.[71] The apparent conclusion is that these three presitigious judicial bodies on this occasion hurried through their programme, imposed no formal punishments, and managed only to add eight cases to the work-load of the succeeding session.[72] As for the role of the gaol deliveries and peace sessions in the control of violent crime, it is instructive to analyse the charges in these cases. The three indictments alleged breaking and entering. One of the prisoners was charged with assault and rape, another with breaking, entering, and rape, and two others with rape. Four were in gaol on suspicion of felony, and one to give security of peace. Thus no more than twelve cases related to any kind of violent crime, even counting rape/abduction, and assuming (against the probability) that all felonies involved violence.[73] Of these twelve cases, four were determined, as acquittals.

Thus, as with King's Bench, the apparent inefficiency of gaol delivery and peace sessions contrasts strangely with their undeniable

[69] See e.g. Feb. 1428 and July 1437; but the time could be even shorter. In Feb. 1430 the 6 counties were toured in only 9 days.

[70] JUST 1 1539 and JUST 3 219/3 m 132 and mm 154–5.

[71] JUST 3 206 m 14^r.

[72] Cf. Pugh's calculations of the duration of 11 trials at gaol deliveries in the period 1292–1302; the average number of minutes per trial was 15.8 (if justices sat together) or 31.6 if they sat singly. The highest figure (assuming the justices sat together) was 35 minutes, the lowest 9.1 ('The Duration of Criminal Trials in Medieval England', in E. W. Ives and A. H. Manchester (eds.), *Law, Litigants and the Legal Profession* (London, 1983), 104–15).

[73] See Ch. 3 for an examination of the dubious nature of 15th-cent. rape charges.

popularity—litigants used them enthusiastically, sheriffs, justices, and juries attended them diligently. Peace sessions particularly must have been a thriving legal institution in the county. In King's Bench and gaol delivery, 1422–42, 1,353 indictments came from the peace sessions—49.4 per cent of all gaol delivery cases, and 36 per cent of Rex side cases in King's Bench (62.8 per cent of those cases where the origin of the indictment is given). In terms of numbers of cases sent to superior courts, their nearest rivals (and those at a distance) were the courts of the liberty of Bury St Edmunds, and the oyer and terminer of 1427.[74] We know that peace sessions were held frequently. By statute, they were assigned to the weeks following Epiphany, Easter, the Translation of St Thomas, and Michaelmas. Over the period 1422–42, therefore, 504 peace sessions should have been held. As Table 2.7 shows, datable records from King's Bench and gaol delivery establish that 230 days' sessions took place in this period, including twelve which coincided with gaol deliveries.[75] We know that this number of days is incomplete, since the total is less than that recorded in the pipe roll records of payments to justices of the peace (Table 2.8). Adding the other 240 gaol delivery sessions at which we may presume peace commissioners to have sat would produce a total of 470 East Anglian peace sessions in the period—only thirty-four short of the number to be expected if the quarterly sessions were strictly observed.[76] Considering that this number is garnered from indirect evidence of the functioning of the peace sessions, it indicates nothing short of remarkable industry on the part of the justices. Further, Figure 2.2 shows that many sessions took place outside the

[74] There were 146 indictments before the seneschal of Bury St Edmunds in gaol delivery records (see Table 2.6); an impressive number, considering they came only from Suffolk, but still only 1.6% of all gaol delivery cases. Only 2 of the 4 oyer and terminer commissions known to have sat in the period (see above, n. 48) sent cases to King's Bench—3 from 1431, and 40 from the 1427 sessions. These comprise only 13.7% of cases on the Rex side of King's Bench.

[75] King's Bench indictments record the date and place of the peace session at which the indictment was taken, generally with the name of the presiding justice followed by '& sociis suis'. The gaol delivery files for most counties note cases as originating 'before the justices of the peace', with no details of time, place, or person; but the records from Suffolk, though they do not contain the lists of justices of the peace sitting at the gaol delivery, do record the dates of peace sessions and the name of at least the principal justice. Thus for most counties the gaol delivery records give the names of the justices who sat at gaol delivery sessions, but little information on other sessions of the peace, while for Suffolk the situation is reversed.

[76] See above, text accompanying nn. 65–8.

TABLE 2.8. *Numbers of peace sessions known from different sources*

No. of sessions known from:	King's Bench	Gaol delivery	Pipe rolls
Norfolk	43	5	47
Suffolk	42	89	78
Cambridge	13	2	79
Huntingdon	8	0	40
Bedford	17	1	20
Buckingham	10	0	16
TOTAL	133	97	280

Note: Total of datable sessions = 133 + 97 = 230.

statutory times—in February, May, June, and December, for instance. Only August, the harvest month, was virtually empty of sessions.[77] Apparently, justices of the peace were prepared to work even harder than was officially required.[78] Also, in large counties, such as Norfolk and Suffolk, peace sessions were held in many places within the county, so that some justices travelled laboriously round the shire in fulfilment of their duties.[79]

This work-load was carried by comparatively few men. Tables A3.1–A3.6 (see Appendix III) give the names of all justices of the peace whom we know to have sat. They show that while in Buckingham and Bedford sixty-six out of sixty-eight commissioners sat at least once, in the other four counties more than half of the available members never (to our knowledge) appeared at all. (In Norfolk only thirteen out of fifty possible justices sat.) Of the total of 133 working

[77] Cf. a Paston memorandum of 1452 alleging against Suffolk's men that 'þe sescionys of þe pees wyth-owte cawse was warnyd in þe myddys of hervest, to grette trobill of the contre whiche was nevere se in Norffolk at seche tym of the yere' (*PL* i. 72). This contradicts Putnam's finding that Aug. sessions were fairly common, despite 14th-cent. petitions against them (B. H. Putnam (ed.), *Proceedings before the Justices of the Peace in the Fifteenth Century* (London, 1938), p. xcvi).

[78] Pipe Rolls' accounts for Cambridge, 1430 (E 372 275) show that the justices were paid for 15 days' work, over a period in which only 3 sessions were required (19 July 1428 to 21 Apr. 1429). Even if we subtract the 2 known gaol delivery dates in this period (24 July 1428 and 25 Feb. 1429), and assume, as Putnam suggests, that quarterly sessions lasted 3 days (*Proceedings before the Justices of Peace*, p. xcvi—but I have found no evidence of such long sessions in the period 1422–42), the conclusion must be that the justices worked 4 more days than they had to.

[79] See below for a discussion of travelling justices in Suffolk.

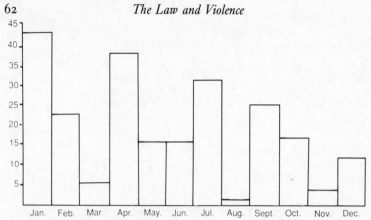

FIG. 2.2   Frequency of peace sessions by month
Note: Months in which quarter sessions were statutory: Jan., Apr., July, and Oct.

justices, an even smaller sub-group did most of the work. If we define as a diligent justice any member of the peace commission who worked at least half the number of days attributed to the busiest member of his commission, then the conclusion is that only two commissioners in Norfolk carried the load of twenty years' work; three in Suffolk, three in Cambridge, five in Huntingdon, seven in Bedford, and eight in Buckingham. Another fourteen commissioners whose careers did not span the twenty years were clearly active in their time—Andrew Botiller in Suffolk (dead by 1430) for instance, or Sir Thomas Tuddenham in Norfolk (first commissioned in 1434). But still it seems that over twenty years, the six counties—especially the large and populous ones, such as Norfolk and Suffolk, which we know sustained many sessions—were mainly served for judicial work by only forty-two people.[80]

These men formed a recognizable social group. Only two of the nine magnates, and one of the eight churchmen, listed on the

---

[80] This confirms Putnam's findings that probably only about one-third of justices commissioned in connection with the records she prints actually sat at sessions (Putnam, *Proceedings before the Justices of the Peace.*, xci). S. J. B. Endelman, 'Patronage and Power; a Social Study of the Justice of the Peace in Late Medieval Essex', Ph.D. thesis (Brown Univ., 1977) finds that about 71% of gentry commissioners sat at least once, but that lawyers were the most active members (44–5). Wright, in *The Derbyshire Gentry in the Fifteenth Century*, finds that the Derbyshire bench was largely staffed by knights, lawyers, and gentlemen, and that 'not only was the county bench the preserve of a small group of justices, but in practice it was firmly under the control of a few working magistrates' (94–5 and 98).

commissions sat more than once.[81] Of the thirty-five knights named, only seven were diligent justices. But thirty-three commissioners were said to be esquires and gentlemen, and nineteen were gentleman lawyers. Of these, eight esquires sat diligently, as did ten lawyers.[82] Obviously the lesser gentry, and particularly the lawyers, tended to staff the peace sessions. Of the two most hard-working justices in each county, one was always a lawyer or at least a man heavily involved in legal business—William Paston in Norfolk, Robert Caundyssh in Suffolk, John Burgoyne in Cambridge, Roger Hunte in Huntingdon, John Enderby in Bedford, and Andrew Sperlyng in Buckingham.[83] This reflects exactly the situation in fifteenth-century Derbyshire, where, according to Wright, the working magistrates tended to be 'professional lawyers and gentry with legal training or experience or both'.[84]

Capably and tirelessly, these forty-two men (who were also active in other areas of local government) travelled round their counties.[85] In Suffolk (the best-evidenced example) Robert Crane moved from Eye, where he held sessions on 18 April 1438 with Sir William Wolf, to Henhowe on the 19th with Robert Caundyssh, and on the 23rd to

[81] The earl of Huntingdon and the duke of Norfolk both sat several times in Bedford; but for a limited period, and probably a specific purpose (see Ch. 6, n. 150). The bishop of Lincoln sat twice in Bedford, again under unusual circumstances (see Ch. 6.2).

[82] The status of many commissioners is unknown, though some were clearly burgesses.

[83] See Tables A3.1–A3.6 (Appendix III). In some cases, this reflects the appointment of lawyers to the quorum—in 1436–7, Thomas Fulthorp, Robert Caundyssh, and Robert Crane, all lawyers, were all on the quorum for Suffolk and were diligent justices. However, John Enderby was a lawyer and diligent justice in Bedford, though never on the quorum (C 66 440 mm 48[d] and 49[d]; cf. Tables A3.1–A3.2). Also C66 424 mm 22[d] and 23[d]; 437 m 36[d] and 440 m 46[d] compared with Table A3.5. Andrew Sperlyng, though not known to be a qualified lawyer, was attorney to Henry Oldcastell (1427), and involved in numerous land and legal transactions: see *CPR, 1422–9*, 409, and *Calendar of Ancient Deeds*, i. 222 and 354; ii. 321; iii. 108; and v. 604.

[84] *Derbyshire Gentry*, 98.

[85] Thirty-one appeared on other types of legal and administrative commission; 19 were in parliament. Nine were escheators and 5, sheriffs, though these offices were hard to combine with a career on the bench. (It should be noted that a further 23 sheriffs came from the group of less diligent justices.) Others held administrative positions such as bailiffs of liberties (Richard Forster and William Fulburne, for the priory and bishopric of Ely respectively), counsel at law to Cambridge town (John Burgoyne), and steward of St Albans (John Barton II, 1408–34); see lists of officials in JUST 3 220/1; C. H. Cooper (ed.), *Annals of the Borough of Cambridge* (5 vols.; Cambridge, 1842–1908), i. 170; J. S. Roskell, *The Commons in the Parliament of 1422* (Manchester, 1954), 150–1; and KB 9 229/2 m 35.

Dunwich, again with Wolf. On 12 December 1440, Crane and Reginald Rous were at Ipswich; on the following two days they moved respectively to Wykhammarket and Beccles, and by 6 January 1441 Crane was back in Henhowe taking sessions with Thomas Higham. Between 1427 and 1431 Caundyssh, Wolf, and Botiller virtually ran all the Suffolk sessions between them, and Caundyssh travelled to all the towns at which sessions were held. They and their fellows tended to keep their places on commission for years at a stretch. Of the eighty commissioners whose death dates we know, fifty-one enjoyed uninterrupted careers on the commission until their deaths; but diligent justices were more likely to have unbroken careers—twenty out of the twenty-eight whose death dates are known were constantly commissioned. Tables A3.1–A3.6 show that they were also consistently present in practice. Their duties were onerous and not particularly lucrative—at 4s. per day, Crane (to our knowledge) earned only £10. 16s. during this period, and Caundyssh's known earnings over fifteen years total just £18. 16s.

Whatever the perceived functions of the peace sessions and gaol delivery, they must have been important to have engaged the dedication of these busy administrators. To be sure, it seems likely that diligence at the peace sessions was one way for a gentleman to render himself an attractive client in the patronage system. William Paston, for instance, according to William Dallyng, was 'with-holde of euery matere' in Norfolk and Suffolk, and took fees from (among others) the burgesses of Great Yarmouth and Lynn, the abbot of St Benet's Hulme, the prior of St Faith's Horsham, and the prior of Norwich.[86] In some cases we know of a man first as a diligent justice, and only afterwards as the retainer of a greater lord. Robert Caundyssh was retained 1433–6 by Sir John Fastolf; but he had been a notable justice of the peace since 1422.[87]

Sheriffs, too, undoubtedly benefited from the fact that their services were vital to any litigant. Comments in the Paston letters show how urgent a matter it was to gain a sheriff's support. As James Gresham reminded John Paston I in 1449, 'meche of a mannes desire þat is in trouble lieth in þe shirrefes fauour'.[88] A sheriff's power operated on

---

[86] *PL* ii. 509.

[87] Fastolf also retained William Yelverton in the 1430s, at exactly the period when Yelverton was becoming a diligent justice, see Smith, 'Aspects of the Career of Sir John Fastolf', 27 and 113.

[88] *PL* ii. 33; cf. ii. 299 and i. 314.

many fronts. In 1461 Thomas Playter wrote to John Paston I that 'at the last cessyons [some hundreds] were not warned, and the schreff excused hym be-cause he cowde not knowe who was officer there.'[89] Thus, a sheriff could forestall indictments altogether, cease process on them or on other suits, influence the composition of juries in a case, and hear cases in his own tourns. No wonder then that sheriffs were venal. As Agnes Paston in 1452 told a friend who enquired 'wheder she myte yeue the sherevys syluer or non', 'if she dede I supposed she shulde fynde hem the more frendly.'[90]

It is thus easy to see how peace commissioners and sheriffs might carry out their arduous labours in the hope of attracting fees from a wide range of people. No doubt a system of general benefit resulted. Patrons had a comfortable assurance of support (should it be necessary) in the local and central courts, justices and sheriffs got the reward of their hard work, and county peace-keeping was done by experienced, well-trained administrators. However, it still remains to be explained why litigation, and the maintenance of the peace sessions, was so important to patrons that they were eager to engage in lawsuits, and to pay those members of the community who were willing and able to sustain the sessions.

Part of the answer lies, I suspect, in the prominence of the law in bestowing authority and honour on individuals in the county comunity. I have argued elsewhere that a claim to honour in the fifteenth century depended largely on the individual's enthusiasm in pursuing the day-to-day business and legal transactions of friends and dependants.[91] As John Paston III wrote to his brother, 'remembyr to sew J. Maryottys chartyr for hys last owtlawry . . . or ellys by my trowthe ye do your-sylf a shame.'[92] Lawcourts of the Middle Ages constituted an openly visible demonstration of legitimate authority.[93] They consisted of

---

[89] *PL* ii. 262.

[90] *PL* i. 38. Cf. the payment of 40s. made in 1432 by the Cambridge burgesses to John Ansty I, the outgoing sheriff, 'In reward . . . for his good behaviour toward the mayor and burgesses in diverse matters' (Cooper (ed.), *Annals of the Borough of Cambridge*, i. 184) and the run of sheriffs listed as the earl of Suffolk's annuitants in British Library, Egerton Roll 8779. See also Bellamy's summary of late-medieval statutes designed to provide remedies at common law for those whose suits over property were hindered by partial sheriffs (Bellamy, *Bastard Feudalism and the Law*, 16).

[91] 'Honour among the Pastons: Gender and Integrity in Fifteenth-Century English Provincial Society', *Journal of Medieval History*, 14 (1988), 357–71.

[92] *PL* i. 549.

[93] See Harding, *Law Courts of Medieval England*, 13, for a succinct statement of this position.

public gatherings of those people—sheriff, justices, constable, jurors, and suitors—who accepted the authority of those who held the court, and (ultimately) of the king who appointed them. No wonder that it was at the 'sesschyonys' in 1461 that William Yelverton conveyed a stern reminder from the king to the Norfolk gentry to cease factional quarrels, and settle their differences before their courts, or their monarch.[94] Here, the court became literally the place where the king's peace was proclaimed. From the central court of King's Bench to the smallest manor court (the holding of which signified the right to hold the land) law-giving imparted authority. This was explicit in the quarrel over the Pastons' claim to the wardship of Thomas Fastolf of Cowhaugh. Bartholomew Elys, as a representative of John Paston I, came to a court at Cowhaugh specifically to challenge the keeper of it, one Bernard, charging him to 'seas and kepe nouthir court nor lete, for ye haue non autoryte'. When Bernard refused to budge, Elys publicly interpreted this as 'forsybly ye put vs from oure pocession', and warned the tenants to pay no suit nor service to the court and its holders.[95]

Courts were thus arenas for the display of authority. They occupied an intriguing position between the worlds of written and oral culture. On one hand, the language of the courts was Latin or French; to manipulate or administer the law, one had to be *literatus*, in the strict sense. Writing was a vital, and authenticating, element in court procedures. The King's Bench was known as a court of record; significantly, at the Cowhaugh court Bernard offered to allow Elys to sit beside him, 'but not to wryte'. From the public's point of view, the court procedures were rendered remote and untouchable by the use of the dual mysteries of writing and Latin. Courts could be parodied, but not controlled, by the illiterate; and even parodies of the courts were seen, in the fifteenth century, as immoral and destabilizing. The play 'Mankind' contains an excellent satire on written legal mumbo-jumbo ('Here ys blottybus in blottis, | Blottorum blottibus istis'); but it is spoken by the fiendish character Mischief, who also mocks Mercy's latinate sermonizing, and leads Mankind to despair and damnation.[96] Yet the courts were not just bastions armed with literate

---

[94] *PL* i. 277; cf. the 17th-cent. use of assizes as forums for the king's judges to make policy speeches (Cockburn, *History of English Assizes*, 3, 65, and 67–9).

[95] *PL* ii. 103–4.

[96] *The Macro Plays*, ed. M. Eccles (EETS, 262; 1969), 175–6; cf. 155.

authority. They were also public rituals of authority, where anyone might come and observe the struggle for status of the gentry of the county, and the exercise of power by one class over another. Hassell Smith considers that the status deriving from a place on the bench at peace sessions was one of the principle rewards of the office in sixteenth-century Norfolk.[97] In 1437 and 1439 in Bedford, two gentry factions nearly came to blows over the right to be seen to be administering justice.[98] Not only court-holders, but all participants in the legal process were involved in this assignment of honour by litigation. Proceedings in the courts became the matter of county rumour, to the detriment or otherwise of a gentleman's status. James Gresham wrote to John Paston II in 1471 to urge him to greater diligence in dealing with the suits out against his men because 'It is a peyne to your weel-wyllers to here your men called in exigendes'.[99]

Thus the status even of those gentry who were absent from the courts could be enhanced or undermined by the proceedings there. The courts were not mere engines for the punishment or redress of wrongs; they were the forum in which fifteenth-century gentry, either in person or through their clients, proved their status—rightly or wrongly holding property, strong or weak, influential or powerless— before the intent gaze of their peers and dependants.

For both plaintiffs and defendants, the advantages of the legal system lay in the many opportunities it gave for belittling or outwitting opponents, to their public detraction. Plaintiffs could use writs of trespass, bills or appeals, have the defendant (or perhaps better still, the defendant's servants) indicted in the peace sessions or other local courts, and could remove indictment to King's Bench if the chances of a favourable hearing seemed better, or if such a move would inconvenience the defendant. If all else failed, a petition to the Chancellor could result in the defendant being ordered to appear *sub poena*. Defendants could manipulate legal inertia to their advantage, persuading the sheriff to make no arrest, or to delay the return of the writs of exigent, or the procuring of a jury. Time gained in such a way might wear out the patience or resources of an appellor, persuade a plaintiff to an out-of-court settlement, allow the purchase of a pardon,

---

[97] A. Hassell Smith, *County and Court: Government and Politics in Norfolk 1558–1603* (Oxford, 1974), 60.
[98] See Ch. 6.2.
[99] *PL* ii. 405.

or generally render the plaintiff, in the eyes of contemporaries, ridiculous and powerless. Defendants too could petition in Chancery, or in their turn have an indictment removed to King's Bench. The plethora of courts and procedures available advantaged everyone— even the poor might hope to pursue cases in manor courts or sheriffs' tourns. Yet local courts had limited powers; they could only amerce, and could hardly compel a defendant not in the vicinity to attend. The well-off litigant, who could bring a case before a number of courts simultaneously, thus overwhelming an opponent's vigilance and resources by sheer multiplication of procedures, stood to gain most of either justice or honour. Osbern Mundford, for instance, in 1452, proposed four separate ventures to remedy his undignified loss of Brayston:

I write to þe King at þis tyme and to oþer my gode lordes for to be kepte in my pocession . . . And if so be þat I may not haue my pocession ayene . . . I wol take an accion . . . of forsable entre in my name and my wifes for our title, &c, and an accion of trespasse for dispoiling of my godes . . . and assisse of a *nouel disseson* jn my sonnes name . . . for to trye þe title and ende debate.[100]

No wonder, then, that lawsuits were snugly integrated into the general procedures of dispute and competition, such as arbitration and violence. As Thomas Denys put it, 'plee, trety' and 'werre' might equally be means to peace.[101]

So well entrenched were the courts in the ordinary life of the gentry that any quarrel tended to take on the ritual nature of the courts themselves. A Paston memorandum of the 1440s recounts a meeting between Edmund Paston and John Hauteyn, who came to lay claim to the Paston manor of Oxnead. The gatekeepers told Hauteyn he could not come in, and Edmund Paston invoked the authoritative character of the law by telling him that 'it where best declarying of his evydence in Westminster Hall'. Hauteyn then 'seyd to hem that come with hym, "Serrys I chargge yow bere record how that I am kept owth with strong hand".' Not only was he appealing publicly to witnesses to 'bear record' as a court would, but he quoted from the action for forcible entry ('with a strong hand' for *manuforti*).[102] The courts' social

---

[100] *PL* ii. 78.

[101] See epigraph at head of this chapter.

[102] *PL* ii. 522; cf. the statute 8 Henry VI c. 9. This is a good example of how a legal formula which might be taken to imply violence against the person was in fact applied to a non-violent quarrel.

influence in fifteenth-century England may thus have been even greater than their judicial role.

What was the relationship between law and violence in this period? Obviously the courts' main function was not the punishment of violent crime. In gaol delivery sessions, nearly 90 per cent of cases involved no violence. Presumably, since many of these cases came from the peace sessions, normal quarter sessions dealt with at least the same proportion of non-violent cases.[103] It is true that Putnam found some peace sessions recording a greater proportion of violent than non-violent offences;[104] but this is by no means the case with all her records.[105] Well over half the allegations—62 per cent— in King's Bench 1422–42 were of misdeeds which were not necessarily violent, such as asporting goods, depasturing land, and maintenance. Even if all remaining allegations were, incredibly, true, we could only deduce that the legal records do not provide good evidence for an upsurge of violent crime in the fifteenth century.

Yet though they are comparatively silent on the issue of violent crime, the legal records are eloquent of force justified by the law. Violence was explicit and formal in the legal process. Force was surely used to arrest suspected felons.[106] Once arrested, a suspect could be imprisoned while awaiting trial, under conditions which were sometimes harsh enough. Twelve prisoners awaiting gaol delivery in this period died before their cases were ever heard.[107] In Suffolk in 1426 two men were indicted for having arrested John Starlyng of Lakenheath, and kept him in prison for two weeks, bound 'cum ferris & cordis' so that he died.[108] Once in court, prisoners who refused to

---

[103] And see Ch. 1, n. 22, for Kimball's edition of early 15th-cent. Shropshire peace rolls.

[104] Putnam, *Proceedings before the Justices of Peace*, 176 (Somerset, 1338–41).

[105] e.g. ibid. 123 (Norfolk, 1372 and 1375–9), where homicides and assaults comprised about half the presentments for felony and trespass, but both categories were outnumbered 2 to 1 by allegations of economic offences. However, it is difficult to make firm conclusions about Putnam's evidence in view of her rather vague terminology (how many is a 'large proportion' of homicides, for example?). Cf. B. Geremek's figures from late-medieval Parisian lawcourts; though some of his court records show a preponderance of the offence of brawling, in at least 2 courts, theft comprised at least 60% of the allegations (*The Margins of Society in Late Medieval Paris*, tr. J. Birrell (Cambridge, 1987), 49, 55, 58, 60, 61).

[106] Cf. the death of John Helvy, see Ch. 4, n. 49.

[107] See Table 2.6.

[108] JUST 3 206 m 12ʳ; the case was dismissed on the grounds that the court at which the indictment was taken was not empowered to hear indictments of homicide.

plead could be subjected to *peine forte et dure*. As for punishments, the law allowed no non-violent sentence for convicted felons. Hanging was the penalty for felony; petty traitors could be drawn and hanged, high traitors hanged, drawn and quartered, women traitors and relapsed heretics burned, penitent heretics flogged. These were only the punishments of the central courts; borough customs prescribed more grisly ones. At Lydd in the fifteenth century, pickpockets and cutpurses could be nailed by the ear to a post and made to cut themselves free. At Sandwich, homicides could be buried alive. Dover felons sentenced for stealing church goods might be 'brend in the forhed with the key of the chirche'.[109] Ecclesiastical and manorial courts could impose lesser corporal punishments.[110] I have argued above that justices of the peace and gaol delivery may have used imprisonment (unofficially) as a milder form of forceful punishment.[111] Finally, a convicted felon might become an approver—that is, turn king's evidence and appeal his associates in crime. These charges might be traversed by the defendant and determined by a jury, or decided by formal battle between appellor and defendant. In the latter case, violence was literally the factor by which the case was judged. The practice was not obsolete, as the chronicler's account of the 'foule batayle' between approver and defendant in London 1455/6 shows.[112]

Naturally, this theoretical rigour was modified in practice. Some forms of legal violence were rare.[113] I know of only one defendant who did not plead, and then the jury swore that he was prevented by 'natural infirmity', and need not submit to pressing. The case was remanded.[114] If twelve prisoners died in gaol, twenty-three escaped (see Table 2.6), which argues that conditions cannot have been hopelessly severe. There were ways of avoiding legal execution. If acquittal or out-of-court settlement were unobtainable, a defendant might plead clergy (if male), pregnancy (if female), or turn approver.

---

[109] M. Bateson (ed.), *Borough Customs* (2 vols.; Selden Society, 18 and 21; 1904–6), i. 57 and 74–8.

[110] See *The Historical Collections of a Citizen of London*, ed. J. Gairdner (Camden Society, NS 17; 1876), 182 and 185 (hereinafter referred to as *Gregory's Chronicle*) for 15th-cent. pilloried offenders in London.

[111] See above, text accompanying nn. 63–4.

[112] *Gregory's Chronicle*, 199–202.

[113] e.g. *Selected Historical Essays of F. W. Maitland*, intro. H. Cam (Cambridge, 1957), 51, argues that sentences to the pillory or tumbrel for breaking the assize of bread and beer were commonly commuted to amercement.

[114] JUST 3 212 m 9ʳ.

Of these, the plea of clergy was the best way for a condemned man to save his life—forty-seven defendants in gaol delivery successfully used it. This amounts to only 14.7 per cent of those convicted in gaol delivery; but there is no record of anyone failing the reading test, and only one appellor protested that his defendant was bigamous, and therefore could not be a clerk.[115] But plea of clergy was not, of course, available to women. Their equivalent—the plea of pregnancy—was much less satisfactory. The conditions were more difficult to fulfil, and the stay of execution only temporary. Nevertheless, the two women in the gaol delivery records who pleaded pregnancy used the time gained to obtain pardons.[116] Least effective of all was to turn approver. Aside from the risks of battle, if anyone appealed by an approver was acquitted by jury, the approver was automatically sentenced to execution. Understandably, only fourteen East Anglian convicts turned approver in either King's Bench or gaol delivery in this period. Of these, nine were eventually executed on failure of an appeal, and the fate of four others is unknown. The single survivor escaped by pleading clergy. (Perhaps the appeals which gave his fellows only a short respite may have allowed him time to learn to read well enough to pass the test.)[117] There is no evidence that the actual trial by battle survived in East Anglia in the fifteenth century; indeed, the fascinated horror with which the chronicler treats the London affair may indicate its rarity throughout England.[118]

Yet the law relied, implicitly, on force and injury at almost all stages of process—bringing prisoners to court, compelling them to plead, deciding the truth of a charge, punishing malefactors. In practice, this meant that the law authorized the use of violence by the private individuals, mostly local gentry, who managed the legal procedures. There were no full-time professionals to serve writs or make arrests.

---

[115] JUST 3 210 m 28^r; though this objection to the plea of clergy was well established in legal practice (Bellamy, *Criminal Law and Society*, 116).

[116] JUST 3 210 m 16^r and 212 mm 15^d–16^r.

[117] William Pesecod was first arrested on suspicion of murder in 1436, and turned approver and pleaded clergy (on the failure of his appeal) in 1437 (JUST 3 209 m 39^d and 210 m 22^r). Cf. L. C. Gabel, *Benefit of Clergy in England in the Later Middle Ages* (Northampton, Mass., 1929), 65 ff. for the increased use of the literacy test in the 14th and 15th cent., and pp. 72–3 for 2 cases in Edward III's time of prisoners apparently attempting to learn to read while in gaol.

[118] See above, n. 112. F. C. Hamil, 'The King's Approvers: A Chapter in the History of English Criminal Law', *Speculum*, 11 (1936), 255–6 could find only 2 15th-cent. examples of approvers' battles and thinks the 1456 duel was the last ever.

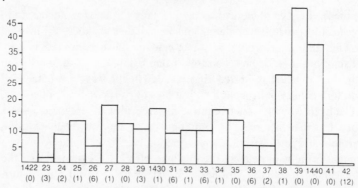

FIG. 2.3   Number of executions from gaol deliveries per year
Note: Figures in brackets give numbers of deliveries for which no record survives in
each year.

Hence it must often have been difficult to distinguish justified arrest
by servants of sheriffs or peace commissioners, from private attack; or
distraint of goods from robbery. Richard Welles, for instance, accused
a group of men in King's Bench of abducting one of his servants with
force and arms. They claimed that they had been helping the
constables to arrest the man legally. Similarly, Thomas Alcok denied
that he had assaulted John Castell, but said that he had tried to arrest
him for assault of someone else 'virtute officij sui'.[119] This confusion
of roles was not overlooked by fifteenth-century gentlemen seeking
justification for attacking an enemy; as Thomas Denys candidly
remarked, 'if I made any felaship agayn Twyer I can haf no colour
now the shirref and I be oute'.[120] The law, then, may have functioned
less to punish violence than to determine who was authorized to use
it.

Hanging verdicts in court were not frequent—only two out of 2,248
cases in King's Bench finally recorded a death sentence, and the 248
sentences of execution recorded in gaol deliveries represent only 10
per cent of the verdicts given. Nevertheless, on the figures, an average
of two felons were hanged each year in each East Anglian county.
Though the number varied widely from year to year (see Figure 2.3)
still most East Anglians must have known of hangings as a normal,
though infrequent occurrence. Examination of the crimes for which

[119] KB 27 727 m 71ʳ and 729 m 69ʳ; see also the case of William Dallyng (Ch. 5.2).
[120] *PL* ii. 234.

these convicts were executed brings to light some interesting paradoxes. For instance, it is clear that homicides ran a much greater risk of receiving the death sentence than those involved in less violent crimes. In the gaol deliveries, 104 cases of murder resulted in thirty-eight death sentences (36.5 per cent). This can profitably be compared with the rate of executions in the 1,315 cases which alleged no violence against the person—only 204, or 15.5 per cent. Apparently, fifteenth-century law-enforcers took a very serious view of homicide. Yet it must be emphasized that because of the overwhelming preponderance of non-violent offences coming before the gaol delivery, actual numbers of executions for non-violent offences outnumbered those for murder, 204 to 38. Thus, though the courts were apparently willing to make homicides pay for their deeds with their own lives, spectators of executions would more frequently see this legal violence used to combat such non-violent crimes as petty larceny. Even more telling is the comparison between alleged homicides and hangings (see Tables 2.1, 2.3, and 2.6). A total of 165 charges of homicide came to the King's Bench and the gaol deliveries between 1422 and 1442.[121] A total of 250 people were eventually sentenced to be executed. Of course this alone cannot prove that the law killed as many people in the fifteenth century as did crime. There may have been extensive underreporting of homicides. Putnam's cases suggest that at peace sessions hangings were rarer than presentments of homicide.[122] Nevertheless, it is clear that legal execution was a not inconsiderable factor in the incidence of violence in fifteenth-century East Anglia. In these public killings, justified violence was literally the function of the courts.

What then do the court records tell us about violence in fifteenth-century East Anglian society? Though many of the cases in King's Bench allege the use of force and arms, these are exactly the suits which were, it seems, routinely used in the course of transactions which had nothing to do with violent crime.[123] Even in gaol delivery,

---

[121] See Tables 2.1, 2.3, and 2.6; and these figures may include some double counting, since allegations of the same crime might be brought to both courts.

[122] Putnam, *Proceedings before the Justices of Peace*; see her summaries of classification of offences and results of the proceedings, *passim*. See also E. Powell, 'The King's Bench in Shropshire and Staffordshire in 1414', in Ives and Manchester (eds.), *Law, Litigants and the Legal Profession*, 97–100—here, a large number of indictments for homicide led to almost no convictions.

[123] Cf. e.g. Robert Ostelyn's suit against the earl of Oxford, above, n. 10.

where the cases presumably represented allegations of actual crime, most of the misdeeds involved no violence against the person. In the frequent cases of larceny, it is even doubtful whether any force against property were at issue. In short, the surviving legal records provide little evidence of a high level of violent crime in society.

But the level and quality of violence in a society cannot be measured soley by its illegal aspects as represented in the lawcourts. We have good reason to suppose that the legal records are selective. The gentry appear in them very frequently as plaintiffs, justices, judges, and victims of violence, but very rarely as violent offenders. The law was, for gentlemen, both a forum and a tool for the achievement of honour and status. In some ways the legal system allowed them also to use violence under the guise of law in pursuit of these ends. When we consider violence perpetrated under the law, the records give a vivid picture of a world in which some sorts of violence against the person, however infrequent, were yet considered legitimate and normal. The gentry of fifteenth-century East Anglia ordered forcible arrests, painful imprisonment, and public death-sentences without remorse or question.

To appreciate the logic behind these paradoxes, we need to know more about the presuppositions and motives of the law-enforcers. What did the community who ran the courts—the plaintiffs who brought suits and appeals and arranged indictments, the sheriffs who pursued cases (or allowed them to lapse), the justices who jogged diligently around the counties taking indictments, ordering arrests, and remanding criminals to prison—what did these people think they were punishing? What forms of disorder did they believe they were putting down? Why did they consider public execution an appropriate way of doing so? We need to know more precisely how the fifteenth-century East Anglian gentry who staffed the courts applied the violent sanctions of the law, and what tacitly assumed notions of the role and place of violence in society informed their legal practice. It is on these questions that the next two chapters will, I hope, shed some light.

3

VIEWING VIOLENCE: THE CONCEPTUAL CONTEXT OF VIOLENCE IN FIFTEENTH-CENTURY ENGLAND

The legal system may have acted, tacitly and in part, to distinguish those justified in exercising violence from those who were not. But this hypothesis in turn raises the question, how were the distinctions made? How did the judges, juries, litigants, and defendants decide to resort to, or refrain from, force; whether to report violence to the courts, and how to deal with it once it was there? To understand their decisions, we need to comprehend their standards. What made violence justifiable? What types of violence were approved? Was there a moral scale of violence, as the peculiar path of homicide cases in the courts would suggest? How equally were moral standards applied to different sections of the community?

It is clear initially that in the fifteenth century, as in the twentieth, violence could imply more than physical action. We talk of 'doing violence' to a belief, though assault and battery can hardly be exercised on an idea. The kinds of non-physical violence recognized in the fifteenth century were different, but the concept was ancient and potent. It was a theological commonplace to include among the prohibitions of the commandment 'Thou shalt not kill' such causes of dispute and slaughter as 'fals witnesse berynge', 'lesyngis-makynge', 'diffamynge', and 'bacbytynge'; and also such workings of spiritual violence as suicide of the soul by mortal sin, or the spiritual murder perpetrated by priests who neglected to preach right doctrine or gave 'euel esaumpulle' to their parishioners.[1] In legal terms the process on

---

[1] *Dives and Pauper*, i/2, ed. P. H. Barnum (EETS, 280; 1980), 1 (hereinafter referred to as *Dives* 2). This section deals with the 6th (or, according to the author of the work, the 5th) commandment, against homicide. See also the *Lay Folks' Catechism*, ed. T. F. Simmons and H. E. Nolloth (EETS, 118; 1901), 47 and 49; and J. Myrc, *Instructions for Parish Priests*, ed. E. Peacock (EETS, 31; 1868), 29. See also J. Shaw, 'Corporeal and Spiritual Homicide, the Sin of Wrath, and the "Parson's Tale"', *Traditio*, 38 (1982), 281–300, which traces the varying classifications of spiritual homicide from the 12th-cent. canonists to the vernacular traditions of the later Middle Ages.

a writ was the same, whether it alleged threaten(d violence ('tales et tantes minationes de vita sua mutilacione memororum suorum ... imposuit') or actual assault ('vi et armis in X insultum fecit et ipse verberavit et vulneravit').[2] Presumably all these forms of non-physical violence were subject to the same moral judgements as corporeal violence.

Some forms of physical violence were thought to be not merely justifiable, but meritorious. The excellent description of Edward IV in battle ('he mannly, vigorowsly, and valliantly assayled them [and] ... with great violence, bett and bare down afore hym all that stode in hys way') is only one instance in the great traditional literary theme of knightly violence.[3] The praiseworthy violence of chivalry pervaded the romance literature before and during the fifteenth century. Thus, the fifteenth-century English version of 'Partonope of Blois' opens with a review of the knightly qualities of Partonope's ancestors, evidenced by their violent pursuits.

> Ector was hardy and þer-to full lyghte,
> Off all þe worthyeste knyghte; ...
> On the grekes he made grette a-sayes,
> So worthy was none after hys dayes

while Clovis

> ... proued hym-selfe a nobelle knyghte.
> Grette werre he held alle hys lyfe.

Malory's 'fyers' fighters are well known.[4] Sir Degrevant appeared as a 'knight | That was both hardy and wyght | ... dowghty ... of dede'; in his successful fight with a neighbouring earl, the opponents were described thus:

> Both with spere and sheld
> Wyghtly wepenes þey weld
> And ferysly þey fyght.[5]

---

[2] See, for instance, *Clerk* v. *Kerdeston*, KB 27 701 m 53ᵈ; and *Talbot* v. *Tynwhite*, KB 27 693 m 38ʳ.

[3] *Historie of the Arrivall of Edward IV*, ed. J. Bruce (Camden Society, OS 1; 1838), 20.

[4] *Partonope of Blois*, ed. A. Trampe Bodtker (EETS, ES 109; 1912 for 1911), 3 and 12 (cf. also the long description of Partonope's fight with Sornegour the Dane, 145–62). See also e.g. Sir Thomas Malory, *The Tale of the Death of King Arthur*, ed. E. Vinaver (Oxford, 1955), 32, 44, 50, and 52.

[5] *The Romance of Sir Degrevant*, ed. L. F. Casson (EETS, 221; 1949), 3 and 19.

The authors did not shrink from retailing the gruesome details attendant on chivalric glory. As the *Laud Troy Book* says of Lamedon, 'Many he greued and al to-hewed; | That he was kny3t, ful wel he schewed.' Lydgate agrees that the battle for Troy was so fierce that 'of þe blood þat was schad of newe | þe grene soile chaungyd hath his hewe'.[6] Metham describes Amoryus at a tournament, where

> at the fyrst metying Amoryus this odyr gan smyght
> Vp-on hys umbrere; that the spere-hed lefft in hys brayn,
> And so schet hym ouer hys hors on the pleynne
> Dede.[7]

Nor is this triumphant catalogue of carnage confined to works of fiction. In one Agincourt song quoted by a London chronicler, Henry V and his knights take up the roles of Degrevant or Lamedon:

> Hontyngdon and Oxforde bothe,
> Were wonder fers all in þt fyght; . . .
> Thorow hem many on to deth were dight
> The Erles fowghten wt mayn & my3t,
> Rich hawberke thei rofe and rente.

Similarly, as the Agincourt carol has it,

> Than went oure kinge with alle his hoste
> Thorwe Fraunce, for alle the Frenshe boste:
> He spared, no drede, of lest ne moste . . .
> . . . .
> There dukis and erlis, lorde and barone,
> Were take and slaine, and that well sone . . .[8]

Vernacular chroniclers of the fifteenth century were liberal with tales of 'manly' warriors inflicting crushing defeats on their enemies, sometimes with grimly humorous detail. According to the author of *Gregory's Chronicle*, for instance, Andrew Trollope was wounded in the foot at the second battle of St Albans. When he nevertheless was knighted immediately after the battle, he remarked,

---

[6] *Laud Troy Book*, ed. J. E. Wulfing (EETS, 121–2; 1902), 43; *Lydgate's Troy Book* pt. 1, ed. H. Bergen (EETS, ES 97; 1906), 133–4.

[7] 'Amoryus and Cleopes', in *The Works of John Metham*, ed. H. Craig (EETS, 132; 1916), 37.

[8] C. L. Kingsford (ed.), *Chronicles of London* (Oxford, 1905), 120–1; *Medieval English Lyrics*, ed. R. T. Davies, Faber edn. (London, 1963), 169.

My lorde, I have not deservyd hit for I slowe but xv men for I stode stylle in oo place and they come unto me, but they bode stylle with me.

The same chronicler described Montague at the battle of Hexham thus:

loo, soo manly a man ys thys good Erle Mountegewe, for he sparyd not hyr malysse, nor hyr falssenysse, nor . . . treson, and toke meny of men and slowe many one in that jornaye.[9]

Henry V's epitaph in the *Proceedings of the Privy Council* named him 'invictissimus Rex flos & decus omnis milicie'; while letters to him from the mayor and aldermen of London spoke of his 'noble knyghthode' and praised the fact that he 'knightly auentureth for the rigth and welfare of vs alle'.[10]

The violent and destructive activities of fifteenth-century knights were thus surrounded by so great a cloud of laudatory adjectives— worthy, worshipful, manly, doughty, invincible, fierce—that no disap- proval could touch them. Further, chivalric slaughter extended from humans to the animal world. Good knights loved hunting; even their battles were often pictured as a form of the chase, the knights themselves taking the character of noble beasts of prey. Thus, of Partonope's ancestor Clovis, we are told 'Nexte dede of armes he loued bestes | To hunte' and Partonope himself first shows his worth in a hunt where he

> Pullud owte hys swyrde lyche a manne,
> And ffreshely to thys bore he ranne
> Be-twyn was then a grette stryfe,
> Butte yet the boore there loste hys lyfe.

Sir Degrevant loved to '. . . brynge þe dere to þe grounde'. Amoryus, at his tournament, acquitted himself 'as a fers lyon', while Lamedon, at Troy

> When he saw his men fleyng, . . .
> He ran thedur as a lyparde,

---

[9] *Gregory's Chronicle*, 214 and 244; see also 211. Also *The Brut*, pt. 2, ed. F. W. Brie (EETS, 136; 1908), 367, 450, and 454 (hereinafter referred to as *Brut*); 'Bale's Chronicle', in R. Flenley (ed.), *Six Town Chronicles* (Oxford, 1911), 117, 144, and 147; Kingsford (ed.), *Chronicles of London*, 141 for a very few of the possible examples.

[10] *Proceedings and Ordinances of the Privy Council of England* (1386–1542), ed. Sir N. H. Nicolas (7 vols.; Record Commission: London, 1834–7), iii. 3 (hereinafter referred to as POPC); R. W. Chambers and M. Daunt (eds.), *A Book of London English 1384–1425* (Oxford, 1931), 69 and 75.

And sclow Gregeis here and there
As a lyon fers and fere.[11]

This image lends to knightly violence the magnificent transcendence of moral judgement implicit in a force of nature. As the right of a lion to hunt is unquestionable, so is the right of a knight to slay his enemies. As the lion displays his proper splendour in hunting, so does the knight in battle. Justification by natural law was explicitly recognized by William Worcester, who wrote in his *Boke of Noblesse* that 'as ire egreness, and feernesse is holden for a vertu in the lion, so in like manere the said condicions is taken for a vertue and renomme of worship to all tho that haunten armes'.[12] In this scheme of the universe, knights and lions, being both fighting species, are naturally comparably fierce.

Yet any appeal to nature as a universal justifier may conceal deeper social values. In this case, one may fairly ask what image of nature allowed fifteenth-century English people to incorporate human violence so readily and comfortably within its bounds? The answer, I believe, is that they regarded nature as the product and realm of a violent authority. God himself, who 'created neuer thynge, but that he gaf to it suche vertue as it ought to haue' was clearly, on occasion, a violent god.[13]

God's violence, however, was neither indiscriminate nor unpredictable. It acted in two related, but distinct, ways. First, God punished sinners, both directly and indirectly. John Myrc, in his festial sermons, speaks of a God who, hearing the false testimony of a mother against her son and St Andrew, sent an immediate bolt of lightning which 'brant þe modyr to colys yn syght of all men'. The author of *Dives and Pauper* asserts that God's word alone quite possibly sufficed to slay Ananias and Sapphira, the early christian embezzlers; while Thomas Gascoigne relates a miracle of the time of Eugene IV in St Paul's, Rome—

unus Catelanus cucurrit ad ymaginem Sancti Pauli ibi in illa ecclesia, et dixit, 'Ad quid portas tu gladium? ego volo habere gladium tuum'; et conabatur

---

[11] *Partonope of Blois*, 14–15; *Romance of Sir Degrevant*, 4; 'Amoryus and Cleopes', 34; *Laud Troy Book*, 42–3. See also Lydgate's reference to the 'sturdy champeoun' at Henry VI's coronation procession as 'sterne as a lyoun' (*The Minor Poems of John Lydgate*, pt. 2, ed. H. N. MacCracken, EETS, 192; 1934), 633.
[12] ed. J. G. Nichols (Roxburghe Society, 1860), 4.
[13] *Caxton's Mirrour of the World*, ed. O. H. Prior (EETS, ES 90; 1913), 145.

auferre a manu ymaginis Sancti Pauli, et, Deo tunc operante in ymagine, cum gladio illo percussit caput ejusdem miseri Catelani et divisit caput ejus in medio in duas partes usque ad mentum ejus.[14]

These are all churchmen's views; but the idea that God would infallibly discover and punish sin was prevalent also among the laity. The author of the *Brut* notes of a murderer that 'he fledde, and wolde haue goon his weye; but God wold not so; for murdour woll com oute; and so he was take.' This is only one example of a view which according to Whiting was proverbial in the fifteenth century.[15] According to Margery Kempe, Christ, like the God of the Old Testament, told her that 'I send hem [people who will not turn from their sin] prechyng & techyng, pestylens & bataylys, hungyr and famynyng . . . & many oþer tribulacyons'.[16]

Secondly, as secular authors frequently asserted, God supported the righteous in violent action. Edward IV provides the example—he killed his enemies 'trustyng verely in God's help'. At Agincourt, St George appeared in the air, fighting for the English. The Yorkist newsletter of the battle of St Albans has the duke of York declare in his pre-battle speech that 'God that is [in] Heven knoweth than our entent is rightful and true. And therefore we pray unto Al myghty Lord Jesus these wordes—Domine sis clipeus defensionis nostrae.'[17] Since he won the ensuing battle, the readers were clearly intended to assume that God had lent a favourable ear to his prayer.

God could thus be represented as uncompromisingly bloodthirsty. Yet fifteenth-century thinkers had difficulty in reconciling all appearances of violence with God's will. The author of *Dives and Pauper* has Dives ask his instructor, 'sith God byddyþ þat no man schulde slen vnriȝtfullyche why suffryth God so mychil warre ben in erde & so manye bataylyys?'. The answer given is that

---

[14] J. Myrc, *Festial*, pt. 1., ed. T. Erbe (EETS, ES 96; 1905), 7; *Dives 2*, 49, and Thomas Gascoigne, *Loci e libro veritatum*, ed. J. E. Thorold Rogers (Oxford, 1881), 206.

[15] *Brut*, 474; B. J. Whiting, *Proverbs, Sentences and Proverbial Phrases* (Cambridge, Mass., 1968), M 806–7.

[16] *The Book of Margery Kempe*, ed. S. B. Meech and H. E. Allen (EETS, 212; 1940), 48.

[17] See above, n. 3; 'A Carol of St George', in *Medieval English Lyrics*, 185, and *Brut*, 377–80, 554–8, and 596–8; and *The Paston Letters*, ed. J. Gairdner (6 vols.; London, 1904), iii. 26.

mychil folc is worþi to deyyn & wil nout stondyn to þe lawe of pes, þerfor God
hat ordeynyd . . . þe lawe of swerd & of cheualrye to bryngyn hem to pes with
þe swerd þat wil nout obeyyn to þe pes by þe lawe of charite & of resoun.[18]

This is comparable with Margery Kempe's notion that violence is the
only effective answer to human sin and disobedience. To fifteenth-
century minds, indeed, peace and violence formed a profoundly
intertwined dichotomy. It was a common literary theme to place peace
and unjust war at opposite poles of good and evil. As Lydgate wrote
in his 'Praise of Peace', 'Al werre is dreedful, vertuous pees is good.'
Yet it was equally commonly asserted that just war was the most fitting
and effective means of bringing about 'vertuous pees'. Thus Lydgate
saw no incongruity in lauding Henry V's 'prowesse and noble chival-
rye' in the French wars, as part of his 'Praise of Peace'. As the end of
his *Troy Book* makes clear, this war was to bring unity and peace to the
two realms of England and France.[19]

It seems, indeed, that the beneficial effects of violence were more
easily accepted in the fifteenth century by analogy with the peculiar
saving power of the violence done to Christ in his passion. Lydgate's
reflections on the nature of peace include a letter-by-letter analysis of
the Latin word 'pax'. 'P' stands for prudence, 'a' for 'Augmentum'
and 'Auctorite'; and

> X for Χρυσ moost digne of reverence
> Which on a cros by mortal violence
> With blood and watir wrot by a relees
> Of our trespacys and for ful confidence
> With hym to regne in his eternal pees.[20]

The violence done to Christ was thus the heart and origin of all true
peace. Likewise, the contemplation of Christ's sufferings had an
effect—sometimes extremely precise—on personal salvation. As one
fifteenth-century poet wrote,

> O! Mankinde,
> Have in thy minde
> My Passion smerte,
> And thou shall finde
> Me full kinde.

---

[18] *Dives* 2, 54.
[19] *Minor Poems of John Lydgate*, 791; cf. Whiting, *Proverbs*, 67, and below, n. 68. See
also Harriss (ed.), *Henry V*, 23.
[20] *Minor Poems of John Lydgate*, 786.

Another has Jesus advising those tempted to the deadly sin of anger,

> When thou art wroth and wolde take wreche,
> Kepe well the lore that I thee teche:
> Thoro my right hond the naile goth—
> Forgif, therfore, and be not wroth.[21]

For Margery Kempe the power of Christ's passion translated all earthly violence into edification; she records that she learned to weep for Christ's death if she saw a man or beast wounded, 'er ȝyf a man bett a childe be-for hir er smet an hors er an-oþer best wyth a whippe.'[22]

If the acknowledgement of the violence done to Christ was seen to be of paramount importance in one's salvation, the violence itself, though not good, was necessary and beneficial in its effect. Furthermore, there are instances where fifteenth-century writers seem to link Christ's passion with other righteous forms of violent action, including the power of God to judge and punish. It is, for instance, 'Wyþ . . . woundes fresch and rede' that Christ comes 'To deme þe quyke and þe dede' in the articles of faith outlined by Myrc. And Thomas Gascoigne praised the great works of God because

fecisti plurimos homines mori in Anglia emittendo sanguinem per os, per nares, per oculos, per ungues, per juncturas, et per secessum, scilicet in illis partibus corporis per quas horribiliter jurare consueverant scilicet per oculos Xti . . . per sanguinem Xti, per cor Xti preciosum per clavos Xti in suis manibus et pedibus.[23]

In the one case, Christ's wounds appear as an integral part of his authority, in the other, God's justification for the punishment derives ultimately from the pre-eminence of His son's passion, and contingently from human blasphemy against the suffering Christ.

Fifteenth-century people had, it seems, a profound sense of the necessary place of violence in the universe, confirmed beyond question—sanctified, almost—by the violence suffered and used by God. Any orthodox fifteenth-century lay person could hardly have professed

---

[21] *Medieval English Lyrics*, 168 and 208; cf. also the *Lay Folks' Catechism*, 21.

[22] *Book of Margery Kempe*, 69.

[23] Myrc, *Instructions*, 17 (cf. 14 and 26); and Gascoigne, *Loci e libro*, 12.

complete pacifism without claiming to be holier than God Himself.[24]
Peace was highly valued—'Jesu! for thy mercy endelesse, | Save thy
pepill and sende us pesse,' prayed a poet in 1500, echoing Richard of
Caistre a century before.[25] But God's ways to peace were not
necessarily pacifist; and humankind, created, with all nature, to fulfil
God's purposes, was therefore bound to undertake active violence.
This was especially true of kings and knights, called by nature to war;
God hates a coward knight, asserted John Audelay.[26]

Yet even common people could become God's instruments to
punish sinners or uphold the righteous. The *Brut*, recounting the
executions of Richard II's henchmen by Henry IV, notes that the duke
of Exeter was arrested by 'the commons of the Contre' who 'smote of
. . . [his] hede'. This execution was then ratified *de facto*—they
'brought hit to London vppon a pole, And hit was sett on London
Brigge.' *Gregory's Chronicle* for 1463 records that when Edward IV
rode north, attended by the 'fals duke' of Somerset,

> the comyns a rosse uppon that false traytur thee Duke of Somersett, and
> wolde have slayne hym with yn the kyngys palys. And thenn the kynge with
> fayre speche and grete defeculte, savyde hys lyffe for that tyme, and that was
> pytte, for the savynge of hys lyffe at that tyme causyd mony mannys dethys
> son aftyr.[27]

It seems that the chronicler would have thought the commons justified
had they succeeded in lynching the duke.

The violence of God, though it might enjoin violence on mankind,
also provided strict guidelines for its exercise; ungodly kinds of
violence were quite unjustifiable. As we have seen, God's violence
could be of two kinds, punishing the wicked and supporting the
righteous, but His motive throughout was the peace, protection, and
welfare of His people. His power and absolute moral supremacy went
hand in hand. Earthly violence, to fit God's purposes, had to conform

---

[24] The slightly different cases of clerics and heretics are discussed below, text
accompanying nn. 105–6 and Ch. 4, text accompanying nn. 52–6. See also K. Haines,
'Attitudes and Impediments to Pacificism in Medieval Europe', *Journal of Medieval
History*, 7 (1981), 369–88, for a wide-ranging survey of medieval ambivalence towards
pacificism.

[25] *Medieval English Lyrics*, 262 and 148; see also Lydgate's poem praising peace (n.
19 above), and Launcelot's view in Malory, *Tale of the Death of King Arthur*, 51.

[26] See nn. 11–12 above; and *Medieval English Lyrics*, 172.

[27] *Brut*, 392; and *Gregory's Chronicle*, 221. Note that M. Hicks, 'Edward IV, the Duke
of Somerset and Lancastrian Loyalism', *Northern History*, 20, (1984), 29–30, points out
that this tale must be a chronicler's construction.

to this paradigm. For example, new knights of the Bath were charged to 'suffir noo murdreris nor extorcioners of the kyngis pepill with in the Contre there ye dwelle but with yowre power ye schalle lete doo take them and put them in to the handis of Justice.'[28] In the *Historie of the Arrivall*, Edward IV, godlike himself in his ability to punish rebels and establish just authority, through 'the helpe and grace of Allmyghty God . . . and by his full noble and knyghtly cowrage, hathe optayned two right-great crwell, and mortal battayles' against 'rebells' and those 'maliciously disposed'. In consequence, the writer would have the readers believe, 'He shall appeas his subgetes thrwghe all his royalme; that peace and tranquillitie shall growe and multiplye in the same.' Most vernacular chronicles, when they praised good knights, were careful to specify that they fought against malice, against the unrighteous, or against national enemies.[29] The author of *Dives and Pauper*, hammering home the point, states that God has given to lords 'þe swerd to punchyn schrewys' and that 'whan þe knyȝt fiȝtynge in his ryþth & for þe ryȝth sleth his aduersarie' it is 'manslaute . . . don for nede & for helpe of þe comounte & for sauacion of hem þat ben vngylty.'[30]

In essence, then, the paradigms of human violence implied three things. First, just violence was to be carried out by someone in a right relationship with authority. This was because all authority came ultimately from God; a claim to be acting on God's behalf would therefore be more convincing if the agent could be seen to be acting under established authority. Secondly, just violence must be done for a good motive; for example, to ensure the peace and welfare of people powerless to compass these things for themselves. This led to an insistence by fifteenth-century theorists on the need to examine minutely the motives of manslayers. Their concern was not the twentieth-century legal one of whether homicide or merely assault was intended; rather they were at pains to determine whether the killer acted for justice and the public good, rather than for private gain or pleasure. Thus, *Dives and Pauper* specifies that for even legal execution to be just,

[28] A. Harold, Viscount Dillon, 'On a MS Collection of Ordinances of Chivalry of the Fifteenth Century belonging to Lord Hastings', *Archaeologia*, 57: pt. 1. (1900), 68.

[29] *Historie of the Arrivall*, 39–40; see also *Gregory's Chronicle*, 224 (quoted above, n. 9); 'Bale's Chronicle', 144; and *The Chronicle of John Hardyng*, ed. H. Ellis (London, 1812), 393–4.

[30] *Dives* 2, 13 and 36.

þe entencion of þe iuge & of þe pursueris & þe offyceris ben riȝtful, þat þei slen hym in sauacion of þe riȝt & for sauacion and example of oþre, nout for lykyng of venchance ne of cruelte, nout hauynge lykyng in his peyne.[31]

Similarly, the Yorkist newsletter of St Albans claimed that York, when forced to fight, bade his men consider 'yn what peryle Ingelonde stondes inne ... therefor euery man help to her power for the ryght ... and ... quyte us lyke men in this querell.'[32] The last clause is significant. Fifteenth-century writers quite commonly stressed the manner in which a battle or other act of violence was carried out, apparently because the good motives of the agents might be judged by their outward demeanour. Manly knights, for instance, met their enemies 'in playne felde' or 'in myddys of the fylde'; they did not sneak up and attack treacherously and furtively, as one pursuing an unrighteous quarrel might do.[33]

These two prerequisites of just violence together impinged on the third—that just violence could be undertaken only against certain people. The wicked were the prime targets, but the necessity for an agent of violence to act under authority inhibited the exercise of just violence against a social superior. A king, for example, held God-given authority, and his subjects could hardly be right to oppose such authority violently. This accounts for the fact that according to the Yorkish newsletter of St Albans, York asked Henry VI to be 'good and gracyous sovereyne Lorde to his legemen, whech with al ther power and mygth wille be redy at alle tymes to leve and dye with hym in his rigth'. He claimed to have come to St Albans not to oppose the king, but only to take charge of 'hem whych hav deserved deth' (the duke of Somerset). Similarly, Hardyng would have his readers believe that the Yorkists at Northampton 'came as worthy warriours | ... to been the kyng his socours'.[34] Clearly, real violence against a king could not be openly declared because of its inherent unrighteousness. On the other hand, the necessity for the agent of violence to act with a good motive—the protection of the powerless—could forbid attack on the common people. A fifteenth-century 'Diatorie' urges, for instance, 'To poore folk do þou no violence.' The satirical 'Sage Fool' in his

---

[31] Ibid. 36–7; cf. Shaw, 'Corporeal and Spiritual Homicide', 285, for the long ancestry of this notion.

[32] *Paston Letters*, iii. 27.

[33] See below for examples of this unjustified type of violence.

[34] *Paston Letters*, iii. 26 (Gascoigne, *Loci e libro*, 203, offers a very similar explanation); *Chronicle of John Hardyng*, 403–4.

mocking testament to the reversal of good social order, bequeaths to his master's almoner 'my Babyll; Be Cawse when he delyueryth your Almys A-monge the pore pepyll they prese on hym & thene he betis them with hys Staffe þat the Blode Ron Abowte there erys'.[35] According to one chronicle, before the battle of Northampton, Warwick ordered his troops that 'no man shuld laye hand vpponne the kyng ne on the commune people, but onely on the lordes knyghtes and squyers.'[36] The effect of this alleged prohibition would be to ensure that violence was directed only against those who, under the rules of the system were undeniably fair game—those fellow fighters to whom Warwick and his knights owed no allegiance, and whom they were not bound by the laws of chivalry to protect.

The only exception to this policy of amnesty towards the poor and helpless was, of course, that a king, knight, or gentleman might chastise the people for their own good. The author of *Dives and Pauper* talks of knights bringing the obstinate 'to pes with þe swerd'. The vicar of Sporle wrote to John Paston I in 1450 about a fine of one noble which both of them evidently felt to be a quite unmerited punishment for a man who 'chasticed a servante of hes . . . and drow blod on hym'.[37] Such exceptions still fall within the system I have outlined—to chastise the lower orders for their improvement was part of the duty of the righteously violent.

This ordering of violent action bears close resemblance to the well-known late-medieval guidelines for the just war, of which the *Boke of Noblesse* speaks, and which are summed up in *Dives and Pauper* as 'a ry3tful cause, a ry3tful intencioun, & autorite of a lauful prynce'.[38] The need for right authority is the same in both war and general violence, as is the prerequisite of a pure motive; and the right intention and right cause specified for a just war imply the need for the discrimination of targets which fifteenth-century people thought should be exercised in all cases of violent action. Thus the ancient debate over the nature of just warfare merged in the fifteenth century

---

[35] *Manners and Meals in Olden Times*, ed. F. J. Furnivall (EETS, 32; 1868), 56; *Treatises on Precedence and Courtesy, English and Foreign*, ed. F. J. Furnivall (EETS, ES 8; 1869), 78.

[36] *An English Chronicle of the Reigns of Richard II, Henry IV, Henry V, and Henry VI*, (1377–1461), ed. J. S. Davies (Camden Society, OS 64; 1855), 97 (hereinafter referred to as *English Chronicle*).

[37] *Dives* 2, 54; and *PL* ii. 59.

[38] *Boke of Noblesse*, 6–7; and *Dives* 2, 55.

with the problem of violent action as a whole. The two issues shared so many assumptions that it is difficult to see how they can validly be separated. For instance, Russell's remark that 'the theologians often conflated the spiritual war of virtue against vice with physical warfare'[39] would apply equally well to fifteenth-century ideas of civil violence.

Such an ethic legitimated certain sorts of violence so successfully that the exercise of force became, like holy war, 'not merely just, but justifying'.[40] A knight could be known by his exercise of chivalric violence; Lamedon's slaughter of the enemy, unassisted by other evidence of righteousness, witnessed to his true knighthood.[41] Besides, God's chosen instruments of violence had, so to speak, credit in hand. Since they were by nature likely to be both righteous and violent, condemnation of their proceedings could be only cautiously attempted. The author of *Dives and Pauper*, discussing the responsibility of a prince's subjects to serve him in war, allows that they might be justified in refusing to serve if he were clearly embarked on an unjust cause for bad ends; but only if they were *absolutely* sure of the prince's wickedness, insanity, or ungodliness. If there were any shadow of doubt in the matter, the prince must be given the benefit of it.[42]

This credit granted to the perpetrators of chivalric violence may account for the fact that the writers of romances evidently felt little need to justify explicitly the apparently gratuitous butchery in which their heroes often engaged. The author of *The Romance of Sir Degrevant*, for instance, was clearly more interested in retailing Degrevant's bloody encounters with a neighbouring earl than in justifying his motives, though the readers are briefly told that he intended to protect his tenants. Similarly, according to Metham, it was only in the intervals of his busy schedule of tournaments that Amoryus saved the citizens of Dorestre from a troublesome dragon.[43]

These theories of allowable violence inevitably set the parameters of unjustifiable violence. Obviously, violence undertaken in ways directly contrary to the system could never be approved. If a true

---

[39] F. H. Russell, *The Just War in the Middle Ages* (Cambridge, 1975), 293; but comparisons with the 15th-cent. theory of violence can be drawn in many places throughout.

[40] M. Chibnall, *The World of Orderic Vitalis* (Oxford, 1984), 147.

[41] See above, n. 6.

[42] *Dives* 2, 56; the obedience owed to the God-given authority of the prince influences this decision, since the same latitude does not apply to knights and friends of the prince 'nout soget to hym be obedience'.

[43] *Romance of Sir Degrevant*, 9–25; and *Works of John Metham*, 44–57.

knight's motives might be discerned by his honourable manner of proceeding, a false knight could be known by his cowardly and treacherous approach to, and despatch of, his enemies. One vernacular chronicler, for instance, described how in 1419 the Dauphin 'ffalsly and vntrewly and ayenst alle maner Lawe off Armes mordrid the . . . Duk [of Burgundy]' by allowing one of his noblemen treacherously to slay the duke, kneeling before him. Similarly, it is recorded that Earl Douglas of Scotland came to England in 1455 because the Scots king 'hadde vnmanly and traytourly slayne the sayde erle hys brother vnder sauf conduct'. In Lydgate's version of the death of Lamedon at Troy, Hercule's 'cruel violence' consisted in casting Lamedon's head 'Among þe hors, . . . | Withoute pite or any reuerence'.[44] None of these killers lived up to the standards of good knighthood.

Similarly, if public-spirited motives justified violence, unworthy ones damned it. The author of *Dives and Pauper* noted that no battle should be undertaken 'ne for non malyce for to ben venchyd ne for non cruelte & lykynge to schadyn blood . . . & for her wickyd entencion God suffrith men to be ouyrcomyn' even in a 'ryȝtful cause'.[45] On the issue of the righteous cause itself, the *Boke of Noblesse* states that

whan tho that wolde avenge have noo title, but sey Vive le plus fort [that] is to sey, Let the grettest maistrie have the feelde . . . in soche undew enterprises their can be thought no grettir tiranny, extorcion ne cruelte.[46]

Likewise, when law is overturned, all authority for violence disappears; it then becomes unjustifiable. John Paston III wrote to John Paston II, telling him of the enormities perpetrated by Yelverton's men, in these terms: 'for what so euyr they do wyth ther swordys they make it lawe . . .' The disgraceful result of this radical defiance of constituted authority was, according to John III, that 'Ther dar no pore man dysplese theym'.[47] The whole system of lawful hierarchy had been upset, with predictable consequences; the ostensible protectors of the people had become their oppressors.

Finally, violence directly contrary to God's law was naturally inexcusable, as Cain found to his cost. The *Boke of Noblesse*, too, urged its readers to 'kepe the lawes of God, for in doubte that ellis God

---

[44] Julius B II, in Kingsford (ed.), *Chronicles of London*, 72–3; *English Chronicle*, 70–1; and *Lydgate's Troy Book*, 139–40.

[45] *Dives* 2, 55.

[46] *Boke of Noblesse*, 7–8.

[47] *PL* i. 532.

wulle suffre oure adversaries punisshe us withe his rodde.'[48] It is partly in these terms that the author of *Dives and Pauper* condemns suicide—everyone is a servant of God, and to deprive God violently of one's service cannot be allowed.[49]

Thus the language of chivalry and righteous violence—godly, manly, lawful, rightful, worthy, fierce—inevitably drew behind it a vocabulary of opposites and pejoratives—ungodly, cowardly, unrightful, tyrannous, traitorous, cruel—which might be used to define and condemn the wrong sorts of violent action.

Yet this was not the only language available for the castigation of fifteenth-century violence. Legal formulae enriched the denunciation of unjust force. The formal pleas of the lawcourts were stereotyped and not designed to distinguish violence from non-violence; but they were well known, and evidently had significant connotations. Suing out a writ of trespass *vi et armis* was the commonest means of bringing a case to law;[50] even women, who rarely appeared in court, knew the correct terms. Elisabeth Clere interrogated a suspect tenant of hers as to whether he had ever alleged to her enemies 'þat my [Clere's] men come in-to his place with force and armes'. Presumably both she and the tenant appreciated the slanderous power of the description.[51] Similarly, indictments for more serious crimes (assault, murder, attempted homicide) provided a rich pejorative vocabulary. As Kaye has shown, the terminology distinguishing those cases of homicide which were thought to be particularly reprehensible, and therefore not pardonable *de cursu*, was by no means settled in the fifteenth century. On the basis of statute, administrative, and case evidence, Kaye argues that after 1380, the term *felonice interfecit*, commonly used to denote inexcusable homicide, was joined by the phrase *et murdravit*, whose old meaning of slaying by secrecy, by night, by stealth, or by ambush, had then recently been revived.[52] However, this fine distinction

---

[48] 'Mactatio Abel', in *The Wakefield Pageants*, ed. A. C. Cawley (Manchester, 1958), esp. 9–13; and *Boke of Noblesse*, 56.

[49] *Dives* 2, 51.

[50] See Table 2.2.

[51] *PL* ii. 199.

[52] J. Kaye, 'The Early History of Murder and Manslaughter', *Law Quarterly Review*, 83 (1967), 383–8. Sir W. Holdsworth, *A History of English Law*, (16 vols.; London, 1903–66; 4th edn., London, 1934; repr. 1966), iii. 314–15 (hereinafter Holdsworth) agrees with Kaye on the identification of murder with secret homicide in the late 14th cent. Cf. the use of the term by the London chronicler of 1419 to denote killing by treachery (above, n. 44).

between two sorts of culpable homicide, whose punishments and possibilities of pardon remained the same, did not survive long. Clerks in the fifteenth century tended to use the phrases 'felonice interfecit' and 'murdravit' interchangeably, or, more commonly, together.[53] Kaye believes that throughout the period, the phrase 'ex malicia praecogitata' meant, at its most precise, only that a felony had been committed 'wilfully', 'deliberately', or 'wickedly'.[54] The upshot of this lack of strict definition appears to have been, in part, that a great breadth of pejorative terms was available to clerks, litigants, and the public, in describing homicides and other acts of violence. Of the six indictments of homicide against the Batemans, for instance, all specify that they slew ('interfecerunt') the unfortunate John Broun, but some add 'et murdraverunt' as well.[55] Legal charges of all sorts frequently concentrated on the unworthy motives of malefactors, with a view to establishing the presence of stealth, treachery, or ambush ('X . . . iacuit in insidiis . . . ad verberandum . . . Y'). For further effect, the phrase 'ex malicia praecogitata' might be added to these details, whether the charge involved homicide or not. Henry Baily, allegedly, 'ex malicia praecogitata iacuit in insidiis ad interficiendum' John Ferrour, but only succeeded in beating him up.[56] Indictments might also show care to describe the physical circumstances of the accused— what weapons they used, what company they had; for these could witness to their ill intent. Robert Kyng and Joan Aleyn, for instance, were indicted in Cambridge in 1430 because they 'iacuerunt in insidiis *cum gladiis & dagardis* . . . ad verberandum & interficiendum [Thomas Kyngston] ex eorum malicia'.[57] When murder was allegedly done or threatened by more than one person, arms-carrying was often indicated by the phrase 'modo guerrino arraiati & armati', which implied a warlike motive inappropriate to peacetime.[58] Some indictments may even have been artistically constructed around such damning phrases. In the peculiar case against William Cuttyng, he was alleged to have

---

[53] Kaye, 'Early History of Murder and Manslaughter', 569–70; and see the evidence of Putnam, *Proceedings before the Justices of the Peace*, p. cxvi.

[54] Kaye, 'Early History of Murder and Manslaughter', esp. 372 and 392–3. Holdsworth believes that the phrase came to define murder from less serious forms of homicide at this period (*Holdsworth* iii. 314–15), but Kaye's evidence, and that from King's Bench cases 1422–42, tells against this view.

[55] See Ch. 5.3.

[56] KB 9 232/1 m 81.

[57] KB 9 1046 m 40 (emphasis mine).

[58] See e.g. the Bateman indictments (Ch. 5.3).

poisoned Robert Thomas by giving him a drink mixed with powdered glass 'cum aliis venenis'. The indictment states that he gained access to Thomas by breaking into his house 'ex malicia praecogitata . . . vi & armis', with swords and staves.[59] There is no suggestion that he forced Thomas to drink the mixture with threats of assault, though it is explicitly stated that he gave him the drink there and then. The indictment makes no sense as it stands—why would an intending murderer come to his victim's house armed as for fighting, and incur a charge of forcible entry, if he could in fact persuade his victim by other means to take poison? Yet if Thomas died by the sword, why allege poisoning? The most probable explanation is that the charge of armed entry, with all its evocative details, was inserted to blacken the character of the accused.[60]

Such phrases and concepts were incorporated into everyday discourse with telling effect. William Paston, in a draft memorandum to the arbitrator of his quarrel with Walter Aslak, claimed that Aslak had threatened to murder him and his servants, just as one John Grys had been done to death in Norfolk some years before. Paston lent authority to his description of this 'orrible' murder by salting it freely with English versions of good legal terms—'felons and brekeres of the Kynges peas', 'of malice and jmaginacion forn-thowght', 'felonowsely slowen and mordered'.[61] No doubt, as a notable lawyer, he might be expected to have such courtroom phrases ready to his pen. But Margaret Paston, too, described Yelverton's men in 1469 as riding 'like men of werre' ('modo guerrino', perhaps?). Her son acknowledged the force of legal formulae in public opinion when he wrote to his brother, warning him, when gathering Norfolk men to impress the earl of Oxford, to 'be ware off on payn and that is thys: Heydon wyll off craffte sende amonge yow par case vj or more *wyth harneyse* fore to sclandre yowre felawschep wyth seying that they be ryotous peple'. Taking up the legal emphasis on arms-bearing as a clue to intention, he advised his brother, 'Requere the gentelmen . . . that iff any men . . . bere any suche harneyse to do them leue it, ore any glysteryng byll.'[62]

---

[59] KB 9 224 m 2 and KB 27 673 Rm 4ʳ.

[60] It would, for instance, have the effect of making the crime technically homicide in the course of felony. In any case, it is probable that forensic science at the time could not promise a high rate of success to simple charges of poisoning.

[61] *PL* i. 8.

[62] *PL* ii. 336 and 432 (emphasis mine).

In legal terms arms-bearing also helped to distinguish a particular form of justifiable violence—homicide in self-defence. The statutory definition of self-defence laid the strongest emphasis on the perpetrators' unwillingness to commit the deeds, as witnessed by their circumstances. Technically, to be sure of winning the case, the defendant had to be attacked, flee as far as possible, and strike the fatal blow with a chance weapon as a last resort. This tough set of conditions was clearly seldom met, and Green considers that pleas of self-defence which did not match the requirements could yet succeed in the fourteenth century.[63] The fifteenth century saw such cases too; but even when the self-defendant was said to have carried arms, it seems that juries sometimes made a comparison between the weapons carried by the defendant and by the victim, and assessed the defendant's guilt accordingly. William Hervy, for instance, was allegedly armed with a staff when his attacker 'violenter' struck him with an iron pitchfork. He killed his assailant; but the jury acquitted him on a plea of self-defence.[64] Technically they were wrong; but they were probably influenced by the legal notion that intention was the principle by which cases might be judged, and that weapon-carrying indicated intention. The law itself thus recognized degrees of evil in violence.

Occasionally, the condemnatory vocabulary of legal records mirrors literary usage almost exactly. Both genres, for instance, roundly vilified violence against helpless innocence. A King's Bench indictment recorded an assault on Simon Bocher and the brutal killing of his infant son John 'super mammas . . . matris sue . . . lactantem'. These words reflect Lydgate's description of the 'merciles' Greeks sacking Troy—'children soukyng at her moder brest | þei mordre & sle'.[65]

Legal concepts and phraseology thus contributed to the formation and expression of fifteenth-century views on unacceptable violence; but provided no clues as to its causes and contexts. To understand how this question was tackled in late-medieval England, we must turn back to the literary sources.

These, not surprisingly, show that the origins of unjust violence were thought to lie in a breakdown of that natural and God-given order which justified right violence. The very language used to

---

[63] Green, 'Societal Concepts of Criminal Liability for Homicide', 676–80.

[64] KB 27 666 Rm 1ʳ; see also the case of Thomas Chapeleyn (*sine die* because of alleged defects in the indictment—KB 9 223/1 m 82 and KB 27 668 Rm 8ᵈ).

[65] KB 27 676 Rm 4ʳ; cf. *Lydgate's Troy Book*, 140.

condemn anti-social violence is revealing. The battle of Shrewsbury, for instance, was 'one of the wyrste bataylys that evyr came to Inglonde' according to the author of *Gregory's Chronicle*, precisely because it was the 'unkyndyst' (that is, most unnatural)—a civil war, in which father and son, brother and cousin, slew one another.[66] Likewise the Didcot parson, alleged by his parishioners to be 'unkynde', was called so not only because he tried to raise the price of a rick of straw which the parish wanted to buy, but also because he maintained men to ambush and assault his congregation.[67] Violence in these cases was a form of rebellion against nature itself, and involved a wilful turning away from God's purpose in nature. The author of *Dives and Pauper*, lamenting the state of the nation, feared that 'God wile maken an ende of this lond, for we louen no pees ... but oure lykyngge is al in warre and wo, in mordre and shedyng of blood'. He replies with grim irony to Dives's query as to the lack of modern martyrs, claiming that there are 'þese dayys martyris al to manye', for 'þey sparyn neyþer here owyn kyng ne her buschopys, no dignyte, non ordre, no stat, no degre, but indifferently slen as hem lykyth ...'[68] The mark and origin of unjust violence is its rebellion against all hierarchical order; Pauper's horror of this cries out in the phrase 'indifferently slen'. Culpable violence, it seems, arises when humans discard the hierarchical rules which enable the exercise of violence with proper discrimination.

Such rebellion against God and nature may appear in many forms. Popular revolt was an obvious example, in which the people (not on the whole seen as naturally vested with the power to exercise violence) made unauthorized attempts to take over the role of their natural leaders. Vernacular chroniclers, for example, were cautiously willing to acknowledge the justice of the people's protests in Cade's rebellion, up to the time when the commons began to exercise forceful executive authority.[69] Cade's behaviour on his entry to London provoked some of the harshest criticism. One chronicler remarked that he

rood aboute the cite beryng a nakid swerd in his hand, armed in a peire of brigaundynez, weryng a peire of gilt sporis, and a gilt salat, and a gowne of

---

[66] *Gregory's Chronicle*, 103–4; cf. *Brut*, 549. The description also echoes biblical accounts of the chaos of the last days before the second coming of Christ—cf. Matt. 10:21–2.

[67] *Stonor Letters*, 1. 68–9.

[68] *Dives and Pauper*, i/1, ed. P. H. Barnum (EETS, 275; 1976), 148 and 208–9 (herinafter referred to as *Dives 1*).

[69] e.g. 'Bale's Chronicle', 130; *Gregory's Chronicle*, 190; and *English Chronicle*, 65.

blew veluet, as he hadde be a lord or a kny3t—and yit was he but a knaue,—and hadde his swerd born befor him.

Another says that he rode into the city 'wt grete pride, And at london stone he strak upon it lyke a Conqueror'. Cade's arrogance, according to the chroniclers, masked his real purpose of violent robbery and tyranny.[70] In other words, the culpable violence of this rebellion sprang from a wilful denial of heavenly and human laws—in fact, from sin. Yet fifteenth-century people acknowledged that the sins which gave rise to violence were not confined to the subjects of authority. If lords and knights failed to fulfil their duty of protecting the people by the exercise of justice, popular rebellion was only to be expected. Friar John Brackley wrote to John Paston I about the punishment of notorious evil-doers, asserting that 'Si ista indilate et cum omni possibili celeritate cicius non reformaueritis, timendum valde supponitur de insurreccione plebis . . .' John Hardyng, advising Henry VI, noted the difference between his reign and his father's, in that Henry V

> . . . kept the lawe and pese
> Thurgh all Englonde, that none insurreccion
> Ne no riotes than wer withouten lese.[71]

Even local lawcourts, representatives in their turn of godly and human order, might be seen as satanically subverted if they failed to do justice. An indictment against Geoffrey Waryn, for assault and 'contumelious words' against Richard Potter, alleges that Potter was a capital pledge of the Yaxham leet in Norfolk; and that Waryn, convinced that Potter and his fellows had unjustly amerced him, appeared at the leet of February 1440, assaulted Potter, and claimed that he and other 'hedborwes of the last lete' had 'soten abowte your verdyte makyng at that day *as a company of devels & nout as men*'. Whatever the rights of Waryn's particular case, in his eyes, clearly, injustice was literally devilish. In this instance it apparently resulted in recourse to violence.[72]

---

[70] *English Chronicle*, 66; *The Great Chronicle of London*, ed. A. H. Thomas and I. D. Thornley (London, 1938), 182 and 184 (hereinafter referred to as *Great Chronicle*); R. Fabyan, *The New Chronicles of England and France*, ed. H. Ellis (London, 1811), 622, and 'Vitellius A xvi' in Kingsford (ed.), *Chronicles of London*, 159.

[71] *PL* ii. 206; and C. L. Kingsford (ed.), 'Extracts from the First Version of Hardyng's Chronicle', *English Historical Review*, 27 (1912), 744.

[72] KB 9 234 m 27 (emphasis mine). The clerk, either wishing to be accurate, or despairing of translating Waryn's idiom, gives the insults in the speaker's 'lingua materna'.

The specific sin which in fifteenth-century terms most directly caused violence (both intended and realized) was naturally wrath. Among the questions to be asked by the confessor concerning wrath, Myrc suggests, 'Hast þow in wraþþe any mon slayn | Or holpe þer-to by thy mayn?' According to the *Lay Folks' Catechism*, wrath is

a wykkyd sterynge of boldness of herte. whe-þorwȝ a man couytys to make wreche or wykkydly venge hym on his euyn-cristyn. And of þis comys stryuynge and chydynge with men; fals othys and many fowl wordys slaundrys, for to for-do a mannys good fame, fyȝtyng and felony and ofte man-slawȝter.[73]

Yet even wrath must be seen as more than a simple, sufficient and immediate cause of violence. In fifteenth-century terms, to succumb to wrath involved a wilful surrender to the forces of unreason and godlessness. That godliness and reason went together in the fifteenth-century mind is sufficiently obvious; in *Dives and Pauper* we read that 'Goddis lawys and holy chyrche lawis ben as resonable and as goode as þe kyngis lawis,' and in the play 'Wisdom', Lucifer attempts to seduce the Soul from God by urging that 'The *wyll* of þe Soule hathe fre dominacyon | Dyspute not to moche in þis with reson'.[74] Moreover, fifteenth-century authors linked wrath with will, as opposed to reason, or 'wit'. The writer of a poem on the moral life advises 'Lete neuere þi wil þi witt ouer lede | Of wraþful wordis euermore be ware.' Myrc counsels the confessor to ask the penitent 'Hast þow any tyme be wroth so | þat þy wyt hath be a-go?'[75] In this scheme, then, surrendering to wrath automatically involved a turning away from godliness and reason.

There was even a fifteenth-century sense that wrath could so deprive people of their senses as to render them less than rationally human. A saying from the end of the fifteenth century has it that 'A man that is malyciously wroth is for the tyme half wode'; and a proverb from 1400 runs that 'Wraththe is a wodeschip that turneth man in to beeste.' Certainly there are many fifteenth-century examples of angry people being likened to wild beasts—'As angered as a boar', 'as wood as a boar', 'wroth as a wode bore', 'Wode in his wrathe, wild as a lion', 'As wood As any tigre'. There is even a proverbial phrase 'As wroth

---

[73] Myrc, *Instructions*, 35–6; *Lay Folks' Catechism*, 91.

[74] *Dives 1*, 160; *The Macro Plays*, 130 (emphasis mine).

[75] *Manners and Meals*, 34; Myrc, *Instructions*, *35;* Whiting, *Proverbs*, W 704; see also Shaw, 'Corporeal and Spiritual Homicide', 294–5, on wrath as spiritual disorder in pre-15th cent. theology and literature.

as the wind'.[76] Here is the reverse side of the laudatory references to knights as beasts of prey.[77] Though the imagery allows the perpetrators of violence to be seen as blameless natural agents, it carries the less comfortable connotation that violence may be bestial rather than human in character, inimical to the rational godliness which marks true humankind. The continual linking of wrath and bestiality surely implies that wrath and humanity—and wrath and sanity—do not consort naturally together, and that people who give way to wrath thereby step out of their human nature, denying their reasonable allegiance to God. Wrath itself might be literally fiendish. Myrc's advised penance against it was that the penitent consider

> How aungelus, when he ys wroth,
> From hym faste flen and goth,
> And fendes faste to hym renneth,
> And wyþ fuyre of helle hys herte breneth,
>
> . . . And makeþ hym syche as þey arn,
> Of goddes chylde, þe deueles barn.[78]

The connection between wrath, madness, and hell is particularly significant because it seems that indiscriminate violence was taken to be a distinctive sign of madness. Whiting notes a saying of 1400 comparing someone to a 'wod hound that biteth and knoweth not his owne maister'. Self-inflicted violence, ('al aȝenys kende', as the author of *Dives and Pauper* puts it) would be, according to Wyclif, the inevitable result of giving a weapon to a man 'in a frenesie'. Margery Kempe records that in her insanity 'Sche wold a fordon hir self many a tym . . . in-to wytnesse þerof sche bot hir owne hand so vyolently þat it was seen al hir lyfe aftyr.' She claims to have been tempted to this unnatural violence by the Devil. In impressing on her readers that the woman she later cured was truly insane, she quotes the husband's story that 'Sche wyl boþe smytyn & bityn & þerfor is sche manykyld'.[79]

Several themes, then, combine in one consistent system. Good

---

[76] Whiting, *Proverbs*, I 54, W 705, B 388–92, L 326, T 290, W 299; cf. *PL* ii. 120—John Howard is described as 'wode as a wilde bullok'.

[77] See above, text accompanying nn. 11–12.

[78] Myrc, *Instructions*, 48–9. Cf. the sense that unjust judges were more like devils than men (above, n. 72).

[79] Whiting, *Proverbs*, H 571 and *Dives 2*, 51; Whiting, *Proverbs*, M 90; *Book of Margery Kempe*, 8 and 178.

violence, inspired by God, was just and discriminating in its objects. Bad violence might therefore be identified precisely because it was either indiscriminate or wrongly directed. Lack of discrimination, and misdirection came from disregarding, or overturning, God's natural order. This viewpoint led to some ambivalence in assigning blame for unjust violence. On the one hand, sin could lead to violence either through ambition, arrogance, and disobedience, or through a failure to use one's wit to overcome wrath and resist the temptations of the Devil. On the other, madness might produce violence without the responsibility of the insane, who did not know what they were doing, and therefore could not be said to show criminal intent. In 1445 a Devon jury refused to convict a man of arson, not because they disputed the facts of the case, but because they believed that he was 'furiosus et extra memoriam suam' at the time, and therefore that 'the felony was not done of malice.' This verdict was accepted, and the man recommended to the king's grace.[80] The juxtaposition of wrath and madness made responsibility a difficult matter to determine. On the one hand, wrath could be resisted by wit; on the other, it was clearly no easy thing to overcome.

Myrc's solution to it is by no means as simple as the remedies he proposes for some other deadly sins, such as thinking of the grave for pride, and saying a paternoster thrice daily for sloth. Again, madness, inasmuch as it is produced by devils, may be resisted by the virtuous while the wicked fall into it. This assumption infuses Gascoigne's terrible cautionary tale of a rapist who 'cum cultello suo scidit membra secreta et ventrem unius puellae xj annorum' so that 'cito postea puella mortua est'. Gascoigne puts this in the context, first of the consequences of sin (due, apparently, to the debilitating effects of 'Luxuria', the man 'concumbens cum ea non potuit cognoscere eam carnaliter'); secondly, of civil rebellion (he says that the man was one of those taking part in the 'magna insurrectio' of 1450); and thirdly of madness ('et ipse vir Belial, ie sine jugo rationis . . .')[81] Thus, though the man was acting insanely, Gascoigne believed him to be at least partly to blame for his own madness. Possibly, then, the only type of violence unequivocally beyond human responsibility was that done directly by fiends, who, as Myrc said, could both 'reryn wyndys, and

---

[80] *CPR, 1441–6*, 389.
[81] Gascoigne, *Loci e libro*, 138–9.

castyn downe trees and howses', and 'reron debate and maken
manslaght'.[82]

To sum up, bad violence could be categorized and distinguished in
a number of related ways. It was at base the product and concomitant
of disorder and disobedience; it sprang in the context of chaos,
disorder, and inhumanity; it defied the hierarchical authority principles of allowable violence; it was indiscriminate or badly directed; it
was carried out by those whose motives were bad, who set themselves
up to act in opposition to moral law and king's peace, and who carried
arms where the exigencies of chivalry did not require it; and it was
done dishonourably, by treachery, trickery, and lies.

We may still ask whether unjustifiable violence was a matter of
degree. The unsurprising answer is yes; for violence was judged by its
hierarchical context. It was, for instance, clearly less criminal to offend
against inferiors than superiors, presumably because offence against
superiors implied that radical disobedience to social order which
spawned almost all illicit violence. Thus, 'fightyng, oreble chydyng,
makyng of debates, drawyng of knyves' may never have been wholeheartedly approved; but when they were done in a lord's hall, in
offence of his lordship, their gravity increased such that the wrongdoers were to be put instantly in the porter's ward or the stocks. To
strike anyone in Westminster hall, before the king's judges, was such
affront to their authority that the perpetrator was liable to lose the
offending hand.[83]

This hierarchical view of violence bore hardly, though not invariably, on those lower on the authority scale, such as women and
servants. Not *all* crimes against women and servants were felt to be
justified; and some exercise of violence was allowed to them. Thus, in
1439, William Atte Halle, a Bedfordshire labourer, was condemned
to hang for poisoning his wife Alice with 'arcenyk'; while in 1438 a
coroner's jury stressed that Joan Chapeleyn had been defending
herself against rape and murder by Everard Legard when she hit him
so hard with a wooden candelabrum that he died. The trial jury
accordingly acquitted her, swearing that in the course of his felony,

---

[82] Myrc, *Festial*, 259, cf. 150.
[83] *A Fifteenth-Century Courtesy Book*, ed. R. W. Chambers (EETS, 148; 1914), 15;
and Kaye, 'Early History of Murder and Manslaughter', 375. See also the rules for the
household of Edward IV's son (1473), quoted in N. Orme, *Education and Society in
Medieval and Renaissance England* (London, 1989), 187.

Everard 'seipsum super candelabrum . . . interfecit'.[84] The principles that homicide (especially by stealth) particularly deserved punishment, and that self-defence was allowable against felonious attack, operated as usual here. Nevertheless, women and servants were less likely to find justified objects for their own violent action, and more likely to have violence perpetrated against them in the name of some unexceptionable purpose, such as justifiable chastisement. I have remarked on the casual acceptance by the Pastons of a man's right to have chastised his servant and 'drow blod on hym'; but it must also be noted that the protest against the master's fine was upheld by this apparently unanswerable question—'[he] asked hym if a man myth not betyn hes owyn wyfe'.[85] In 1440 Henry Mayster of Norwich accused a fellow merchant, Richard Ayfield, of abducting his wife Joan. The defence pleaded that Joan had gone to live with Ayfield (apparently her son by a former marriage) because Henry beat her so severely that the blood flowed 'to her ankles'. In this case, Joan successfully escaped domestic violence for at least a short period—the mayor, coroner, and a sheriff of the city were involved in counselling the couple, and were said to have given Joan leave to go to Ayfield until they could construct a final 'concord' between husband and wife. Presumably they thought this a particularly bad case of wife-beating; but it is unlikely to have been unique, and Mayster's suit of abduction demonstrates the legal difficulties a battered wife might face if she tried to escape her plight.[86] Similarly, John Hothom, a Suffolk apprentice, brought a plea of assault against his master John Lyoun. But Lyoun was probably guilty rather of administering over-harsh discipline to his servant; for Hothom also alleged that Lyoun had forced him to carry such heavy loads that his back had become permanently bent. In this case, apparently, violence was effectively concealed behind accepted forms of good service and wholesome correction. The fact that Hothom's only redress was through the writ of trespass *vi et armis*, which could apply to a large and varied collection of civil and criminal actions, violent and non-violent, highlights the unwillingness of the period to distinguish, and provide means for dealing with, such injustices.[87] It is

---

[84] For Atte Halle, JUST 3 220/2 m (6) S1 and JUST 3 210 m 29ᵈ; for Chapeleyn, JUST 3 220/2 m (9) S1 and JUST 3 210 m 29ᵈ. In Chapeleyn's case, xenophobia may have been a factor—her assailant was stated to be a Frenchman.

[85] *PL* ii. 59.

[86] KB 27 717 m 78ᵈ and 718 m 87ᵈ.

[87] KB 27 710 m 7ᵈ.

true that a late fifteenth-century legal opinion laid it down that a
master who killed his servant (or a lord his villein, or a schoolmaster
his clerk) in the course of chastisement, was guilty of felony, since it
behoved such people to 'moderer lour correction en tiel forme qe tiel
misaventure nensuera'.[88] But this was presumably of little comfort to
those in Hothom's position, whose masters stopped short of murder.

The law of rape/ravishment itself posed systematic problems for
women subjected to violence; not least because of the total lack of
distinction between the two crimes.[89] Allegations of ravishment might
be distinguished by the inclusion of the charge of asporting goods;
and some cases clearly alleged only abduction and asporting goods.[90]
But in others, the plain formula 'rapuit & abduxit' was used to signal
cases where only ravishment—without possibility of rape—was the
issue.[91] This conflation of offences which varied widely in the quality
of violence to which the victim was subject, hardly indicates great
concern for the protection of women, or the punishment of genuine
rape. Indeed, Post remarks that the statutes of Westminster 'turned
the law of rape into a law of elopement and abduction'. This may have
been in line with common practice; according to Walker, thirteenth-
and fourteenth-century cases of ravishment quite commonly achieved
monetary compensation for the woman's family rather than the
punishment of the ravisher.[92] However as Post points out, the statutory
provision that a woman's relatives could prosecute the abductor
whether the woman had consented with him or not, certainly seems to

---

[88] This opinion was apparently attributed in the 17th cent. to Serjeant Kebell, who
died in 1500, see Kaye, 'Early History of Murder and Manslaughter', 570. Kebell
himself may have been influenced by the canon law tradition here; Raymond de
Peñafort laid it down, in such a case, that a master disciplining his pupil must not use
excessive force, see N. Hurnard, *The King's Pardon for Homicide before A.D. 1307*
(Oxford, 1969), 70.

[89] I use J. B. Post's distinction between rape (forcible coition) and ravishment
(abduction without necessarily implying forcible coition)—'Ravishment of Women and
the Statutes of Westminster', in J. H. Baker (ed.), *Legal Records and the Historian*
(London, 1978), 150–60.

[90] e.g. KB 27 664 m 44[d], 660 m 19[r], 666 Rm 32[d], and 659 m 45[d]; and KB 27 673 m
1[r] and KB 9 240 m 27.

[91] As in the two cases of abduction of a ward by the child's mother—*Henry and Anne
Inglose v. Alice, widow of Henry Reppes* (abducting her son John; KB 27 661 m 92[d]) and
John Grey of Ruthyn v. John Berney of Reedham and Margery Mautby (abducting Margaret
Mautby; KB 27 692 m 48[r]).

[92] Post, 'Ravishment of Women', 160; S. S. Walker, 'Convicted Ravishers: Statutory
Strictures and Actual Practice in Thirteenth and Fourteenth Century England', *Journal
of Medieval History*, 13 (1987), 237–50.

have made the law even more useful to husbands trying to recover goods stolen by their runaway wives, or fathers trying to prevent their daughters' marriages to unwelcome and mercenary sons-in-law.[93] Thus the law, to a certain extent, side-stepped the question of the punishment of violent rapists.

Interestingly, the issue of the woman's consent to ravishment evidently remained of some importance even after the statutes of Westminster. Perhaps families found abduction hard to prove if a woman agreed with her abductor, and if no loss of goods could be demonstrated. In this case, it would be in the abductor's interests to have the woman certify her willingness to elope. John Paston I, for instance, heard that Jane Boys had denied that she resisted ravishment, and became instantly pessimistic about the chances of a lawsuit on the issue—'I fere that her frendys shuld sew the more feyntely.' Seeking to counteract her damaging admission, he compiled a list of proofs of her unwillingness, including such heartrending examples as

whan she was bounde she callid vpon her modyre, wheche folwyd her as far as she myght on her feet, and whan the seid Jane sey she myght goo no ferther she kryid to her modyre and seid that what so ever fel of her she shuld neuer be weddyd to that knave, to deye for it.[94]

But in view of the pressures on her, her admission of consent can hardly have been unexpected; and considering the small likelihood that the law would be able to extricate her from her predicament, one must perhaps hope that Paston was wrong about her resistance.

Even in those cases where coition, rather than abduction, was clearly alleged, it seems that the law was not often used to punish rape. Many cases apparently concerned only seduction, fornication, or adultery. (The term 'fornicando' is actually used in the indictment against John Eleyne for the 'rape' of Margaret Marchaunt.) Two cases in the Norwich guild-hall in December 1440 suggest that a rape charge could be used to punish the customers of a prostitute, with (perhaps) the advantage of protecting the honour of the woman's husband. For John Turner and Thomas Speryng were each indicted of breaking into Richard Hervy's house, within three weeks of one another, attacking his wife and 'ipsam ... carnaliter cognovit'. Both were fined 2s. for the offence, as were two other 'rapists' of Margaret

[93] J. B. Post, 'Sir Thomas West and the Statute of Rapes, 1382', *BIHR* 53 (1980), 24–30.

[94] *PL* i. 69–70.

Fedymend at the same sessions.[95] It is hardly likely that Beatrice
Hervy was so unlucky as to have been chance-raped by burglars twice
in so short a time.

The rape charge was also possibly used to admonish sexually-erring
clerics. At least five defendants out of twenty-seven cases known to
concern coition from King's Bench and the gaol deliveries in this
period were clerics.[96] In all King's Bench cases of rape/ravishment,
thirty-seven clerics appear among the 216 defendants—a much higher
proportion (17.1 per cent) than among defendants generally.[97] The
details of some cases confirm the impression that the defendants were
thought to be merely breaking their vows of chastity. It was alleged
that Richard Smyth, former vicar of Stradbrook, and brother-in-law
of Margaret Smith, attacked her one Sunday ('insultum fecit') and
raped her. However, the same indictment also stated that over the
seven years before and after the given date, he had repeatedly slept
with her, which was 'against natural brotherly honour' and a 'perni-
cious example'. This phraseology suggests that the moral aspects of
the case—rather than Margaret's willingness, or the possible force
levied on her—were taken to be the major issue. In the indictment
against Thomas Pydyngton, parson of Sudbury, there is no evidence
that Joan Bailly, 'filiam suam in deitate', ever objected to the fact that
in the preceding year he slept with her 'quandocumque sibi placuerit'.
William Robyns, a Norfolk clerk, was indicted in 1435 for alleged
rape of a widow. He was also accused of heresy, and since at this time
the charges against Norfolk lollards record their unanimous opposition
to clerical celibacy, he was possibly only practising what he preached.[98]
Finally, the amazing case against Robert Stafford, chaplain, alleged
that he broke into Brusyerd abbey, assaulted Katherine Brigge, one of
the nuns, '& ipsam . . . rapuisse voluit'. That is, he suggested to her
that 'non est mortale peccatum concubere cum muliere pro eo quod
humanum & naturale est', backing up this pragmatic case with a

---

[95] KB 27 692 Rm 7[d]; and N & NRO case 8, shelf a.

[96] KB 27 675 Rm 2[r] (Stephen Esthawe), 725 Rm 6[d] (John Walpole), 727 Rm 5[d]
(William Haytor), JUST 3 219/1 m 38[r] (Roger Whyssh), and KB 27 731 m 77[d]
(Thomas Bettys). Examples of clerical defendants in other cases which do not certainly
concern coition can be found in KB 27 653 Rm 5[r], JUST 3 219/1 m 4[r], 50/12 m 33[r],
219/2 m 5.

[97] Cf Table 2.5.

[98] KB 9 938 m 83 KB 27 684 Rm 6[d]; KB 27 699 Rm 9[d]; cf. *Heresy Trials in the
Diocese of Norwich, 1428–31*, ed. N. Tanner (Camden Society, 4th series, 20; 1977),
17.

theological discussion on the veniality of the sin. His ulterior purpose throughout was, allegedly, to persuade Brigge to hand over valuable jewellery which was in her keeping.[99] In none of these cases does it seem that the object of the prosecution was to punish rape. Rather, the indictment of rape was used as a means of bringing into King's Bench cases of moral dereliction which were normally outside its scope.[100]

This does not prove that fifteenth-century people thought lightly of genuine rape. Gascoigne's censorious passage, and the execution of Thomas Elam for homicide in the course of attempted rape, indicate the opposite (at least in cases where the woman died.)[101] Yet the legal records do suggest that a charge so open to use against all sorts of non-violent abuses of law and morals must have lost some of its edge against genuine cases of forcible coition. Rape victims could hardly feel that the law provided a specific remedy for them. In the terminology of the law, punishing violence against a woman was made to appear no more important than chastising a number of moral infringements, of varying seriousness.

Indeed, the maintenance of an ordered system of power in fifteenth-century England required the upper orders of society to countenance a certain amount of violence against their social inferiors. Dives asks Pauper, for instance, whether it is a greater sin to kill one's parents or one's wife. Pauper answers that 'Boþe ben greuous synnys & mychil aȝenys kende'; but nevertheless feels compelled to distinguish between them—'it is mor synne & more aȝenys kende' to slay the parents from whom a man has his beginning, 'and also if he sle ony of hem he forfetith opynly aȝenys two comandementis of God, þe ferde & þe fyute'. The moral hierarchy of violence must be maintained, at the expense of wives' safety. A more practical case confronted Richard

---

[99] KB 27 676 Rm 2ʳ.

[100] The purpose of taking these cases to King's Bench rather than to the church courts is obscure. It cannot have been to impose heavier punishments because few rape defendants were convicted (Thomas Elam, Ch. 4, n. 34, is the only one known in the gaol delivery records); and convicted clerics could plead clergy and escape punishment (e.g. Roger Whyssh, JUST 3 219/1 m 38ʳ). A case is known where in the year of a visitation, the parishioners made no complaint of their vicar, though in the same year he was indicted for assault and rape (C. Harper-Bill, 'A Late-Medieval Visitation—the Diocese of Norwich in 1499', *Proceedings of the Suffolk Institute of Archaeology*, 34: pt. 1 (1977), 46). Possibly the odium of appearing on a charge of rape in the secular courts was a form of unofficial punishment visited on delinquent clergy.

[101] Above, n. 81 and Ch. 4, n. 34.

Cely in 1478. His wife was accused of having insulted one Thomas Blakham; Richard, justifying his position, wrote that if he had found the accusation true, 'Y wold haue had corrected her þat she shuld haue remembred it duryng her lyf.'[102] Whether Cely in fact beat his wife or not, his right to do so was clearly essential to the maintenance of his status among his fellows. Similarly, I know of no fifteenth-century case in East Anglia where a woman was physically branded for adultery or fornication. But public threats of mutilation apparently served the purpose of symbolically branding women as immoral. In 1444 Norfolk rumour reported that John Heydon had denied paternity of his wife's last child, threatening 'þat he xuld kyt of here nose to makyn here to be know wat sche is'.[103]

This hierarchical context of morality justified the legal definition of a master's murder by his servant, a cleric's by his spiritual inferior, and a husband's by his wife, as petty treason; a notion which was taken literally. Margery Andrewes, accused only of complicity in the murder of her husband Walter, was nevertheless condemned in 1434 to be burned as a traitor.[104]

I have described this system of violence as if it were all-embracing. Naturally, this is too simple. It was, for instance, chiefly a secular hierarchy. Its rules did not apply to churchmen, who were theoretically debarred from practising violence in any form. The author of *Dives and Pauper*, observing that 'god forbedeth hem [clerics] þe swerd', goes on to outline the theory in all its rigour. No priest should take part in battles or armed games, even in wars against the heathen. No priest may take any part in condemning anyone to death, nor help in any execution. No priest may slay anyone in self-defence unless the situation was such that he could not save himself by flight, and even then enquiry should be made as to whether he fell into such extremity by his own folly. To provide a woman with contraceptive medicine is manslaughter for a priest; if a priest should send a child on an errand to a river, and the child drown, the priest is to be treated as a man-slayer. The only case in which priests may bear weapons is 'whan þei

---

[102] *Dives 2*, 54; *The Cely Letters 1472–1488*, ed. A. Hanham (EETS, 273; 1975), 15.

[103] *PL* i. 220; a similar threat was allegedly made by a priest to his mistress in 1491 (from an ecclesiastical court in London, quoted in P. Hair (ed.), *Before the Bawdy Court* (London, 1972), 90).

[104] KB 27 690 Rm 3ʳ. Thomas Tatenell, allegedly her lover and the murderer of Walter, was convicted, but pleaded clergy. See also Green, 'Societal Concepts of Criminal Liability for Homicide', 693.

passyn be perlious pas to afesyn þeeuys', and even then 'þei owyn nout smytyn.' The author's justification for this is that God wishes church-men to be 'men of pees of mercy & of pyte', while 'schadyng of blood & manslaute is token of vnpacience, of vnpes, of wretthe & of cruelte.' True to the long medieval tradition that divided the upper classes between those who fought and those who prayed, this theory set churchmen in a special relationship with God, quite outside the system of violence which nevertheless had God at its head.[105] While kings and knights were called to imitate and implement God's just vengeance, churchmen must represent His mercy, forswearing all violence, godly or otherwise. Such dualism pre-empted the need to explain why God should not wish all His subjects to be 'of pees . . . mercy & . . . pyte', and how it came about that secular judges and knights should run the danger of becoming 'disposyd to cruelte' by the bloodshed which their office or rank entailed.[106]

Similarly, the moral hierarchy of violence depended on the exercise of reason and discrimination. Its provisions were therefore hard to apply to those incapable of reason. The insane, as I have pointed out above, were sometimes held not responsible for any violence they committed.[107] But the position of children, too, was equivocal, since fifteenth-century people believed that children were not reasonable, and did not have the firmness of purpose on which moral sense was based. As Caxton's *Book of Courtesye* has it, the child

> Stondeth as yet vnder in difference
> To vice or vertu to meuyn or applye.[108]

No one denied that children could be angry—'Soone meued and soone fiȝtinge' as Lydgate put it. But in view of their natural lack of reason, they could not be said to commit violence wilfully, and the fifteenth century was reluctant to believe that any real harm could follow children's anger. 'Wraþþe of children is ouercome soone | . . . In her quarel is no violence' continued Lydgate.[109] Yet equally clearly, children could not remain in this state of moral neutrality; such lack

---

[105] *Dives* 2, 37–46; cf. G. Duby, *The Three Orders: Feudal Society Imagined*, tr. A. Goldhammer (Chicago, 1980), esp. 79 and 296–8.

[106] The author of *Dives* 2 alleges (p. 40) that the priests of the Old Testament, who could both judge and execute, thereby ran the risk of becoming cruel.

[107] See above, n. 8/0.

[108] ed. F. J. Furnivall (EETS, ES 3; 1868), 3.

[109] 'Stans Puer ad Mensam', in *Manners and Meals*, 31–2; cf. Whiting, *Proverbs*, C 203 for three similar statements.

of perception in an adult would imply dangerous liability to tempta-
tion.[110] One common answer to the problem of imprinting wit, reason,
and rectitude onto the 'waxe' of childish nature was chastisement.[111]
In one sense, this can be seen as an extension of the pervading
fifteenth-century view that violence could be met, subdued, and
transformed into peace by more violence. In another, it was outside
the system altogether; though undertaken for the eventual good of the
child, and fully allowable, it was not really either supporting righteousness or punishing sin. It was merely a precautionary measure,
undertaken because an appeal to reason could not be made to
irrational children. They must instead be trained in an almost
Pavlovian way. 'A rodde reformeeþ al her necligence', thought Lydgate. Another poet wrote

> As a scharppe spore makyth an hors to renne
> . . . Ry3t so a yerde may make a chyld
> To lerne welle hys lesson, and to be myld.

It is true that N. Orme distinguishes, in fourteenth-century literature,
a current of thought which advocated more lenient treatment. Yet
references to normative corporal punishment abound in the school
exercises of the fifteenth century. Schoolboys in Bristol, for instance,
were required to translate into Latin the following salutary sentence:
'3yf jon my felow were y-bete as ofte as he doþ deserue hit, with-out
dowte he wold be come a gode chyld and an hesy wyth-yn a fewe
days.'[112]

Yet the fear that this blameless chastisement might run uneasily
close to real violence shows clearly in the privy council's worries over
the treatment of the infant Henry VI. Were his preceptors to regard
him as a king (not to be touched) or a child (requiring to be beaten)?
So knotty was this dilemma that the council was forced to issue an
official decision in favour of beating the child. His nurse was
warranted, in his name, 'de nous resonablement chastier de temps en
temps ainsi come le cas requerera saunz ce que vous serrez par celle
encheson molestee grevee ou en damagee par temps avenir'.[113] Thus

---

[110] See above, text accompanying nn. 74–81.

[111] *Caxton's Book of Courtesye*, 3.

[112] 'Stans Puer ad Mensam', in *Manners and Meals*, 31–2; and 'Symon's Lesson of
Wysdome for Chyldryn', ibid. 402; Orme, *Education and Society*, 233–47, 96, and 104.

[113] *POPC* iii. 143.

the fine distinction between justifiable chastisement and treasonable assault was affirmed.

Children and churchmen to some extent fell outside the main scope of the hierarchy of violence. Jocular violence, on the other hand, might temporarily reverse the normal workings of the system while leaving its fundamental architecture undisturbed. In a poem from the end of the fifteenth century, a birched schoolboy, complaining that his master beat him till he bled, wishes that he were a hunter, all his books hounds, and his master turned into a hare. The comic figure of Noah's wife, boxing her illustrious husband's ear, was well known in medieval drama; and in the play 'Mankind', New Guise too has a wife who 'ys my master | I haue a grett wonde on my hede.' In the Wakefield pageant of Cain and Abel, Cain has a comic servant who mocks his master at every turn, hits back when Cain hits him, and cheerfully volunteers when Cain (trying to pull rank) says, 'I am thi master. Wilt thou fight?' Again, in 'Mankind', New Guise and Mischief are represented as comically escaping from their just punishment; one was nearly hanged, but the halter broke, and the other was put in chains, which he proceeded to break, kill the gaoler, and take his widow. In all these cases, the underdog or the unrighteous are allowed briefly to emerge as the equal of their masters, and to trade blows on common terms. But the joke would be no joke in the absence of the prevailing norm, which the authors sometimes take care to reaffirm. New Guise and Mischief are diabolical characters; the beginning and end of the Wakefield pageant show clearly that Cain and his boy are both the Devil's servants.[114]

It is also true that writers produced humourous scenes about violence which directly reinforced the system. In the second shepherd's play of the Wakefield cycle, Mak the sheep-thief, a little too clever for his own good, ends up being tossed in a blanket by the shepherds he sought to deceive. Mankind, at one stage in the play, beats away his three tormentors with a spade.[115] Presumably, fifteenth-century audiences liked seeing rough justice done for law and order's sake.

Despite these areas of flexibility within the system, some problems

---

[114] *Manners and Meals*, 403; *Everyman and Medieval Miracle Plays*, ed. A. C. Cawley, 2nd edn. (Everyman, 1957), 35 and 45; *The Macro Plays*, 162 and 174–5; and *The Wakefield Pageants*, 1–2 and 12–13.

[115] Ibid. 60; and *The Macro Plays*, 166.

remained in the practical application of the theories. It is clear that it was often difficult to determine which of two outwardly similar, but morally very different, categories, an action belonged to. The very system of violence and power demanded of some people behaviour which could easily be either misconstrued as culpable, or used as a cloak for culpable violence. A lord was expected to be attended by a retinue which could serve him honourably in time of war; the problem was to tell when a retinue was *unjustifiably* warlike. Knights and gentlemen allowably and necessarily gathered together for hunting, or to attend a court day. But John Paston I recognized the ambiguous nature of such gatherings when he complained in 1454 that a company of men 'come vndur colour of huntyng' to besiege the manor of Brayston.[116] In practice, the motives of armed men were more difficult to determine than the legal records might imply; John Dam records, in a letter of 1448, a confrontation between Gunnore and Margaret Paston in the course of the debate over Gresham manor. The immediate issue was whether Margaret's men should go armed with 'wyfeles and . . . jackes'. Margaret maintained that the weapons were purely defensive and therefore legitimate—'for it was seid that she shuld be plukkyd out of here howse.' But Gunnore apparently felt equally sure that he could rightly demand that they leave off their armour. In a 'stately' manner, he replied that 'but if thei left here aray it shuld be plukked from þem'.[117]

Even the commons could enter this arena of confused roles. As I have noted, occasional punitive violence by the commons was allowed—for instance, to protect a king.[118] This concession once made, it was for the individual to identify good violence from bad. Robin Hood's exploits in the outlaw ballads, for instance, though perhaps not as socially aware as later centuries made them, could appear moral in fifteenth-century terms. He punished the wicked, was a manly and successful fighter, and claimed to be a supporter of the king's law.[119] No wonder, then, that the name of Robin Hood might be used by the violent in justifying their actions. A group of yeomen and labourers in Norfolk in 1441 allegedly armed themselves with jacks, swords, staves, and cudgels, and camped on the road at Southacre, waylaying travellers, threatening to murder Sir Roger Harsyk, and singing the song 'We arn Robynhodesmen war war

---

[116] *PL* i. 79.   [117] *PL* ii. 30.   [118] Above, n. 27.
[119] J. C. Holt, *Robin Hood* (London, 1982), 10–11, 123–5, and 142–5.

war'.[120] Whoever framed the indictment presumably thought it worth-while to include this detail as proof of criminal intent; but equally the accused evidently felt Robin Hood to be a good role-model.[121] The confusion as to whether setting out to punish one's enemies with force was actually authorized and allowable in any one instance produced this uncertainty. This in turn was possible because the criteria for judging any one case were partly superficial and easily imitated. Good knights might be known by their openly warlike mien; from this it was easy to slip to the belief that a warlike character (such as Robin Hood displayed) was its own justification.

Other forms of confusion could arise. The explanation given by the city of Norwich of the events of the so-called 'Gladman's insurrection' is a case in point. It draws on the notion that common people had a right to gather in the streets for festival and 'disporte'. The citizens acknowledged that Gladman rode through the streets in procession, but alleged that only Sir Thomas Tuddenham's and John Heydon's perjury made it appear 'that thei [the citizens] shuld an ymagined to a made a comon rysyng'. Other accounts suggest that this version is disingenuous, to say the least, and it certainly does not explain all the unrest in Norwich during the late 1430s and early 1440s.[122] But if it is a lie, it is all the more significant, since it indicates what the governing body of Norwich felt would be a plausible means of explaining away a riot. They must have realized how closely public merry-making and public disorder may resemble each other, and how the two may merge; and they were prepared to use the muddle produced by this similarity of categories to exculpate themselves.[123]

From this alone, it is clear that fifteenth-century East Anglians recognized different categories of violence, each with a distinct moral identity. These moral values performed vital social functions. The Norwich citizens tried to exonerate themselves from serious charges of rebellious riot by manipulating the categories of violence into which

[120] KB 27 737 Rm 5ʳ. I have been unable to find any song corresponding to this opening in the surviving corpus of Robin Hood literature.

[121] Cf. the case of Roger Marshall, in Staffordshire in 1498, who also adopted the name Robin Hood when embarking on a piece of only dubiously justifiable violence (Holt, *Robin Hood*, 58 and 147–9).

[122] G. Johnson (ed.), 'Extract from the Books of the Corporation of Norwich', *Norfolk and Norwich Archaeological Society*, 1 (1847), 299; but see Ch. 6.2.

[123] See E. Le Roy Ladurie, *Carnival in Romans*, tr. M. Feeney, Penguin edn. (Harmondsworth, 1981), ch. 7 for an examination of the interrelationship of revelry and riot.

their actions might fall. Paston stigmatized Aslak, using the language of the courts to lump him with a group of brutal murderers. Sir Miles Stapilton, anxious to boost his status as an honourable knight, patronized Metham, whose tale of Amoryus and Cleopes ends by asserting that 'As notabyl storyis off manhod and chyualrye' might be told 'Off knyghtys now lyuyng'—instance, that 'wurthy werryur', his patron.[124] Sir William Oldhall commissioned a book of hours which portrayed him kneeling in armour before the image of St George slaying the dragon, that ancient symbol of the evil and godless forces in the universe.[125] Could any more succinct statement of his allegiance to the values of right violence be imagined?

Besides these particular uses, the moral structure of violence acted to uphold the entire (theoretical) system of godly, hierarchical social order. Violence was explicitly justified as God's sanction against His rebels. This sanction was placed in the hands of upper-class males, who were thus responsible for maintaining order—protecting the innocent and meting out appropriate chastisement to the wicked. Their violence was both instrument and sign of their power. People of lower status, such as women and servants, tended to be justified in suffering, rather than executing, violence. This in itself served to debar them from the exercise of power. It was unthinkable that a woman, or a 'knaue' could lay claim to the knight's godly authority.[126]

I have tried, in this chapter, to show the conceptual side of this structuring of power by moral violence. The practice remains to be analysed. In my next chapter, I shall discuss the use made by the law of this hierarchical violence. The following chapters will show how, in individual instances, the intertwining factors of law, violence, and power were put to use by fifteenth-century English people.

---

[124] *The Works of John Metham*, 77–8. Stapilton seems to have been sensitive on the subject of his honour; John Paston I thought 'knavyssh knyght' a good insult to apply to him, and accused him of spreading denigrating rumours in turn about his, Paston's, 'kynred' (*PL* i. 95).

[125] British Library, Harley MS 2900, fo. 55ʳ. The image was no doubt familiar—cf. the earl of Lancaster and St George (book of hours, *c.*1322 Bodleian Library, MS Douce 231, fo. 1), and the first Garter King of Arms with St George (Bruges Garter Book, British Library, Stowe MS 594, fo. 5ᵇ).

[126] See British Library, Harley MS 6563, fos. 88ᵛ–87 (marginal grotesque of a woman fighting a snail, early 14th cent.); also charges of immodest dress, and cruelty, levied against Joan of Arc (P. Champion, *Procès de condamnation de Jeanne d'Arc: Texte, traduction et notes* (2 vols.; Paris, 1920–1; Slatkine Reprints; Geneva, 1976), i. 55, 71–2, 104, and 367. For knaves, see above, n. 70.

4

VIOLENCE IN PUBLIC: APPEARANCES AND PUNISHMENTS IN THE COURTS

If any truths have emerged in the preceding chapter about the beliefs of upper-class fifteenth-century East Anglians, we should expect to see them realized in the lawcourts. For the gentry, either as plaintiffs or as officers of the law, were responsible for bringing most cases to the courts; and an important function of the courts was to provide gentlemen with a forum in which to prove their honour.[1] I have argued that the use of allowable violence, and the punishment of reprehensible violence, were both vital in the demonstration of status and authority. If this was so, we should be able to see the lawcourts fulfilling both these functions.

At first sight, however, the evidence that King's Bench punished violent, as opposed to non-violent, crimes is equivocal at best. As I have pointed out, it is not even easy to tell, in any individual case, whether a crime of violence against the person was actually alleged or carried out. On one hand, writs of trespass which came to the court necessarily alleged the use of 'force and arms', whatever the charge involved. (To quote a particularly ludicrous example, it was said of Ralph Joys in 1434 that he had, with force and arms, swords, staves, etc., torn up a bond of obligation.)[2] On the other, appeals of robbery (which should technically have concerned robbery with violence) may have been brought in cases of theft merely to enable the victim to recover the stolen goods.[3] Verdicts, particularly adverse ones, were almost fabulously rare in King's Bench, apparently indicating that the court did not function to punish either violent or non-violent crime. Process on writs in King's Bench was the same whether or not violence was alleged.[4] How can any legitimate deductions about fifteenth-century constructions of violence be drawn from

---

[1] See Ch. 2.   [2] KB 27 691 m 50^r.
[3] See Ch. 2, n. 29.   [4] See Ch. 2, text accompanying nn. 5–6.

TABLE 4.1.   *Progress of cases in King's Bench*

	Plea side (minus appeals)		Rex side	
	Violent (513 cases)	Non-violent (1,365 cases)	Violent (119 cases)	Non-violent (191 cases)
% defendant appeared	61.8	43.4	86.6	71.7
% reached end of process	6.6	5.1	67.2	61.8
% guilty verdict	4.5	3.4	3.7	1.1

this unpromising material? Can we go beyond the individual case record?

Perhaps strangely, it seems we can. We may legitimately assume, to start with, that the function of King's Bench was less to punish criminals than to achieve certain stages in the legal process which would bring pressure to bear on the defendants. We can distinguish those cases which actually alleged violence against the person (such as assault, mayhem, homicide) from those which alleged mere damage to property (such as depasturing, felling wood, asporting goods). No doubt many allegations were, to say the least, inexact. We can rarely tell to what extent an indictment or plea was genuine, collusive or malicious.[5] Yet a statistical consideration of hundreds of these cases brings to light elusive but positive indications that violence and non-violence were differently treated in the fifteenth-century courts, judging by the stages to which these cases proceeded.

Table 4.1 gives the results of a comparative examination of the progress of cases actually alleging violence against the person, as distinct from those which merely claimed damage to property. Whichever side of King's Bench we look, treatment of cases alleging personal violence differed from that of other cases. Charges of violence against the person attracted a slightly greater percentage of guilty verdicts, reached an end more often, and were much more likely to obtain the appearance of a defendant. These percentage differences are, in the

---

[5] See examples in Ch. 2.

strict statistical sense of the word, significant.[6] The contingency co-efficient between cases alleging personal violence, and appearances of the defendant is 0.162 in the Rex section, and almost exactly the same (0.160) in the plea section.[7] The number of appeals is too small for a contingency co-efficient to be profitably calculated, but the percent-ages are nevertheless similar.[8] Fifty-six appeals were brought in King's Bench, and a high proportion (thirty or 53.6 per cent) reached an end. Even if we discount those inconclusive cases where the defendant was acquitted because the appellor failed to appear, the percentage of verdicts was 28.6.[9] Of the fifty-six appeals, thirty-five unequivocally alleged violence against the person, and twenty-one of these (60 per cent) reached an end. The remaining twenty-one cases, which alleged crimes of doubtful violence,[10] showed only nine verdicts (42.9 per cent).[11] Clearly, the normative actions of fifteenth-century plaintiffs and law-keepers emerge from the invisibility of the individual case, in the light of these statistical trends. What deductions can we draw from them?

Two red herrings must be cleared from the path here. It might be argued that cases alleging violence tended to attract more verdicts

---

[6] I use the calculation for contingency co-efficient, which measures the strength of a relationship between 2 variables. If we take, for instance, the proportion of verdicts reached in cases of alleged violence against the person, calculating the contingency co-efficient will show by how much the proportion exceeds that which might be expected if there were no relationship between these variables. A contingency co-efficient of 0 indicates no relationship between the variables; one of 0.707 shows a perfect relationship. Significant relationships are ranged between these two figures. See R. Floud, *An Introduction to Quantitative Methods for Historians*, 2nd edn. (London, 1979), 133–45.

[7] The co-efficients between verdict rates and allegations of violence against the person are slighter, but still noteworthy—0.029 for plea side cases and 0.048 for Rex side.

[8] The contingency co-efficient will show significance only where large numbers of cases are involved. The reason for this is comparatively simple. Suppose, in the example given in n. 6 above, the total number of cases tested were very small, and the degree of relationship not perfect. This would mean that there would be very few verdicts—maybe only 2 or 3—above the number which might be expected if there were no relationship between the variables at all. To allege a significant trend, based on 2 or 3 cases, would be nonsensical, since there might very well be no common factor between them. Because of this, there is no point in calculating contingency coefficients for the tiny numbers of guilty verdicts, or for the 56 appeals which appeared in King's Bench.

[9] See Ch. 2, text accompanying nn. 30–1.

[10] Such as rape/ravishment and robbery, see Ch. 3, text accompanying nn. 91–100.

[11] Percentages in such a small group of cases are statistically meaningless; I quote them only for the sake of giving a very rough basis for comparison with other King's Bench cases.

because they appeared more often in the Rex side of King's bench and among appeals. The proportion of charges of violence in Rex side King's Bench was 38.4 per cent; in appeals, it was 62.5 per cent. These can be compared with the meagre 27.5 per cent of plea side cases which even alleged any personal violence. Similarly, the proportion of cases which came to an end in Rex side as a whole was very high—63.6 per cent, as against the 53.6 per cent of appeals, and the miniscule 5.4 per cent of other plea side cases. Does the apparent difference between cases alleging violence and other cases in fact reflect only the varying practices in different sections of the court's work?

I doubt it. For one thing, the progress of cases alleging violence is distinctive *within* each section of the court. For another, such an argument ignores the motives which brought the cases to court. If cases alleging personal violence were subjected especially to those processes which gave fair hope of yielding a verdict, it is fair to suggest that the choice of process was deliberate. It seems that in these cases, participants were more eager to sue out writs of *certiorari*, sheriffs (or their subordinates) were more willing to execute writs, constables to arrest, and juries to appear. Perhaps the high rate of appearances and verdicts in Rex side and appeals cases was a result, rather than a cause, of the fact that they dealt with cases of violence.

But what if Rex side cases more frequently secured a defendant and a verdict because writs of *certiorari* were more often sued out by defendants intent on pleading pardon or certain of acquittal?[12] The successful completion of such cases would imply not that plaintiffs or the courts showed a great desire to detect and survey unacceptable violence, but that the court structures could be used by the perpetrators of violence to right themselves formally in the eyes of the law. This hypothesis can be tested by examining the categories (violent or non-violent) in which those cases fall that were most likely to have been brought in by the defendant. Following Post's reading, writs of *certiorari* brought by the defendant were probably confined to cases which ended in the defendant pleading a pardon or making a fine. In all likelihood, the category is even smaller. Surely such defendants would not sue out a *certiorari* long before they had the necessary pardon. If then the defendant did not promptly appear to plead a

---

[12] See Ch. 2, n. 40.

TABLE 4.2. *Rex side cases ending in pardon or fines*

	Violent	Non-violent
Pardon pleaded in same term	10	9
Pardon pleaded later	13	4
TOTAL	23	13

pardon, we may reasonably assume that it was the plaintiff who brought the case to court.[13]

There are, to start with, remarkably few Rex side cases ending in pardons or fines—only thirty-six out of 310 cases apparently brought by *certiorari* (11.6 per cent). In Table 4.2 the comparative numbers of pardons pleaded in the same term and pardons pleaded later are set out both for allegedly violent and for non-violent cases. If this admittedly small set of figures is to be believed, over half the defendants in cases alleging personal violence could not produce their pardon until some considerable time after the case was brought to King's Bench. Less than one-third of defendants in cases where no personal violence was alleged were in a similar predicament. It appears that perpetrators of violence were driven to buy pardons by the diligence of plaintiffs, who forced them to appear in King's Bench. Defendants who had only damaged property, or threatened property rights, were left comfortably to assert their blameless public status by suing out their own writs of *certiorari*.

It seems, then, that fifteenth-century plaintiffs and court officials showed a decided interest in bringing defendants charged with violence into the court and obtaining a verdict in these cases. Why then was the verdict so seldom a guilty one? What did the court, or the community, gain merely by bringing suspected felons before the law, to let them go unpunished?

I suggest that the answer depends on the simultaneous power and ambiguity of violence in fifteenth-century life. Violence was inevitable—indeed laudable—in maintaining right social order; but unlicensed violence might destabilize the very order it should protect. The king's courts, as instruments and demonstrations of royal authority, were vitally concerned with the maintenance of this order. In these

[13] See Ch. 2, text accompanying nn. 37–9.

circumstances, one of their primary roles must have been to test charges of violence. Whether they eventually reached a verdict (guilty or otherwise) was in some senses of secondary importance. The first necessity was to bring suspected offenders before the court, where their very presence was an acknowledgement of the courts' authority to pronounce on cases of violence. Before the king's justices, violent actions could be rightly classified, and innocence validly pronounced. Furthermore, courts generated power and status, in part, by imposing order on chaos.[14] Royal power, and by implication the power of the administrative hierarchy, was enhanced by the king's being seen to do justice against violent wrongdoers.[15] In this context, it is understandable that gentry plaintiffs in King's Bench, and the officials of the court itself, felt that it was vital to bring violent offenders to court to answer for their alleged crimes. Any violence freely performed without sanction or question of the courts *ipso facto* detracted from their authority; any alleged violence brought before them enhanced it.

The evidence from gaol deliveries is less complex. Since verdicts were commonly achieved there, it is possible to compare the outcomes of cases of alleged violence to those of cases where non-violent crimes, such as larceny, were alleged. It is immediately clear that allegations of personal violence were treated more seriously than other cases. Defendants in cases of violence against the person ran a fair risk of facing a death-sentence.[16] A verdict of execution was passed in forty-four cases of the 210 which alleged personal violence—over one in five or 21 per cent. By contrast, only 204 out of the 1,315 cases of non-violent crime (15.5 per cent) ended with a hanging verdict.

In law as in theory, there were clearly shades of reprehensibility in cases of violence. In both King's Bench and gaol delivery, homicide was the crime contemporaries were most anxious to examine and most willing to punish. The sixty-one homicide cases in King's Bench all came by appeal or *certiorari*, but their verdict rate was even higher than in Rex side cases and appeals generally—forty-three cases or

---

[14] See Ch. 2, text accompanying nn. 93–6. In 1525 when the marquis of Dorset was sent to quell the Coventry enclosure riot, one of his first efforts to combat this outbreak of disorder was to hold special ceremonial sessions of the peace nearby at Kenilworth (C. Phythian-Adams, *Desolation of a City: Coventry and the Urban Crisis of the Late Middle Ages* (Cambridge, 1979), 256).

[15] See Ch. 1, n. 5.

[16] Though not all death-sentences resulted in a hanging—defendants might plead clergy or obtain a pardon.

70.5 per cent, reached an end. The presence of this group of cases must therefore be a major factor in the high rate of completion among Rex side cases and appeals. It was for murder, or complicity in murder, that the only two known death-sentences were handed down in King's Bench.[17] In gaol deliveries, more than one-third of the 104 cases of homicide attracted a death-sentence—thirty-eight cases or 36.5 per cent. These thirty-eight cases represent over 86 per cent of the forty-four executions for crimes involving personal violence. The horror of homicide may seem very understandable; but it is worth asking why homicide, out of all violent crimes, attracted such a high rate of punishment, and what sorts of homicide were particularly deprecated.

One obvious point is that murder struck directly not only at human, but at divine order. Homicide offended God in two distinct ways. First, as the author of *Dives and Pauper* points out, 'man is mad to þe lyknesse of God & so manslaute is opyn wrong don to God, in þat . . . his ymage [is] despysyd & distryyd.'[18] Secondly, God alone, as the maker, protector, and lord of all mortals, had the right to decide when life should end. He might delegate this power to lawful judges; but to usurp the privilege violently and illegally was effectually to rebel against divine rule (just as to kill someone under the king's protection was to defy the king's authority).[19] This may in part account for the unusual harshness of the courts when faced with this crime.

Nevertheless, it is clear that punishment of all homicides was not the purpose of the courts. In both King's Bench and gaol delivery, more accused homicides escaped the death penalty than suffered it. As with other forms of violence against the person, the courts operated to oversee cases of violence; to bring them within the scope of constituted authority, and distinguish the allowable from the totally unjustifiable. This then raises the question, how did the law-keepers distinguish one homicide from another?

In legal theory, almost all homicide had been considered culpable since at least the thirteenth century; this did not mean, however, that all homicide was equally to be punished. Indeed, homicide was classified broadly into three categories, depending on what punishment the slayer deserved.

---

[17] See Ch. 2, n. 43.

[18] *Dives* 2, 32.

[19] See ibid. (manslaughter is wrong because God's 'seruant is so slayn'); Ch. 3, text accompanying nn. 14–19 and 28–30; and Holdsworth, ii. 47.

The first category was justifiable homicide. In the case of an execution ordered by a competent court, or the death of a convicted felon while resisting arrest, or the killing of a trespasser by foresters or parkers in the course of an arrest, the homicide was not culpable, and no criminal action could lie against the killers.[20] These narrow provisions were apparently strictly upheld in the later middle ages. St German in his *Doctor and Student*, for instance, made a fine distinction between the legitimacy of simply killing someone outlawed for murder or felony on *any* occasion, and killing the same person *in the course of an arrest*. The latter, done 'by auctoryty of the kynges lawes', was justifiable; the former was not. Furthermore, he points out, if the killing took place during an arrest under a capias in an action of debt or trespass, it was not justifiable, and the killer could be indicted.[21] There was evidently no leeway in the matter of the legal standing of the victim in such cases; only a convicted felon or an outlaw could be killed. In 1422 Henry Veel was slain during an attempt to arrest him, together with John Bateman, to face trial for the murder of John Broun. No doubt because both were as yet untried, the constables involved were apparently loath to take responsibility for Veel's death.[22]

The second category consisted of homicides pardonable as a matter of course. This comprised accidental homicides—killing by misadventure—and homicide in self-defence. I have already dealt with the rigid provisions governing killings *se defendendo*.[23] Homicide by misadventure was defined as accidental killing in the course of some lawful action, such as cutting down one's own trees or shooting at the butts. Bracton, apparently drawing heavily on canon law, laid it down that such crimes were culpable, but pardonable—the accidental slayer 'deserves but needs' a pardon.[24] Accordingly, the Statute of Gloucester (1278) laid down the procedure by which all who had slain in self-defence or by misadventure had nevertheless to appear in the royal courts, to face a jury which could pronounce on the pardonable nature of the crime, and to receive the justices' recommendation to the king's mercy.[25]

---

[20] Ibid. ii. 358 and iii. 311–12 and 604.
[21] *St German's Doctor and Student*, ed. T. F. Plucknett and J. L. Barton (Selden Society, 1974), 265.
[22] See Ch. 5.3.
[23] See Ch. 3, n. 63.
[24] Holdsworth, ii. 259 and iii. 313; N. Hurnard, *The King's Pardon for Homicide before A.D. 1307* (Oxford, 1969), 69–70 and 73–4.
[25] Ibid. 281; and Holdsworth, iii. 312.

All remaining homicides fell into the last category—felonious slaying, which was culpable and for which no pardon as a matter of course could be issued. Whether, and to what extent, there were legal distinctions within this category of homicide has been long debated. Some historians have suggested that from the fourteenth century, murder, defined as homicide *ex malicia praecogitata*, comprised a separate type of particularly reprehensible homicide.[26] However, Kaye's evidence on the non-specialized uses of the terms 'murder' and 'ex malicia praecogitata' in the late-medieval courts, and his examination of fourteenth-century attempts to delimit pardons *de cursu*, tells against this view.[27] Significantly, all culpable homicides alike were subject to capital punishment until at least 1497. Even then, the statute 12 Henry VII c. 7, to 'make some offenc[es] petty treason', was intended only to bar some homicides from pleading clergy. The legislators did not, as has sometimes been claimed, distinguish between premeditated murder and other forms of felonious homicide; indeed, in the casual fashion typical of the fifteenth century, they used the compound phrase 'murdred and slayne' to describe the crime they had in mind. Their purpose, apparently, was to ensure that servants who killed their masters, in defiance of divinely instituted social order, should not escape their just punishment as petty traitors. The statute was prompted by the crime of one James Grame, a yeoman, who had slain his master, a gentleman named Richard Tracy. The legislators felt that Grame was typical of those who 'wilfully co[m]mytte purpensed murdre, in sleyng their Maister or their immediat Sov[er]eign', and to discourage such outrages laid it down that he and any other lay people committing this crime were to be drawn and hanged with no claim to benefit of clergy. Clearly, the statute-makers thought this type of homicide to be particularly evil and deserving of the ultimate punishment. But as evidence of a fifteenth-century legal distinction between murder with malice aforethought and other forms of homicide, it is unconvincing.[28]

---

[26] Cf. ibid. ii. 451, and the summary of the debate given by Kaye, 'Early History of Murder and Manslaughter', 366–72.

[27] Ibid. 369–95 and 569–71. See also examples from 15th cent. East Anglia (Ch. 3, text accompanying nn. 55–7).

[28] See Holdsworth, iii. 314, as compared to 12 Henry VII c. 7 (*The Statutes of the Realm*, ii (London, 1816; repr. 963), 639). J. Bellamy examines the significance of the statute in his *Criminal Law and Society in Late Medieval and Tudor England* (Gloucester, 1984), 130–1. Why this particular crime prompted the legislation is not entirely clear. If Grame had indeed killed his master, the offence was already petty treason, without statutory definition. Bellamy believes that 'he had not murdered his master but only plotted his

Nevertheless, there were persistent attempts throughout the four-teenth century to reassert the definition of the wide category of homicides which were not pardonable *de cursu*, apparently because it was thought that the Crown was too free with its pardons.[29] The 1390 statute to this effect specified murder, homicide by ambush or assault, or in general by malice aforethought as the range of culpable homicides. Kaye suggests, no doubt rightly, that the ancient use of 'murder' to mean secret or stealthy killing had reappeared here, but that the basic intent of the act was to comprehend, not divide, the category of culpable homicide.[30] It seems that late-medieval opinion detected finer shades of heinousness in crime than did the law itself.

It is already clear that the lawcourts acted as an embodiment of that authority which simultaneously justified, and was sustained by, right violence. The sentences of the law made homicide justifiable; accidental killing might be pardoned, but only if the killer came in person to accept the ruling of the law. Killing secretly, maliciously, feloniously, outside the public deliberations of the law, was fully culpable. The definitions of the law distinguished right homicide from wrong.

This surely produced a situation which encouraged anyone mounting a serious appeal or indictment for homicide to ascribe to the act as many as possible of the stated characteristics of culpable killing—for instance, by using such terms as 'insidiando', 'felonice interfecit et murdravit', and 'ex malicia praecogitata', or by constructing a picture of the crime which witnessed to stealth, or malice aforethought, or both. Equally it was the business of juries to allot each case under their scrutiny to its appropriate category of homicide. Contrary to our notions of a jury's role, their primary function was not to decide who had committed the crime, but to say what sort of act had been committed. Thus, not only did a medieval coroner's jury answer first the question whether the

---

death' (p. 131) though the statute clearly states that Tracy was 'by him [Grame] and his purpensed assent. . . murdered and slayne'. Perhaps the difficulty was that though Grame had *planned* the murder while in Tracy's service, he was no longer Tracy's servant when he committed the deed; hence the phrase 'wilfully assentid and purpensed the murdre of . . . Richard Tracy . . . *then* his maister' (emphasis mine). This would leave a doubt as to the exact nature of the felony, which might require resolution by statute. See Kaye, 'Early History of Murder and Manslaughter', 569 for 15th-cent. confounding of the terms of murder and homicide.

[29] Ibid. 377–9, and Hurnard, *The King's Pardon for Homicide*, 324.

[30] Kaye, 'Early History of Murder and Manslaughter', pt. 1, *passim*.

death had been caused by felony, misadventure, or nature before proceeding to the question of who, in the case of homicide, had done the deed; trial juries too, as we shall see, tended to scrutinize indictments with a view to deciding the type of death dealt out, rather than the true identity of the killer.[31] This is useful for the historian, since it is in these decisions we can, sometimes, discern the juries' adherence both to legal categories of homicide, and to the moral rules of just and unjust violence.

In many of the cases on record in East Anglia 1422–42, insufficient details are given to allow us to judge the principles on which the juries made their decisions. But where a full indictment survives, it is generally clear that juries upheld the conditions of hierarchical violence by a sophisticated use of the provisions of the law. A few examples will make this clearer.

In Norfolk in 1434, a servant of Thomas Lowell called variously Elesius Tomesson (or Johnson) or John Elyos, was indicted for the death of the 18-year-old Richard Tarcel. The indictment stated that the murderer had asked the young man to walk with him to a field to inspect Lowell's horses. When they got there, '*ex malicia praecogitata*' he killed Richard with a hedge stake and hid the body in the ditch. At the gaol delivery of July 1435, Richard's uncle, William Tarcel, appealed the killer, using such phrases as '*insidiando et ex insultu et malicia praecogitata*' which implied culpable homicide. Tomesson/Johnson/Elyos was condemned to hang.[32] Similarly, the long indictment on the body of Richer Lound of Norfolk stated that Richard Fayrcok had conspired with Martin Budde, Lound's servant, to kill him. When Lound disturbed the pair plotting in his hall, Fayrcok attacked him with a sword, crying, 'Now I have what I want,' and killed him, Budde standing by in his support. The two men allegedly carried the body into a garden next to the hall, dug a grave six-feet deep among the trees, threw in the body, filled the hole, and replanted the ground 'subtiliter' to prevent discovery of the corpse. Both were condemned, though Martin escaped his punishment by pleading clergy (thus providing a classic case of what the statute-makers of 1497 tried to prevent).[33] Again, in the Norfolk gaol delivery of 1439, an indictment was presented

---

[31] R. F. Hunnisett, *The Medieval Coroner* (Cambridge, 1961), 20–2.

[32] JUST 3 209 m 13ʳ and 220/1 m (68) S2.

[33] JUST 3 220/1 pt. ii (77) S7 and JUST 3 209 m 3ʳ; and see above, n. 28. Note that there may have been a long-standing quarrel. In Easter term 1425, Lound sued out a writ of trespass against Fayrcok in King's Bench (KB 27 656 m 50ʳ).

against Thomas Ilom or Elam, a Rougham labourer, who, it was said, attacked Margaret Perman, trying to rape her, broke three of her ribs and bit off her nose. She died of the infection of this wound; and Elam, judged to have murdered her, was duly sentenced to death.[34]

All these cases display at least one of the classic features of culpable homicide. As the indictment jury told it, the attack on Tarcel was well-planned, and the murderer hid the body; both of which implied murderous stealth and malice aforethought. Fayrcok could hardly be said to have planned the exact crime, but the account makes it clear that his long-term intention was criminal, and the horrid story of the secret burial is surely meant to suggest killing by stealth. Elam was clearly alleged to have killed Margaret Perman, feloniously—that is, in the course of felonious assault. A similar pattern is reflected in the two convictions recorded in King's Bench, where Isabella Cutte appealed her husband's murderer for acting '*insidiando in insultu et ex malicia sua praecogitata*', and Margery Andrewe and Thomas Tatenell were presented for conspiring to ambush and kill Margery's husband Walter as he came innocently homewards from his day's work.[35] The descriptions of all these cases left no doubt that the perpetrators of the deeds were guilty of culpable homicide under the terms of the law; in most they had also offended the hierarchical principles of right violence, by murdering husbands or masters, or by killing their victims secretly, cowardly, deceitfully, and for unjust reasons.

Conversely, the indictment of William Pikeman, a Suffolk shepherd indicted for killing Edmund Gosse in March 1431, is an exemplary case of the statement of homicide in self-defence. The jury said that Gosse assaulted Pikeman with a staff, and drove him to a river-bank, from which he could retreat no further. In their opinion he could not have saved his life without attacking Gosse. He was accordingly remanded to await the king's pardon.[36]

This is not to say, of course, that juries were invariably accurate in their accounts and judgements of homicides. On the contrary, it is likely that the courts functioned also as a place for the trial jury to legitimate a story concocted by the indictment jury. Certainly, Green found instances of juries apparently skilfully constructing and manip-

---

[34] JUST 3 210 m 7[d].

[35] KB 27 666 m 38[r] and 690 Rm 3[r].

[36] JUST 3 209 m 22[d]; cf. also JUST 3 219/1 mm 53[r] and 55[r], and JUST 3 201 m 6[d], for a similar case against Robert Bast in Suffolk, 1422.

ulating accounts of culpable homicide and self-defence to free (or condemn) defendants whose case might not technically warrant it.[37] Yet there is also at least one case where the defendant (or his lawyer) seems to have been too wary of breaching the strict rules governing pardonable self-defence to trust to this gambit. Considering the death of John Lambe, in 1427, the coroner's jury produced a fair approximation of the case for self-defence. Lambe had assaulted Thomas Chapeleyn, the defendant, with a staff, intending to kill him. Chapeleyn duly fled as far as he could, and when he turned at bay was felled to the ground by a blow from Lambe's staff. So far so good; the next part of the story fulfils the rules less perfectly. Chapeleyn drew his knife to ward off another blow, and in the course of doing so, 'nesciente' struck Lambe in the leg and killed him. A true self-defender was supposed to be unarmed, and to strike the death-blow with a chance weapon. Though armed defendants were pardoned in this period, Chapeleyn was evidently reluctant to trust to such precedents. Instead he pleaded a technical insufficiency in the indictment and safely attained his *sine die*.[38] Nevertheless, the jury's account of his act seems to show that they considered the killing not fully culpable and were prepared to give him the chance to obtain an easy pardon.

Those cases where juries apparently manipulated their indictments or verdicts to suit a desired legal category, are valuable evidence of the types of crime which juries were either anxious to condemn or willing to pardon. One such concerns the killing of Robert Ele of Norfolk, 22 June 1434. William Talloir, evidently a neighbour of Ele's, was appealed by the widow and indicted by the coroner's jury. They alleged that Talloir had sat up from 2 a.m. in his house '*ex malicia sua praecogitata*' waiting for Ele to come by; which he did at 4 a.m., bound for his work at Edward Kervyle's, carrying his spade. Talloir saw him, came out, attacked him, wrested the spade from him, and brained him with it. Talloir's wife Margaret was said to have urged him to the deed, for unspecified motives.[39] This exciting tale fits the category of culpable homicide with almost suspicious perfection. The story of long planning between Talloir and his wife, and the wait overnight, add to the presumption of criminal intent. Crimes

---

[37] Green, 'Societal Concepts of Criminal Liability for Homicide', 675–93.
[38] KB 27 668 Rm 8ᵈ; Ch. 3, n. 64.
[39] JUST 3 220/1 m (70) S1 and 209 m 11ʳ.

committed at night were thought to be particularly furtive and reprehensible.[40] At the same time, the account implies ambush, and finally homicide in the course of felonious assault—two more water-tight reasons for considering it fully culpable. Though it made no difference to the legal status of the case, the jury took care to specify that the victim was innocently and laudably going about the duties of his station in life.[41] The only appropriate detail missing is a charge that Talloir tried to hide the body; maybe it was common knowledge that he did not.

Yet despite its well-tailored air, the story is not entirely self-consistent. It is not clear how Talloir's accusers knew that he had hidden in his house overnight (though this detail might have been drawn out of Talloir by examination). Even more inexplicable is the allegation that a murderer of such foresight came out with no weapon of his own (not even any of the agricultural tools which he must, as a husbandman, have possessed), and thus had to rely on his victim to provide the blunt instrument. One cannot help wondering if Talloir killed Ele in a much fairer, and more spontaneous, fight than the indictment suggests; in which case, his neighbours made sure he would die for it by embroidering the story with elements which they knew suggested murderous action.

Conversely, one coroner's jury displayed a positively reckless disregard for the strict requirements of the law in deciding that the killing of Robert Bury by Robert Wryghte in May 1427 fell into the category of self-defence. They stated that Bury and Wryghte, a parker of Lydgate, were travelling home together, Bury riding and Wryghte on foot. They came to a pond by the highway and fell into dispute; whereupon Bury, 'furore repletus' tried to ride Wryghte into the water. Wryghte fended him off with his 'wyfele'.[42] Bury grabbed the blade of the wifle, thus seriously injuring his own hand. Apparently further enraged by this he pushed on, whereupon Wryghte struck him

---

[40] Green, 'Societal Concepts of Criminal Liability for Homicide', 693.

[41] Compare similar features in the indictment of Andrewe and Tatenell; above, n. 35.

[42] It is not entirely clear what a wifle was. The *OED* defines it as a 'dart, javelin, spear; a battle-axe'. It appears in a King's Bench case against William Sheldrake as a 'wyfle vocatur bil' (KB 27 666 Rm 124^d); in another, the weapons of an attack are given in two indictments respectively as 'longpykes & Glyves' and 'a wyfyl' (KB 27 721 Rm 21^r). In Robert Bast's case (above, n. 36) the weapon is given as a 'baculo vocatur wevyll'. It may have been a generic term for a long-handled blade, which would fit the context well.

again on the head, and killed him. The jury said that he had acted '*se defendendo*'; it was thus pardonable homicide.[43]

The coroner evidently found this account unsatisfactory. Indeed it was, since it met none of the conditions for self-defence. Far from being the unarmed victim of attack, Wryghte had a very effective weapon. It was the unfortunate Bury who was apparently unarmed. It is nowhere stated that Bury meant to kill Wryghte, nor that Wryghte tried at all to escape (though setting the scene of action at a pond may have served to recall the rivers which formed an effective barrier to self-defendants in other cases).[44] Nor is it suggested that Wryghte did not know what he was doing when he struck the fatal blow. The coroner, therefore, was (unusually) recorded as asking the jury whether Wryghte might have evaded death without killing Bury; but they replied firmly 'no', and Wryghte was allowed mainprize until his pardon of 24 June 1430. The single phrase '*se defendendo*', supported by the jury's determination, saved him.

These juries had apparently made their own decisions on the heinousness of the crime before putting it in a form more or less acceptable to the courts. The particular basis for their judgements is not clear; we do not know why Talloir's neighbours wanted him dead, while Wryghte's preferred him to live. Indeed, members of juries (even when lists of their names survive) were generally such obscure men that we cannot discover their past histories, preferences, or relationships to the defendants. Nevertheless, a broad view of jury decisions suggests that the moral hierarchy of violence had some force in their deliberations. The relative status of murderer and victim was clearly a factor. Husband-murderers and servants who killed their masters could expect little mercy. Margery Andrewe was condemned to be burned, and it was noted that Richard Tarcel was killed by a servant. In the case of Richer Lound, the jury emphasized twice over that Martin Budde had '*false & fraudulenter*' deceived his 'good master'. They also took care to point out that had he acted '*ut fidelis serviens*', Lound would never have been killed. Clearly, such defiance of the hierarchy horrified them.[45] Juries may have been sympathetic to the unfortunate issue of a fair fight between equals—most of the self-defendants seem to have slain men of approximately their own

---

[43] JUST 3 207 m 8^d and 209 m 17^r.
[44] Green, 'Societal Concepts of Criminal Liability for Homicide', nn. 17 and 23.
[45] JUST 3 220/1 pt. ii (77) S7.

standing. But they were horrified by cases where the victim was of higher status than the murderer, or where the victim had no real chance of self-defence because of the malicious cunning of the assailant. This may explain the exoneration of Robert Wryghte. Whatever the merits of the case as pardonable homicide, it was at least clear that Bury had not been attacked by surprise or subterfuge, and that the fight was between two men of approximately equal status and abilities. In such cases, the hierarchical justification of violence gave no presumption of innocence or guilt to either side. In some sense, violence between equals was unthreatening, morally ambiguous; the decision might safely rest on the individual merits and motives of the participants.

This was not so in cases of unjust violence exercised on the innocent and helpless. William Smyth/Joye was tried in January 1439 for having broken into John Miller's house with weapons of war and attacked and killed Joan Warrok, aged 9. The indictment is in terms of premeditated murder (*ex malicia praecogitata*), in the course of armed felony; though the fact that the actual murder was said to have been done with a wooden candelabrum may throw doubt on the allegation of arms-carrying. This nevertheless indicates that the jury thought the killing of a helpless child to be unpardonable.[46]

In such cases, the nice distinctions of fifteenth-century theory showed plainly in practice. Violence against masters by their servants was thought particularly reprehensible, and juries put it in the most damning terms possible. Violence against the powerless was allowable for good motives, but culpable for felonious ones. Killers who outranked their victims perhaps stood a better chance of escaping legal condemnation of their crimes, as the cases of the deaths of Emma Joket and Alice Body may indicate. John Joket was indicted by a coroner's jury, and at the peace sessions, for murdering his wife. A circumstantial account was given of how he put poison—'Ratonesbane'—in her food, and (in one indictment) how he was abetted by Margaret Norfolk, whom he later married. But the trial jury recategorized the death as natural, stating that Emma had been gravely ill for some time, and had died 'nullo alio modo'.[47] It is, of course, possible that both indictments merely reflected malicious gossip; but

---

[46] JUST 3 210 m 19^d.
[47] JUST 3 209 m 15^r, KB 9 227/1 m 37, and KB 27 698 Rm 7^r. In the gaol delivery he and his abettors were acquitted.

it is equally likely that the trial juries were loath to convict a man of wife-murder. Similarly, when Alice Body/Shepperd died in March 1438, there was clearly some contemporary uneasiness about the cause of death. The coroner's jury stated that in August 1437 William Mylys had broken into her house 'ex malicia praecogitata' and beaten her so severely on her arms and body that she never recovered. Yet when Mylys finally appeared at the gaol delivery of 1440, the trial jury refused to take up such issues as whether Mylys had in fact administered a beating, and if so, whether it was justified. Instead, they simply stated that Alice had died 'ex infirmitate naturali', and Mylys went free.[48] What the truth of the matter was is now impossible to discern. There is not even any evidence to show what relationship existed between Mylys and Body. However, it seems clear that there was never any question of convicting him of either murder or assault; one must suspect, again, that the main point of the case, from the court's viewpoint, was to assert the right of the law to review, and judge, cases of alleged violence.

It is interesting to note that in at least one case, a trial jury apparently preferred to use the method of reclassifying a death as due to natural causes rather than argue for justifiable homicide. The gaol delivery in Cambridge in 1429 heard, in the coronial indictment against Richard Sutton and others, that Sutton, a serjeant, had tried to arrest John Helvy, and when he fled, had struck him with a staff on the back of the neck, and dragged him to gaol where he subsequently died. This may seem a textbook example of justifiable homicide. Yet the coroner's jury referred it to gaol delivery as possibly felonious, presumably because John Helvy was a suspected, rather than a convicted, felon. The trial jury, evidently intent on saving Sutton from the consequences of his actions, then blandly affirmed, not that the killing was justified, but that Helvy had died 'ex subita infirmitate'.[49] This solution neatly avoided the need to enquire into the exact reasons for Helvy's arrest, while yet allowing Sutton to exercise with impunity whatever violence his rank and office might require.

Fifteenth-century juries were thus called on to make fine moral decisions about the function of violence in cases of homicide; and in general, they classified killings which did not offend the structure of divine and earthly order as either pardonable homicide, or not

---

[48] JUST 3 212 m 11.   [49] JUST 3 8/13 m 1ʳ.

homicide at all. They had also to judge whether the killer was capable of intending to disrupt the natural order.[50] Insanity, for instance, precluded a guilty verdict. On the death of Beatrice Mogyll, her neighbours attested in court that during the previous year, her husband William had been troubled '*maligno spiritu*', and had to be kept in iron fetters with an iron lock. One morning, Beatrice herself unlocked them; an hour later he attacked her with an axe and killed her. No verdict was recorded; he was merely remanded to the next gaol delivery.[51]

It seems, then, that the law was brought delicately into play to combat the disturbing forces of unruly violence. Those who committed homicide—even if it were finally pardonable—had to come dutifully to the king's courts to have their actions examined and categorized. To the law belonged the authority to state whether a homicide was easily pardonable or not. Culpable homicide was not only defined by the law, but recognized by the juries as radically offensive to the principles of social hierarchy. In these cases, the hanging verdicts of the law overwhelmed offence and restored order in real life, as surely as did the righteous swords of the knights of romance in literature. If hierarchy was to be upheld, servants and wives who killed their masters, or murderers who would not meet their victims in equal battle, had to be eliminated from the system with exemplary public disgrace. If violence was to be vindicated by its power to protect the needy, the law had to deal violently to protect murdered children.

This context makes some sense of the violent punishment of heretics which also took place in fifteenth-century East Anglia at this time (though cases of heresy, being the province of the church, hardly ever appear in the records of the central courts).[52] Of the seventy-three defendants on charges of heresy noted by Tanner, twenty-five were sentenced to public whipping. Three heretics were burned in

---

[50] Bracton wrote that neither an infant nor a madman could be held criminally liable (Holdsworth, ii. 259; cf. the 15th century view on children and violence, Ch. 3, text accompanying nn. 108–9.

[51] JUST 3 212 m 5ᵈ; cf. Ch. 3, n. 80. Unfortunately, the records of the succeeding gaol delivery do not survive.

[52] A rare case appears in a Suffolk gaol delivery of 1430; Elias Heyward, a Norfolk cleric, was accused of sheltering felons and holding Lollard views, such as that priests could lawfully marry, that unbaptised infants might be saved, and that the relics of a saint such as St Thomas à Becket were no more to be reverenced than any common bones. He was released to his ordinary (JUST 3 209 m 16 ʳ,ᵈ).

Norwich in 1428.[53] The whippings were probably not intended to injure, since they could be suspended or reduced in cases of age and debility.[54] But they were, as Tanner rightly points out, deliberately made as public as possible. The penitents were to appear at their parish church on Sunday, or in the market of their local town.[55] Heretics not only questioned the orthodox structures of the Church, thus threatening the notions of relationship between God and human-kind on which the moral system of violence depended; they also specifically denied any role to righteous violence. One of the charges against the Norwich heretics was that they believed all killing to be wrong, even executions for theft, homicide, or treason.[56] Such resistance to the orthodox legal sanctions maintaining justice and order had to be met and overwhelmed by just force.

So far, I have concentrated on the treatment of homicides, and other violent crimes in the lawcourts, since these show most directly how fifteenth-century people translated their theories about morally reprehensible violence into practice. On the other hand, the realization of their notions of just violence can be well illustrated by an analysis of their use of death-sentences to punish non-violent crime.

In terms of the scale of the exercise, the hanging of non-violent offenders was an even more important function of the courts than the execution of those convicted of violent crime. It is true that a greater proportion of violent, than of non-violent, crimes attracted death-sentences. But allegations of non-violent offences were so much more common than indictments for assault, mayhem, robbery, or homicide that their comparatively small proportion of death-sentences nevertheless outnumbered those for crimes of violence against the person. Of 248 executions ordered in the gaol deliveries, 204 or 79.1 per cent, were for non-violent offences such as housebreaking or theft.[57]

This number represents only 15.5 per cent of the 1,315 cases.

---

[53] *Norwich Records*, ii. 66 gives the expenses for buying and carrying wood for the burning of William White, William Waddon, and Hugh Pye.

[54] Tanner, *Heresy*, 181 and 200—Thomas Mone and Isabella Chapleyn. Tanner points out, however, that Mone may have got his remission for wealth rather than weakness (pp. 24–5).

[55] Ibid. 23.

[56] Ibid. 15.

[57] This category does not include robbery, which legally implied violence against the person. There were comparatively few cases of robbery in the East Anglian gaol delivery records, see Table 2.6.

Obviously, then, either a large proportion of indictments were mistaken, or hanging was seen as an inappropriate punishment for most non-violent crime, even where the offence was technically felonious and therefore capital. Certainly, rape or ravishment rarely attracted punishment, though it was a not infrequent charge; in July 1436 at Henhowe, for instance, there were four cases alleged, but only one man was found guilty, and he was a parson who pleaded his clergy.[58] Only certain types of non-violent felonies, it seems, induced juries to hang the perpetrator.

Closer examination of the indictments against the condemned suggest that it was, in the main, repeated thefts of substantial value which tended to condemn the perpetrators to death. In practice the hanging value of stolen goods seems to have been well above the 12*d.* limit which defined capital felony from amerciable trespass. Over half the defendants—118—were said to have stolen goods worth over a pound (and over one-third, goods worth £2 or more). Clearly this was not the minor pilfering of temporary necessity. The thieves took such things as livestock; Geoffrey Semer made off with seventy-six sheep worth £3.16*s.* in 1430; in 1425 William Glegg took two horses and harness worth 20*s.* from Adam Clerk. John Werman, a Bedfordshire labourer, was arrested in possession of three horses, two of which— worth 26*s.* 8*d.*—were not his own. The twenty-two sheep stolen by John Frensshman, a Bedfordshire labourer, in 1438, were priced at £1.16*s.* 8*d.* In 1422 John Gerard, a Suffolk yeoman, was said to have stolen two lots of cattle worth a total of £4. 10*s,* while in 1424 Henry Barkere stole four bullocks, allegedly worth 4 marks, and a horse worth 20*s.* In 1439 in Huntingdon, Benedict Lawerens's two stolen horses yielded him 25*s.*[59]

Other thieves took substantial amounts of coin and plate. William Clerke and Robert Holywode, two Bedfordshire labourers, allegedly robbed Sir John Wenlok of 4 gold marks in 1429. Even this was a small haul compared to the £40 worth of gold and silver which Richard Forest, a Norfolk labourer, allegedly stole from Edmund Couper. Richard Webstere was indicted for taking a chalice from a church worth 20*s.*; and Robert Pax stole £10 worth of silver. When John Mowere, a Norfolk yeoman, was hanged for theft in 1433, his

---

[58] JUST 3 209 mm 29[d] and 32[r].
[59] JUST 3 209 m 1[d], 210 m 30[r], 206 m 2[d], 207 m 16[r], 206 m 8[d], and 210 m 28[d].

chattels included two silver salt-cellars, eleven silver spoons, and two gold and two silver-gilt rings. He was clearly no small-time operator.[60]

Some of the condemned may have had local histories of crime, as indicated by indictments which alleged more than one offence.[61] In rare cases, as in that of the unlucky Walter Margery, captured in possession of a picklock, the indictment itself gives evidence of criminal history.[62] Margery did the best he could for himself by turning approver, but was hanged when one of his appellees was acquitted. John Curle, a labourer from Great Plumstead, Norfolk, had several encounters with the law before he was finally condemned to death in February 1439. He first appeared in the gaol delivery of July 1425, charged with three counts of theft (to the value of £9) and one of rape. The same allegations appeared in King's Bench in Michaelmas 1425, together with the allegations that he was a 'communis raptor mulierum.' In the 1427 oyer and terminer before Humphrey of Gloucester, it was alleged that he was indicted for various felonies, and his case was remanded until the next gaol delivery. He must have been released at some later stage, for in February 1439, he was in trouble again, accused of extensive robberies from the Wilton family in 1438; also of arson and theft in 1424. This time the jury showed no mercy.[63]

Not all of, and only, those defendants who had histories of stealing on a large scale were sentenced to death. There are counter-examples to both generalizations. John Olyver's only known occupation was 'theff', but he was nevertheless acquitted of the more serious charges of arson and robbery in February 1433.[64] In July 1429 John Deye, a Norfolk yeoman, was released even though it was alleged that he had stolen three horses worth 10 marks, and was a 'common thief'.[65] Conversely, John Curre, of Huntingdon, was condemned to hang on

---

[60] JUST 3 219/5 m 8ʳ, 210 m 6ʳ, 219/5 m 140, 209 m 2ᵈ, and 209 m 8ᵈ.

[61] JUST 3 207 m 20ᵈ and 219/5 m 8 against William Clerke and Roger Holywode; JUST 3 207 mm 20ʳ,ᵈ against Gilbert Spenser and John Mille, and m 4ᵈ and JUST 3 219/5 m 140 against Richard Webstere, JUST 3 209 m 5ʳ and 220/1 pt. ii m (75) against William Wychyngham, and JUST 3 209 m 14ᵈ and 220/1 pt. ii m (67) against William Atte Hill, for example.

[62] JUST 3 212 m 17ʳ,ᵈ.

[63] JUST 3 219/3 m 239; KB 9 936 m 11 and KB 27 669 Rm 9ᵈ; JUST 3 50/12 m 32ʳ; JUST 3 210 m 8ʳ and 220/2 m 242.

[64] JUST 3 209 m 6ʳ.

[65] JUST 3 207 m 5ʳ.

one charge of theft of goods worth only 4*s*.[66] But overall, the defendant with a history of stealing expensive goods was clearly the most likely candidate for a hanging verdict.

The function of this kind of legal violence was surely to protect the goods of the richer and more powerful orders of society from the depredations, not of the poorest classes (who might steal necessities such as foodstuffs and firewood from their neighbours) but of those members of the community just below them in social standing and wealth.[67] These people, by pertinaciously transferring significant amounts of gentry property to their own use, attacked the nicely graded system of social distinctions in the simplest and most direct way. They removed from the rich the outward signs of their status. I do not suggest that they stole from consciously revolutionary motives; no doubt they did it for money, just as the juries who condemned them probably thought of themselves as the protectors of property rights rather than explicit social conservatives. But the fact remains that as the system worked, it tended to provide a striking reinforcement of the doctrine that distinctions of power and wealth were to be rightly preserved by the exercise of authoritative violence. I have found no cases in the gaol delivery records of gentry executed for theft, though it is impossible to believe that all upper-class fifteenth-century East Anglians were of stainless financial probity. Gentry crimes against property went to a gentler forum—King's Bench plea side, where honour was satisfied by ritualized legal interchanges, and executions were virtually unheard of.

To sum up, it is clear that the lawcourts functioned in a number of ways to construct and reinforce the linked systems of ordered violence and power in fifteenth-century society. On a simple level, the gaol deliveries punished, with exemplary violence, those moderately substantial citizens who attacked the property of the wealthy; in terms of the numbers of people executed, this was probably the main function of the death-sentence in East Anglia in this period. In terms of contemporary perceptions, however, it may be that the more vital role of the courts was to bring to execution those guilty of the crime which most clearly symbolized the dissolution of human and divine order—

[66] JUST 3 210 m 28^r; see also the case of John Talbot, labourer, of Waterbeach in Cambridge, in Feb. 1436 (JUST 3 7/4 m 2^d).

[67] Cf. Z. Razi's comments on the 'frequent' presentment of poorer villagers in their manor court for thefts of food and firewood (*Life, Marriage and Death in a Medieval Parish* (Cambridge, 1980), 78).

culpable homicide. This is shown by the comparatively high proportion of homicide cases that resulted in death-sentences. Overall, the courts took care to kill a noticeable number of East Anglians each year. Executions, whether they involved the hanging of felons or the burning of heretics and traitors, were highly public affairs. We may well suspect, therefore, that the maintenance of order and the generation of political power was the issue at stake, rather than the preservation of human life.[68]

These were the direct ways in which the lawcourts worked to reinforce social order. There were others. The justices of gaol delivery who ordered the executions took on the godlike power of exercising just violence, striking the guilty dead. Presumably the justices of the peace who sat with them (well-known local gentlemen, every one) shared this awesome glory in the sight of their contemporaries. Even in the milder forum of King's Bench, every defendant charged with violence who was successfully brought under the scrutiny of the court witnessed to the fact that the king's court was the authoritative tribunal for establishing the parameters of just and unjust violence. Again, the fact that gentry disputes over property were fought out decorously in King's Bench, while the crimes of lesser people came to gaol delivery, meant that in literal daily practice there was one sort of law for the rich and another, harsher, sort for the less powerful. Since the workings of the court extended into the provinces, to the activities of the sheriffs, bailiffs, and constables, by which the county community judged the relative honour and influence of its gentlefolk, these distinctions were constantly reinforced throughout the East Anglian community.

In all these ways, from the brutal exhibition of legal violence at the gallows, to the cobweb subtlety of county rumour and litigation, the practice of the law was vital to the maintenance of hierarchical power and authority.

So far we have surveyed the ways in which law and violence were conceived and used in the fifteenth century from a very general viewpoint, ranging over late-medieval literature, law, theology, and chronicle-writing, as well as the thousands of cases which passed through the King's Bench and gaol deliveries, 1422–42. It is now

---

[68] Cf. Michel Foucault's brilliant explication of the functions of early-modern torture and execution, in his *Discipline and Punish: The Birth of the Prison*, tr. A. Sheridan (Harmondsworth, 1979), 47–69.

time to sharpen the focus—to examine, in the context of individual cases, how fifteenth-century East Anglians behaved within the complicated system of social order which informed their world. In the next chapter, five case-studies will be used to analyse the motives for, and meanings of, allegations of violence in fifteenth-century East Anglia.

5

FIVE CASE-STUDIES

What a picture of the violent mode in which our ancestors
suffered their animosities against one another to burst forth!

(Sir John Cullum, *History of Hawsted and Hardwick*,
1st edn. (London, 1748), 105)

5.1 The Diggers; Inglose v. Haldeyn *et al.*

The remarkable ordinariness of this affair qualifies it to head a
collection of case-studies. Like most of the cases of alleged violence
which came to King's Bench from East Anglia, it originated in
Norfolk, was sued by a writ of trespass *vi et armis* on the plea side,
and concerned property rights.[1] The plaintiff, Sir Henry Inglose (a
noted Norfolk soldier and administrator) was clearly a man who
believed in prosecuting for his rights; he was the most enthusiastic
user of the court in the period 1422–42, appearing as plaintiff in
thirty-nine cases, thirty-three of which involved property matters.[2] A
familiar status gap separated plaintiff and defendants; Inglose accused
Richard Haldeyn, John Attewelle, John Lynstede, and nine others, all
husbandmen at Dilham (his main manor) of illegally cutting turf on
24 May 1433. His (or his attorney's) use of the writ of trespass led to
the unconvincing assertion that this misdeed was achieved with
swords, staves, and other weapons.[3] The single unusual feature of the

---

[1] See Tables 2.1 and 2.2.

[2] Inglose was lieutenant-admiral for the seas from Thames to Berwick by Sept. 1428
(*CPR, 1422–9*, 502); justice of the peace for Norfolk in 1424 and 1428; named on two
commissions to inquire into the misgovernment of Norwich in 1433 (*CPR, 1429–36*,
349 and 351) and on a commission of array in 1436 (ibid. 521). See also A. R. Smith,
'Aspects of the Career of Sir John Fastolf (1380–1459)', D. Phil. thesis (Oxford, 1982),
108–9.

[3] KB 27 690 m 76^d and 691 m 42^r; cf. Tables 2.1 and 2.5.

case is that it reached a verdict.[4] In this instance, the power of the suit to produce out-of-court settlement was not wholly effective.

At the case's first appearance, the defendants' attorneys asked for time to consider the plea, and were granted until Hilary 1434. Haldeyn, Lynstede, and Attewelle all appeared then, and with attorneys for the remaining defendants, entered a standard defence plea—that the charge misstated the amount and value of the turf dug, and that they had rights over the land anyway. At some stage before the jury gave their verdict (recorded in Easter 1435) the defendants boldly petitioned the Chancellor.[5] They willingly admitted that they and their ancestors had been 'sesyd at the wyll of the lordes of dylham', but claimed that they had 'had comone of turbarie [right to cut turf] syn tyme that no mynde rennyth' until Sir Henry Inglose had 'putte hem oute of her said landes and comone wythoute cause'. Predictably, but perhaps not untruthfully, they alleged that they could not fend off his suits of trespass, because 'the said landes ben holden of hym at his Will'.

Who actually had the greater right over these turf-diggings, we cannot now discover. The jury, at any rate, stated that the tenants had no claim to common, and should pay damages of £40. This decision initiated the tedious process of getting them to pay. The sheriff was ordered to bring them to make settlement in Easter and Michaelmas 1435, and Easter 1436, and was himself still being ordered into court to explain his failure to do so in Hilary 1437.[6] It seems, however, that during this period, some compromise must have been reached. When the jury verdict was to be given, Inglose dropped charges against three of the defendants, and on 4 July 1438 he waived his right to damages from all but John Lynstede (at that time in the Marshalsey).[7] Lynstede eventually made a 20s. fine in Michaelmas 1438; perhaps he was the group's scapegoat.[8]

The details of this case, scant and commonplace as they are, suggest again that law, and not primarily violence, was the medium of dispute. There is no evidence in the form of charges or petitions of assault or menaces, that Inglose's tenants had actually used violence to assert their claims; and Inglose did not try to impose on them the severe

[4] Cf. Table 2.3.
[5] C 1 10/24.
[6] KB 27 696 m 8[r], 698 Rm 10[d], 700 m 74[r], and 743 Rm 22[d].
[7] KB 27 691 m 42[r].
[8] KB 27 710 fines m 1[r].

punishments fairly freely available at gaol deliveries and peace sessions. Once the case came to court, the defendants accepted the necessity of dealing with it in a business-like way. They hired two good lawyers to plead for them (William Norwich and John Borle were both frequent pleaders in King's Bench) and presented a well-worded petition in Chancery (the phrase 'syn tyme that no mynde rennyth' translates well the common-law usage of prescriptive title).[9] They also avoided heavy damages. Their peaceful methods cannot indicate either lack of determination or a collusive suit, since normally the case would never have come to a verdict; presumably only the defendants' stubbornness kept it in court.[10] Inglose too apparently regarded the matter as routine, delegating the running of the case to the experienced Norfolk lawyer Adam Mundeford. An overview of King's Bench records for this period gives the impression that much of the apparent lawlessness of the age was nothing of the sort. The analysis of this case can only confirm such a view.

What it seems to show is the eagerness with which people turned to the law, not to provide a solution for their problems, but to act as a forum for ritualistic exchanges concerning the relative power and justification of the parties to a dispute, and as a ratification of the outcome of the tussle. This attitude towards the law evidently pervaded many classes of society. The Dilham husbandmen, perhaps emulating their landlord's litigatory skill, took up with consummate ease the challenge he set them. He put pressure on them by a charge in King's Bench. They wasted no time trying to avoid appearance, probably calculating rightly that a man of Inglose's standing could easily persuade the sheriff to pursue arrests or outlawries.[11] Instead, they countered his charges very appropriately, and proceeded to apply a persuader of their own—the Chancery petition. For a Chancery subpoena had the power to bring even so great a man as Inglose before the court, as surely as if he had been the lowliest defendant compelled by the sheriff's men to attend sessions in the county. This threat to Inglose's standing may have induced him to settle more leniently with most of his recalcitrant tenants. No doubt he won. The jury decision in a court of record would stand against the tenants'

---

[9] Sir W. Holdsworth, *A History of English Law*, 2nd edn. (London, 1937) vii. 344.
[10] See Table 2.3.
[11] The fact that John Lynstede was in prison in London in 1438 is probably an index of Inglose's power to secure his defendants.

claims from then on, and Lynstede, who had fought so well for his claims, was both imprisoned and fined. But Inglose won not (as far as we know) by an irregular use of violence, but because the law confirmed a settlement in accord with his superior influence and authority. His opponents were defeated; but apparently neither destroyed nor disgraced.

The law in this case thus operated peacefully to reaffirm the hierarchical rights and responsibilities of the late-medieval land-owning system. That violence lay behind, and justified, this hierarchy, is true; but the details of its day-to-day workings were matters of quasi-political debate, in which both tenants and landlord might use the law peacefully to their advantage.[12]

The law, however, contained sound provisions for justifying violence.[13] The next study illuminates the by-play to which these provisions might give rise.

5.2 An Opportunists' Quarrel; John Bekeswell v. William Dallyng

Between 1415 and 1450 in the southwest corner of Norfolk lived two minor gentlemen—John Bekeswell and William Dallyng. Their lands, at Bexwell and Fordham respectively, were barely three miles apart. Bekeswell was styled 'gentlemen', and once 'armiger'. Dallyng may have been rising socially; first known as a husbandman, he was later styled 'franklin' and once, 'gentleman'.[14] Yet his daughter and presumed heiress married a neighbouring yeoman (William Gyllour of Ryston) and he remained, socially, one step below Bekeswell.[15] Neither held any major county office.[16] However, both were active at

---

[12] See Ch. 2.

[13] See Ch. 2, text accompanying nn. 106–12 and 119–20.

[14] *CCLR, 1454–61*, 63 and KB 27 699 m 53ʳ for Bekeswell; KB 27 654 Rm 18ʳ (Michaelmas 1424), KB 27 723 Rm 24ʳ, 726 m 61ᵈ, and 723 m 59ʳ for Dallyng.

[15] *CCLR, 1441–7*, 127 (charter of his lands by Dallyng to his son-in-law and daughter and others, 1 Aug. 1441, memorandum of acknowledgement Feb. 1443).

[16] Such as sheriff, or justice of the peace. John Bekeswell of Norfolk should not be confused with the John Bekeswell who was a justice of the peace in Huntingdon in 1429, and owned land in Huntingdon and Bedford in 1436 (E 129 240/268). The Huntingdon man was presumably 1 of 2 John Bekeswells who were dead by Oct. 1438 (C 1 9/485).

lower levels of officialdom. Dallyng was undersheriff in 1422, 1429, and 1438, and sub-escheator in 1439–40. In 1427 he was commissioned to investigate concealed wardships and marriages in Norfolk and Suffolk.[17] Bekeswell was named with Sir Simon Felbrigge and others on a 1437 commission to investigate alleged wool-smuggling from Norfolk, and also appeared on a commission *de walliis & fossatis* in 1452. He was a feoffee and associate of greater men, such as Sir Robert Ponyngges,[18] and, at least by 1441, bailiff of the abbey of Ramsey, empowered to hold the abbot's tourns at Stradsett and Clacklose Hill.[19] To some extent the areas in which the two men held land overlapped—Dallyng owned messuages in Bexwell.[20] This background of close peer co-existence provides the context for a series of offences alleged against Dallyng by Bekeswell in the year following the Michaelmas term of 1441.

The supposed crimes range from 1428 to 1441, but the concentration of suits into one year suggests that the actual dispute came to a head late in the period. To summarize, in Michaelmas 1441, Bekeswell brought a bill to King's Bench, alleging that on 3 October 1429 Dallyng had illegally arrested him, and only released him on payment of £10.[21] On 5 October 1441 Bekeswell and Thomas Halle took indictments at the abbot of Ramsey's tourn at Clacklose Hill, that on three occasions between 4 December 1434 and 12 August 1441, Dallyng had abetted and protected known felons. (Two of them had allegedly stolen goods from Bekeswell.) In one instance, John Walpole had been arrested by the constable of Downham Market on suspicion of felony. Dallyng allegedly came with a body of men *modo guerrino*, assaulted the constable, and rescued the prisoner. Another indictment at the same tourn blamed the rescue on William Gyllour, Dallyng's son-in-law, with Dallyng as accessory. These cases were removed to the Rex side of King's Bench in Trinity 1442.[22] Meanwhile, in Hilary 1442 Bekeswell accused Dallyng, again in a bill, of trespass on his lands at Bexwell and Crimplesham with force and arms, depasturing,

---

[17] KB 27 654 Rm 18[r], 709 Rm 19[d], 722 m 108[d], and 723 Rm 24[r] and m 59[r]; and *CPR, 1422–9*, 467.

[18] *CCLR, 1441–7*, 435 and *CCLR, 1422–9*, 335–6.

[19] KB 9 240 m 62 and KB 27 725 Rm 25[r]; but Blomefield, *History of Norfolk*, vii. 516 says that he was steward of the abbot of Ramsey in Wimbotsham in Henry V's time.

[20] See above, n. 15.

[21] KB 27 722 m 108[d].

[22] KB 9 240 m 62[r] and KB 27 725 Rm 3[d].

and cutting down woodland, between 1 December 1438 and 16 November 1441. In Easter 1442 Bekeswell turned his attention to Gyllour, suing a writ of trespass (with depasturing and woodcutting) in Bexwell and Crimplesham from November 1428 to February 1441.[23] Finally, in Michaelmas 1442, Bekeswell brought an appeal of robbery, repeating that Dallyng had sheltered those who robbed him in 1434.[24]

Similar charges had been laid against Dallyng before 1441. In Michaelmas 1424 presentments from two separate peace sessions at Lynn and Norwich in 1423 appeared in King's Bench Rex side. They alleged that 28 August 1419, Dallyng had broken into the property of Lady Margery Clyfton, assaulted her and her servants, and illegally taken twenty sheep; that 7 May 1422 he had 'sine ... warranto' arrested one William Blyth and taken 26s. 8d. from him; and that 14 September 1422, as undersheriff, he had released a well-known counterfeiter. He was eventually acquitted of all these charges.[25]

Other suits followed Bekeswell's. In Hilary 1442 Thomas Watson alleged that Dallyng and three other men had stolen cattle (14 August 1439). The defendants pleaded that the 'theft' was in fact legal distraint carried out by the escheator and his servants in connection with an outlawry proclaimed in 1437. In the same term, a Rex side case appeared against Dallyng for defrauding the king of goods. Again, Dallyng pleaded that he had merely undertaken to sell the goods of a proclaimed outlaw as part of his duties as sub-escheator.[26]

Thus, Dallyng may have been commonly suspected of using his office to feather his nest and pay off his scores. Yet the fact that these cases appeared in King's Bench, rather than the more punitive gaol delivery, suggests that his accusers did not intend to invoke severe punishment on him. Further, of all the cases against him, the only two on which he was convicted were the trespass on Bekeswell's lands, 1438–41, and the theft of Thomas Watson's cattle. In the first, the jury awarded Bekeswell sizeable damages of £20, disregarding Dallyng's plea that Bekeswell had agreed to give him the timber. In the second, Watson was awarded damages of over 7 marks (duly paid in February 1446). Bekeswell also won his case of trespass against

[23] KB 27 723 m 79[d] and 724 m 28[r] and 730 fines m 1[d].
[24] KB 27 726 m 61[d].
[25] KB 27 654 Rm 18[r].
[26] KB 27 723 m 59[r] and 723 Rm 24[r].

Gyllour, who paid 100s. damages in Michaelmas 1443 (Dallyng standing pledge for him). This is peculiar, granted that bills and writs of trespass did not commonly come to verdicts, especially guilty verdicts. Appeals pursued with any vigour were much more likely to reach an end;[27] yet Bekeswell's appeal of robbery against Dallyng fizzled out with the non-appearance of the jury.[28] As for the other charges, Dallyng was acquitted of all three allegations of abetting felons which came up in Trinity 1442, and the suits for unlawful arrest of Bekeswell and embezzlement of the king's goods never reached a verdict because no jury appeared.[29]

This is not to say there was no truth in these charges. To the imprisonment issue, Dallyng pleaded that though he was entitled as undersheriff to arrest Bekeswell (who had, he said, been presented for receiving stolen cattle at the peace sessions of 12 June 1428), he and Bekeswell had afterwards settled the affair by arbitrement before Laurence Braunche, at London. The award ordered that Dallyng give Bekeswell a meal worth 20d. in settlement of all disputes between them. Arbitrements were not commonly pleaded in defence in King's Bench; and though Dallyng might have invented the plea, placing the arbitrement in London so that a London jury would have to be gathered to give a verdict on it (to the annoyance of his Norfolk adversaries) it is equally likely that the award did take place, and that Dallyng, since he paid a settlement fee, was at fault to some degree.[30]

Similarly, though both Dallyng and Gyllour were acquitted of the alleged violent rescue of John Walpole in 1441, a third indictment taken before William Paston and others in Norwich, 9 April 1442, sheds light on the case.[31] This indictment alleged that Dallyng received Walpole, knowing him to be a thief and adulterer; it made no mention of the violent rescue specified in the indictments before Bekeswell.[32] Unfortunately, whoever drew up the charge mistakenly

---

[27] See Tables 2.2–2.3, and Ch. 4, n. 9.

[28] See Tables 2.2–2.3, and Ch. 4, n. 9, as compared to KB 27 726 m 61[d] and 730 Rm 100[d]. See also Ch. 2, text accompanying nn. 29–32, for the use of appeals in vexatious litigation.

[29] KB 27 722 m 108[d] and 725 m 44[d]; KB 27 723 Rm 24[r] and 732 Rm 2[d].

[30] Only 20 pleas of arbitrement were made in the period 1422–42; but see also E. Powell, 'Arbitration and the Law in England in the Late Middle Ages', *Transactions of the Royal Historical Society*, 5th series, 33 (1983), 63 for arbitrements pleaded as a bar to further legal action.

[31] KB 27 725 Rm 3[d].

[32] KB 27 725 Rm 6[r].

dated the crime the year after the indictment, enabling Dallyng to procure an easy *sine die* by pleading error. However the existence of the accusation suggests that Dallyng may genuinely have been at fault in his dealings with Walpole, but that the indictment of October 1441 represents a heightening of the real misdemeanor by Bekeswell (then just starting his campaign against Dallyng).

Verdicts in King's Bench were always uncommon, but in general, cases alleging violence stood a better chance of achieving a verdict than those which did not.[33] It is curious, then, that in the Bekeswell/ Dallyng dispute only those charges directly relating to property rights rather than violent crime yielded a guilty verdict. This suggests that Dallyng's possible abuse of his official position was in Bekeswell's eyes peripheral to the main issue—presumably property rights. In pursuit of his ends Bekeswell cheerfully embarked on the daunting array of diversionary suits appropriate to the legal system within which he worked. He may have purposely allowed some charges to linger in King's Bench at the stage of calling the jury, to retain some hold over his adversary.

Exactly what was the basis of the dispute is now difficult to tell; but the evidence suggests that Dallyng, too, tried to use the law to dislodge Bekeswell's hold on his land. On 28 January 1437 an inquest was taken at Bokenham Castle before Sir John Clyfton and Thomas Derham on whether John Bekeswell was native-born English. It was alleged that Walter Walyngton, born in Flanders, had in 1385 acquired land without licence, in Bexwell, from John Bekeswell the elder; and that John Bekeswell, Walter's son, was himself born out of England. His land acquisitions in Bexwell, Fyncham, and other nearby places, 1422–42, would thus have been illegal. Bekeswell promptly appeared to ward off this threat to his livelihood, claiming that Walter Walyngton his father was born in Surrey, and had acquired Bexwell manor by marrying Margery, daughter of John Bekeswell the elder.[34] That Dallyng was involved in this attempt to undermine Bekeswell's right to his lands is indicated by the later accounts of Bekeswell himself. In one Chancery petition, he claimed that Thomas Derham, the holder of Crimplesham manor (about half a mile from Bexwell) procured the inquiry, ('by cause þe seyd John askyd of þe seyd Thomas derham

---

[33] See Ch. 4, Table 4.1 for the comparative probabilities of gaining a verdict in violent and non-violent cases.

[34] C 44 26/6.

land rent And othyr thyngs the qwyche is his inheritaunce').[35] However, another petition referring to the same inquest laid the blame on the 'informacon & sterryng' of Dallyng, who had also 'manast & thret' to 'let & hyndyr hym [Bekeswell] in his seyd travers swyng' if he were not bought off.[36] It sounds as if both Dallyng and Derham had reason at this stage to throw doubt on Bekeswell's right to hold his lands—Derham to avoid paying rent, Dallyng because of the property dispute which lay behind his illegal entry into Bekeswell's property in 1438.[37] Possibly they co-operated against Bekeswell for mutual profit. This idea receives some oblique support from the fact that they certainly appeared together in Michaelmas 1436, in a case of debt against Edmund Wichyngham in Common Pleas.[38] Bekeswell, however, managed to mobilize some powerful friends against Dallyng, if not against Derham—on 2 March 1442, a commission was issued to Sir John Clyfton, William Goderede, Sir Thomas Tuddenham, John Heydon, and Bekeswell himself, to investigate Dallyng's dealings in the matter of the inquisition on Bekeswell's alien extraction.[39]

Violence in these affairs (if indeed there were any) must have taken place within the bounds of legal process. *If* Dallyng were guilty of distraining Thomas Watson's goods unlawfully, and arresting Bekeswell without due cause, then some show of force may have been used to obtain the goods and the prisoner. Aside from this, the quarrel seems to have been pursued with very sophisticated legal techniques. Dallyng's use of the knotty question of Bekeswell's citizenship is an example. One must also guess that Dallyng conveyed his lands to his daughter and son-in-law in August 1441, to evade any charges which Bekeswell (then presumably threatening his campaign of litigation) might levy on them.[40] No doubt it was when Bekeswell realized this in Easter 1442, that he took to suing Gyllour as well.[41]

Yet legalized violence had its effect on the dispute. Apparently, Bekeswell was able to pursue his cases against Dallyng with such success only because by Michaelmas 1441, Dallyng was already

---

[35] C 1 10/324. The petition goes on to assert that the matter had been arbitrated in Bekeswell's favour, but that Derham refused to keep the award.

[36] C 1 12/100. Bekeswell also complained that Dallyng had been appointed to arbitrate a dispute between Bekeswell and 2 other men, had taken from him bonds of agreement to keep the award, and had then neither made the award nor returned the bonds.

[37] See above, n. 23.

[38] CP 40 703 m 86ᵈ.

[39] *CPR, 1441–46*, 77.

[40] See above, n. 15.

[41] See above, n. 23.

imprisoned in the Marshalsey. He may have remained there for most of the ensuing year.[42] Bekeswell was thus enabled to bring bills against him, which Dallyng was forced to traverse, rather than simply avoiding the case by non-appearance. Since he was already in gaol, it cannot have been Bekeswell's charges which brought him there. From other evidence, it seems that at this stage, Dallyng had fallen foul of the powerful Norfolk lobby for the earl of Suffolk. A Paston memorandum of 1451 concerning the crimes of Suffolk's main supporters in the county, Sir Thomas Tuddenham and John Heydon, speaks of the 'prisonyng of Dallyng', and notes that one of Tuddenham's men 'toke of Wylliam Dallyng at Norwyche v mark for smytyng of hese feteris whan he was there in preson Ao xixo'.[43] It seems that Dallyng the undersheriff had experienced the very irons which he helped to load on others; and that Bekeswell took advantage of his temporary helplessness to bring his own business to a successful conclusion.

After 1443 no signs of the quarrel emerge. Probably Bekeswell, having gained convictions over the trespass on his lands, and thus secured his rights, was prepared to let other matters go. Possibly Dallyng was unwilling to risk further imprisonment at the hands of Bekeswell's powerful friends, and was satisfied with the acquittals he had gained in his Rex side cases.

However we assign the doubtful guilt or innocence of each party, the case gives valuable insights into the relationship between law and violence in fifteenth-century disputes. The quarrel may never have concerned violent misdeeds. Force, if it was used in the affair, must have been done under pretext of legality—theft and trespass masquerading as distraint, assault and extortion as legal arrest. Bekeswell surely used his position as bailiff of the abbey of Ramsey to promote damaging indictments against Dallyng, and Dallyng was possibly rightly accused of misusing his position as undersheriff and subescheator to rob and harass his opponents. But if so, the violence in the affair was legalized, implicit, and off-stage. Even Dallyng's imprisonment could have been technically legal—Sir Thomas Tuddenham, as a justice of the peace, was entitled to issue warrants for

---

[42] KB 27 722 m 108^d, and KB 9 240 m 62.

[43] *PL* ii. 526. This is a partisan document connected with the oyer and terminer against Suffolk's supporters after his death; but where it fits other evidence so well and fortuituously, it may be believed. Note that Tuddenham and Heydon were named on the commission apparently obtained by Bekeswell in 1442, to investigate Dallyng's dealings, above, n. 39.

arrest. In fact, the case demonstrates neatly the working out, in sober provincial practice, of the strict moral order of violence described in Chapters 3 and 4. Violence could only be justified if it occurred in the context of right authority, and with the purpose of maintaining order and justice. No wonder then that less reputable forms of violence were carried out under colour of the administration of justice. The local community wielded the procedures and sanctions of the law; this meant that the law was likely to be used partially. Either Dallyng's opponents suffered from the forces of law and order which he could muster, or Dallyng himself was caught by the fact that the execution of his duties could be represented as criminal action. This shady side of law and order was evidently tacitly accepted by fifteenth-century people. The banditry of mercenary soldiers did not shake their faith in the values of chivalry; no more did the misuse of legal sanctions undermine their confidence in the law.[44]

5.3 John Broun's Body; or The Bateman Murder Case

So far the case-studies seem to suggest that lawful dispute-settlement was endemic in late-medieval England. However, the murder of John Broun, a dyer and franklin of Barrington, Cambridge, on 21 October 1422, seems at first sight very different. There is no doubt that a man died in the course of a quarrel, and the records of the affair apparently show that his death typified both indefensible violence as the fifteenth century recognized it, and the disorder and thuggery of late-medieval society as historians have represented it. Six separate juries presented the case to the justices of the peace at Cambridge, 18 March 1423. Their indictments, though formalized into two types, express in the strongest available terms the horror of the deed. One set of indictments alleges that John Bateman of Bury Hatley,[45] gentleman, and Richard Bateman, of Harlton *modo guerrino arraiati et armati* and *ex malicia praecogitata* lay in ambush to slay John Broun at Meldreth; the other, that the pair were *insidiatores viarum* who lurked at Meldreth *tam per diem quam per noctem*, pursuing their hapless victim. The

---

[44] M. Keen, *Chivalry* (New Haven, Conn., 1984), 224–37.
[45] Now known as Cockayne Hatley, Bedford; but in 1422 John Cokayn the justice had only just bought the manor, and the old name still applied.

indictments were removed into King's Bench by Michaelmas 1423, with the addition that these crimes were done *per procurationem et abbettamentum* of Ralph Bateman of Harlton, gentleman.[46] There could be no clearer example of the definition of murder as killing by ambush or stealth, with criminal intent witnessed by arms-carrying. Further, the patent rolls for 20 November 1423 record a commission of oyer and terminer, issued to investigate the Batemans' misdeeds; first the murder of John Broun (also of Simon Aylmere and Henry Veel, at Clavering in Essex), and secondly the alleged assault and wounding of Nicholas Caldecote, the outgoing escheator of Cambridge, in the course of his duties.[47]

Superficially, the transaction seems to be pure criminal law—dangerous criminals on the one hand confronted jury indictments on the other. Yet the fact that the charges came to King's Bench rather than gaol delivery should raise suspicion that negotiation, rather than punishment, was the object of the legal exercise.[48] Further, if John, Richard, and possibly Ralph Bateman were well-known violent criminals and habitual *insidiatores viarum*, one would expect them to appear more than once in legal records.[49] But there is no evidence of prior criminal history. The only legal affairs in which members of the family had been demonstrably involved were probably civil ones—two cases of novel disseisin in which Ralph's brother William was a defendant, and a supersedeas in a case of trespass by a John Bateman in 1379.[50] This paucity of criminal background does not reflect the youth of the offenders—John Bateman was certainly adult by 1394 and possibly by 1375, Ralph by 1375 and Richard by 1410.[51] Either these rather elderly suspects had evaded the law all their lives, or they had suddenly plunged into violent crime.

Finally, and perhaps most tellingly, in view of the high appearance and verdict rates for allegedly violent crime (especially murder) in King's Bench Rex side, almost nothing came of this flurry of legal

---

[46] KB 9 203 mm 45 and 46; KB 27 650 Rm 4ᵈ.

[47] *CPR, 1422–29*, 173–4.

[48] See Ch. 2.

[49] See Ch. 4, p. 131, and compare the case of John Belsham, below.

[50] C 1 5/171 and JUST 1 1520 m 10ᵛ; and *CCLR, 1377–81*, 326. There were at least 2 John Batemans alive in the family at this stage (see *CCLR, 1381–5*, 409 and *CCLR, 1409–13*, 111). It is impossible to tell either the exact nature of the alleged offence, or whether the perpetrator was the same John Bateman accused in 1422.

[51] *CCLR, 1392–6*, 252, *CCLR, 1374–7*, 228, and *CCLR, 1409–13*, 111.

activity.[52] No evidence suggests that the oyer and terminer commissioners ever sat. The principal defendants never appeared in court, even though two were arrested.[53] When the King's Bench case came up, only Ralph Bateman was there. Since he was an accessory rather than a principal, his case could not be tried, and he was allowed mainprize. Writs returned in Hilary 1424, Michaelmas 1425 and 1426, Trinity 1427, Hilary and Trinity 1428, Hilary 1429, and Easter 1431 reported the disappearance and finally outlawry of John and Richard, and the non-attendance of Ralph (for which his mainpernors were fined).[54] But this was the sum of the law's achievements.

Does this perhaps reflect a lack of sufficient money or ability on the part of the Batemans' accusers to see the case through? Apparently not. True, John Broun's son, a poorer neighbour of the Batemans, might have found the costs and troubles of litigation hard to sustain.[55] But the case, once brought in the Rex section of King's Bench, did not require a plaintiff. In any case, it appears that John Broun junior was not the only, nor even the main, mover of the actions. He never appealed the Batemans for the death of his father, though it was his right to do so. It was Nicholas Caldecote, claiming to be the victim of the Bateman's assaults, who presumably obtained the oyer and terminer commission, and he perhaps organized the arrest of John Bateman and his accomplice Henry Veel. He also sued a writ of trespass against the Batemans in Michaelmas 1422, which appeared in Hilary 1424 as an allegation of assault. In Trinity 1423 he brought a suit of trespass against the Batemans and a certain Alexander Child, draper, of London.[56] None of these cases proceeded beyond the calling of exigents; yet Caldecote was clearly capable of seeing any case through to a conclusion, had he chosen to do so. He was a lawyer whose work brought him into contact with such influential men as Sir Walter de la Pole and William Alyngton.[57] His positions as escheator and justice of the peace suggest that he was a competent man of

---

[52] See Table 4.1.

[53] SC 2 171/53—the manor court roll for Clavering, 9 Nov. 1422, which records the arrest.

[54] KB 27 651 Rm 13ʳ, 658 Rm 27ᵈ, 662 fines m, 665 Rm 5ʳ, 667 Rm 1ʳ, 669 Rm 12ᵈ, 671 Rm 13ᵈ, and 680 Rm 2ʳ.

[55] In 1428 he held two-eighths of a fee in Barrington (*Feudal Aids*, i. 183).

[56] KB 27 646 m 1ᵈ and 651 m 40ᵈ; and KB 27 649 m 1ʳ.

[57] See below, text accompanying nn. 71–5.

affairs. By 1436 he held land in Cambridge, Essex, and Huntingdon worth at least £50 per year.[58]

The closer the analysis, the more this affair resembles a typical King's Bench case, in which a plaintiff brought a bewildering variety of allegations against his opponents, in order to gain, not a result at law, but an advantage in an outside dispute. Punishment for murder cannot have been the main aim of the proceedings; no one apparently thought it worthwhile to pursue the malefactors beyond an outlawry. Ralph Bateman, at least, seems to have been quickly accepted back into the county community—a bare four years after the alleged crime, he witnessed a quitclaim with Caldecote![59] No doubt John Broun did indeed die at the Batemans' hands rather than from natural causes, since John Bateman and Henry Veel had evidently fled over the border of their own shrievalty to Essex by early November, rightly fearing arrest. But apparently the crime was thought by contemporaries to have mitigating circumstances.

How, then, could John Broun have become involved in a dispute so desperate as to lead to his death? Broun was a near neighbour of the Batemans, and judging from his fairly frequent appearances as a witness in Barrington deeds, a prosperous and respected citizen.[60] He may have been involved in legal business in a small way; he received a gift of goods and chattels with that well-known figure of the East Anglian legal scene, Robert Caundyssh.[61] His relations with the Batemans seemed essentially business-like. He was said to have joined John Bateman in enfeoffing some Barrington land to Edmund Bendyssh, and he witnessed a quitclaim made by Ralph Bateman to John Cokayn, Sir Walter de la Pole, Nicholas Caldecote, and others, of Ralph's Harlton manors.[62] It was this transaction which apparently involved him in the dispute over Harlton between the Batemans and Caldecote, which led directly to his death.

The trouble with the Harlton property stemmed from the Bateman's family history. Ralph's father William, a successful lawyer and justice

---

[58] E 129 240/268. Since this was a declaration for tax purposes, it is likely to be under- rather than over-estimated.

[59] *CCLR, 1422–29*, 315 (Dec. 1426).

[60] Trinity College Cambridge MSS, Wren Library, BI Dc 12, 15, 16, and 18 (1410–19).

[61] *CCLR, 1409–13*, 410; and cf. Ch 2, pp. 63–64, and Table A3.2.

[62] Trinity College Cambridge MSS, BI Dc 24 (though the actual record is of May 1439, and is therefore recording transactions at least 17 years old). See also *CCLR, 1419–22*, 131–2.

of the peace in the late fourteenth century, bought land in Bedford, Harlton, and Essex; unfortunately, his four sons all survived him, a contingency his resources were insufficient to meet. Ralph got Harlton, the most substantial property—two manors and their attached lands. The Essex manor of Little Sampford went to William the younger, who nevertheless tried to claim a share of Harlton.[63] John had lands in Bury Hatley, Bedford, which can never have been extensive; he does not seem to have lived there, and is sometimes said to have been of Cambridge, or of Harlton.[64] The fourth brother, Richard, apparently had no patrimony, and lived with Ralph.[65] At one time Ralph must have supplemented the family finances by trade—in 1394, Sir William Castellacre owed him £288 for merchandise bought in the staple of Westminster; as late as 1412, Ralph owned London property worth 13s. 4d. per annum.[66] But no further evidence of business activities appears. Harlton must have been, henceforth, the family's mainstay.

But Harlton was not free from dispute. Aside from William's claims (not settled until 1411), the heiress of the Flambards, one of the families who sold the manors to William Bateman the elder, prosecuted Ralph in Chancery in 1407, alleging that the full purchase price had never been paid.[67] In this position, the Batemans might have done well to arrange affluent marriages, pursue careers in law, or at least assure themselves of influential aid in lawsuits by diligent service to greater men. Unfortunately, this seemed beyond their capacities. We have no evidence that any of the brothers married. Ralph's trade is the only known career among the four of them. Neither John nor Richard held any official or legal position. Ralph did; he was justice of the peace in Cambridge from 1392–1414, and of Cambridge town up till 1418, but whether he ever sat at sessions is unknown. Although he was named on various administrative commissions, he never held any key position, such as sheriff, and his activities apparently declined

---

[63] JUST 1 1520 m 10ʳ.

[64] He owed suit at the manor court of Bury Hatley, but consistently defaulted (Bedford Record Office, BW 1248 and 1250). See also KB 9 235 m 50, and *CPR, 1422–6*, 173.

[65] Ibid. and KB 27 650 Rm 4ᵈ.

[66] *CCLR, 1392–6*, 359, and E 179 144/20.

[67] JUST 1 1520 m 10ʳ, and JUST 1 1543 m 25ʳ. This claim was repeated in the final transfer of land to Alexander Child in 1432, when families claiming to have been feoffees of the Flambards were involved (ibid., JUST 1 108/10, and CP 40 786 m 130ʳ).

towards 1420.[68] Admittedly, he must have been at least 64 at his last appointment to the peace commission, which might be taken to explain his subsequent disappearance from it. But as I have noted above, it was unusual for a man to be dropped from peace commissions, especially if he were an energetic magistrate, whatever his age.[69] Ralph's only known contact with the more prominent and active members of the county community in the second decade of the century was as a witness to their land transactions.[70] This does not argue a close identity with the county governing élite.

As Ralph Bateman declined in power and influence, Nicholas Caldecote was rising. He was evidently a much younger man (adult in July 1399 and alive until 1443).[71] He was first a commissioner of the peace in Rutland around the turn of the century. But by 1406 he was named as attorney to Sir Walter de la Pole, and in 1410 made him a gift of all his chattels.[72] In 1417 he was commissioned with other prominent East Anglians (such as William Alyngton, Roger Hunte, and John Ansty) to investigate a murder case.[73] From 1422–3 he was escheator. His association with de la Pole appears to have continued in 1421, when they shared the Bateman quitclaim, and in 1433, the Boefe quitclaim.[74] De la Pole was well worth knowing, a cousin and feoffee of the earls of Suffolk, a knight of the shire three times before 1421 and four times after, a distinguished diplomat, and (perhaps more important from Caldecote's viewpoint) sheriff in 1423–4.[75]

The ageing Ralph Bateman apparently came to an agreement with these two powerful men, together with John Cokayn the justice and others, in Michaelmas 1419. Perhaps he was tired of the constant struggles over Harlton, or desperately short of money; perhaps he no longer felt competent to deal with the property. Whatever the truth, he apparently first demised the property to Caldecote and his friends

---

[68] See his subsidy commission, 1412, and commission of array, 1419; *CPR, 1408–13*, 378, and *CPR, 1416–22*, 210.

[69] See Ch. 2, pp. 63–4.

[70] e.g. he witnessed the Gernoun quitclaim to Caldecote and others in 1419 (*CCLR, 1419–22*, 40).

[71] *CCLR, 1396–9*, 519, and *IPM* iv. 216.

[72] *CPR, 1405–8*, 248, and *CCLR, 1409–13*, 168–9.

[73] *CPR, 1416–22*, 84. This is the sort of commission that Ralph Bateman had been on earlier, see *CPR, 1399–1401*, 516.

[74] *CCLR, 1419–22*, 131–2, and *CCLR, 1429–35*, 289.

[75] J. S. Roskell, *The Commons in the Parliament of 1422* (Manchester, 1954), 172–4.

for ten years, then quitclaimed it to them in January 1421. This quitclaim was witnessed by John Broun.[76]

Unexpectedly, this did not complete the transfer of property. By 27 July 1422 Ralph had brought an assize of novel disseisin against Edward Tyrell, Nicholas Caldecote, John Broun, and a number of others over the Harlton lands. That a serious quarrel had blown up between Ralph Bateman and Caldecote is shown by the size of the securities of peace they exchanged—Ralph got a £20 bond from Caldecote, and had himself already given security of £100.[77] Clearly he had either changed his mind about allowing Caldecote and his friends to take possession of the manor, or that had never been his intention. Perhaps he was forced into making the quitclaim; or his brothers objected to the project; or he expected to be re-enfeoffed of the lands for his lifetime, and was disappointed; or he was simply dissatisfied with the price paid.[78] Faced with this awkward situation, he took the only two possible courses—he brought the action of novel disseisin, and he found (possibly from his erstwhile London contacts) an alternative purchaser for the lands—Alexander Child, the London draper, who in 1423 was accused of trespass at Harlton by Caldecote, and who by 1428 was said to own the manor.[79]

His prospects, however, were not good. Legal actions required money, time, influence, and expertise to reach a successful conclusion. The Batemans probably did not have much money, were certainly running out of lifetime, and had the cream of the county's influence and expertise opposing them.[80] Besides, the undoubted fact that he had made the quitclaim to the supposed trespassers hampered him badly. And if the list of defendants in Ralph's actions can be trusted, John Broun, witness of the quitclaim, had understandably decided to give his voice in support of the powerful men opposing Bateman.

Exactly what happened when John Broun was killed three months

---

[76] *CCLR, 1419–22*, 131–2.

[77] JUST 1 1533 m 3.

[78] Caldecote had allegedly once reneged on an arrangement to receive lands while re-enfeoffing the original owner, see Agnes Wynslowe's petition in Chancery, C 1 7/48.

[79] See above, n. 67 also *Feudal Aids*, i. 183.

[80] Aside from those mentioned, Warin Ingrith, a very hard-working Cambridge attorney in King's Bench, had joined the group. The Batemans might have appealed to some other great local figure, such as Sir John Tiptoft, either to support their claim, or to bring the parties to arbitration; but Caldecote was probably a friend of Tiptoft's (he was named as his attorney in 1426); *CCLR, 1422–9*, 223.

after the suit was brought is impossible to discover; but it seems most likely that the Batemans either set out to stop the mouth of this inconvenient and renegade witness, or perhaps simply killed him, inadvertently, during a quarrel over the stance he had taken.

The response was quick—by the 9 November, John Bateman, and his associate Henry Veel, had been arrested at Clavering, in Essex.[81] But the next move of the Batemans' adversaries was to pursue not the murder, but the property dispute. On 6 February 1423, Caldecote and Ralph Bateman gave bonds of £100 to abide the award of four arbitrators in the matter.[82] On 24 February, a counteraction of novel disseisin was brought against Bateman by Edward Tyrell.[83] Not until 18 March 1423 did the indictments against the Batemans for murder first appear; in the following November, the oyer and terminer commission laid the responsibility not only for the murder of Broun, but also for the deaths of Simon Aylmere and Henry Veel on the Batemans; and on 9 March 1424 an Essex jury belatedly registered an indictment against them for killing Aylmer and Veel.

These last two allegations are dubious at best. The Clavering court roll which records the arrest of John Bateman confirms that Veel was his accomplice by listing his possessions, together with Bateman's, as those of a captured felon. The roll also states that Veel was slain, but carefully refrains from naming his killer.[84] In the absence of any reason for Bateman to kill his companion, and any discernible link between the Batemans and Aylmer, and in view of the suspicious delay between the supposed crime and the indictment, it may be that both Aylmer and Veel were killed unintentionally in fighting during the arrest, and that their deaths were laid to the Batemans' charge to exonerate the Essex constables and to further Caldecote's purposes.

The whole sequence suggests that the property was Caldecote's main concern; and perhaps that Broun's death was, and was known to have been, the accidental result of a fight, rather than fully intentional murder, though it fell outside the strait legal definition of homicide by

---

[81] KB 9 203 m 46 (last indictment) and KB 27 665 Rm 5ʳ.

[82] A. H. Thomas (ed.), *Calendar of Plea and Memoranda Rolls preserved among the Archives of the Corporation of the City of London at the Guildhall, A.D. 1323–1482* (6 vols.; Cambridge, 1926–61), 4. 149–50.

[83] JUST 1 1543 m 24ʳ.

[84] SC 2 171/53. It is recorded that 2s. 4d. had been taken out of Veel's ready money, to pay for his burial 'eo quod ipse interfectus fuit'.

misadventure.[85] Caldecote's response to the death seems to have been to offer an arbitration on the property dispute. The string of carefully inconclusive legal actions on the alleged murder, the counteraction of novel disseisin, and the fruitless oyer and terminer, may then be seen as a methodical series of persuaders, applied to break down the Batemans' resistance to a settlement.

Caldecote's position compared to that of the Batemans seemed impregnable. After their outlawry, for instance, John and Richard would have been debarred from bringing actions in court; and Caldecote could apparently hold over them a plausible homicide charge. Yet the outcome of this unequal trial of strength was less clear-cut than one might expect. Certainly the Batemans sustained losses. John Cokayn, for instance, evidently benefited by John Bateman's outlawry; his will of February 1428 bequeaths land that had been Bateman's.[86] Yet the final owner of the Harlton lands was not Caldecote, but Alexander Child; and when he eventually bought the property in 1432, Ralph Bateman (then aged at least 78) was named among the supposed disseisors, and must therefore have retained some rights in his father's lands.

However we reconstruct the killing of John Broun, one thing is certain—the Batemans were not acting as the unruly gentry retainers of any overmighty magnate, systematically indulging in reckless violence in defiance of a feeble law-system. Nor were they part of a criminal subculture. Even if the killing was intentional, what impelled them was apparently no inherent love of violence, but the desperate defence of their livelihood. They were caught in a trap compounded of their parents' fecundity, their chronic land-shortage, their apparent failure in worldly affairs, and the administrative miscalculation of having rashly quitclaimed Harlton to so sharp an operator as Caldecote. None of these faults or misfortunes disqualified them from respectable gentry society. Possibly, too, they chose, in John Broun, the right person to attack—an opponent subordinate to them in status and wealth, whose death would warn their adversaries of their determination to defend Harlton, without conspicuously violating the principles of hierarchically justified violence. Clearly Caldecote, for

---

[85] Note again the absence of an appeal from Broun's family. See Ch. 4, n. 24, for the legal definition, and text accompanying nn. 42–4 for a possible case of jury sympathy for a killer who slew his opponent in a fair fight.

[86] M. McGregor (ed.), *Bedfordshire Wills proved in the Prerogative Court of Canterbury, 1383–1548* (Publications of the Bedfordshire Historical Record Society, 58; 1979), 8.

all his ambitions, was unwilling to press matters against them to any drastic conclusion, or even to ostracize them completely.[87] Perhaps the death of one of his supporters warned him to proceed carefully; perhaps he was simply unwilling to damage the web of county connections and relationships in which both he and the Batemans lived.

Violence occurred in Bateman's quarrel with Caldecote; but the Batemans, as an established gentry family, and members of a class entitled to deal out necessary punishment, were never themselves severely punished for what may have been an accidental killing. John Broun's death went unavenged, partly because Nicholas Caldecote preferred to have land rights rather than strict justice, and partly, it seems, because of the perceived imperative of gentry solidarity. Indeed, the Batemans' one essay into violence apparently became only another bargaining point in the business world of their county.

5.4 The Constable's Murderer; the Career of John Belsham

The Batemans were not, to our knowledge, habitual criminals; and they apparently kept their niche in the community of Cambridge gentry. But John Belsham, gentleman/armiger of Hadleigh, Suffolk, seems to have led a consistently dangerous life, isolated from, and disliked by, his peers and neighbours.[88] From 1422 to 1439, he was accused of fourteen separate crimes, including three murders and six assaults. He was appealed of murder twice, indicted interminably before justices of the peace, brought several times before justices of gaol delivery, and outlawed 1428–32. His affairs were no property disputes, fought out decorously in King's Bench; Belsham's opponents did their best, from 1427 onwards, to have him punished. With all allowance for the doubtful accuracy of fifteenth-century allegations, it seems that Belsham did perpetrate a number of violent crimes.

In chronological order, his alleged wrongdoings were: September to November 1422, counterfeiting at Hadleigh; 28 January 1425, poisoning John Legat, son of a neighbouring landowner; January 1426, counterfeiting gold coins; 30 September 1426, assault of

---

[87] See above, n. 59.
[88] The lawcourts record him as either gentleman or armiger (KB 27 685 Rm 5^d).

William Grove; 30 January 1427, counterfeiting, assault of John Lyon and murder of Willian Sugge; 5 October 1430, assault of John Jakelot; 21 July 1432, assault of Thomas Gyffard; 1 October 1437, assault of Robert Fakenham; 28 November 1437, murder of Alice Lowell; 29 December 1437, assault of Walter Sparwe; 1 December 1438, breaking and entering, and asporting the goods of Maurice Lowell; and 2 December 1438, breaking and entering, and asporting the goods of Sir William Wolf.

The allegations, however, were not made in sequence. The first crime to be officially recognized was the murder of Sugge in 1427. The general oyer and terminer of 11 June 1427 took indictments against John Segrave and Thomas Jakelot, gaolers, for allowing Belsham to escape while he was in their custody to answer for Sugge's murder. Both indictments state that he was arrested 6 March 1427 in Essex, and escaped after being brought to Ipswich gaol on 4 May.[89] Six separate indictments of the murder were made before the oyer and terminer itself, and in Michaelmas 1427, Emma, Sugge's widow, appealed Belsham of murder in King's Bench.[90] This group of actions was the first known attempt by Belsham's contemporaries to bring him to justice; it resulted only in his outlawry in April 1428. Apparently Belsham had not stayed to argue the case. He set sail to join the duke of Bedford's forces at Calais, and remained there from February 1428 to September 1429. This prudent absence enabled him, after a decent interval, to get a reversal of outlawry on the grounds that he could not have appeared to answer the charge from France.[91]

The next series of accusations runs from 9 June 1431 to 25 April 1435. In 1431 an oyer and terminer held before the earl of Suffolk, William Paston, John Howard, and others at Henhowe heard three more presentments of Belsham for Sugge's murder, and the allegations of counterfeiting in 1426 and 1427. Sessions before the seneschal of Bury St Edmunds at Stowmarket, 29 January 1433 and 18 January 1434 took indictments for the assaults of John Reynold in 1425, William Grove in 1426, John Lyon in 1427, John Jakelot in 1430, and Thomas Gyffard in 1432; as well as another indictment for

---

[89] KB 27 665 Rm 18[d] and 666 Rm 7[d]. Presumably the arrest was made on suspicion, or following a coroner's inquisition which has not survived.

[90] KB 27 693 Rm 1 and 666 m 74[r].

[91] KB 27 685 Rm 5[d] (plea made in Trinity 1432). He proffered a letter from the lieutenant of Calais, confirming his presence in the English camp.

the murder of Sugge.[92] In peace sessions before Sir William Wolf and Robert Caundyssh on 25 April 1436, he was twice indicted for the poisoning of John Legat. All these charges, except the last, were finally brought into King's Bench in Trinity 1434—not, apparently, by Belsham, who was in the Marshalsey at the time.[93] But the jury failed to appear in the case; and like a large minority of his fellows in such circumstances[94] Belsham used the respite to gain a pardon (19 June 1437) which covered all crimes up to 2 September 1431, and allowed him to go free.[95]

This series of charges is interesting in that all but two of the crimes mentioned were supposedly committed before June 1427. Why, if this were so, were the indictments not brought before the oyer and terminer of that year, together with the allegations of the murder of Sugge? And what induced Belsham's opponents to take up the hunt after a lapse of at least three years? True, from his escape in May 1427 to his return to England in 1429, Belsham was presumably safely out of the sight, mind, and reach of his Suffolk victims and neighbours. But though this may account for the lack of indictments between 1427 and 1430, it does not explain the non-appearance of these charges at the 1427 oyer and terminer. I suggest, therefore, that the real purpose of these indictments was to enforce, finally, some punishment for the murder of Sugge. That this offence rankled with local juries (or their instructors) is indicated by its four appearances in 1431–4. But the accusers were hampered by the fact that Belsham, having been outlawed for the crime, could not be tried for it again. Possibly, then, local law enforcers sought out (or manufactured) other charges to lay against him, any of which, if proved, would have hanged him. Certainly they seem to show the fear and aversion which Belsham's actions provoked in his community, which apparently compelled him to purchase a pardon rather than face a trial jury.

From at least 1434 to 1438 Belsham may have spent considerable time in prison.[96] This could account for the lack of both indictments

---

[92] KB 27 693 Rm 1.

[93] The 1435 indictments were not heard in King's Bench until Hilary 1438 (KB 27 707 Rm 3ᵈ).

[94] See Ch. 2, text accompanying nn. 40–1.

[95] He pleaded the pardon in Hilary 1438 (KB 27 693 Rm 1). It was apparently overlooked that this would not technically apply to the assault of Gyffard, which took place in July 1432.

[96] KB 27 693 Rm 1ᵈ (Trinity 1434) and 707 Rm 3ᵈ (Hilary 1438); both state that he was in the Marshalsey.

and alleged crimes in this period. But in 1438, the accusations began again. A series of peace sessions from 23 April 1438 to 3 March 1439 took indictments of the assaults of Fakenham and Sparwe, the murder of Alice Lowell in 1437, and the thefts from Maurice Lowell and Sir William Wolf in 1438; they also revived what must, at best, have been an old tale of Belsham's counterfeiting in 1422.[97] For the murder of Alice Lowell, Belsham was again gaoled, at Bury St Edmunds, at least from 21 July 1438 (the date of the gaol delivery session). But when the gaol delivery reconvened on 20 February 1439, it was the sheriff who produced him, rather than the Bury St Edmunds gaoler, John Lardener. On examination, Lardener admitted that 8 September 1438 the duke of Norfolk had come to Bury gaol and ordered Lardener to deliver Belsham up to him. Lardener claimed to have objected to this, in the absence of a mandate from the king or his justices. The duke then presented him with two choices, to hand over the prisoner, or have him taken against his, Lardener's, will ('invito'). For 'fear and terror' of the duke, Lardener promptly acquiesced; only afterwards did he receive letters from Norfolk warranting the transfer.[98]

On 19 February 1439, Belsham was rearrested at the order of Robert Caundyssh and Robert Crane, who during the peace sessions at Henhowe were informed by Sir William Wolf that despite numerous indictments against him, Belsham was at large nearby.[99] But by 24 July 1439 he was again out of Lardener's custody, this time because a close letter dated 18 April had commanded Belsham to be in Chancery on 10 May 1439 for examination. From there he was returned to the Marshalsey. Nothing further is known of Belsham's career, except that he was acquitted of counterfeiting, and stealing from William Wolf, in King's bench in 1441.[100] Since no new crimes were alleged against him, it seems that either his activities were curtailed in some way not involving official punishment, or his opponents received some acceptable satisfaction.

The contrast between Belsham's affairs and those of Inglose and his tenants, or Dallyng and Bekeswell, or even the Batemans, is immediate. Belsham was not involved in a short-term dispute; none of the charges against him suggest that landownership was at issue;

[97] JUST 3 210 m 17, KB 27 717 Rm 9ʳ, and KB 9 232/1 m 98.
[98] KB 9 232/1 m 98; cf. also JUST 3 220/2 m 181.
[99] JUST 3 220/2 m 165.
[100] JUST 3 210 m 17 and KB 27 717 Rm 9ʳ.

his opponents, rather than harassing him with suits of trespass in plea side King's Bench which could conveniently be allowed to lapse, did their best to indict him at sessions where real punishment took place; and where this failed, to remove the indictments to the Rex side of King's Bench, where adverse verdicts were obtainable. Belsham himself escaped such verdicts not because the cases were allowed to lapse, but because he showed extraordinary skill at removing himself from the country, and buying much-needed pardons. In other words, his contemporaries treated him as a dangerous criminal.

It is true that by 1439, Belsham felt that he had a personal quarrel with Sir William Wolf, member of parliament, commissioner of oyer and terminer and of array, and one of the three most active justices of the peace in Suffolk in the 1430s.[101] In February 1439 it was Wolf who apparently urged the justices of the peace at Henhowe to rearrest Belsham. The justices' account of the occasion states that when Belsham was brought before them, he lost his temper, shouting 'furibunda voce' that it was all the fault of the 'treacherous' Wolf ('totem hoc causavit ipse proditor . . . [Wolf] sedens vobiscum') and calling for the arrest of Wolf's servant, William Andrew. When Andrew called Belsham a liar, Belsham 'furiose' retorted that the lie was Andrew's, and drawing his dagger, would have killed him had not three other men intervened.[102]

But Belsham's whole career cannot be explained in terms of a private feud with (or persecution by) Wolf. By 1439, indeed, Wolf had good reason to oppose Belsham; for Alice Lowell, Belsham's alleged victim of 1437, had been the wife of one of Wolf's servants. Maurice Lowell, from the scanty evidence to hand, was apparently a fairly prosperous and certainly hard-working figure in the lower echelons of the local legal hierarchy. He could afford to take a case to King's Bench in 1442. He was bailiff of Samford hundred, he sat on juries, made arrests, and was one of the good and honest men who saw to it that mainpernors had their defendants in court.[103] As such, he must have been a valuable servant to Wolf. Not surprisingly, Wolf seems to have marshalled his legal forces to the help of Lowell. He sat at the series of four peace sessions in 1438–9 which heard the indictments against Belsham not only for the Lowell murder, but also for the

---

[101] *CCLR, 1429–35*, 271; *CPR, 1429–36*, 132–3 and 523; and Table A3.2.
[102] JUST 3 220/2 m 165.
[103] KB 9 229/2 m 37, KB 27 677 m 60^r, 686 Rm 6^r, and 723 m 25^r.

assaults of Fakenham and Sparwe; and he supported the appeal made by Alice's son John.[104] Belsham replied to this rush of indictments in 1438 by alleging unspecified treasons against Wolf in the court of chivalry, some time before 11 November 1438.[105] Consequently Wolf was put under surety in Chancery. Wolf and Lowell replied with a petition to the king, 13 July 1439, which resulted, a week later, in a commission to the justices Cottesmore, Fray, and three others to investigate the whole affair.[106] But Wolf, probably as a result of the accusation in the court of chivalry, had already been deprived of his peace commission (his name was missing from the commission of October 1438); he was never to be reinstated, even though no treason was ever proved against him.[107] Surely Wolf had good cause to feel persecuted by Belsham, rather than *vice versa*. True, some links between Belsham and Wolf apparently existed before the attack on Lowell's wife in 1437. According to the inquisition held on Belsham's lands when he was outlawed, he held part of them from Wolf.[108] Wolf was also named on the oyer and terminer commission headed by the earl of Suffolk, which took a number of indictments against Belsham in 1431, and it was before Wolf and Robert Crane that the indictment of poisoning John Legat was taken in 1435.[109] But it is not even certain that Wolf was among the 'sociis suis" who assisted the earl of Suffolk, William Paston, and Sir John Howard at the 1431 oyer and terminer. And both these events succeeded the first rush of indict-

---

[104] KB 27 717 Rm 9ʳ and Wolf's petition of 1439 (E 28/62 m 70).

[105] *CPR, 1436–41*, 265, where Sir Henry Brounflete was commissioned to try the case. (Note that Belsham called Wolf a 'traitor' in 1439.)

[106] E 28/62 m 70 and *CPR, 1436–41*, 316–17.

[107] He remained active in county affairs until 1444. Oddly enough, though his last known peace commission was 28 Aug. 1438, Wolf is known to have sat at several sessions in 1439 (KB 27 717 Rm 9ʳ, 721 Rm 20ʳ, and E 101 575/33 (sheriff's accounts)). Perhaps his county colleagues were reluctant to lose his experience, and simply ignored the official commission; it is clear from the account of Belsham's arrest that the justices continued to take advice from him. His association with the earl of Suffolk (see below, nn. 113–14) is also probably relevant. His last known official position was on commission of arrest in Feb. 1444 (*CPR, 1441–46*, 246). He apparently died shortly afterwards (the death of his widow is recorded in 1446—*IPM* iv. 226).

[108] KB 27 671 Rm 1. Earlier links between Wolf and Belsham are unlikely, in that Wolf was not a native Suffolk man. William Worcester (*Itineraries*, ed. J. H. Harvey (Oxford, 1969), 358 and 360) says he came from Wales, was in the retinue of Thomas duke of Exeter, and was knighted by the duke of Clarence in Paris. He was thus probably a career soldier. He gained lands in Suffolk by marrying the widow of William Wyngfield, sometime between 1418 and 1425 (British Library Cotton charters xxix. 30 and Harley charters 58.D.12; and KB 27 655 m 21ʳ).

[109] *CPR, 1429–36*, 132–3 and KB 27 693 Rm 1; KB 27 707 Rm 3ᵈ.

ments against Belsham by a number of years. Since Belsham seems to have taken to violent crime eight years before Wolf appeared to oppose him, and there is no other individual known to have any personal quarrel with him, it seems unlikely that Belsham was the persecuted victim of private vendetta.

In fact, there is evidence of his long-standing antagonism to any officer of the law. Examination of his victims shows that a number were base-level law enforcers. Sugge was constable of Hadleigh; so was John Lyon, whom Belsham allegedly intimidated into neglecting his duties. William Grove may have been, then as later, bailiff of Hadleigh.[110] Of the victims of the assaults and robberies later alleged against him, John Jakelot was presumably a relative of the Thomas Jakelot who had once arrested Belsham; Maurice Lowell was, as I have pointed out, a busy figure in local law enforcement. What exactly lay behind these attacks on the officers of the legal establishment cannot be established. Maybe Belsham was simply attempting to avoid arrest. Certainly it was later alleged that he had been a counterfeiter since the autumn of 1422,[111] and he was also indicted for counterfeiting in 1426–7 (one presentment called him a 'communis fabricator . . . monete domini Regis' and gave details of the nobles he made out of copper 'ad similitudinem boni auri.'[112] Counterfeiting was included in the treasons specified by the statute 13 Edward III st. 5 c. 2. Faced with the unpleasant punishments for treason, Belsham may have had good reason to fear arrest by the local constables. On the other hand, the alleged assault on Jakelot did not take place until 1431, after Belsham had escaped punishment for counterfeiting and for the murder of Sugge. This suggests sheer revenge as a motive for some of Belsham's violence.

Interestingly, the nature of the battle between Belsham and the law changed over the fourteen years from which records survive. Until 1430 it seemed local and low-scale. His alleged victims were men of lower status, from his home town; the attempts to bring him to justice were made by his neighbours, only fortuitously helped by the general

---

[110] For Lyon, see KB 27 693 Rm 1; but this allegation was commonplace in charges of menace. For Grove, see JUST 3 209 m 29^{d} (1436).

[111] KB 27 717 Rm 9^{r}. However, this is one of the less reliable allegations. The indictment was not taken until 1439, before Sir William Wolf. At best it represents jury memories of long-distant events; at worst mere gossip which the jury was directed to certify.

[112] KB 27 693 Rm 1.

oyer and terminer of June 1427. Belsham himself made no attempt to organize powerful county opinion to his support, but simply fled, first to Essex, and when that proved too close for safety, to France.

Perhaps from 1431, certainly from 1435, he attracted the notice of the more prestigious William Wolf. This meant that he was no longer evading arrest by local men, but dealing with many indictments taken before, and possibly at the instance of, an influential county administrator. Moreover, Wolf may have brought an element of even greater patronage to the situation, since he appears to have been an associate of the earl of Suffolk. His land at Cotton was near the earl's residence at Eye, and was perhaps held of Suffolk.[113] He appears with other known Suffolk supporters (such as Tuddenham and Robert Lyston) on a jury list of Hilary 1440.[114] Certainly, Belsham's response to this new scenario was of greater sophistication. As well as attacking Wolf's supporters (such as Lowell) and buying a pardon, he became a client of the duke of Norfolk, whose direct intervention sprung him from gaol in September 1438. Since Wolf had already clashed with Robert Wyngfield, an old associate of the duke of Norfolk,[115] the stage was set for a confrontation between the two major patronage groups in fifteenth-century East Anglia. The transactions between Wolf and Belsham moved abruptly from the local arena to some of the highest tribunals in the land—Chancery, and the court of chivalry. Wolf and Lowell's petition to the king received an immediate response.[116] Wolf's disappearance from the peace commission may have been at the instigation of Norfolk, seeking to reduce Suffolk's influence in East Anglian legal affairs. It is possible that a compromise was made, to the effect that Norfolk would guarantee Belsham's future good behaviour, in return for the removal of the diligent and pro-Suffolk

---

[113] It appears to have reverted to Suffolk after Wolf's death (though it came originally from Wolf's wife, see above, n. 108); W. A. Copinger, *The Manors of Suffolk* (7 vols; London and Manchester, 1905–11), iii. 215 and 252. Harriss finds that most of the duke of Exeter's retainers were drawn to the earl of Suffolk after Exeter died in Dec. 1426, though Wolf was retained by Cardinal Beaufort (*Cardinal Beaufort: A Study of Lancastrian Ascendancy and Decline* (Oxford, 1988), 164).

[114] KB 27 715 m 62ʳ. For Lyston as a Suffolk supporter, see *PL* ii. 22.

[115] He accused Wyngfield of assault at the peace sessions at Ipswich in 1436 (KB 27 717 Rm 32ᵈ), and eventually got 200 marks damages awarded (KB 27 718 Rm 7ʳ). For Wyngfield's connection with the duke of Norfolk, see R. Virgoe, 'Three Suffolk Parliamentary Elections of the Mid-Fifteenth Century', *BIHR* 39 (1966), 186, and Ch. 2, n. 24.

[116] See above.

Wolf from the peace sessions.[117] Such an agreement would presumably have involved saving Belsham from the consequences of any outstanding charges. Certainly the only known instance of his facing a jury was in 1441; he was acquitted, perhaps with Norfolk's support.[118]

This must raise the question of whether bastard feudalism did in fact promote violence, as its detractors claim. It does at least seem that Belsham escaped just punishment by attaching himself to a great lord. Yet Norfolk cannot be said to have ordered, or enticed, Belsham into a life of violent crime, since there is no evidence of connection between the ducal family and Belsham in 1427, when the allegations of crime started. (Besides if Belsham was a retainer of any great lord in 1427, why was he compelled to flee overseas?) At most, the developing tension between the duke of Norfolk and the earl of Suffolk in the 1430s perhaps gave value to Belsham's anti-social activities, and enabled him to attach himself to Norfolk. This situation may not be typical of bastard feudalism as a whole.

Furthermore, what distinguishes Belsham from his less combative neighbours, is not his connection with a magnate. Other men—such as Sir William Wolf, the Pastons, John Bekeswell, Reginald Rous— were more or less certainly retainers of one or other of the great East Anglian lords. Yet they carried out their disputes peacefully, both using and demonstrating their power in and through the law.[119] The great difference between these men and Belsham is Belsham's conspicuous lack of friends of his own rank. He seems to have been isolated from—even ostracized by—his local society as early as 1427. It is significant that by then Sugge, Lyon, Segrave, and Jakelot were all trying to arrest him, since, as I have noted, county authorities were not usually enthusiastic in their pursuit of suspects; indeed they could be actively discouraged from making an arrest by the victim's influential friends.[120] Unusually among fifteenth-century defendants, Belsham was never indicted with any named associate.[121] The most the indictments venture to suggest was that unknown persons acted with

---

[117] Though Suffolk appears to have replaced Wolf on the peace commission with Reginald Rous, an annuitant (British Library, Egerton Roll 8779 and *PL* ii. 518) who was first commissioned 6 Apr. 1439, and thereafter attended sessions diligently, see Table A3.2.

[118] KB 27 717 Rm 9ʳ.

[119] See *PL* ii. 517–19 for an account of such an affair; the writer claimed he had suffered heavy losses at Rous's hands, but never alleged any violent action against him.

[120] Ch. 2, nn. 12–13 and n. 23.

[121] See comparative figures of plaintiffs and defendants, Table 2.5.

him in the attack on William Grove.[122] A servant of his, John Marshall, was arrested in July 1438 on suspicion of felony, but was remanded until the next gaol delivery and there acquitted for lack of indictment; so there was clearly no feeling among Belsham's accusers that Marshall shared great responsibility for Belsham's misdeeds, or deserved any heavier punishment than a short prison term.[123] No mainpernors ever appeared for Belsham; there is no record of any friends or neighbours acting as his securities; no one apparently wanted him as feoffee, or even witness.

This seems to indicate two things. The first, that isolation might itself produce violent crime; lack of peer support presumably reduced Belsham's chances of settling any quarrels, or overcoming any financial difficulties, by legal means. The second is that Belsham's society as a whole apparently did not accept or support his actions, and cannot have thought them normal or allowable. Indeed, the reaction to his various crimes provides an index to the contemporary perception of violence.

Of all Belsham's misdeeds, the one which clearly provoked most reaction from the largest number of people was the murder of Sugge. It led to the most indictments, and was the only crime which his opponents tried, for twelve years, to bring home to him, even after he had been outlawed and pardoned for it.[124] I suggest this was because of Sugge's position as a servant of the law. If there is one outstanding attitude of mind demonstrated in these case-studies, it is the respect in which the law was held, and its high place in the community as a forum of honour, and a means to try debates. But the legal system could fulfil these functions only if there were a consensus within the community to uphold and support the law and its servants. This is not to say that no illegal acts were ever perpetrated, or that the rules of the law were never bent to serve individual interests. But it is true that the county gentry community continued to supply, readily, the skilled pesonnel to staff the peace sessions, the shrievalty, the courts of the liberties, and the coroners' positions. Their friends and servants were co-opted to act as bailiffs, undersheriffs, constables, clerks, and all

---

[122] KB 27 693 Rm 1.

[123] JUST 3 220/2 mm 185 and 168.

[124] Ten separate indictments survive, plus the appeal of Sugge's widow. Sir William Wolf also thought it worth mentioning in his petition to the king in 1439 (E 28/62 m 70). My thanks are due to Dr G. L. Harriss, who first drew my attention to this document.

other necessary functionaries of the various courts. Diligently these men examined cases, arrested suspects, returned writs, heard (and perhaps sometimes wrote) indictments, punished felons. When pursuing their own disputes, they did not always act with probity; but they tended to stick rigidly to the legal rules of the game, answering plea for plea, entering seriously into bonds of agreement, suing out their own writs as appropriate. In short, every case they brought to court, however tortuous its progress there, upheld the authority of that court, and witnessed to the participants' tacit acceptance of the authority of the court and its officers.

Belsham's actions defied this consensus. He killed an officer of the law (apparently to prevent him from doing his duty); he would enter into no debate under legal form. This radical rejection of so important an element in the ordering of fifteenth-century gentry life was unacceptable to his contemporaries, who apparently felt, dimly, the threat that it posed to their well-organized authority structures. The murder of a law-enforcer in order to facilitate criminal behaviour could never be justified by fifteenth-century standards of righteous violence, which demanded the altruistic maintenance of justice and peace. No wonder that by this standard, Belsham stood condemned in public opinion.

Significantly, the murder of Alice Lowell, another innocent victim of Belsham's vendetta against law-enforcers, provoked another strong reaction.[125] Milder and more short-lived responses followed the accusations of assault and counterfeiting. On the whole, it seems that it was Belsham's murderous violence directed against the very system of the law which his contemporaries reprobated.

The case also illustrates the difficulty of enforcing legal punishment on a criminal who would not submit to the system. According to the allegations, Belsham stood to be hanged several times over. His local support seems to have been minimal; he did not even dare face a jury until 1441, when his acquittal was probably due to the duke of Norfolk's influence.[126] The difficulty seems to have been not enforcing his appearance in court (for he appeared several times) nor establishing his guilt (since most of the cases never reached that question); but

[125] Wolf's influence in bringing this case to the notice of the courts must not be overlooked. On the other hand, Wolf had to convince his contemporaries to support any campaign against Belsham, a task presumably facilitated by Belsham's anti-social behaviour.

[126] KB 27 717 Rm 9ʳ.

that the system offered loopholes to man of his abilities and standing. Military service in France acted as an escape from his entanglements just as the Scots wars did for the Folvilles and Coterels a century earlier.[127] Pardons could be granted which frustrated the normal course of the law. When all else failed, a powerful patron could remove the case (and the prisoner) altogether from the jurisdiction of the local and criminal courts.

This case does not prove that such escape routes were normally, or even often, used by fifteenth-century criminals. Maybe Belsham was exceptionally cunning; he was certainly fortunate in having the French wars, and the developing tension between the duke of Norfolk and the earl of Suffolk, to use to his advantage. Nevertheless his career shows some of the opportunities offered by the legal and social structures of the time to an enterprising wrongdoer.

Yet even this is perhaps too bleak a view of fifteenth-century law-keeping. For Belsham's opponents showed no impatience at their apparent failure to bring him to justice. There is no sign that, disillusioned with the law, they took to using his own violent tactics against him. Can it really be that they clung loyally to a system of justice which offered them absolutely no rewards? Hardly. Belsham (technically) evaded punishment; he did not come off scot-free. Aside from his forced absence from England in 1428–9, and the loss of his lands while he was outlawed (1428–32), he was in the Marshalsey for some time in 1434, 1438, and 1439, and in local prisons for varying periods between 1427 and 1438. Thus, using purely legal means, his neighbours managed to put Belsham safely out of the way for at least two years, and to deprive him of landed revenue for four—all without ever gaining a conviction in the courts. Had Norfolk not appeared to upset this course of events, the same trends might have continued indefinitely.

In other words, the battle between crime and the law was a complex one. The legal system did not necessarily operate by achieving an official punishment of crime. Instead, at a local level, it was used by both the criminal and the law-abiding as a tool to gain results not explicitly promised by the law, but of great value to the interested parties. No one succeeded, before 1439, in preventing John Belsham

---

[127] Stones, 'The Folvilles', 120–1 and 129, and Bellamy, 'The Coterel Gang', 711–13.

from carrying out violent crimes; but the local community curtailed his activities all the same.

As I have argued above, the influence of great patronage disputes on Belsham's violent outbreaks seems limited. If anything, Norfolk may have succeeded in cutting short his criminal career. This, however, tended to remove the control of criminal violence out of the sphere of local influence altogether; which may have had detrimental long-term effects. The intervention of magnates in local peace-keeping might help to downgrade the importance of the local consensus of law-keeping which functioned so briskly in the early fifteenth-century East Anglian communities. County gentry corporately administered and supported the actions of the law. If this power—with all its attendant rewards of status and justification—were taken from them, then the whole structure of county order would be at risk.

These case-studies have, I hope, shown that violence was anything but normative in the disputes and litigation by which fifteenth-century East Anglians ordered their position and their affairs. Nevertheless, it existed—as sanction (and perhaps as sanctioned force) in the Beke-swell/Dallyng quarrel; as an attack on legal order in Belsham's case; as (perhaps) a continuation of litigation by other means in the Batemans' disputes. The problem that remains for the historian is to distinguish these cases from the others, to suggest what factors turned a non-violent dispute into a violent one, and how the well-ordered conceptual and social structures of the fifteenth century enabled these factors to operate. Ideally this should be investigated by analysing the antecedents and progress of a number of disputes in which violence was never alleged, as a control group. Unfortunately, quarrels which neither used nor alleged violence tended, *ipso facto*, not to generate sufficiently substantial and long-lasting records to furnish a case-study. I have therefore included one of the few cases of this kind for which anything like sufficient information survives.

5.5 The Gentlemanly Dispute; William Clopton and Robert Eland

The quarrel between William Clopton, esquire, of Suffolk, and Robert Eland, esquire, of Raithby, Lincolnshire, concerned the ownership of the manor of Hawstead, about three miles south of Bury St Edmunds.

According to the best existing account of the affair, Clopton bought this manor in 1414–15 from his cousin Sir William Clopton;[128] but it had come, in the mid-fourteenth century, from one John Fitz-Eustace.[129] Eland's wife Elizabeth was a descendant of FitzEustace; by 1429, Eland was claiming to possess a charter dated 1 July 1343 by which Hawstead was entailed to the FitzEustace heirs for ever.[130]

The FitzEustace family had made prior attempts to challenge the Cloptons' possession. In Easter 1408 in King's Bench, the record appears of a process in Common Pleas from Easter 1402 to Michaelmas 1405 between Sir William Clopton and John FitzEustace *et al.* on a charge of breaking and entering, woodcutting, and asporting goods, in September 1397. The jury had declared Clopton the owner, and awarded damages of £23; the case came to King's Bench only because FitzEustace had not paid.[131] By 1408 he had been outlawed for non-appearance, which perhaps prevented further prosecution of his claims.

No further reference to the dispute occurs until 23 November 1428. By then, Robert Eland must have stated his claims to the new Clopton owner, proffering in support the 1343 charter, and a power of attorney to deliver seisin of the same date. In reply, Clopton had evidently accused Eland of tampering with the documents, for Eland took his case to the court of chivalry, alleging that Clopton said he had set his seal to forged documents 'encontre honeste & gentilesse d'armes'.[132] The duke of Norfolk was ordered to bring Clopton to answer the charge.

What became of this case is unknown, but in the 1430 Easter term, Clopton and William Galyon in their turn sued Robert Eland and Roger Bernardeston (a gentleman neighbour of Clopton's at Kedington) for attempting to disturb Clopton's possession of Hawstead by publicizing forged documents. Eland pleaded a minor error in the indictment (querying the spelling of Raithby in the original bill); Bernardeston that the documents were genuine. Though juries were called from Suffolk and Lincoln to determine the case, it was still

---

[128] Sir J. Cullum, *The History of Hawsted and Hardwick*, 1st edn. (London, 1784), 101 (see genealogy on facing page).
[129] J. Gage, *The History and Antiquities of Suffolk: Thingoe Hundred* (London, 1888), 417.
[130] KB 27 676 m 54ʳ (Easter 1430).
[131] KB 27 588 m 32ʳ.
[132] British Library, Harleian MS 1178 fo. 44ʳ.

undecided in the Michaelmas term of 1433.[133] But it had evidently
done its work—Eland had been persuaded to come to negotiation.
The matter was settled by an arbitrement of 28 October 1433, made
by Clement Denston (archdeacon of Sudbury), Richard Alrede, and
Robert Peyton.[134] This itself was the culmination of a series of
negotiations; it mentions that the disputed documents 'were put in
daying divers tymes er then we the seid arbitraitors medlyd therwith'.
These preliminaries involved prominent East Anglian legal figures—
Robert Caundyssh, Thomas Fulthorpe, and William Goderede.

Denston and his fellow arbitrators took their job seriously. Having
examined the document 'ageyn the sonne at our leyser', they decided
that 'it was lyke to have be wrete beforn, and was rased of that letter,
and sith wreten ther on aȝen with a dede and a feble ynke to seme
old.' They also examined 'olde men aboute Hausted', who denied any
entail to Elizabeth Eland's benefit. To finish the affair officially, an
entry appeared in the feet of fines for 1433–4 between Clopton and
Galyon on one hand, and Robert and Elizabeth Eland on the other,
after which it seems from the absence of any further references that
Clopton enjoyed undisputed possession of the manor.[135]

The question stands, why did Eland's apparent desire to possess—
and Clopton's to defend—the manor of Hawstead not lead to any
accusations of violence (even of trespass, like those against John
FitzEustace in 1397)?

It must be admitted at the outset that we cannot be sure that Eland
was mounting a serious attempt at a takeover. If he were, his chances
of success were almost invisibly small. His opponent, Clopton, was a
very well-to-do man; he engaged in a number of land transactions in
south Suffolk, 1422–40; his epitaph described him as 'dapsilis et
largus'; and his son John could contribute handsomely to the lavish
rebuilding of Melford church later in the century.[136] He also had a
number of useful friends. William Galyon, his associate in the case,
had been escheator in 1431–2. Clopton himself had at least one

---

[133] KB 27 676 m 54.

[134] Cullum, *History of Hawstead*, 109–10.

[135] W. Rye (ed.), *A Calendar of the Feet of Fines for Suffolk* (Suffolk Institute of
Archaeology; Ipswich, 1900), 295.

[136] Ibid. 288, 293, 294, 296, 298, and 299; W. Parker, *The History of Long Melford*
(London, 1873), 127 and 131 (there is some confusion here as to whether William
Clopton esquire, or William Clopton knight, is meant, but the death date—cf. *IPM* iv.
234—establishes the epitaph as belonging to the esquire). The chapel built with John
Clopton's money can still be seen at Long Melford.

property deal with Clement Denston and Richard Alrede, two of the eventual arbitrators, and he seems to have been a close friend (or perhaps even relative) of Robert Caundyssh, the indefatiguable Suffolk lawyer.[137] It seems odd that Eland should consent to having the matter arbitrated by his opponents' supporters; but his other options were little better. If he had in fact forged the document, even neutral arbitrators would not have served his turn, and if he had allowed the King's Bench case to proceed, the forged documents would most probably have been examined, and exposed, there. Perhaps, therefore, Eland's motive was less to take over the manor than to set a price on his document for nuisance-value. The feet of fines entry for 1433–4 implies that money changed hands between Clopton and Eland. If this interpretation is correct, then the case was a minor, gentlemanly attempt to screw some money out of a long-dead property dispute. Since Eland was willing to be paid off and Clopton was perfectly able to pay, there was no necessity for violence on either side.

But even if the property was really in dispute, the case was not one where the honour or status of the participants was at risk. Unlike the disputed properties at Bexwell and Harlton, Hawstead was not the main livelihood of either party. No one, it seemed, could regard it as the heart and symbol of family prosperity and respectability. Clopton's home manor, inherited from his father, was at Kentwell in Long Melford.[138] Apart from his Raithby property (the extent of which is unknown) Eland apparently held land at Willsthorp worth 50s. a year.[139] The Hawstead revenues (calculated at a solid £11. 14s. 8 d. in 1358) were a tempting addition, but no more than that, to both men's incomes.[140]

There was little incentive, then, for either Clopton or Eland to try to push the other into such extremities that violence offered the only

---

[137] For Clopton, Denston, and Alrede, see Rye, *Feet of Fines, Suffolk*, 294 (1433). Alrede was a noted lawyer, justice of the peace, and civil servant, see S. J. B. Endelman 'Patronage and Power: A Social Study of the Justice of the Peace in Late Medieval Essex', Ph.D. thesis (Brown University, 1977), 217–18. Clopton and Caundyssh were involved in common property transactions in 1433, 1435, and 1438 (Rye, *Feet of Fines, Suffolk*, 294, 296, and 298). Parker, *History of Long Melford*, says that Caundyssh married Clopton's daughter Elizabeth. This is doubtful, since he gives her birth date as 1423–4, and Caundyssh was dead before 1439 (*CCLR, 1435–41*, 336). But Caundyssh is depicted in a stained-glass window in Long Melford church, so it is possible that there was marriage-relationship between the families.

[138] Cullum, *History of Hawstead*, 101.

[139] *CCLR, 1441–7*, 105.

[140] Gage, *History of Suffolk*, 417.

way out. In any case, granted that they lived in separate counties, this would have been a difficult task; the aggressor would require some power in the central legal or administrative system to harm so distant an opponent. But neither Clopton or Eland were heavily involved in county or central administration. Clopton may have been on the peace commission in 1422 (unless one of his namesakes is meant)[141] and was named on two special commissions of gaol delivery in 1433 and 1435; Eland was twice on the commission *de walliis & fossatis* in Lincolnshire, and that is all.[142] Neither had sufficient legal pull to harass a man from another county into a hopeless position, or even to use extensive violence under cover of legal sanctions. Indeed, a quarrel at such long distance was hardly amenable to settlement by use of local force.

Nor could it be significant in terms of the power and prestige of the participants. There was no real underlying struggle for public recognition, as there probably was between Bekeswell and Dallyng, or even between the Batemans and Caldecote. It would not have redounded to Clopton's credit had he lost the case; yet his visible standing in Suffolk would hardly have altered. Enemies of Eland in Lincolnshire might have rejoiced at the failure of his claim, but could not deduce from it that he was a spent power at home. Indeed, the dignified progress of the case, with Eland's appeal to the honourable court of chivalry, and the final agreement by fine, preserved the honourable image of both gentlemen. In short, the economic, geographic, and administrative status of the participants lessened the risks of the quarrel for each and gave them leeway to operate non-violently.

Violence, as I have tried to show in my study of its conceptual and social context, was closely linked to legitimation and hierarchical status. A man of rank could—indeed must—use certain sorts of honourable violence honourably, if only in order to demonstrate his status. Violence was the sanction upholding the ordered system within which people recognized their superiors and inferiors with comfortable precision. Situations where someone's standing was unclear, or was challenged, must therefore have been likely contexts for violence. The Batemans were hanging precariously to the edge of financial and social success; Caldecote's attempt to direct the future of their main

---

[141] See Cullum, *History of Hawstead*, 101; the genealogy shows at least 2 other contemporaneous William Cloptons.

[142] *CPR, 1429–36*, 278 and 476; and *CPR, 1422–9*, 468, and *CPR, 1429–36*, 273.

manor apparently inspired them to violent retaliation. Dallyng and Bekeswell were competing for one tiny niche in the echelons of the lesser gentry in Norfolk. The issue confronting them was who could best manipulate his standing in the legal system to the disadvantage of the other. Each apparently used arrest and imprisonment to down-grade both the financial and social status of his competitor. Even Belsham, according to the account of his arrest at gaol delivery, reacted particularly strongly and violently to being called a liar—an imputation most damaging to his honour as a gentleman.[143] Perhaps what particularly enraged him, when he was confronted with the ill-fated William Sugge's warrant for his capture, was that men of his rank were rarely prosecuted, and almost never arrested; so that to submit to the constable would have seemed a damaging admission of loss of status.[144] No one's status was seriously at issue between Clopton and Eland; no wonder then that their quarrel was composed with such calm propriety.

Violence in fifteenth-century quarrels seems generally to have been a last resort, which occurred more often in allegation and implication, than in reality. Where law and arbitrement would serve (as they did between Clopton and Eland, and Inglose and his tenants) fifteenth-century antagonists were quick to use them. The Batemans tried legal means before they turned to assault. Dallyng and Bekeswell, if they used forceful sanctions, did so strictly within the letter of the law. The very fact that law and violence were so inextricably entwined tended to limit and control violent actions—to turn them into well-directed channels and rituals, with their own plainly defined non-violent alternatives and escape routes.

This is not to say that violence never occurred. To ignore the fact that men of higher status could, on occasion, literally get away with murder is to do scant justice to the memories of the unfortunate John Broun, William Sugge, and Alice Lowell. The question is, whether such violence was normative; and an analysis of the cases seems to show that it was not. Both John Bateman and John Belsham fled the county after committing their crime, rightly fearing an indignant

---

[143] See above, n. 102; also J. Pitt-Rivers, 'Honour and Social Status', in J. G. Peristiany (ed.), *Honour and Shame: The Values of Mediterranean Society* (London, 1965), 34 for a discussion of the relationship of lies to honour, and my 'Honour among the Pastons; Gender and Integrity in Fifteenth-Century English Provincial Society', *Journal of Medieval History*, 14 (1988), 357–8.

[144] See Ch. 2, text accompanying n. 25, and Table 2.5, and text accompanying n. 50.

reaction from their neighbours. Belsham, at least, appears to have been something of an outcast from the county com nunity, feared and ostracized by his peers. Though neither Bateman nor Belsham were hanged for homicide, both were outlawed, and Belsham spent considerable time in prison. Their survival, then, seems to indicate not that murder was viewed as a common and acceptable occurrence, but that the gentry community may have been reluctant to impose the most violent sanctions of the law on fellow upper-class males. In short, violence within and without the law was ordered within a strict hierarchical framework. Only (and rarely) outside these limits, did unacceptable, destabilizing violence take place.

6

COMMUNITY VIOLENCE:
TWO CASE-STUDIES

No analysis of law and violence in fifteenth-century East Anglia can be complete without a study of the outbreaks of group violence which are commonly said to have occurred in Bedford and Norwich at this period. The quarrels of the Lords Grey and Fanhope at the peace sessions in Bedford in 1437 and 1439, and the alleged urban riots in Norwich (1437 and 1443) have been taken by historians as striking illustrations of the violence inherent in fifteenth-century society, the unruliness of gentlemen retainers, and the lawlessness of magnates, whose quarrels disrupted civil government and helped to drive the nation into civil war. Thus, for Griffiths, the confrontation between Grey and Fanhope in 1437, which escalated into an 'armed affray' and 'disrupted the king's sessions', together with the 'truly serious' Norwich riots of 1437, provided evidence that 'by 1437 the foundations of [political] stability were cracking'. Likewise the Bedford disturbances, he thought, were 'of a sort not uncommon in aristocratic England'. The editors of the Norwich records felt that the city's internal problems were exacerbated because 'it was a time when violence and contempt for justice reigned supreme throughout the land'. The 'lawlessness of the times and the intervention of powerful and unscrupulous agitators from outside' combined with factionalism in the city government to produce urban chaos. For Storey this very intervention by the earl of Suffolk in the affairs of Norwich formed an elegant demonstration of the thesis that the fall of the Lancastrian dynasty was hastened by magnates maintaining quarrels which spread to encompass the whole political community.[1]

Fifteenth-century accounts seem to show that contemporaries too

---

[1] Griffiths, *Henry VI*, 147 and 570–2; Hudson and Tingey (eds.), *Norwich Records*, vol. i, intro., pp. lxxxiii and xciv; Storey, *End of the House of Lancaster*, app. 3. It should be noted that Storey, in particular, has pointed to the existence of a number of important documents, of which he provides an illuminating account. My interpretation of the events in Norwich, however, differs from that of Storey at almost all points.

thought that violence had really occurred. The events in Norwich in 1443, for instance, were described as a 'magna insurrexio' by one chornicler, and as a 'common insurrection and disturbance of all the liege subjects of the lord king' to which the perpetrators came 'riota & routa', in an indictment in King's Bench. What precise meaning the writers attached to such terms as 'riot' is, however, less easy to assess. As Bellamy points out, the statutes on riot from 1361 to the time of Henry VI covered all sorts of offences, from 'boisterous wrongdoing' to peasant rebellion, including armed gentry quarrels and forcible entry of lands. Certainly the purpose of the statute 13 Henry IV c. 7 seems to have been to define not riot, but the means whereby it could be dealt with. The statute laid it down that in the case of any unlawful assembly, at least two justices of the peace, together with the sheriff or undersheriff, should arrest the participants immediately, using the 'power of the county'. The justices and sheriff could then record what they had seen, their record having the force of a conviction. If they could not arrest the wrongdoers, they should hold an inquiry within a month after the riot, and determine the case according to law. If by this means the truth could not be established, the justices and sheriff could certify the king and council of the deed, and the certification would act as a presentment. In law, then, riots were distinguished as much by the peculiar procedure (justices' certification) which they elicited, as by the sorts of actions involved. Three justices' certifications survive from Bedford and Norwich in the 1430s; one from Norwich in 1437, the others from Bedford in 1439. On these grounds alone the events would be classed by contemporaries as riots; however, whether they can be classed as riotous by historians, how much violence was actually involved, and what their significance was—political and otherwise—remains to be seen.[2] The final two case-studies will examine the events in Norwich and Bedford in the light of these questions.

[2] 'John Benet's Chronicle for the Years 1400–1462', ed. G. L. and M. A. Harriss, *Camden Miscellany*, xxiv (Camden Society, 4th series, 9; 1972), 189; the indictments are in KB 9 84/1 mm 3–4 and 10–13, and KB 27 728 Rmm 24 ff., and 729 Rm 6, m 14ʳ, m 18, and m 28. See also J. Bellamy, 'The Late Medieval World of Riot', in his *Criminal Law and Society*, esp. 54–61, and the statute 13 Henry IV c. 7.

6.1 The Bloodless 'Riots': Norwich, 1437 and 1443

The surviving accounts of the disturbances in Norwich are almost entirely legal; indictments from 1443, and a justices' certification from 1437. In 1443 indictments made only a month after the outbreak of hostilities between the city and the Benedictine priory of Norwich alleged that leading aldermen of the city (Robert Toppes and William Asshewell) armed themselves and their followers with swords, bows and arrows, axes and lances, and stormed into the guild-hall where the mayor and other aldermen were sitting in assembly.[3] They then took away the chest containing the corporation's seal. Over the following four days, they collected 'ingenia & bellorum machinas' to besiege and mine the priory, broke the prior's prison and freed two prisoners, and threatened to burn or bombard the priory and kill the monks unless they returned to the besiegers a copy of an agreement made between the city and the priory in 1429 over various jurisdictional and property rights. They also closed the city gates to the king's ministers as if in time of war. Accounts of these events outside the lawcourts are extremely scanty; apart from the reference in Benet's chronicle, only one London chronicle relates how in Norwich 'the comons aroose, and wold have ffired and sawtyd the abbey, and have destroyed the prior . . .'[4]

Similarly, our knowledge of the 1437 'riot' is based on a justices' certification, which states that eight of the twenty-four aldermen of the city, led by Robert Toppes, John Caumbrigge, and John Gerard, with other prominent citizens, came together on May Day and 'excited a gret Rowte' of over 2,000 servants and foreigners, in order to exclude other aldermen and citizens from the mayoral elections. Another alderman, William Grey, claimed to have been assaulted by a group of rioters, who also threatened Richard Brasier, the sheriff, 'of bodyly harm yf he come in to the Gildhall that day'. When the sheriff tried to arrest one of the crowd, they in turn rescued the prisoner and 'plukked and toke awey the . . . shirreves dagar from his girdel, seying that thei shuld suffre noman to be arested that day.' Thomas Ingham,

---

[3] For Asshewell, Toppes, and other participants of the alleged 'riots', see the brief biographies in Appendix II. The mayor at the time was William Hempstede.

[4] KB 9 84/1 mm 3–4 and 10–13, and KB 27 728 Rmm 24 ff, and 729 Rm 6, m 14ʳ, m 18, and m 28; 'John Benet's Chronicle', 189; MS Cleopatra C iv, in Kingsford (ed.), *Chronicles of London*, 151.

a justice of peace, attempted to intervene; the crowd reportedly answered, 'trede don that grotbely to the ground'. Lest the court should overlook this shocking insolence, the certifiers painstakingly pointed out that this involved 'namying the seyd Thomas Ingham grotbely'. The current mayor. Robert Chapeleyn, with his loyal aldermen, two royal commissioners (the bishop of Carlisle and John Cottesmore the justice) and two hundred 'wel ruled comoners of the . . . citee', then tried to proceed to the guild-hall; but were stopped in the market-place by 'riotous puple'. The aldermen Robert Toppes, Edmund Bretayn, and William Asshewell were allegedly

stondyng among the same riotous puple . . . comfortyng and steryng hem to make affray . . . In so meche as . . . Edmund Bretayn seyd unto the . . . puple . . . abyde awhile til thei com to us ward and than set on them.

Despite an appeal by the commissioners, the crowd then assaulted the plaintiffs, and 'to ther power wold suffre no freman of the . . . citee to come to the . . . eleccion but suche as were of their oppinyon'.[5]

These circumstantial accounts have hitherto gone almost unchallenged.[6] Yet in the course of this study it has become increasingly clear that legal allegations, far from presenting objective realities, were themselves conditioned by the structures and functions of the law, and the motives and purposes of the disputing parties. In the case of the Norwich 'riots', it is arguable that neither the indictments nor the certification can be taken at anything like face value. The 'riot' of 1437 may well have been a legal fabrication, constructed to serve the interests of one of two groups competing for power in the city government; the events of 1443 can perhaps be better understood as rituals designed to legitimate one group of the city's rulers in opposition to the claims of the Norwich priory to authority over some of the city's territory. When examined in the context of the long dispute between city and priory, and the internal divisions in the city's governing bodies, both events demonstrate well the intricate role of law, negotiation, and public display in competitions for status and power. Both show how potential disorder was incorporated within the framework of legal and social expectations, to serve intitially the pretensions of one or other group, and ultimately the purposes of divine and social order.

---

[5] KB 9 229/1 m 106 and KB 27 707 Rm 4ʳᵈ.

[6] Storey, for instance, clearly believes that the 1437 certification recorded an actual riot (*End of the House of Lancaster*, 220).

The starting-point for this argument is the anomalous absence, in these two 'riots', of any injuries, let alone fatalities. No coroners' inquisitions recorded unusual deaths at this time; no private litigation resulted in guilty verdicts of assault against any participants; no damage to property—except to the prior's prison—was ever alleged. A 'violent riot' without damage or casualties is surely unusual in either fifteenth- or twentieth-century terms. Furthermore, there is no evidence either of a popular seizure of power, or of the intervention of armed magnate retainers. What then was the nature of these events?

To understand this, we need to analyse the context of the allegations of riot in some detail. The quarrels which generated them took place in the atmosphere of tense, close association between urban and ecclesiastical powers which nurtured many medieval disputes.[7] The priory of Norwich was geographically attached to the town; the very territory within the city walls was invaded by that of the priory, which held Tombland and Ratonrowe in front of the cathedral precinct, Holmstrete along its northern edge, and the liberty of Normanslond in the Ward-over-the-Water (see Map 6.1). The priory also had charters to rights in the suburbs and villages surrounding the city, such as Bracondale, Trowse, Lakenham, and Eaton, and could hold, and receive tolls and profits from, an annual Pentecost fair in Tombland.[8]

In the first known conflict between the city and the priory, in 1272, a fight of obscure origins provoked a major assault on the priory and cathedral, parts of which were burned down. Thirteen people died in the attack, and at least thirty citizens were hanged in reprisal.[9] By the mid-fifteenth century this tale had disappeared from the public records. Only the threatened burning of the priory in 1443 hints at its tenuous survival in folk tradition. Throughout the fourteenth century,

---

[7] See M. D. Lobel, *The Borough of Bury St. Edmunds* (Oxford, 1935), esp. 16–17, 24–9, 33–5, 44–55, 82–8, 123–7, 145, and 156–9; S. Reynolds, *An Introduction to the History of English Medieval Towns* (Oxford, 1977), 115–16 posits that ecclesiastical authorities made particularly restrictive landlords—'It is . . . notable how largely towns subject to ecclesiastical lords figured in the disturbances of periods like the 1260s, 1326–7 and 1381.' (See also 134 and 183.) For a striking earlier European example, see Guibert of Nogent's account of the revolt at Laon, in J. Benton (ed.), *Self and Society in Medieval France* (New York, 1970), 145–90.

[8] *CPR, 1436–41*, 552–3.

[9] N. Tanner, *The Church in Late Medieval Norwich, 1370–1532* (Pontifical Institute of Medieval Studies; Toronto, 1984), 141. On the score of casualties, this might reasonably be called a riot.

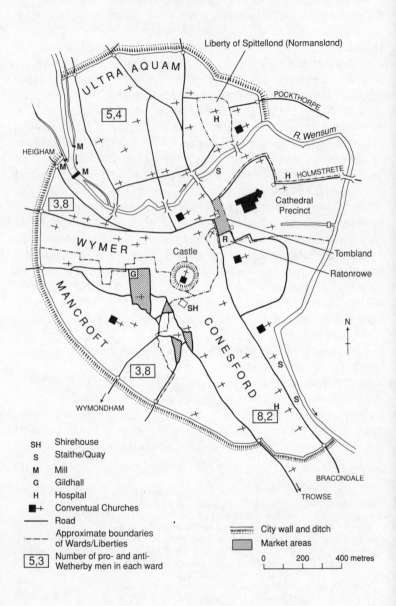

MAP. 6.1　Features of Norwich and distribution of disputing parties

sporadic outbreaks of anti-priory hostility occurred.[10] But a sequence of confrontations which seems to provide a logical context for the events of 1437 and 1443 starts in 1404.

In that year, the city gained its charter, which apparently rendered the city's powers and boundaries more, rather than less, ambiguous and contentious. It was concerned to distinguish the extent of the city's legal and administrative territory from the royal jurisdiction in Norfolk, rather than from the liberties of the priory. Thus, Norwich officers were to have rights over all the city, 'cum suburbis & hamlettis suis', except for the castle and the shirehouse, which remained an administrative part of Norfolk.[11] This phraseology allowed the city to claim rights to grazing, fishing, and (most importantly) court-holding[12] in the hamlets of Trowse, Bracondale, Lakenham, and Eaton, and to jurisdiction in Tombland, Ratonrowe, Holmstrete, and Normanslond; just those areas where the priory was prepared to defend its chartered liberties.[13] Regarding internal government, the charter was most precise in defining the privileges accorded out of the king's hand to the rulers of the city. Thus it specified that the citizens 'may choose yearly from themselves a Mayor, who shall be the King's Escheator; and . . . may choose yearly from themselves 2 sheriffs', and recorded what profits these officers might take, what legal cases they might hear, and so on. The anxious distinctions of royal and communal authority are nicely elaborated in the definition of public ritual:

The Mayor may have a sword carried erect before him in the presence of all magnates and lords except the king. The sergeants at mace of the mayor and the Sheriffs may carry gilt or silver maces with the king's arms even before the king within the Liberty[14]

All this, though essential from the king's viewpoint, did nothing to settle either the structure of internal elections or the claims of the priory. Over the next ten years, serious disputes arose within the city between the twenty-four 'prudhommes' and the sheriffs, and the commonalty of the city. The main issue was the relative powers of each group in the election of the mayor. In 1414 both parties submitted to the judgment of Sir Thomas Erpingham, under whose

[10] Tanner, *The Church in Late Medieval Norwich*, 145.
[11] Hudson and Tingey (eds.), *Norwich Records*, i. 31–6.
[12] See Ch. 2.
[13] See above, n. 8.
[14] Hudson and Tingey (eds.), *Norwich Records*, i. 31–2.

guidance a composition (14 February 1415) was achieved. This laid down the election procedures and duties of city officers. The election of the mayor was to be attended by twenty-four aldermen and the sixty common councillors; all citizens living in the city, except for foreigners, could 'frely come' to the guild-hall at the time; the mayor and the aldermen were to retire to an inner chamber, while the common speaker asked for two nominations from all the people in the hall; and the nominations, written down by the speaker and six of the common council, were to be conveyed to the mayor and aldermen, who voted individually and secretly to the common clerk, the recorder of the city, and the common speaker.[15] In case of deadlock, the mayor's vote counted for two. In many ways, the system was well thought out and equitable. The power of the mayor and the aldermen was balanced by the fact that the commoners elected their own speaker, nominated candidates for the mayoralty, and appointed one of the two sheriffs. The document also carefully stiuplated that the twenty-four aldermen could do nothing to 'bynde or charge þe Cite' without the assent of the commonalty.[16]

Though royal sanction for this composition was not granted until two years later, it apparently succeeded in temporarily reconciling the conflicting parties; for no further adjustments to the system are recorded until 1424. In that year an indenture was drawn up between the mayor, sheriffs, and aldermen, whose terms were clearly intended to promote a united front among the twenty-four, even in the matter of elections. Not only was it enjoined on aldermen not to sue any quarrel against their fellows, or to be party in any dispute against them, but they were forbidden (with what one can only feel was excessive political naïvety) to 'werkyn . . . among the comon puple of the citee, steryng ne excityng no maner of mater to be chosen to any offys'. The authors optimistically suggested that city officers might thus be chosen 'pesably . . . withoute coloure of mayntenaunce'.[17]

By 1414 then, there were groups of individuals, if not parties, disputing city elections; and we know that by 1417 the city had challenged the rights of the priory over the hamlets outside Norwich, and the liberties within it. They had evidently used the well-estab-

---

[15] If the assembly were unable to agree on 2 names, the 60 common councillors were to decide.

[16] Hudson and Tingey (eds.), *Norwich Records*, vol. i, intro., pp. lxiii–lxx and 93 ff.

[17] Ibid. lxx and 109–12.

lished paths of litigation to test their powers; that is, city officers had set out to hear cases in hamlets such as Trowse and Bracondale, and to present the prior of Norwich for obstructing Holmstrete. The priory countered legal challenge with legal rebuff, by obtaining an inquisition on encroachments on the king's geldable, held at Cringleford before Edmund Oldhall, escheator of Norfolk, on 7 October 1417. All the alleged encroachments in fact concerned the attempts of the city officers to demonstrate their supposed rights in public; and it is clear from the indictments that public ritual was part of this process. In order to claim fishing rights at Trowse, for instance, the mayor, sheriffs, and aldermen allegedly went on an official fishing expedition, and having caught their token fish, paraded back to the city, singing and shouting, 'We are in possession by right and by our liberties of this City of Norwich we have caught them'. The meeting finished with a ceremonial fish-distribution to the citizens.[18]

Three conclusions arise from this evidence. First, and most obviously, the inquisition, though supposedly upholding the king's legal rights, was actually a weapon used by the priory to fend off the claims of the city. Technically, this succeeded; the jury swore that the hamlets in question had never been suburbs of the city, and that the sheriffs had no right to present the prior for obstructing Holmstrete. Secondly, this was clearly only one interchange in a quarrel with long possibilities. The law was used not as an authority to settle the dispute, but as a tool for each side to probe the strengths and weaknesses of the other, and for both to demonstrate publicly their status, power, and commitment. Thirdly, the city at least was alive to the value of public ritual as justification and authorization. I need not rehearse here all the arguments on the political power of the procession in the Middle Ages; but it was undoubtedly great. Processions acted out, in real time, space and flesh, an image both of divine order and of social hierarchy.[19] This was well appreciated in fifteenth-century England, as Phythian-Adams brilliantly shows in his analysis of Corpus Christi and Midsummer processions in Coventry.[20] The Norwich aldermen

---

[18] Ibid. 320–4.
[19] See e.g. Duby, *The Three Orders*, 68, and R. Darnton, 'A Bourgeois Puts His World in Order; The City as Text', in *The Great Cat Massacre and Other Episodes in French Cultural History* (New York, 1984) (I owe this reference to Dr David Garrioch). See also R. Trexler, *Public Life in Renaissance Florence* (New York, 1980), pt. 3, esp. 249–64.
[20] C. Phythian-Adams, 'Ceremony and the Citizen: The Communal Year at Coventry

who went fishing so impressively at Trowse were simply appropriating the authoritative value of a procession to their own ends. Perhaps the distribution of the fish even appealed to the biblical—and therefore highly authoritative—image of the post-resurrection Christ feeding the disciples.[21] Whatever the allusion, the dispute clearly took place on a sophisticated level of symbolic interaction. Any apparent appeal to violence must be viewed in this context.

However, the jury's verdict at Cringleford proved a poser to the city. This is clear from the part played by the inquest records in the prolonged negotiations between the priory and the city over their respective jurisdictions in 1426–9. On 21 February 1426, the city assembly deputed six of its members, including Thomas Ingham and Thomas Wetherby, to treat with the prior over the inquest findings.[22] The surviving 'view of account of the Treasures of Norwich and of the commonalty money' for 1429–30, illustrates vividly the impressive scale (and cost) of activities generated by the negotiations.[23] In all, the city spent nearly £70 on the matter in the four years 1426–9. One alderman, Thomas Wetherby, was apparently deeply involved in these expensive transactions. The account includes such items as 13s. 4d. paid to John Hauke and William Yelverton 'de consilio cum' Wetheby, for treating with the prior over two days: 46s. 8d. to Hauke and Edmund Fuller for staying fourteen days in London on the city's business;[24] £10. 13s. 4d. to Thomas Rolf, Robert Caundyssh, and Thomas Derham and their servants, while they were giving legal advice to the city (at Wetherby's suggestion); and money to pay for letters sent to the executors of Edmund Oldhall, the escheator who

---

1450–1550', in P. Clark and P. Slack (eds.), *Crisis and Order in English Towns 1500–1700* (London, 1972), esp. 63; see also the many references to royal processions in London in 15th-cent. vernacular chronicles (e.g. *Gregory's Chronicle*, 112 and 160, *Brut*, 380, 557–8, 425–6, and 491).

[21] John 21: 9–14.

[22] N & NRO case 8, shelf d, Assembly Roll 1420–6.

[23] N & NRO case 7, shelf d. This document is apparently unique in the Norwich records of 1420–50. It did not record ordinary city expenses (cf. Hudson and Tingey (eds.), *Norwich Records*, ii. 65–7); only the extraordinary cost of entertaining noble guests and pursuing the dispute. Why it was specially made, or specially preserved, is unknown, but in view of the succeeding internal strife in the city, it may have been used to support charges against Wetherby and his friends for financial mismanagement of the negotiations.

[24] Hauke was clearly an associate of Wetherby (see below). Fuller was probably the alderman styled sometimes Bretayn, and sometimes Bretayn/Fuller.

took the Cringleford inquisitions.[25] The city employed not only some of the most active and eminent East Anglian lawyers of the time (Heydon, Caundyssh, Yelverton, and Derham) but also London notables such as Thomas Rolf and Thomas Greswold.[26] Hard bargaining, sustained by solid legal research, characterized the dispute in this period.

Yet the results must have been disappointing to many citizens. On 20 December 1429, William Worstede the prior and Robert Baxter the mayor of Norwich sealed an indenture of agreement between the two bodies, the contents of which told heavily in the priory's favour. The prior's rights over the hamlets and the disputed city streets were reasserted; moreover, a rent of 4*s.* a year was to be exacted from the city in return for grazing rights in the hamlets. The only concessions made by the prior were that the city's officers and justices of the peace could act in the disputed areas in matters not touching the right of the priory. Since the right of the priory involved the claim to hold legal proceedings in those areas, it is difficult to see how the city officers could have taken advantage of this offer.

Certainly, whether or not the priory's claims were justified, some citizens were, then or later, bitterly disappointed with this supposed settlement. In 1443 the 'rioters' allegedly demanded the return of this indenture in the words 'ye monkes 3e charlys bryng out youre balled prioure and that chartr *that Robert Baxster . . . and other solden* to William Worstede'.[27] Similarly, the London chronicler of 1443, perhaps repeating a version of the affair current in merchant circles, spoke of the indenture as 'falce contryved evydence, that were seled . . . wt the comon sell vnwetyng of hem [the city] but thorow a prior of old and certayn falce aldermen . . . that now aryn dede.'[28] The immediate effect of sealing the indenture appears to have been to refocus the conflict. From 1429–38 the overt dispute was not between the city and the priory, but between two opposing factions within the city government, one of which was thought by the other to have gone over to the side of the priory. The first unequivocal signs of this division occurred at the mayoral election of 1433.

---

[25] On 10 Feb. 1428 the city assembly issued a writ to Oldhall's executors to deliver up all documents connected with the inquest (N & NRO case 17, shelf b, Book of Pleas, fo. xxx^d.

[26] See Tables A3.1–A3.2 for the activities of these men on peace commission.

[27] KB 27 729 Rm 28^d (emphasis mine).

[28] Kingsford (ed.), *Chronicles of London*, 151.

After that election, at which Richard Purdaunce was eventually chosen,[29] the new mayor and his officers returned a *certiorari* to Chancery stating that John Hauke, John Querdlyng, John Belhagh, Thomas Fysshlok, and John May were guilty of various misdemeanours and abuses of office in the city.[30] All were associates of Thomas Wetherby, the outgoing mayor and mainstay of the 1426–9 negotiations with the priory. By 25 February 1434, Purdaunce and the five supposed miscreants had appeared in Chancery, and promised to abide by an award on the dispute in the next city assembly. Though Wetherby's five friends submitted to the fine then imposed, he himself would not do so. He refused to keep a series of days granted to him in March 1434; at which the city assembly lost patience, and 'in detestacion of . . . wilful and malicious attemptyng and doyng agayn þe charte of þe liberte' decided in his absence that he should pay a staggering £100 fine, and 'lese his liberte of þe . . . cite for evermore'.[31]

This was a serious attempt to eject Wetherby from the city government. (It may have seemed the only way to get rid of him, since aldermen, once elected, had life-tenure.)[32] It is tempting to speculate that the so-called 'malicious . . . doyng agayn þe charte of þe liberte' referred to shady dealings with the priory in 1426–9; but maybe Purdaunce and his fellows only meant Wetherby's handling of the 1433 election. Whatever issues lay behind this rift in the city government, Wetherby was determined to fight tenaciously for his position. His reply to the attempt to unseat him was an object lesson in the creative use of administrative rules for individual ends. He submitted a deposition to the chancellor, giving his own version of the 1433 election, in order to prove that Purdaunce was unconstitutionally elected, and hence that all his subsequent official acts were invalid. Wetherby's story, dating from the spring of 1434, is therefore the first of two which fortunately survive concerning the election.

Wetherby stated that at the election he had heard 'gret noysyng'

[29] Cf. the saga of the election dispute, below.

[30] N & NRO, case 9, shelf c. This exemplification of all proceedings in connection with Thomas Wetherby contains all documents relating to the issue, unless otherwise stated. Cf. also C 49 49/8, the Chancery record of the proceedings (my attention was drawn to this document by Andrew King). Querdlyng, Hauke, Fysshlok, and May complained in Chancery in Nov. 1433 that they were kept from the city assemblies and elections (C 244/9 m 24).

[31] In comparison, the mayor's fee for a year of office was 50 marks (Hudson and Tingey (eds.) *Norwich Records*, ii. 65).

[32] Ibid. i. 97.

among the commons at the nomination of mayoral candidates, but on sending to know the reason, had met John Querdlyng, the common speaker, coming to convey the news that the commons were 'fully accorded' on the nomination of William Grey and John Gerard. Grey was duly elected, and led home in procession by Wetherby, the outgoing mayor, as custom demanded. However, after Wetherby, with the city's recorder and the aldermen, had gone home to dine and 'after mete redyn oute for her desporte', 'diverse persones' returned to the guild-hall, kidnapping one of the sheriffs and some of the aldermen on the way, and tried to 'compell hem to make newe eleccion'. On their refusal, some of the commons themselves chose John Gerard for mayor, while others broke the chest where the common seal was kept and used it to certify Richard Purdaunce as mayor.

Purdaunce and his associates, forced to respond, in turn claimed that Querdlyng was not elected common speaker, but co-opted secretly by Wetherby and his associate John Hauke; and that Wetherby's handling of the election included many other irregularities. He 'procured and excited diverse Aldermen and many comoners longe tyme before þe day of eleccion with thretyng wordes' to vote for Grey.[33] He did not withdraw to the inner chamber as he should have done, and knew that Richard Purdaunce and John Gerard were nominated, as it 'openly appered . . . by the partyng of þe seid comones in the hous'. At this, he 'maliciously' rebuked the assembly, and retired to present a faked bill of nomination of William Grey to the aldermen. Some 'substantiall comoners' were sent to require the aldermen not to proceed; Wetherby replied that he 'wold not here hem'. He and Querdlyng threatened to stab one of the ambassadors. When Wetherby returned to the commons to announce the election of Grey, 'þe most part of the Commens . . . answerd . . . holy with oon voys nay nay nay we named never William Grey'. Wetherby persisted in leading away the new mayor, but most of the aldermen and wealthier commons remained in the hall, calling for their own nominees. The aldermen then sent two of their number to Wetherby, asking him to 'reconsile þe people in such wyse þat þey myght have þat that longeth to hem of reght'. Only after Wetherby refused, did the aldermen consider themselves justified in choosing Richard Purdaunce for themselves; which election, they claimed, was done 'after the fourme and effecte'

---

[33] Thus contravening the provisions of the indenture of 1424, see above, n. 17.

of the 1415 composition, 'with out any compulson or constreynyng, or any manere of reryng of any of the kynges peple pesibly with out any riote, affray or offence of þe lawe'.

So far, both groups had attempted to gain power by justifying themselves in the eyes of law and government. Each appealed to Chancery to authorize them as upholders of the city's constitutional precedents. But Wetherby did not stop at this. From 1433 to 1437 he apparently tried persistently to pack the city institutions with his own supporters, and oust those of the opposing party. In 1432–3, three Wetherbys—John, Richard, and Walter—entered the prestigious guild of St George, together with Thomas Ingham, later a known Wetherby supporter.[34] In 1436, when Wetherby's friend William Grey was alderman of the guild, Sir Thomas Tuddenham, John Heydon, Richard Monesle, Richard Brasier, and the current mayor, Robert Chapeleyn, were all admitted; and (unusually) all but Chapeleyn seem to have had their entry fee remitted.[35] In the same year, Chapeleyn sponsored the admission of Christopher Straunge (probably, like Tuddenham, a supporter of the earl of Suffolk) as freeman of the city. By the following year, he was alderman of the city, possibly replacing Richard Purdaunce, who died in 1436.[36] It may be that 1436, when his friend Chapeleyn was mayor, was a turning-point in Wetherby's fortunes. Certainly Walter Gefferey was then expelled from the St George's guild because, allegedly, he had 'outered ungoodly language' of five other members, one of whom was Wetherby's friend Belhagh.[37] And perhaps the Thomas Broun who alleged in Chancery, 1436–7,

---

[34] N & NRO surveyors' accounts of the guild of St George, case 8, shelf e, 1430–7. For the prominence of this guild, see Tanner, *Church in Norwich*, 78–81, and M. Grace (ed.), *Records of the Gild of St George in Norwich 1389–1547* (Norfolk Record Society, 9; 1937), intro., 7. John Wetherby, gentleman, servant of Thomas Wetherby, was presented in the guild-hall in 1441 for assaulting William Asshewell and others on behalf of the prior of Norwich and Thomas Wetherby (N & NRO case 8, shelf a). He also appears in CP 40 727 m 449[d] (Michaelmas 1442) as 'formerly of Norwich, gentleman'. A John Wederby was a feoffee and close friend of John Brown of Wymondham when the latter died in 1465 (see PCC wills, 13 Godyn), but may not have been the same as the Norwich man. A Walter Wetherby appears in CP 40 645 m 282[r] (Easter 1422) as the yeoman brother of John of Attleburgh, yeoman; also 10 years later as 'of Wicklewood, yeoman'; Ralph Lord Cromwell was then suing him to render reasonable account (CP 40 685 m 93[r]). Nothing is known of Richard Wetherby.

[35] N & NRO case 8, shelf e, 1430–7. Storey thinks that the earl of Suffolk was also admitted 'about 1435' (*End of the House of Lancaster*, 219), but this seems to be an error. The guild did, however, make him a gift.

[36] Book of assembly proceedings, N & NRO case 16, shelf d, fo. l[r].

[37] Grace (ed.), *Records of the Gild of St. George*, 39.

that Robert Chapeleyn had 'of malice and yvel will' assigned him to join Humphrey of Gloucester's expedition to Flanders, and had him fettered in prison for eleven weeks when he refused, was the same man who later appears opposing Wetherby and the prior.[38] Chapeleyn may have tried to reinstate Wetherby as alderman by dubious means. A case in King's Bench, Easter 1443, alleged that in January 1437 he had fabricated a 'blaunchartre' and fraudulently procured seals for it by threats—'yf ye will not seale it I shal certifie yow for ryseres'. He had then written in the charter that Thomas Wetherby was an alderman and citizen of Norwich.[39] The alleged threat is particularly significant in view of the fact that Wetherby's opponents were indeed certified as 'ryseres', just four months later. Certainly Wetherby took steps to authorize his position by reference in a court of record—in Michaelmas 1436 he described himself, in an action of debt in Common Pleas, as 'alderman' of Norwich.[40] In December 1436 Benedict Joly and others complained that John Hauke, despite being banned from all offices in 1433, had become undersheriff by the 'couyne and procurement' of Wetherby and the 'tender affection' of Richard Brasier and Walter Crumpe, the sheriffs.[41]

As a result, Justice William Goderede was sent to Norwich to investigate this last allegation on 2 January 1437. Examined by Goderede, all twenty-four aldermen agreed with Joly's statement, except Richard Brasier and Richard Monesle. Goderede's exemplification of all proceedings involving Wetherby and his associates, which appeared 14 March 1437, therefore upheld the position of the anti-Wetherby group. It also apparently alerted the central government to the possibility of dispute at the next mayoral election. Accordingly, a week after the issue of the document, a large assembly at Norwich heard the earl of Suffolk declare that the young king, on hearing of 'divysyon and debate' in the city, had sent him to 'examyne the causes . . . and cese and redresse the occasyon ther of', or to certify to the

---

[38] C 1 70/108. For Gloucester's foray into Flanders, see K. H. Vickers, *Humphrey Duke of Gloucester: A Biography* (London, 1907), 248–53. A Thomas Broun, alias Snarler, was mentioned in the 1437 certification and indicted in King's Bench in 1443 (KB 27 728 Rm 25ᵈ).

[39] KB 27 728 Rm 22ᵈ. The original indictment (in the guild-hall before William Paston) was not made until Michaelmas 1439; Chapeleyn thought it worthwhile to purchase a pardon for the offence in 1446.

[40] CP 40 703 m 252ᵈ.

[41] Exemplification of proceedings in connection with Thomas Wetherby (N & NRO case 9, shelf c).

king the names of those fomenting discord. The earl dictated a form of agreement to settle all disputes since 1433. The common seal, kept out of its accustomed place since May 1433, was to be returned; all writings relevant to the quarrel were to be nullified; Wetherby was not to sue anyone for matters arising from the debate; and he, Fysshlok, Hauke, Querdlyng, Belhagh, May, and William Grey were to be restored to their positions as freemen (or aldermen) of the city.[42]

Though all present were said to have affirmed this 'settlement', it was clearly biased in Wetherby's favour. It assumed (what his opponents denied) that the common seal had been misused, and effectively ignored the conclusion of Goderede's recent investigation. It forced controversial officials back on to the city, and posed tricky problems regarding Wetherby's position, since in 1437 there were already twenty-four aldermen without him. How the city's institutions were to function with a twenty-fifth, or who should step down in his favour, were conundrums that Suffolk did not bother to explain.

Wetherby himself took immediate advantage of the ruling, making a return to Chancery as alderman of the city on 15 April 1437.[43] But his indignant opponents did not submit quietly. Two days later, the privy council ordered Wetherby to appear before them on 24 April. This was probably connected with a 'bille' (exact contents unknown) the origins of which Humphrey of Gloucester was asked to investigate; if so, some of Wetherby's opponents may have been the authors.[44] Evidently as a result of their interview with Wetherby, the council were convinced that troubles would break out at the next mayoral election on 1 May. They hurriedly appointed the bishop of Carlisle and John Cottesmore as overseers to ensure a peaceful election, and threatened a seizure of the city liberties if any disturbance occurred.[45]

In the circumstances, this was likely to be a self-fulfilling prophecy. The election was clearly to be a showdown between two groups of city rulers. The anti-Wetherby group had gained power with great difficulty four years since, and had apparently lost ground badly in 1436.[46]

---

[42] Book of assembly proceedings, N & NRO case 16, shelf d, fo. 2; 54 citizens, including 18 aldermen, attended.

[43] He was still using this to exemplify his position in 1440, when a Chancery writ mentions this return (C 241/229 m 11). Robert Toppes, then mayor, saw through the ruse, and returned that Wetherby was not an alderman at that time.

[44] POPC v. 15.

[45] POPC v. 17–18, and CPR, 1436–41, 86 (commission dated 26 April).

[46] See above, pp. 186–7.

Its members might well feel aggrieved at Suffolk's partisan interference, and apprehensive of Wetherby's possible election tactics and probable means of exacting vengeance were he to win the election. Wetherby, on the other hand, was determined to regain his position. He was not young (he died in 1445) and perhaps saw in this election his last chance to re-establish a privileged position in the city.[47] Thus both parties needed to prevent the other from packing the election. But the losing party had great incentives to claim that some disturbance had occurred, in hopes of upsetting the winner, and benefiting from the promised seizure of the liberties. Since this is precisely what Wetherby's associates did claim, in the certification of 1437, after they had lost the election to the rival candidate John Caumbrigge, the document is hardly unimpeachable evidence of the existence of a riot.[48] We should note that Wetherby had once before alleged electoral interference in pursuit of his own aims.[49]

Some features of the document itself tell against it. Why, to start with, was it not an indictment? The certifiers (Robert Chapeleyn as outgoing mayor, Thomas Ingham, John Dunnyng, and Thomas Wetherby as justices of the peace in Norwich, and Richard Brasier as sheriff) were careful to conform to the statutory provisions on certification. They claimed that they dared not arrest the rioters at the time 'for dred of ther deth', and could take no presentment later because the jury was similarly terrified. But fifteenth-century jurors were more often bribed than threatened away from their duties.[50] Further, at least three of the jurors (Geoffrey Quyncy, John Belhagh, and John May) were known Wetherby supporters (Quyncy claimed to be an injured party). Is it credible that Wetherby could get his own men on a jury, but not protect them should they make an indictment? It seems more likely that the certification was made because to overturn the election it was necessary to allege riot, and one distinguishing feature of riots was the peculiar legal process of certification.[51] An added bonus, from the certifiers' viewpoint, was that this

---

[47] See W. J. Blake, 'Thomas Wetherby', *Norfolk Archaeology*, 32 (1961), 60–72. The earliest date at which we know he was adult is 1413. He was therefore at least 45 in 1437; but since in 1413 he was a rich enough merchant to buy a manor at Cringleford, he was probably older.   [48] See above, n. 2.

[49] See above, p. 18.   [50] See Ch. 2, text accompanying nn. 45–7.

[51] See above, n. 2. Storey seems not to have realized that the document was a justices' certification—he calls it 'not a formal judicial record' (*End of the House of Lancaster*, 220).

method allowed the allegation to be made by only four people, rather than a full jury.

The outcome of the certification does nothing to inspire trust in its account. True, the council carried out its promise of seizing the city liberties into the king's hand, appointing John Welles, a London alderman, as keeper of the city in place of the newly elected mayor, John Caumbrigge.[52] On 15 June 1437, Caumbrigge, John Gerard, Robert Toppes, William Asshewell, and five other alleged rioters were called before the council, which nevertheless recorded no discussion of the certifiers' account of the affair until 12 July.[53] The council then decided to exile Robert Toppes to Bristol; but the same meeting also sent Thomas Wetherby, Christopher Straunge, and William Grey, all on the side of the certifiers, away from Norwich.[54] By 18 November, these rather sluggish deliberations on the supposed 'riot' were complete—the council decided that the liberties should be restored, and an 'indifferent' man chosen to act as mayor until next May. They then selected John Caumbrigge, who cannot possibly have been indifferent.[55] This decision must have been influenced by the report of their own commissioners, who had been present on 1 May; which indicates that they at least had observed no riots there. The certification led to no legal proceedings except an appearance in King's Bench in Hilary 1438, when Toppes came to plead a convenient supersedeas, which ended the process.[56]

The affair can thus hardly be called a riot. However, its place in the internal strife in Norwich at this period can be gauged from the private suits which followed it. All these suits were apparently initiated by John Heydon. He sued writs in King's Bench in Michaelmas 1437 against William Asshewell and Edmund Bretayn *et al.* for assault and menaces on 1 May; and against Robert Toppes, John Gerard *et al.* in Common Pleas (Hilary 1439) and King's Bench (Hilary 1440) on a similar charge.[57] In the last case he was eventually awarded 400 marks damages. In Hilary 1439 Robert Suker, William Asshewell, and

[52] Hudson and Tingey (eds.), *Norwich Records*, vol. i, p. lxxxvi.

[53] *POPC* v. 33 and 45.

[54] *CCLR, 1435–41*, 94.

[55] Ibid. 142; though John Welles continued to act with John Caumbrigge until 1439, see B. Cozens-Hardy and E. A. Kent, *The Mayors of Norwich, 1403–1835* (Norwich, 1938), under the year 1438.

[56] KB 27 707 Rm 4[r].

[57] Respectively, KB 27 706 m 116[r]; CP 40 712 m 124; and KB 27 715 m 62[r]. I owe the Common Pleas reference to Ms Diana Spelman.

Edmund Bretayn appeared in King's Bench on the charge that Suker had, on 1 May 1437, broken a bond of peace made to Heydon in April 1437 (Asshewell and Bretayn were his mainpernors). This case dragged on until Michaelmas 1443, the defendants arguing that the bond was not technically sound.[58] The defence plea in the 1440 case shows that the issue was whether Toppes and his fellows had illegally prevented Heydon, who was named in the certification as recorder of the city, from attending the 1437 election; the defendants pleaded that the guild-hall was the property of the mayor and aldermen, who had a right to expel non-citizens from it. Why should Toppes and his friends have attempted to exclude Heydon from the election? The answer appears in a scrap of evidence from the presentments against the duke of Suffolk's supporters in Norfolk at the 1450 oyer and terminer. There it was alleged against Heydon that while he was recorder of the city, he disclosed to the prior of Norwich evidence on which the city based its case against the priory. For this, the mayor and commons 'dischargid the said Heydon of the said condicion of recorder'.[59] This must have happened before 1 May 1437, for the book of assembly proceedings notes then that William Yelverton was chosen recorder.[60] No wonder that Heydon alleged as a grievance in his lawsuits that he had been prevented from holding assizes in the city.[61]

That there was a conflict of interests at the election of 1437 is indisputable. My contention is, however, that the heart of this supposed 'riot' may have been John Heydon's attempt to dispute, ritually, his dismissal from office, by his official attendance at the election. No doubt he was refused entry, perhaps somewhat rudely. But the rebuff was then heightened into a legal accusation of riot with the support of Wetherby, whose party stood to gain by alleging disturbance of the elections. Once again, the process we perceive is not overt violence, but an intricate political ritual of justification,

---

[58] KB 27 711 Rm 17ᵈ and 714 Rm 48ʳ.

[59] Hudson and Tingey (eds.), *Norwich Records*, i. 345; cf. also no. CCCVII. Some of the charges at this oyer and terminer were clearly unfounded; a fragment in the N & NRO puts the responsibility for the disturbed election of 1433 (misdated to 1436) onto Tuddenham and other Suffolk supporters (case 9, shelf c). But the supporting evidence in Heydon's case seems to indicate the accuracy of that indictment. A similar charge against Heydon appears in the city's attempted self-exculpation after 1443 (G. Johnson (ed.), 'Extract from the Books of the Corporation of Norwich relative . . . Gladman's Insurrection', *Norfolk and Norwich Archaeological Society*, 1 (1847), 296–7).

[60] N & NRO case 16, shelf d, fo. 3ᵈ.

[61] KB 27 715 m 62ʳ, and 706 m 116ʳ.

authorization, and patronage, involving law as well as public ceremonial.

In the struggle for control of the city, the stance of the participants towards the priory was clearly a distinguishing feature of the two groups. Wetherby, Heydon, and his friends, were, or were thought to be, secret supporters of the priory. Asshewelle, Toppes, and their comrades evidently saw themselves as patriotic upholders of the rights of their city against the encroachments of the priory. This emerges clearly in the pattern of the city–priory disputes in the years 1436 to 1443.

In 1436 the quarrel with the priory had, it seems, been in abeyance for some years, for no records of any clash of interests survive from this period. Perhaps the internal politics of the city prevented concerted action against the priory. Perhaps Prior Worstede, having gained his satisfactory legal settlement of 1429, could afford to be lenient over small breaches of the agreement in practice, and generous in his definitions of what constituted those 'matters not touching the right of the priory' in which the city officers could act in his domains.[62] But Worstede died in 1436; his successor, John Heverlond, apparently espoused a more rigorous policy.[63] He was also, after 1437, facing a section of the city government hostile to his claims, which had temporarily gained the upper hand over their opponents, in the aftermath of the 1437 dispute. From this time on, a string of offences to the priory's rights were alleged against prominent citizens of Norwich. In Easter 1438, Heverlond brought an action in King's Bench against Edmund Caly, a Trowse franklin, William Dunnyng, a Norwich merchant, and others, for poaching in his free warren at Trowse in 1437.[64] On 30 December 1440 the prior and two of his servants were in turn presented before the city justices of the peace for assaulting a servant of the city sheriffs in November 1440 and rescuing from him a man he had just arrested on a plea of debt.[65] In

---

[62] See above p. 183 for the terms of the indenture.

[63] His election was confirmed 12 Oct. 1436 (F. Blomefield, *An Essay towards a Topographical History of the County of Norfolk* (11 vols; London 1805–10), iii, 604.

[64] KB 27 708 m 17ʳ. An Edmund Caly enfeoffed land in Trowse in 1403 (Blomefield, *History of Norfolk*, v. 459); so there may have been personal elements to this suit. But it would not be surprising if the city aldermen and Caly combined together in this instance against the priory; cf. also N & NRO DCN 79/2 (city's servants sued for false arrest in Holmestrete leet).

[65] N & NRO case 8, shelf a, presentments of assaults before the justices in the guild-hall.

January 1441 the prior evidently requested an *inspeximus* of his charters and rights; for a copy of the Cringleford inquest of 1417 was called into Chancery.[66] The *inspeximus* confirmed the prior's rights over the Pentecost fair, the hamlets outside Norwich, and the liberties within it; but it provoked a strong reaction in the city assembly. An incomplete entry in the book of assembly proceedings for 22 June 1441 shows William Asshewell the mayor formally declaring that Heverlond was acting 'by colour' of letters patent obtained 'upon unjust information'. The assembly had already arranged to circumvent some of the prior's powers—on 15 February 1441, they declared a boycott of the Pentecost fair court. Any citizen of Norwich making a plea there was to be fined 20s.[67] The priory continued its campaign by getting a special commission of oyer and terminer, issued on 30 June 1441, for an investigation into 'errors defects and misprisions in the city of Norwich for lack of good governaunce'. These terms (like 'encroachments on the king's geldable') clearly covered challenges by the city to the priory's authority, since the three commissioners who sat 31 July 1441 at Thetford heard presentments that arrests by city officers in Trowse, Bracondale, Tombland, Holmstrete, and Raton-rowe from March 1439 onwards, were unjustified and illegal. At the same inquest, the prior presented a bill against William Asshewell, the sheriffs, and many leading citizens of the town, such as John Gerard, John Caumbrigge, William Hempstede, and Thomas Ingham.[68]

At this stage, the 1429 indenture, virtually dormant for eight years, gained sudden importance. It provided evidence not only of the prior's rights, but of the city's consent to them; a fact which would stop any defence plea in court. Perhaps because of this, the citizens changed their tactics. They decided, by August 1441, to seek a new agreement with the priory. On 21 August, William Asshewell apparently sent a letter to the bishop of Norwich, confirming an arrangement for the aldermen, the prior, and the bishop to meet in the cathedral church.[69] The recent Thetford sessions were one item on the agenda; but by

---

[66] C 260 146/22 and *CPR, 1436–41*, 552–3.

[67] N & NRO case 16, shelf d, fos. 16ʳ and 14ᵈ. Wetherby, at least, had ostentatiously sued in the court in 1436 (N & NRO, DCN 79/8).

[68] See *CPR, 1436–41*, 574 (cf. above, n. 18). The sitting commissioners were John Fortescu, William Paston, and Thomas Tuddenham; Paston was said, in 1433, to have been taking 40s. a year as a retainer from the prior of Norwich (*PL* ii. 509). The records of the proceedings appear in KB 9 240 mm 35–7 and C 260 146/22.

[69] A damaged draft survives in N & NRO case 9, shelf c.

this stage, the city was also embroiled in disputes with three other ecclesiastical neighbours. The most important of these was with the abbot of St Benet's Hulme, over whether mills built by the city damaged his lands. Another concerned the use of a quay owned by the abbot of Wendling, but rented to the city. The issue in the third dispute, with the abbot of Walsingham, is unknown. All these were to be concluded in the new agreement; for Asshewell, with the sheriffs and aldermen, bound himself on 12 October 1441 to submit to the arbitration of the earl of Suffolk on all quarrels between the city, the bishop, the three abbots, and the prior of the cathedral, up to August 1441. Sometime before the next 23 June, a list of the disputed points was drawn up, presumably as a guide to the arbitrator.[70] The copy we have may be incomplete—it starts abruptly 'Item the same parties be at travers'—but it lists the main issues; the city's new mills, the status of Holmstrete and other lands in Norwich and the hamlets outside, and the prior's right to fair jurisdiction. But Wetherby's group within the city government evidently managed to insert into the schedule some internal issues raised by these external quarrels. In the case of the abbot of Wendlyng's rented quay, the aldermen had apparently tried to subvert his rights by ordering all citizens to use the common staithe. A decision to levy money from the city to pay for legal costs, should the abbot cite it in a plea, had already been made.[71] Wetherby's minority group in the city government must therefore have been responsible for the question whether the 'meir and the more part of the cominalte ayens the Will of the remenaunt' might make an ordinance compelling all Norwich freemen to use the city's quay rather than another; and whether the levy for legal costs might be taken 'of them þt nevere consented to the graunt'.[72]

The appeal to a great lord to settle the internal politics of the city harks back to the famous 1415 composition of Sir Thomas Erpingham.[73] But the results of the 1442 arbitrement were to prove even less harmonious. The tripartite indenture of award, dated 23 June, between the city, the prior, and the abbot of St Benet's Hulme was said to be for 'the more norisshyng and kepyng of good loue and peas' between the parties.[74] Suffolk claimed he had 'harde the

[70] N & NRO case 9, shelf c.
[71] N & NRO case 16, shelf d, fo. 4ᵈ (book of assembly proceedings).
[72] N & NRO case 9, shelf c.
[73] See above, text accompanying nn. 15–16.
[74] N & NRO case 9, shelf c.

compleyntes the answers replicacions allegiaunces evidences and proves' of each side, giving judgment only 'after grete deliberacion and avyse'. Nevertheless the results were patently unsatisfactory to the majority of the city. Suffolk ordered that the city's mills, erected 'to the noysaunce of the freholde' of the abbot and the prior, be removed before next 30 April, at the city's cost. The city was bound in an obligation of £50 to the bishop, £50 to the prior, and £100 to the abbot to do so. The prior's full rights to fair jurisdiction were reasserted. The only mitigating factor was a note that the parties 'can not by assente accorde' over the disputed areas of jurisdiction within Norwich; so a suit was to be brought into King's Bench, that the 'trouthe theryn [might be] knowen by fourme and esie processe in the lawe.' But the collusive action, appearing promptly in Michaelmas 1442, resulted only in another jury verdict against the city's officers.[75]

With this decision, the city's quandary was complete. In any legal judgment, they were hampered by the weight of documentary evidence against them (the Cringleford inquest and the 1429 indenture). Arbitration had only compounded this problem—if the citizens were to seal the 1442 settlement, it would prove another disastrous hindrance to the defence of their claims. But the aldermen, politicians first and last, evidently espoused the belief that a decision is final only until reversed. Their first reaction was not to raise a riot, but to draft an appeal to Suffolk for a 'reformacyon' of the award, on the tactfully phrased grounds that some of the articles were 'ambyguows' and 'wold seme more large than the verray entent of 30ure award was'. They claimed that the award on fair jurisdiction implied giving the prior a franchise in the city, which 'if the meir and comonalte shulde afferme be her comen seel ... it were hard in tyme to kom consideryng that the fraunchise of the ... prior is not 3it determyned'.[76] They also quibbled with the obligation clause, alleging that it was unclear whether an offence against one ecclesiastical body entailed a payment to all three or not. On the back of this document appear two draft petitions to Suffolk, begging him to send Sir Thomas Tuddenham, or others of his council, to come to Norwich at the city's cost and reform the award.[77]

---

[75] KB 27 726 Rm 39ʳ.

[76] Evidently this document was drawn up before the verdict in the collusive King's Bench action.

[77] N & NRO case 9, shelf c.

The city's lawyers also evidently worked overtime to devise legal counters to the award. On 8 October 1442, Hempstede, whose post of mayor included that of king's escheator, wrote to an unnamed lord, desiring his help and advice in what he claimed was a knotty point of law. He was, he implied, dismayed to discover at a recent escheator's inquest in Norwich, 'divers places' held in mortmain, 'at þis day unmortesed'. Needless to say, these comprised areas claimed by the prior to be in his jurisdiction. Hempstede, courteously supposing that it 'was never my lords wyll of Suff.' to cause 'vneesse' to the city by his award, nevertheless professed himself baffled as to where his duty lay in regard to sealing it. 'To þe which arbitrement', he wrote, 'we feer right sor to consent for þe kyngs hurte.'[78]

Suffolk, however, was unwilling to revise his views; there is no evidence that he replied to these baits. The city fell back on inaction. By 1 December 1442, the indenture had still not been sealed, and a special assize was granted to the prior over the city's failure to observe the award.[79] Tension within the city government was clearly running high. On 25 January 1443, a city assembly was called to discuss the sealing.[80] So bitter was the dispute that it lasted until after 5 p.m.; in the end, those commons who were opposed to sealing the award, apparently convinced that the other side would win the debate, invaded the hall, and 'token a wey the Comon Seall to that entent that the obligacion shulde nott be a Sealyd'.[81]

At this point the 'riotous' events described in the indictments of 28 February 1443 took place. One indictment alleges against thirty-nine people (encouraged and abetted by Robert Toppes, William Asshewell, and Walter Gefferey) that they invaded the guild-hall and removed the seal with armed force; after which they besieged the priory and broke the prior's prison. The second states that a total of ninety-eight people, headed by William Hempstede the mayor and the two sheriffs, threatened to burn the priory and kill the monks if they would not hand over the indenture of 1429. This indictment also alleged that one John Gladman rode through the city 'ut regem cum corona ceptro

---

[78] Ibid. (dispute with the Prior and the Abbot of St Benet). The intended recipient may have been the Treasurer, Lord Cromwell, since a day later Hempstede recommended lobbying him for support.

[79] SC 8 6474.

[80] According to an account written in the Liber Albus in 1482; Hudson and Tingey (eds.), *Norwich Records*, i. 348–51.

[81] This account is borne out by the indictments of 28 Feb. 1443 (KB 9 84/1 mm 3–4 and 10–13).

[*sic*] & gladio', with a sword carried before him, twenty-four riders preceding him arrayed like a king's valets with crowns on their sleeves and bows and arrows in hand, and one hundred armed men following after in armed procession 'ad monendos homines in civitate praedicta ad insurreccionem'. The Norwich crowd are said to have broken the prior's stocks, and extorted money from one of the monks, and (significantly) Thomas Wetherby.[82]

Unlike the certification of 1437, these indictments clearly record actual events with some accuracy. The city's own account confirms the removal of the seal.[83] The government response lacked the leisurely and equivocal air of their reaction to the 1437 dispute. The liberties were seized again, and not returned for four years; instead of a fellow alderman, Sir John Clyfton was appointed governor; the corporate fine (apart from individual fines) was 3,000 marks.[84] Two of the more prominent defendants—Robert Toppes and William Asshewell—thought it necessary to buy individual pardons.[85] We know that Gladman's curious procession really took place, for the citizens, attempting to exculpate themselves after 1448, never tried to deny it. Their whole endeavour was to prove it innocent, rather than riotous, by alleging that it was part of the customary 'merth and disporte and pleyes' of Shrovetide, in which citizens of 'sad disposicon', such as Gladman (a man 'true and fethful to God and to the King') might be expected to appear.[86] This was a lie; January 25 fell a good five weeks before Shrove Tuesday in 1443.[87] We must therefore assume that the city hoped, by these means, to palliate an undeniable truth.

The question is thus not whether there occurred in Norwich in 1443 an upheaval which the government found deeply disturbing, but what was the nature of the affair. The answer, I believe, is that it was

[82] Ibid. The charges reached King's Bench in Easter 1443 and were repeated in the next term (KB 27 728 R mm 24 ff., and 729 Rm 6, m 14ʳ, m 18, and m 28). The indictments use 'ceptro' for 'sceptro'.

[83] From the Liber Albus in 1482; Hudson and Tingey (eds.), *Norwich Records*, i. 350–1.

[84] Ibid. i. 355–6; *POPC* v. 229 and 256, 28 Feb. and 30 Mar. (instruction to the duke of Norfolk to make Clyfton governor if the liberties were seized, and order to do so); and E 28/71 nos. 49 and 50 (note that the fine was later reduced to 1,000 marks).

[85] Asshewell on 12 July (KB 27 729 Rm 28ᵈ and Toppes on 27 July 1443 (*CPR, 1441–6*, 189).

[86] Johnson (ed.), 'Extract from the Books of the Corporation of Norwich', 299.

[87] See C. R. Cheney (ed.), *Handbook of Dates for Students of English History* (London, 1970), table 31.

hardly violent, that it did not involve a seizure of power by a normally suppressed populace, and that it never seriously attempted to subvert established authority; therefore it cannot meaningfully be called a riot. It must be re-emphasized that in this affair there was no damage to life, limb, or property except for the breaking of the prior's stocks and prison. Even the threats of violence hardly seem very practicable. Though the 'rioters' organized mines and a gun to lend force to their siege, they had to kidnap Walter Aslak, a neighbouring gentleman and ex-soldier, lead him to the gun, and threaten him with defenestration unless he would aim it at the priory walls and prepare it for them 'sicut usitater est in ffrancia'; which speaks poorly for their revolutionary expertise.[88] There is no evidence that they succeeded, even by these means, in having the gun fired.

The anomalous lack of violence is only one factor which throws doubt on the 'riotous' nature of the affair. As Bellamy points out, 'riot' in the fifteenth century, could imply an uprising of the normally powerless populace; certainly the modern definition of violence presupposes a temporary seizure of power from the control of ruling groups, a sudden fall into lawlessness and chaos, and the prominence of a hitherto subservient section of the community.[89] Was there any reversal of power in favour of the common people in Norwich in 1443?

A survey of named participants of the riot suggests otherwise. Some of the more prominently named rioters, it is true, had not hitherto been among the most powerful men in the city government. Benedict Joly is perhaps typical of those described as having 'the rule of the city' in 1443. Though he may previously have been an active common councillor, he was never mayor, sheriff, or alderman.[90] John Gladman and Robert Suker never held office, and are hardly known outside the records surrounding the riot. Well-known office-holders, such as William Asshewell, Robert Toppes, and Edmund Bretayn were named as abettors of the 'rioters', not active participants. Yet the 'rioters' were hardly lower-class or marginal people. Joly was a chandler, who first appears in the assembly rolls in 1420. Both he and Gladman were paid-up members of that élite fraternity, the Guild of St George.[91] As

---

[88] KB 27 728 Rm 24 ff.

[89] Cf. the *OED* definition, 4a and b, and above, n. 2.

[90] KB 27 728 Rm 24ʳ, and N & NRO case 16, shelf d, fos. 3, 7ᵈ, and 8, for his attendance at assemblies.

[91] N & NRO case 8, shelf e (rolls of surveyors' accounts of the Guild of St George).

a whole, the participants were highly respectable citizens and bur-gesses. Sixteen of the ninety-eight people named in the longer indictment had held some city office (mayor, sheriff, alderman, common councillor, undersheriff, or auditor) and one was constable of a ward. The occupations of eighty-three are known. Of these, only five are designated labourers or servants; there were two gentlemen, five merchants and four lawyers among the supposed 'rioters'.[92] This list, then, confirms the impression given by the course of the dispute—that the outbreak was not an attempt by the powerless to overturn the structures of power, but a struggle between two divisions of the ruling class of the city.

What distinguished these groups was not greater or lesser wealth or respectability. Three known factors divided them; age, loyalty to the policy of individual wards within the city, and most importantly their attitudes towards the quarrel between the city and the priory. That riches were not a significant dividing principle is shown by the wills and financial dealings of both groups. If Thomas Wetherby was said to be 'a man of grete goodes', Robert Toppes cannot have been far behind him—he was one of only six out of all lay testators studied by Tanner to leave bequests to every parish church in Norwich (including £13. 6s. 8d. to St Peter Mancroft), and the only one to leave, besides, substantial amounts to seventeen other East Anglian churches.[93] The wills of such men as William Asshewell (1457) and John Folcard (1464) speak of comfortable circumstances.[94]. In 1430 John Caum-brigge, Richard Monesle, and Thomas Ingham joined, in unusual harmony, to lend £172. 16s. to the king.[95]

Nor were Asshewell and his friends absent from the social institu-tions of the ruling class. The certification of Wetherby's party in 1437 claimed that the election 'riot' was fomented by the 'most party of the Gilde called the Bacherye'; and one version of the King's Bench indictment of 1443 also specifies that members of 'quadam fraterni-

---

[92] The other 67 comprise the wife of another named defendant, 4 scriveners, 4 weavers, 7 fullers, 1 reder, 2 raffmen, 2 shearmen, 4 mercers, 2 drapers, 1 dyer, 4 tailors, 5 souters/cordwainers, 2 hosiers, 3 goldsmiths, 1 smith, 2 carpenters, 2 masons, 1 pewterer, 2 cutlers, 1 graver, 1 butcher, 1 taverner, 2 chandlers, 3 barbers, 2 bowyers, 1 parchmenter, 1 skinner, 2 loders, 2 barkers, and 1 minstrel.

[93] See the Liber Albus account (Hudson and Tingey (eds.), *Norwich Records*, i. 348); Tanner, *Church in Norwich*, 127.

[94] N & NRO wills, Brosyard, fos. 78–9 and 350–1.

[95] *CPR, 1429–36*, 61.

tatem . . . voc. le bachery' took part.[96] No doubt the Bachery was the junior guild; but even if it included members of the anti-Wetherby group, we know that until at least 1434, men who were, then and later, opponents of Wetherby were also active in the senior St George's guild.[97] Benedict Joly, for instance, contributed 6s. 8d. to it in 1429 and was still providing the guild's wax in 1434.[98] The dispute thus took place *within* the St George's guild as much as between the two guilds.[99]

Distribution of the members of the feuding groups by ward, however, does show a striking pattern. As Map 6.1 shows, Conesford was almost solidly behind its leading citizen Wetherby, whereas Mancroft and Wymer were equally solidly against him. (Indeed, two of Wetherby's three supporters in Mancroft—Peter and Richard Brasier—were both also Conesford men and may have owed their allegiance there.) Only the Ward-over-the-Water was equally divided. This suggests that political patronage was deeply embedded in the ward structure of Norwich; apparently, powerful aldermen built up their own empires in their home wards.

There was also, it seems, a distinct age-difference between the two groups. Known death dates for citizens are rare (and birth dates even more so). But we can calculate the ages of the disputing parties in 1437 from the earliest known dates at which they were adult.[100] Table 6.1 gives the results for thirty-three participants.

The bulk of Wetherby's supporters were apparently at least over forty, while by far the majority of his opponents were under that age. Similarly, an examination of the thirty-one known death dates shows that Wetherby's supporters on the whole died earlier than his antagonists; only two out of ten were alive after 1460, as compared to eleven out of 21 of his opponents.[101] Possibly, then, the Norwich government of the 1430s and 1440s was split between a group of formerly powerful, but aging, citizens, gathered around Thomas

---

[96] KB 9 229/1 m 106; and KB 27 746 m 29ʳ.

[97] We cannot check the membership of the Bachery, since no records survive.

[98] N & NRO case 8, shelf e. These accounts also show that Clement Rassh and his wife, John Gladman, and Thomas May were members, and that Richard Purdaunce, John Folcard, and John Goddes all contributed substantially to guild finances.

[99] Cf. Wetherby's attempt to pack the guild and (apparently) expel members from it, above, text accompanying nn. 34–7.

[100] Excluding those of whom 1437 is the earliest known record.

[101] Note that the samples of those whose death dates are known, and those for whom age in 1437 can be calculated, do not necessarily overlap.

TABLE 6.1. *Minimum ages of disputing groups in 1437*

Age group	25–9	30–4	35–9	40–4	45+	Total
Pro-Wetherby	1	3	2	7	2	15
Anti-Wetherby	4	4	8	2	0	18
TOTAL						33

TABLE 6.2. *Death dates of disputing groups*

	1437–40	1441–4	1445–9	1450–4	1455–9	1460–4	1465+	Total
Pro-Wetherby	0	1	3	1	3	1	1	10
Anti-Wetherby	1	1	1	5	2	3	8	21
TOTAL								31

Wetherby, whose platform was to admit the claims of the priory; and a group of men probably about ten years younger, eager to assume control of city policy, and firm in their opposition to the prior.

Increasingly, the whole series of events from 1433 to 1443 resembles, not a history of outbreaks of destablizing violence, but an extended competition between a set of authoritative bodies and personages for legitimacy, status, and power. The very actions undertaken by the participants underline this thesis. Why, for instance, did the 1443 'rioters' damage *only* the prior's prison and stocks? Surely they were influenced by the prevailing fifteenth-century reverence for the legitimating power of public law-enforcement.[102] They felt that the identity of their city, as legitimate corporation as well as territorial entity, depended on their settling the vital point of who was to be *seen* to have the right of holding courts in Holmstrete and the hamlets— whose legal officers were to be obeyed, whose prisoners brought to trial, whose inquests successfully held? Their continued attempts to administer justice in the disputed areas from 1417 onwards were, in practice, claims to power and authority. These challenges were met

[102] See Ch. 2.

on their own level by the priory. Both parties acted out their authority—the priory disputed arrests, arranged for the inquest of 1417, the oyer and terminer of 1441, and the special assize of 1442. The city presented the prior in its own courts, sent its officers to act in his areas of jurisdiction, and finally physically broke his prison and freed his prisoners. This last was a highly charged symbolic action. A fifteenth-century ruler who could not succeed in arresting and punishing wrongdoers could hardly be fit to rule.[103] To deprive the prior of his prison was to prevent him from performing one of his legitimating roles.

The force of ritual action here explains the necessity (in the eyes of some of the citizens) for Gladman's procession. For processions, aside from their wider significance, were potent events in the annual life of Norwich citizens. Not only was the new mayor ceremonially led to his home by the outgoing mayor every year; but there were civic processions at the feasts of All Saints, Christmas, and Epiphany, in which members of all crafts were bidden to attend the mayor, sheriffs, and aldermen in ranked order, to the cathedral. On every St George's Day, the saint's guild went in procession with the mayor and aldermen on horseback in livery, twenty-four priests clothed in red and white preceding them, cantors of the cathedral singing, the bells of the cathedral ringing, and a man dressed as St George, armed and mounted, battling a dragon through the streets.[104] The dragon was an ancient symbol of chaos, disorder, and enmity to the righteous God; its ceremonial annual slaughter triumphantly asserted the victory, in Norwich, of legitimate power over godless anarchy.[105] In this demonstration, the rulers of the city and the priory (as represented by the cathedral cantors and bells) were joined in one. Therefore the mere facts of Gladman's procession, in which ecclesiastical representatives

---

[103] See Chs. 2 and 3.

[104] Grace (ed.), *Records of the Gild of St George*, 16–18, 31, and 67.

[105] J. Le Goff, 'Ecclesiastical Culture and Folklore in the Middle Ages: Saint Marcellus of Paris and the Dragon', in id., *Time, Work and Culture in the Middle Ages*, tr. A. Goldhammer (Chicago, 1980), 159–88, esp. 181, postulates some relatively well-disposed medieval dragons; but the Norwich version seems to have been the antagonistic type. It spouted fire and smoke (in 1428, 2s. 4d. was paid to a man 'ludenti in dracone cum gonne powder', N & NRO case 8, shelf e, 1420–9), and the George, rather than placating it, was instructed to 'make a conflicte with the dragon' on both days of the procession (Grace (ed.), *Records of the Gild of St. George*, 67). The surviving 18th-cent. 'civic snap' (Castle Museum, Norwich) does not have the friendly aspect described by Le Goff.

were conspicuous by their absence, was an assertion of the citizens' capacity to order their world legitimately, on their own, without reference to the power of the prior.

Such pageantry, as Orgel points out, was for the benefit of the participant as much as the spectator—by such means, men showed themselves as they wished to be, and to be seen.[106] We must assume then, that Gladman and his friends—whatever excuses they later made—wished to become, as well as to be seen as, the legitimate rulers of the integral territory of the city. Presumably, this demonstration was also directed towards those citizens, such as Wetherby, who were thought to be jeopardizing the city's identity and freedom by too close an association with the prior's case.

Finally, it must be noted that the city and the priory, at least until 1443, apparently engaged in a competition to be seen as protectors of royal rights. If the priory claimed that the city had encroached on the king's geldable, the city replied by their ingenious argument that the priory was in breach of the statute of mortmain. Clearly both disputants were anxious *not* to be seen as riotous destabilizers of public order.[107]

Nevertheless, this was a competition which the priory won. The legitimating displays of the city, though they may have signified the city's determination to oust the authority of the priory from their territory, risked offending the king, from whom all lay power proceeded. John Gladman's followers were said to be attired like a king's valets; the king's ministers were allegedly shut out of the city.[108] The speed and rigour of the government reaction suggests that the king (or his advisors) appreciated fully the danger of allowing his subjects to fabricate their own authority to rule. Both royal revenues and royal right were at stake—on 14 March 1443, the privy council recorded that the king wished the submission of Norwich to be 'entred [of record] in þe largest & lowest wyse for his honour and worship'; while they later assigned 'monoie ȝt wol growe of þe fines at Norwich' to the victualling of Dieppe.[109] This reflects government fear of loss of authority; it does not actually prove that it was the citizens' intent to disturb the government. There is no evidence to support the accusa-

---

[106] S. Orgel, 'The Spectacles of State', in R. Trexler (ed.), *Persons in Groups* (New York, 1985), esp. 103.

[107] See above, nn. 18 and 78.

[108] See the indictments of Feb. 1443, above, nn. 4 and 82.

[109] *POPC* v. 242–4 and 307.

tion of a London serjeant of arms, engaged in arresting Benedict Joly, that he was a 'traytour' and 'oon of thoo for to make a newe Kyng'.[110] If this were the aim, why did they attempt to portray themselves as the upholders of just authority? Why did the city's representatives, immediately after the 'riot', ride post-haste to London to lobby the king's relatives for a pardon?[111] Indeed, they finally submitted, with exemplary humility, to royal power; seeing themselves less as its opponents than as sharers in its benefits.[112] Their own demonstrations, appealing to sound contemporary principles of hierarchical authority, did nothing to disturb the fundamental tenor of fifteenth-century government.

Nor, apparently, were the supposed rioters motivated by radical principles of ecclesiastical reform. There is a clear distinction between their attitude towards church institutions in general and the Norwich priory in particular. Their wills, far from displaying anti-clericalism, bear witness to marked devotion.[113] Edmund Bretayn left 6s. 8d. to his parish church in 1446, and 33s. to its fabric. Robert Toppes's outstandingly generous bequests have been referred to above. William Asshewell, in 1457, besides leaving money to St Peter Mancroft, and for various charitable endowments, gave 13s. 4d. to the Augustinian friars, 6s. 8d. to the Carthusians in London, 6s. 8d. to a Yorkshire monastery, and 3s. 4d. to two anchorites. All his books were to go to his son William if he would become a priest.[114] These men were not attacking ecclesiastical authority; they were competing for a share of its legitimating power in their home town.

---

[110] Hudson and Tingey (eds.), *Norwich Records*, i. 351. In any case, the making of this accusation may have been a matter of legend rather than fact, since it was not recorded until 1482 (Liber Albus account).

[111] The Liber Albus account states that the mayor and others were in London early in Feb., petitioning the duke of Gloucester to 'be her good lorde' in the dispute (ibid. 351). It also claims that the purpose of the visit was to answer to the council for the Jan. 'riots', which may well be true; but their willingness to appear, and their approach to Gloucester, suggests that they did not admit any guilt.

[112] See ibid. 114–22, for the city's petitions to the bishop of Norwich and the earl of Suffolk to intercede with the king for the return of their liberties, and the draft of the eventual restoration.

[113] In contrast to Storey's view that anti-clericalism must have played a part in the priory dispute (*End of the House of Lancaster*, 218).

[114] For Toppes, see above, n. 93; see also N & NRO wills, Wylbey fo. 136, Brosyard, fos. 78–9 (cf. Aleyn fos. 51–2 and 130–2—wills of Clement Rassh and Robert Blyklyng. The latter, said to have incited the crowd in 1437 and 1443, left 20s. to the nuns of Carrow, 6s. to a monk in St Albans, and 20s. to the monks of Norwich priory itself).

In the long term, the city's policy of calculated public bravado did it no harm. Suffolk's hated award of 1442 never was properly sealed;[115] after 1447 the city repaired the broken mills, argued their case again with the abbot of St Benet's Hulme (1481), and, after renegotiating the dispute with the priory (1517–24), finally brought it to a more favourable settlement.[116]

Violence had its place in this competition for authority. The right to impose violent sanctions on evil-doers, which was one token of authority, was implied in the administration of law. When the city claimed to be justified in arresting suspects and holding courts, they implicitly arrogated to themselves the right to institute whatever violent sanctions the law might allow. Similarly, the military bearing and company of knights witnessed to their just place in the hierarchy of honour and power. The unashamedly martial displays of January 1443 were no doubt intended to appeal to this ethic of chivalric glory. But even these militaristic demonstrations were rare in fifteenth-century Norwich. The threat of violence was used only as a last resort. More typically, law and negotiation served the citizens' ends. A letter of William Hempstede to Walter Gefferey, 9 October 1442, urging him to pursue the reformation of Suffolk's award, aptly sums up the prudent, legalistic, conservative (in the strict sense) approach to politics of these supposed 'rioters': 'take to ȝou as good counsell as ȝe can and be ware of þe sotelte of þe termeȝ and which termes bynde & which not and see sadly þat we spend not our monee for nouȝte'.[117] If this was the habitual tone of the disputants, it is no wonder that even their most flamboyant actions tended to rebuild, rather than destroy, the order of their society.

---

[115] An indenture survives, dated 10 Mar. 1443, between the mayor and aldermen of Norwich and the abbot of St Benet's Hulme (N & NRO case 9, shelf c); but it was proved in 1482 that William Hempstede, the mayor in 1443, could not have sealed it then, since records of the Fleet showed that he was imprisoned there from 13 Feb. to 20 Mar. (N & NRO case 9, shelf d). The Liber Albus account (Hudson and Tingey (eds.), *Norwich Records*, i. 352) insists that Wetherby 'and hys adherents' illegally used the common seal in 1443 to seal obligations to the city's opponents.

[116] Tanner, *Church in Norwich*, 145 and 152–4.

[117] N & NRO case 9, shelf c.

6.2 'Riots' by Accident: Bedford, 1437 and 1439

The fact that within a space of two years, court sessions in Bedford-shire were twice disturbed by armed confrontations, indicates the degree to which law and violence were bound up together in the fifteenth century. It does not show that one necessarily produced the other—at least seventeen undisturbed peace sessions were held in Bedford from 1422–42.[118] But as we shall see, it implies that the decentralized nature of the peace-keeping system allowed opportunities for the peace-keepers themselves to use violence, and—in the case of dispute among the county élite—made force one of the few efficient methods of settling arguments.

A plain recital of the events of 1437, when John Cornewaill, Lord Fanhope, and Reginald Grey of Ruthyn, came with their adherents to Silsoe to contest the right to hold sessions there, can be reconstructed from the privy council's examinations into the affair.[119] From these it is evident that the local community was already deeply divided by 1437, though no disturbance of peace sessions had been recorded before then. Cornewaill and Grey were undoubtedly the two most important landholders in the county. In some respects their careers were remarkably similar. Both had served under Henry IV; both had fought in France under Henry V. Their lands, at Ampthill and Silsoe, were barely three miles apart. Both had been active members of the Bedford peace commission since their return to England in 1422. Thus, though Cornewaill was some fifteen years younger than Grey, neither were newcomers, either to Bedford, or to gentry politics.[120]

On Thursday 16 May 1437 the dispute started, with the issue of a commission to William Luddesop (a diligent Bedford peace commissioner), William Pekke, John Fitz, and Henry of Lye to inquire into felonies, trespasses, insurrections, riots, rebellions, and concealments

---

[118] See Table 2.7.

[119] *POPC* v. 35. The disturbance took place on 21 May 1437 (deduced from the known date of the commission—*CPR, 1436–41*, 87—and the sequence of events as given by the examinee Pekke before the privy council).

[120] For Cornewaill, see A. C. Reeves, *Lancastrian Englishmen* (Washington, DC, 1981), ch. on Cornewaill; for Grey, see *DNB* entry. See also Table A3.5. Cornewaill was created Baron Fanhope on 17 July 1432 (*CPR, 1429–36*, 247); for consistency I name him Cornewaill throughout.

in Bedfordshire, and to make report to Chancery.[121] Both Pekke and Luddesop were clearly Cornewaill's men.[122] With unusual despatch, Pekke arranged for the sessions to be held on the following Tuesday.[123] The place chosen was Silsoe, the site of Grey's main manor in the county.

Pekke and Luddesop apparently turned up for the sessions accompanied by Cornewaill and his 'meyny'. While they were waiting to start, Grey himself, together with a member of his council (John Enderby), appeared at the head of a retinue allegedly numbering anything between 100 and 180 people.[124] Understandably annoyed by Cornewaill's incursion into his home territory, he asked Pekke and Luddesop their business. They showed him their commission, whereupon he announced his intention of staying to 'see what was doo þere þt day'. Pekke claimed that Enderby said that 'þe labour of þe said commision was stolen oute and laboured by nyȝte for to endite þe said Lord Greyes tenants'. This interchange was interrupted by the arrival of John Fitz, another frequent peace commissioner, accompanied by the parsons of Shitlington and Barton. The two clergymen then attempted to arbitrate the matter, suggesting that Cornewaill and Grey should withdraw their men to opposite sides of the town while the sessions were held. Grey (said Pekke) refused, demanding instead that the sessions be adjourned, 'for it wer no worship ... for [him] to departe & þe sessiones to be holden wher þt his tenants myȝt be greved'. Because of 'þinconvenience' or 'þe perell' likely to arise, the sessions were in fact deferred, apparently never to be held. They 'wolde have caused grochgyng' Fitz believed; Luddesop said that the jurors 'durst not have appiered'. The only solid result of the affair, Pekke stated, was that Grey and Cornewaill agreed to 'stande to thaward & arbitrement of certain persones as for þe mariage of a woman & for certain goods etc'.

Though we have no particulars of these hinted-at quarrels, the fact of prior disagreement is beyond doubt. It may well be that the purpose

---

[121] C 66/440 m 20[d]; Griffiths, *Henry VI*, 570 mistakenly says that it was a commission of oyer and terminer, and that it included Sir John Wenlock, who was not apparently named on any judicial commission in Bedford before 1448.

[122] See brief biographies, Appendix II.

[123] According to a later privy council examination (19 June, *POPC* v. 35). Further examinations were held on 28 June and 28 July (*POPC* v. 38–9 and 57–9).

[124] The allegations varied wildly; Pekke gave the numbers as 150–80, Luddesop put them at 100, rising later to 600, and Henry of Lye guessed 110–300 (*POPC* v. 36, 39, and 59).

of the original commission was to procure indictments of Grey's men. There seems little other justification for it. The disorders it was to investigate were never specified, and the normal peace commission (issued, for reasons which remain obscure, on the same day) should have been sufficient to deal with usual county malefactions. The one obvious distinction between the special commission and the peace commission was the allegiance of its membership. The special commission was apparently a mainly pro-Cornewaill group. Pekke and Luddesop were solid Cornewaill supporters; Henry of Lye is an obscure figure,[125] but his attempt to convince the council that Cornewaill's followers came innocently unarmed to the sessions implies a kindness towards Cornewaill.[126] John Fitz seems to be the only true Grey supporter; but though his name was on the commission, someone evidently decided at the last moment to exclude him from the running of the sessions—he told the council that 'he knewe not þt he was a commissioner in þe said [commission] til þt it was þe Tewsday in þe morow tyde þt þei sholde sitte'.[127] Pekke, Cornewaill's man, was entrusted with the preliminary arrangements of the session. Presumably then, Cornewaill's party decided at the last minute that whatever hopes they may have nourished of winning Fitz's support by naming him on the commission were not to be relied upon, and that it was safer to exclude him.

In contrast, the most diligent members of the ordinary peace commission were men either sympathetic to Grey (John Enderby and Thomas Wauton) or possibly neutral, such as Thomas Manningham. Wauton, in particular, was a man of formidable experience, a constant member of parliament since 1397, four times sheriff of Bedford and Buckingham, and a conscientious member of the peace bench. At any normal session, even if he were not presiding, his place on the bench was bound to be high, and his influence strong.[128] No wonder that it was worth Cornewaill's while to secure a different, and docile, set of commissioners, enabling him to take presentments against Grey's

---

[125] His name occurs only once elsewhere in the records, taking the oath against maintaining peace-breakers (*CPR, 1429–36*, 374).

[126] See below, n. 173.

[127] *POPC* v. 57.

[128] See Table A3.5 and the brief biographies in Appendix II. See also A. Hassell Smith, *County and Court: Government and Politics in Norfolk 1558–1603* (Oxford, 1974), esp. 60, for the importance of status and precedence at the peace sessions in Elizabethan Norfolk.

men, and to appear in the prestigious position of administering justice in Grey's own town. Only Grey's timely arrival prevented him from achieving these aims.

Yet Cornewaill refused to give up, and on 12 January 1439 at Bedford a second showdown in court between his and Grey's supporters took place. Fortunately, three separate accounts of this survive. The first is a certification, dated 12 January, returned by the four sitting justices (Sir Thomas Wauton, John Enderby, John Fitz, and Henry Etwell) and the undersheriff (Thomas Stratton). This formed the basis of a suit in King's Bench. A second certification, also pleaded in King's Bench, came from the rival justices Luddesop and Pekke, headed by Cornewaill, on 24 January.[129] The third account comes from the privy council examination of Wauton, Enderby, Fitz, Etwell, and Stratton on 10 and 24 February 1439.[130] All the versions differ, and it is from the variations themselves that the participants' motives in this interesting affair can be reconstructed.

Wauton originally claimed that Cornewaill interrupted the normal peace sessions, at which he had evidently presided with his three fellows. Cornewaill, it was claimed, brought with him 140 men armed with doublets of defence, iron caps, longswords, falchions, and war axes. Some of them stood outside the door of the hall, others crowded in so that the jurors could not approach the bench. Thomas Hasilden, one of Cornewaill's men, then picked a quarrel with Henry Etwell, openly calling him a liar with 'aliis verbis contumeliosis'. Then when a John Hamond, a constable, was accused of letting free a woman felon and selling to his own profit the goods she had stolen, Cornewaill bade him reply to the charge, at which he shouted that it was a lie. The goods in question had been taken from a gentleman named Stephen Creuker, and John Fitzgeffrey, apparently Creuker's relative by marriage, spoke up to defend the charge. Faced with this open quarrel, Wauton exclaimed that 'ibi fuit mirabilis gubernacio', and threatened to defer the sessions. Cornewaill then made him a rude gesture ('pugillum suum erga me . . . praetenso police [sic] inter duos digitos derisorie porrigendo') and said 'te diffido & querelam tuam & totam tuam maliciam', to which Wauton replied, 'diffidacionem tuam

---

[129] E 28 59, nos. 49–50 and KB 27 711 Rm 22^f for the certification of Wauton and his fellows; KB 27 713 Rm 3^f for the certification of Cornewaill, Luddesop, and Pekke.
[130] *Select Cases before the King's Council, 1243–1482* (Selden Society, 35; 1918), 104–7.

hic non reputo'. Cornewaill then sprang up ('surrexit et prosiliit') onto the chequer table and drew his dagger. (Wauton and his friends claimed that they were unarmed.) Cornewaill's supporters, following their leader, drew swords and assaulted some of the crowd. In terror, a mob of people attempted to get out of the hall by way of a flight of steps, and in the crush eighteen named men, five of them said to be Grey's tenants, were killed. Wauton's certification also alleged that some of the casualties could have been saved, but that Cornewaill's men kept would-be rescuers away; and that Cornewaill sent for his attorney, Thomas Kempston, and for the Bedford town coroners, to hold inquests on the bodies, maintaining armed men at the sessions, and thus provoking 'mirabilis infama' throughout all England.

In his certification, Cornewaill predictably alleged that it was Wauton and John Enderby who came to the sessions 'ex malicia' with over eighty men, mostly armed with swords. He claimed that Wauton refused to take presentments from the Bedford juries, proposing to postpone them until the next gaol delivery.[131] When he reprimanded Wauton for being 'too hasty' in this, Wauton replied 'malignandi' that he would complain of Cornewaill, who responded that he would think nothing of such a complaint. He attributed to Wauton the remark 'Ego te et maliciam tuam penitus diffido'. Enderby then drew both his dagger and his sword, whereat all Wauton's men unsheathed their weapons. He admitted to standing on the chequer table, and to seeing his own men with drawn swords, but said it was an attempt to quiet the crowd. However, seeing the weapons, some of the people fled down a wooden staircase, part of which collapsed, killing three of his own servants and fifteen others. Keeping faithfully to the statutory requirements for certifications, Cornewaill alleged that he had tried to have Wauton and Enderby arrested for causing this 'riot', but that they had fled. The fact that, contrary to the statute, neither the sheriff nor the undersheriff lent their names to the certification was, Cornewaill carefully explained, because Thomas Stratton the undersheriff was a godson to John Enderby and wore his livery, and therefore refused to certify.[132]

Under examination by the council, Wauton modified his original statement considerably. He still said that Cornewaill came to the

---

[131] Due on 27 Feb. (JUST 3 210 m 17ᵈ).

[132] Cf. 13 Henry IV c. 7 (above, n. 2). Stratton was also clerk of the peace sessions (*Select Cases*, 106, and E 372 282).

sessions with armed men, but the number, he now thought, was sixty rather than 140, and only two of them came 'within the barre'. The council evidently suspected an attempt either to exclude Cornewaill from the sessions, or to impugn his honour there, for Wauton and his associates were closely questioned over whether Cornewaill had been properly notified of the meeting, and how he had been greeted—had they, for instance done him 'eny reuerence' at his appearance? Wauton said he had not been forewarned, but that when he arrived, Enderby, Etwell, and Fitz all stood up, while he himself 'sitting stille avaled his hode'. (Enderby, examined later, claimed that 'thei stode up alle' at Cornewaill's arrival.) Continuing his examination, Wauton said that Cornewaill attempted to take over the presidency of the sessions—he

sat him doune and called to him John Fitz and William Pek and willed theime to sitte downe by him and the seid Fitz aduised [him] to take unto him Wawton and Enderby for thei were aboue [Fitz] in the commission, and [Cornewaill] answered theim Nay come and yee will the toon shal be wolcome the tother may chese; and this communicacion had thei sat downe to giders.

Evidently Fitz, awkwardly placed between two competing forces, had appealed to the rank-ordering of commissioners.

Asked how the quarrel arose, Wauton omitted all reference to John Hamond's derelictions of duty as constable, and said merely that there had been 'oncurteise langage' between John FitzGeffrey and a servant of Cornewaill's; though he noted that Hamond had replied to the charges against him by saying 'it was fals and so lyued the seid John Fitz Geffray'. He represented the exchange between himself and Cornewaill as follows:

WAUTON. It is the unruliest session that I haue euer sey in Bedford and yif it be not otherwise reuled I wol complaine unto the kynges counseill.
CORNEWAILL. Complaine as yo wole y defie thi manasing and all thine euel will.
WAUTON. I sette litil of thi defiance.

Wauton claimed that he did not actually see Cornewaill draw his dagger, though he saw one in his hand; and professed ignorance as to whether Cornewaill held it with the point downwards, or outwards to strike. He also said that neither Cornewaill nor any of his men struck anyone, and that when Cornewaill stood on the chequer table he strove 'alsoo diligently as euer he sawe man' to keep the peace in the hall. Cornewaill, he said, 'with his oune seruantz lete feleshipped the seid Wawton and other of his felaws unto theire logginges for theire more seuretee'. The other examinees in the main corroborated this account, though Enderby confessed to drawing his own dagger, and said that 'in the tyme of the rumor his man brought him a swerd'. Enderby and Fitz also stated that Cornewaill had not to their knowledge ever had a dagger in hand. Only Thomas Stratton, examined separately on 24 February, alleged that as Cornewaill 'stode upon the cheker borde he made countenance towarde Enderby as he wolde haue smete hem,' but said, 'he smote him not.'

Clearly the account given to the privy council had been laundered. It appears that by February some compromise had been reached between Cornewaill and his opponents, whereby all mention of casualties should be suppressed, Cornewaill credited with attempting to halt the disorder, Hamond's possible constabulary misdemeanours overlooked, and some appearance of unity among the county élite preserved. There was no longer any suggestion that Cornewaill had tried to arrest Wauton and Enderby, or that they fled from the scene. Instead, Cornewaill was represented as their benevolent lord, providing an appropriate retinue for their orderly withdrawal. Of course this was to the immediate advantage of both sides—it was on the grounds of 'divers discrepancies' between the examination and the certifications that the council decided on 7 March 1439 to allow Cornewaill to purchase a pardon. Wauton and his friends, too, were eventually pardoned on the following 30 May, for similar reasons.[133] The story given to the privy council thus functioned as a means of cancelling the actions the participants had caused to be brought in the crown side of King's Bench, which they could not withdraw on their own account. But the compromise was at the expense of the truth. What was the real course of the quarrel, and how does it reflect on the uses of law and violence in the county community?

The fact that both sides agreed on the number of deaths, and tried to throw the blame onto the other, inclines one to believe that there really were eighteen people killed; and since more of these were known to support Grey rather than Cornewaill, it may well be that Cornewaill's men had crowded out their opponents from the front of the hall, forcing them to the back where the crush eventually

---

[133] *CPR, 1436–41*, 246–7 and 282–3.

occurred.[134] Both certifiers agreed that Wauton had threatened (or proposed) to defer at least some of the session business. The hint that he invoked the gaol delivery may indicate that he was afraid of partisan interference, and wanted to secure the authoritative influence of the central court judges.

Corroborating traces of the dispute involving John Hamond also appear outside these records. An indictment at gaol delivery in 1439 alleged the robbery of Stephen Creuker's goods on 6 December 1438 by Katherine Wever; in the appeal which Creuker also made, the goods were alleged to have been in Hamond's keeping.[135] This is not to say that Hamond had definitely sold the goods in dereliction of his duty; but the case was clearly one in which Hamond's motives might be suspect. That he was thought to have used his position consistently to favour Cornewaill, is suggested by a petition he made to Chancery after Cornewaill's death in 1443; there he alleged that other Bedford men 'contynuelly sith the deth of the lorde fanhope knyght whom god assoile have ley in awayte . . . to sle' him, and that sureties of the peace had proved useless because 'they stonde soo in favour with the lorde Grey Ryffyn'.[136] This sounds like a programme of long-awaited vengeance.

In short, the consistent trend of the certifications and examination is to imply that the quarrel at the peace sessions, the indirect result of which was that eighteen people died, was basically over the honourable administration of law and justice. The issues were, for instance, whether Cornewaill or Wauton should have precedence on the bench, and what sort of 'reuerence' should be accorded to Cornewaill; whether Cornewaill's man John Hamond had overstepped his constabulary duty; whether the presence of Cornewaill and his men would undermine the operation of justice in the shire. There is little evidence of other disputes, such as over property, despite the propinquity of Ampthill and Silsoe. Grey's last dispute with the former owners of Ampthill dated from before 1415. Nor can the quarrel have stemmed, as Godber suggests, from purely personal animosity fuelled by Grey's resentment against a newcomer who 'threw his weight around' in

---

[134] Certainly Ralph Clerk, the coroner, named on Wauton's list of casualties, was replaced in office from 1439 onwards, see gaol delivery lists; JUST 3 219/3, 219/5, 220/1, 220/2, and 220/3, *passim*.

[135] JUST 3 220/2 m (7) S2 and S3; Wever was found guilty and sentenced to death (JUST 3 210 m 31ʳ).

[136] C 1 16/712.

county government.[137] For one thing, Grey was not even present in 1439. For another, Cornewaill was hardly a 'newcomer' to Bedford in 1437. He was probably nearly sixty, and had been on the Bedfordshire peace commission since 1406.[138] Although he was intermittently engaged in the French wars from 1412 to 1422 (and was therefore presumably less visible in county affairs)[139] from July 1423 he was an active peace commissioner in Bedford, a member of numerous loans commissions, and a commissioner to ascertain which Bedford men should pay the parliamentary grant of 1431.[140] Besides, Grey was not the aggressor in either case—the original element in the dispute as we know it was Cornewaill's partisan handling of the peculiar commission of 1437. We come back again to two questions; why was the running of the peace sessions such a vital issue to Cornewaill that he was prepared to go to such lengths to dominate it? And why did he choose 1437 as the time to mount his campaign?

It seems that despite his long association with Bedford, Cornewaill had found it difficult to gain a position of influence in the county society. His actions in 1437 and 1439 amounted to desperate—and not entirely unsuccessful—remedies to this situation. Control of county society depended above all on the goodwill of the sheriff and his underlings, and to a lesser extent of other officers such as justices of the peace, coroners, and local law-enforcers.[141] A brief survey of the officers of local government in Bedfordshire from 1422 to 1437 shows that Cornewaill had not succeeded in making these essential connections. In regard to the shrievalty, he owned no land in Buckingham, and must therefore have been unable to influence the choice of the six Buckingham men who held office nine times in the period 1422–37. Of the rest, Wauton was sheriff three times, and John Broughton (later a member of Grey's council) once. The only

---

[137] S. J. Payling, 'The Ampthill Dispute: A Study in Aristocratic Lawlessness and the Breakdown of Lancastrian Government', *English Historical Review*, 104 (1989), 889; J. Godber, *History of Bedfordshire 1066–1888* (Bedfordshire County Council; Bedford, 1969), 132; cf. Griffiths, *Henry VI*, 570.

[138] He was adult in 1401, when his name appears on an oyer and terminer commission to Devon (*CPR, 1399–1401*, 553).

[139] Reeves, *Lancastrian Englishmen*, 153–68; Grey was also occupied in France at this time, see *DNB* entry.

[140] See Table A3.5; his loans commissions were in 1422, 1426, 1428, 1430, 1431, 1434, and 1436; *CPR, 1416–22*, 417; *1422–9*, 355 and 481; and *1429–35*, 51, 125, 354, and 529; see also *CPR, 1429–36*, 137.

[141] See Ch. 2, text accompanying nn. 87–90.

period at which a known Cornewaill supporter held the post was from July to November 1434, when the death in office of James Gascoigne may have enabled Cornewaill unexpectedly to place his candidate. Nor does he seem to have been much more successful in getting his supporters onto the slightly less important commission of the peace. Of his associates in 1439, only two—William Beauchamp and William Luddesop—were commissioned before 1437, and only Luddesop sat at all frequently. Of the coroners, Thomas Chamberleyn, who served from 1425 to 1441, supported Wauton in the 1439 quarrel; Thomas Moreton, a Cornewaill man, did not sit as coroner until the death of Ralph Clerk at the unlucky 1439 sessions provided a vacancy.[142] Perhaps, then, on his return to England in 1422, Cornewaill found in Bedfordshire a closely knit governing community which allowed him no entry.

The geographical distribution of his and Grey's supporters (Map 6.2) confirms this. Cornewaill's supporters were much less widespread in the county than Grey's. Whereas Grey's men were spread over thirty-seven manors, Cornewaill's were found in only sixteen. Grey had twenty-two gentry supporters, of whom only three came from any one place. Five out of Cornewaill's sixteen gentry supporters—and sixteen of his thirty-five non-gentry supporters—came from his own town of Ampthill.[143] Many of them were probably paid servants: fourteen received bequests in his will (1443) as members of his household.[144] Such names as Patrick Irysshman and Matthew Walsshman indicate that some were not local men. It was Cornewaill who brought supporters from as far away as London and Hereford into the dispute. Finally, at Risley and Goldington, even though the gentry were on Cornewaill's side, the lesser men were not. There are no contrary cases of tenants appearing on Cornewaill's side while the gentry were on Grey's. All this suggests that Cornewaill's support in the county was of a peculiar and limited type. He relied largely on his personal following, directly paid for, rather than on a solid network of county interest; and such support as he did have was probably fairly recently gained.

---

[142] For his service, see JUST 3 219/3, 219/5, 220/1, 220/2, and 220/3, *passim*.

[143] Not all participants appear on the map, since the home locations of some cannot be ascertained.

[144] Assuming that the 'Patry' and 'Mathew' mentioned in the schedule of bequests can be identified with the Patrick Irysshman and Matthew Walsshman of the King's Bench record—otherwise 12. See H. Jenkinson and G. H. Fowler (eds.), 'Some Bedfordshire Wills at Lambeth and Lincoln', *Publications of the Bedfordshire Historical Record Society*, 14 (1931), 108–9.

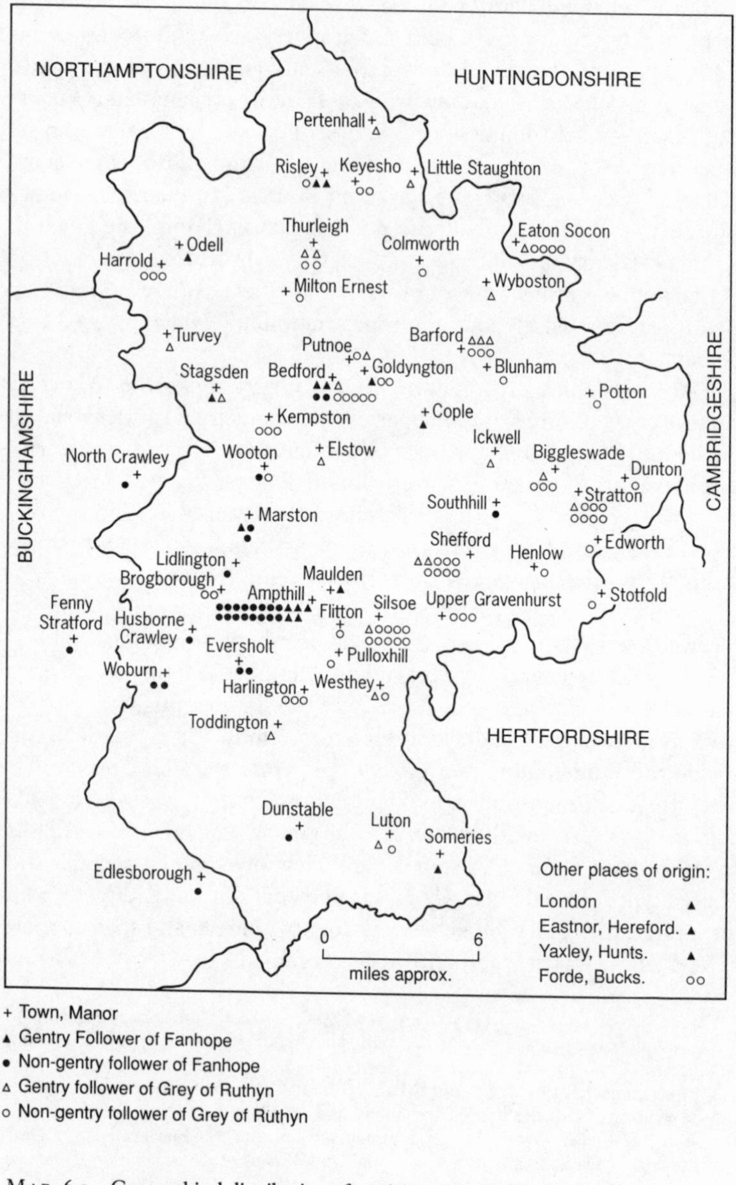
NORTHAMPTONSHIRE
HUNTINGDONSHIRE
BUCKINGHAMSHIRE
CAMBRIDGESHIRE
HERTFORDSHIRE
Pertenhall
Risley
Keyesho
Little Staughton
Thurleigh
Colmworth
Eaton Socon
Odell
Harrold
Milton Ernest
Wyboston
Turvey
Putnoe
Barford
Stagsden
Bedford
Goldyngton
Blunham
Potton
Kempston
Cople
Ickwell
North Crawley
Wooton
Elstow
Biggleswade
Dunton
Stratton
Southhill
Marston
Shefford
Edworth
Lidlington
Henlow
Brogborough
Maulden
Ampthill
Flitton
Silsoe
Upper Gravenhurst
Stotfold
Fenny Stratford
Husborne Crawley
Eversholt
Pulloxhill
Woburn
Harlington
Westhey
Toddington
Dunstable
Luton
Someries
Edlesborough
0
6
miles approx.
Other places of origin:
London
Eastnor, Hereford.
Yaxley, Hunts.
Forde, Bucks.
+ Town, Manor
▲ Gentry Follower of Fanhope
● Non-gentry follower of Fanhope
△ Gentry follower of Grey of Ruthyn
○ Non-gentry follower of Grey of Ruthyn

MAP. 6.2 Geographical distribution of participants in the Bedford 'riots'

Of course he was not powerless in the county legal system before 1437. He seems to have attacked the problem at a lower level. The activities of John Hamond suggest that he had managed to buy some constabular support, and his men are fairly often found on jury panels at gaol deliveries.[145] Nicholas Ravenhull, for instance, was named in February 1428 and February 1436, and John Caldecote in 1425.[146] When James Fynaunce, one of Cornewaill's most trusted clients, was indicted in February 1434 of the murder of Agnes Kempston, Cornewaill had at least six of his men on the panel, and three were eventually sworn.[147] The jury duly found Fynaunce not guilty, and accused another man altogether of the murder.[148] As early as 1427, Cornewaill marshalled his forces to protect Thomas Kempston, the mayor of Bedford, in a protracted quarrel with Hugh Hasilden, another Bedfordshire gentleman.

In this dispute, Kempston was originally accused to having aided and abetted the murderers of John Meskeburgh, a servant of Hasilden's, on 24 July 1427.[149] It was perhaps in retaliation for this accusation that Cornewaill presided at the peace sessions on 15 September 1427 which took an indictment against a number of men for attempting to assault Kempston. When Kempston was indicted at the peace sessions of 22 January 1428, before the duke of Norfolk, the earl of Huntingdon,[150] John Enderby and Hasilden himself, for raising Bedford town against Hasilden, and carrying out a series of

---

[145] Hamond was left 4 marks in Cornewaill's will (ibid. 109).

[146] JUST 3 219/3 m (8) S4 and 220/1 m (11) S3; also JUST 3 219/3 m (8) S2.

[147] Fynaunce was left 20 marks in the will, and given custody of Cornewaill's bastard son Thomas (Jenkinson and Fowler (eds.), 'Some Bedfordshire Wills', 108–9).

[148] JUST 3 220/1 m (15) S, S3, and S4; also JUST 3 209 m 48.

[149] He was eventually acquitted (Michaelmas 1428) (KB 27 668 m 79^r and 671 Rm 3^r). Hasilden had already appeared before the assize judges (30 July 1427) to acknowledge his debt for 'debat. & discordia' between him and Kempston; and by 2 Dec. 1427 the quarrel was so serious that Hasilden was brought before the council to give £100 security of peace towards Kempston (*POPC* iii. 280–1).

[150] The role of these noblemen in the affair is unclear. Hasilden was a tenant of the duke of Norfolk (see *Feudal Aids*, i. 43); and both Norfolk and Huntingdon sat at 8 peace sessions in Bedford at this period, though neither is known to have attended any session in any other East Anglian county to which he was commissioned. It may be, then, that Hasilden was a client of one or both; but no other evidence can be found of any particular connection between the three. Indeed, Huntingdon and Norfolk may have been attending sessions for other reasons; see, for an account of their alleged antagonism at this period, R. Archer, 'The Mowbrays, Earls of Nottingham and Dukes of Norfolk, to 1432', D. Phil. thesis (Oxford, 1984), 258–61. John Enderby was an annuitant of Huntingdon (E 163 7/31/2); but whether this accounts for Huntingdon's presence on the bench is doubtful.

extortions 'colore officii' (August to December 1427), Cornewaill, with Luddesop and John Hamewell of Huntingdon (another of his followers in 1439), stood mainpernor for Kempston.[151]

This case shows well the limitations of Cornewaill's power in Bedfordshire. He had some supporters in official positions (such as Kempston); and by 1439 may have constituted himself as protector of Bedford town interests (he claimed specifically that Wauton refused to take presentments from Bedford juries).[152] He could supply his men with bail, some jury support, and the advantage of his presence at peace sessions. But these facilities were hardly commensurate with his status and position. They were the sort of services that any reasonably prosperous county gentleman might offer his friends. He clearly did not have that lordly influence over the higher echelons of the county administration which could prevent charges from being levied against his people in the first place. Nor could he be said to resemble the ideal of the perfect knight, who from a God-given eminence dispensed at will peace to the innocent and punishment to the guilty. The fifteenth-century belief in the divinely-ordained duty of the upper classes to repress violence and uphold justice entailed the reverse significance—one of the ways to tell a powerful man and a true knight was by his exercise of justice.[153] This link between property, power, and legal authority was widely enforced in the fifteenth-century mind by the system of manor courts.[154] It was also acted out daily by the patrons of the county hierarchy, whose influence in the legal system allowed them to protect supporters and harass enemies through safe legal means, rather than the dubious use of unjustified force.[155]

No wonder, then, that Cornewaill and his men were so concerned to gatecrash the peace-keeping system of Bedfordshire, or that his opponents were determined to keep him out. For each group, the public exercise of justice was vital, both for their real power in the county, and for their status in the eyes of their peers. Clearly, in 1439, Cornewaill intended his entrance to the sessions to be a public drama,

---

[151] KB 27 668 Rm 19[r]. The case disappeared from the King's Bench record with no recorded punishment of Kempston.

[152] See above.

[153] See Ch. 3; also my 'The Legitimation of Power; Riots and Authority in Fifteenth-Century Norwich', *Parergon*, NS 6a (1988), 65–84.

[154] See Ch. 2.

[155] See Ch. 2.

affirming his precedence on the bench by word, gesture, and role-play. The nature of the quarrels that arose in the session, with their repeated 'giving of the lie', and the formal defiance and rebuff between Wauton and Cornewaill, shows clearly that the matter was one of gentleman's honour.[156] As if in a duel, the knightly status of each participant was at stake. The only distinguishing feature of this honour occasion was that it was neither tournament, duel, nor knighthood ceremony—just the ordinary running of a normal element in the structure of county government.[157] Similarly, in 1437 the administration of the legal system was an issue crucial to both parties. Why? Because, had the sessions been held by Cornewaill in Grey's town, Grey's 'worship', along with his tenants' safety, would have been jeopardized; and Grey's lost honour was Cornewaill's gain.[158] Hence Grey's council, countering the commission so ostentatiously displayed by Pekke and Luddesop, claimed that Grey and his supporters on the quorum of the peace commission could 'holde þis day sessiones her . . . & enquer as wel for þe [king] as þei'.[159] So eager were both sides to be seen to be administering justice that it was only with great difficulty—and with reference to the opinion of so eminent a lawyer as John Cokayn—that it was agreed to abandon the sessions.[160]

It may be asked why Cornewaill's aim of increasing both his real and symbolic power in the county was better served in 1437 by his obtaining a separate commission than by having his nominees made justices of the peace. If his influence was sufficient for the one, surely it could compass the other? To a certain extent this point is sound; as we shall see, the strategy did not seem to bring immediate success. Perhaps he had as well a specific purpose in mind, such as indicting Grey's men. Having his own men on the peace commission would not necessarily achieve this, since, as we have seen, Grey commanded the loyalty of some of the most diligent and experienced men on the bench. The dominance of Grey's supporters at peace sessions would also have hampered Cornewaill's quest for visible status. As Fitz's

---

[156] See J. Pitt-Rivers, 'Honour and Social Status', in J. G. Peristiany (ed.), *Honour and Shame: The Values of Mediterranean Society* (London, 1965), for the formulaic character of these honour-terms.

[157] Cf. M. E. James, *English Politics and the Concept of Honour, 1485–1642* (Past and Present Society Supplement, 3; Oxford, 1978), 24.

[158] See above, p. 207.

[159] *POPC* v. 37; see also 39 and 57.

[160] *POPC* v. 59.

comments on the right rank-ordering of justices showed, Cornewaill's nominees, had he succeeded in placing them, might be expected to give place at peace sessions to the pro-Grey establishment for some years to come, the remarkable stability of peace commissions ensuring that the advent of Cornewaill's men would not of itself result in the removal of Grey's.[161] Cornewaill may have thought that both his current quarrels and his county status were best pursued by the issue of a separate commission.

But the reaction of the privy council to the danger of riots arising in 1437 in fact promised only limited success to Cornewaill. First, they made sure that the gaol delivery succeeding the confrontations of 1437 was attended by such prestigious figures as the bishop of Lincoln, the earls of Huntingdon and Suffolk, and the justices John Cottesmore and John Fray, all of whom might be expected to impress the sessions into order and impartiality.[162] In itself, this helped Cornewaill only in so far as it limited the actions of Grey's supporters. Secondly, the affair evidently led the council to make some changes to the peace commission. Though this was potentially in Cornewaill's interest, the changes were in fact in Grey's favour. On 13 June 1437, Sir Henry Brounflete, Henry Etwell, and Sir John Grey joined the commissioners. Brounflete, a king's knight and experienced diplomat, was never named again, and may have been included to keep a governmental eye on the feuding parties.[163] Both Etwell and John Grey, however, must have been Grey's nominees.[164] The council's action here may reflect their dissatisfaction with Cornewaill's part in the 1437 dispute.

After 1439, however, a change of mind is evident. Cornewaill himself evidently thought the examination of 10 February 1439 was favourable to him, since he petitioned the king for an official exemplification to be made of it.[165] The peace commission of 12 March 1439 omitted those notable Grey supporters Enderby, Fitz, Wauton, and Etwell. (John Grey of Ruthyn remained, perhaps because of his close connection with Grey, perhaps because he was not present at the disturbance.) Of these, only Wauton was ever

---

[161] See Ch. 2.
[162] JUST 3 220/2.
[163] Brounflete was appointed ambassador to the general council at Basle in 1434 (*CPR, 1429–36*, 339).
[164] See brief biographies, Appendix II.
[165] E 175 File 4 5.

reinstated, though all were pardoned in May 1439. Even Wauton had to wait until 1443, after Cornewaill's death, to resume his place. It is true that Cornewaill too lost William Pekke from the 1439 commission, but he was reinstated in 1440. It also seems certain that Grey managed to have John Broughton commissioned for the first time in 1439, and may have influenced the choice of Roger Hunte the lawyer, who had last been named on a Bedfordshire commission seventeen years before.[166] But overall the position of Grey's men on the commission was weakened, both numerically, and (perhaps more significantly) in terms of the experience and seniority they could exercise. From this time onward, Cornewaill's supporters seemed to take more prominent positions in the county government. In November 1438, Sir John Wenlock (named on Cornewaill's side in 1437 and 1439) became escheator, and in 1439 he was knight of the shire with William Pekke.[167] It seems that 1439 marked the beginning of Cornewaill's success in upgrading his county status.

Why he chose 1437 as an appropriate time to improve his standing in Bedford cannot be explained with perfect certainty; but a reasonable guess may be made at some of the long-term considerations with which he was juggling. His own chances of survival must have exercised his mind, along with the likelihood of Grey's imminent decease at the age of 75. Sir John Grey, Reginald's heir apparent, had so far played little or no part in Bedfordshire affairs.[168] Cornewaill may have decided that it was time to push his claims in county government, in readiness to fill any power vacuum created by Grey's death. Further, by May 1437, his standing at court was high. He consistently attended council (of which Grey was not a member) and was one of the twenty greatest lenders to the government in the period 1432–42. He was thus well placed to support such a power-play.[169] He may even have believed that county feeling was turning his way, and that a display of power and authority would consolidate his support. Hugh Hasilden, for instance, the erstwhile opponent of

---

[166] J. S. Roskell, *The Commons in the Parliament of 1422* (Manchester, 1954), 193.

[167] J. S. Roskell, *Parliament and Politics in Late Medieval England* (2 vols.; London, 1981), ii. 235.

[168] See above, nn. 120 and 138, and the *DNB* entry for Grey; John Grey was deputy of Ireland 1427–8, and appears on no Bedford commission before 1437. Cornewaill was not to know, of course, that John Grey would predecease his father, dying in 1440.

[169] *POPC* iv. 339–40, v. 6, 7, 9, 13–14, 65–6, 71, 108, 153, 157–9, 163, 167, 173, 210–15, 218–19, and 223, for examples up to 1443. See also A. Steele, *The Receipt of the Exchequer 1377–1485* (Cambridge, 1954), 257.

Cornewaill's attorney, died at some time between 1435 and 1437.[170] His heir, whatever his father's politics, became a strong Cornewaill supporter, described as 'his man' in Wauton's certification of 1439.[171] As the aftermath of 1439 shows, Cornewaill was able to persuade or force even such men as Enderby and Wauton to suppress some truths unfavourable to him at their council examination. By the Hilary term of 1442, John Enderby's son had been sued by his father for offences allegedly committed together with John Gerveys, a gentleman named in the 1439 certification as Cornewaill's supporter, and bequeathed £5 in Cornewaill's will.[172] Perhaps, then, Cornewaill had managed to sway the balance of favour in Bedford county government.

What was the role of violence in this struggle for county authority? No doubt both sides in both 1437 and 1439 brought some armed men to their support, though the determination of each party to minimize the tale of their own weaponry, and exaggerate that of their opponents, makes an accurate assessment of weapon-carrying difficult. In 1437, Pekke alleged that Enderby's 100 to 120 men had 'bowes some bent arowes palatts ... doubletts of defense & gisarmes & polaxes & staves'; his companion Henry of Lye claimed that among Cornewaill's men 'þere were non haberjons but oon þt Wenlok had & on oþer'.[173] But Fitz said that Grey's men 'wer not defensably arraied' and that holding the sessions would have caused bad feeling partly because 'þe Lord Fanhop was arraied & the Lord Grey unarraied'.[174] Wauton's and Cornewaill's conflicting and fluid views of the level of their own, and each other's, armed support in 1439 have already been noted.[175] Probably then some men at both gatherings (though fewer than was alleged) had serious weapons.

But that the intended use of these was to perpetrate violence is by no means clear. Both parties may have recognized the legal implications of arms-carrying—that it helped to establish the intention to assault, riot, or murder. This would explain their strenuous attempts

---

[170] He was named on the peace commission of Jan. 1435, but by May 1437 Thomas Hasilden was described as his heir (*CCLR, 1435–41*, 120).

[171] KB 27 711 Rm 22ʳ.

[172] See above, n. 144; Jenkinson and Fowler (eds.), 'Some Bedfordshire Wills', 109; and KB 27 723 m 61ʳ for John Enderby senior's case (assault and imprisonment of a servant in Sept. 1441).

[173] *POPC* v. 36, 37, and 59.

[174] *POPC* v. 39 and 57.

[175] See above.

to implicate their opponents and excuse themselves in the matter. But it is hard to see what actual exercise of violence can have been contemplated by either Grey or Cornewaill. An open attack on a fellow knight, outside of war, could hardly have been justified by the fifteenth-century moral code of violence, and would not have advanced the claims of either to authoritative status. To our knowledge, no one was actually hurt in 1437, and the only deaths in 1439 were purely accidental. There are no allegations in 1439 that Cornewaill came attempting to assault the justices, or that Wauton's friends attacked Cornewaill, which one might expect if genuine violence had been intended or carried out. Instead, both sides collaborated to suppress the history of the accident before the privy council. No individual actions relating to any of the deaths ever reached the central courts, which indicates that the county community, whatever its various allegiances, accepted a *de facto* verdict of accidental death on the unfortunate victims. Similarly, the brief accounts of the affair which reached the London chronicles and the *Brut* show that the writers thought it an accident—as the *Great Chronicle* puts it, 'at Bedford on the shire day were xviij men atte ones murdred myschevously *withoute ony stroke* in fallyng doune hedeling atte steyer of here shirehous'.[176] All chroniclers put the affair in the context of other natural disasters currently afflicting the realm, such as the death of the earl of Warwick, and a great famine.

The real function of these warlike assemblies, I suggest, was to back up claims of power and status with the panoply of honourable might and the threat of force, rather than to perpetrate violence. Each leader was trying to show, with the maximum of ostentation, that he was the true wielder of the 'swerd to punchyn schrewys'.[177] Each armed retinue demonstrated to the other the strength and valour of their opponent's knightly standing, and his firm commitment to pre-eminence in county business. The threat of violence led not to assault, but to arbitration and compromise. Competition, not aggression, was the order of the day.

It is thus extremely doubtful whether these activities legitimated physical violence. Griffiths thinks they did—that the tenants of greater

---

[176] *Great Chronicle*, 174 (emphasis mine). Note how this illustrates again a very unspecific definition of murder; cf. *Brut*, 507, and *Joannis Lelandi Antiquarii de Rebus Britannicis Collectaneorum*, ed. T. Hearne (n.p., 1715), i/2, 492. (From its subject-matter, this appears to be another version of the *Brut*.)

[177] *Dives 2*, 13; and see Ch. 3.

landowners accepted as commonplace the 'kind of violence to which their superiors were addicted in order to settle their quarrels'. Thus he considers the Bedford disturbance a 'sorry tale' often repeated in Henry VI's reign.[178] But in fact, such ceremonial display of power was appropriate only to the knightly classes; one may doubt whether it was commonly seen by tenants and husbandmen as a role model. The mere threat of real violence caused great apprehension—when the hall erupted into uproar, Wauton called it 'the unruliest session that I haue ever see in Bedford' and threatened to close the sessions. I know of no other disturbances on such a scale at peace sessions in East Anglia from 1422 to 1442, and Wauton's comment, together with the appearance of the incident in chronicles of national affairs, surely indicates that it was thought most abnormal for such knightly competitions of precedence to get out of hand.

Nevertheless, it is significant that violence was the threat which both sides, in the end, found most effective. Others were used—to oppose one court session with another, to report an offender to the privy council—but ultimately it was the threat of violence that prevented possibly partisan sessions from being held, and which persuaded the privy council to act to ensure the integrity of the peace sessions, and to bolster Cornewaill's position in the community. Partly, this was the result of the peculiar circumstances of the dispute. The quarrel itself was concerned with the administration of the law, so neither party could use the law properly to provide a remedy. The decentralized structure of law-keeping (which was effectively in the hands of the local élite) demanded an undivided county establishment for its efficient operation. It was the breakdown of this necessary consensus that in Bedford in 1439 resulted—probably without any murderous intent on the part of the antagonists—in the deaths of eighteen innocent people.

But equally, the quarrels and the deaths were partly the result of the peculiar position of violence in the power-structure of fifteenth-century England. Knightly violence helped to legitimate power. A claimant to authority, though he might not actually harm anyone, had to display publicly the capacity to exact violent redress for injury. Violence was made implicit in government; the quarrels in Bedford in 1437 and 1439 show how this submerged violence could, under

---

[178] Griffiths, *Henry VI*, 136 and 142.

certain conditions, surface to cause an unintended and yet perhaps inevitable tragedy.

In these two instances of large-scale public demonstrations, as in the five studies of individual cases in Chapter 5, it may seem that alleged, rather than performed, violence was the order of the day. Nevertheless, the threat of violence was there; it took its place in the complex interweaving of force, litigation, and display that typified the constant competition for honour and authority in the gentry society of fifteenth-century England.

7

VIOLENCE AND SOCIAL ORDER

It should now be clear that the simple question, 'was late-medieval East Anglia a violent society?' is capable of many true answers. In terms of whether physical violence occurred frequently, the answer may be no. We have little hard evidence that assault, riot, or murder were even commonly alleged. All court statistics show allegations of non-violent crimes vastly outnumbering accusations of violence against the person. Moreover, the case-studies of Chapters 5 and 6 have shown how instances of alleged violence—such as those made by Sir Henry Inglose against his Dilham tenants—have a disturbing tendency to shrink, dislimn, or metamorphose when subjected to historical scrutiny.

Yet as we have seen, the 'violence' of the fifteenth century has played an important role in many of the historical debates concerning late-medieval English politics and society. The repression of violence (or lack of it) has been taken to be the measure of governmental success; the violence of magnates and their retainers has been used to demonstrate and characterize the social and political structures of the age. The violent quarrels of the nobility are still cited as important elements in explaining the outbreak and progress of the Wars of the Roses.[1] If we have little proof that there was a high level of violence in late-medieval England, what becomes of these debates?

To a certain extent, the historiographical focus has already shifted away from these areas. The study of English fifteenth-century provincial societies, for example, was stimulated by the perceived need to analyse the role of bastard feudalism in the counties in bringing about

---

[1] Most recently, S. J. Payling, discussing the effects of the Ampthill dispute on the duke of Exeter's allegiance to the crown, observes that though Storey may go too far in attributing the fall of the Lancastrian dynasty to the effects of magnate quarrels, 'there can be no doubt that these feuds undermined traditional Lancastrian loyalties' ('The Ampthill Dispute: A Study in Aristocratic Lawlessness and the Breakdown of Lancastrian Government', *English Historical Review*, 104 (1989), 881–907, quoting from p. 881).

a breakdown of public order, and the end of the Lancastrian regime. Yet the most recent studies have tended to emphasize not the violence of provincial society, but the uses of litigation, arbitration, and non-violent debate in the maintenance of an ordered local community.[2]

Does this mean, then, that the question of violence has lost its significance? Far from it; for as I have noted in Chapter 1, the realization that the rate of violence in late-medieval England is not accurately discernible leaves unanswered the great questions of the nature and function of whatever violence was practised in fifteenth-century England. Furthermore, this study of the nature of fifteenth-century violence shows clearly that violence and the law were inextricably and intricately connected in late-medieval English society. We have little chance of understanding the purposes and progress of fifteenth-century litigation and arbitration without analysing the role of violence.

In analysing the relationship of law and violence in the fifteenth century, we must first discard the modern tendency to place violence at an opposite moral pole to the law. For fifteenth-century East Anglians, both violence and the law could be used to protect and establish divine, social, and political order. Indeed in many ways violence and the law acted as complementary equals to achieve these great tasks.

That the law in medieval England was both an agent and sustainer of political and social authority comes as no surprise. The structure of feudal land-holding necessitated a close connection between land-holding, law-giving, and political power. To judge cases in a court—whether king's court, peace sessions, or manor court—was a sign of authority; to attend a court to hear judgment of a case, whether as suitor or defendant, was to acknowledge tacitly an acceptance of that authority. Partly for these reasons, as we have seen in Chapter 2, even county peace sessions engaged the eager attention of the provincial upper classes. It was the local gentry who willingly undertook to provide justices of the peace, sheriffs, and other court officials. The reputation and honour of the gentry was to some extent determined by their ability to make effective use of the law in defending both their properties and their servants. No wonder, then, that they were enthusiastic and skilful litigants.

[2] See e.g. Saul, *Scenes from Provincial Life*; Wright, *Derbyshire Gentry*; Bellamy, *Bastard Feudalism and the Law*.

In contrast, the role of violence in constructing and maintaining systems of authority has perhaps been underestimated. Yet as an analysis of the conceptualization of violence shows, the power to judge and punish wrongdoers with immediate violence was, in the fifteenth century, an integral part of the authority of the greatest ruler of all— God. The view that God delegated to earthly knights and magistrates the sword to punish miscreants and protect the innocent was, as we have seen, widespread and orthodox in fifteenth-century England. The exercise of violence, then, was thought to be essential in the maintenance of moral and civil order. Furthermore, fifteenth-century views of violence incorporated the notion that by analogy with the ultimately salutory violence suffered by Christ, which brought peace to all humankind, the forces of right violence could meet and subdue disruption and disorder, transforming them into harmony and peace.

This moral order of violence was quintessentially hierarchical. The power to judge and execute descended from God to kings and knights, and kings in their turn delegated this authority to their judges, justices, and lieutenants. This chain of authority legitimated right violence, whether in the form of a just war, or simply just punishment of the guilty. For both knights and justices, the authority of a lawful monarch, good motives, and good means were the three factors which ensured that the violence they practised would further the divine plan for human social order. Thus the exercise of violence became both the duty and the hallmark of legitimate authority.

Yet how could the justness of any particular violent act be determined? The answer in part was by the king's law. In literal daily practice, the king's justices were empowered to hear complaints of murders, assaults, robberies, and riots, and to bring juries to decide, in any of these cases, whether the violence complained of had taken place, and if so, whether it was felonious or pardonable. If the violence were found to be unjustifiable, then by law the felons were subjected in their turn to a violent death. This is no mere theory. The analysis of gaol delivery verdicts in Chapter 4 has shown that over one-third of alleged homicide cases—often those which violated some principle of social hierarchy—attracted the death-sentence. The theory that unjust violence could be conquered by the use of righteous violence was thus directly reflected in the practice of the lawcourts. Moreover, it should be noted that execution was apparently used to combat not only violent crime, but also non-violent misdeeds—such as the persistent theft of gentry property—which would tend to remove and redistribute the signs of social order.

Violence and law were thus intricately entwined in the process of the legitimation of power and authority. Prospective users of right violence needed the sanction of the law, both in and out of the courts, to legitimize their actions. Thomas Denys knew that the authority of the sheriff could give the colour of righteousness to any attack he made on his enemies.[3] William Dallyng was reputedly expert at disguising robbery and extortion under the dress of official duty, and was himself imprisoned in chains by form of law.[4]

The law had power to distinguish right from wrong violence. Yet the law itself was sustained by the public and open use of violence. As the examination of the quarrels between the prior and the city of Norwich in Chapter 6 shows, the rivals attempted to demonstrate their authority over disputed areas by much-publicized arrests and imprisonments. The law allowed the possibility, in approvers' battles, of violence literally deciding the issue of a case. The ability to impose the violent punishments of the law on criminals was vital to anyone in authority. Thus in Norfolk in the 1420s, Lollards, whose principles denied to rulers the right to punish by violence, were whipped and burned in public reaffirmation of the order of church and state; while in Norwich in 1443, the citizens, seeking to deny the prior any power in their city, took care to break the stocks with which he punished wrongdoers.[5]

Even when no punishment was actually imposed, the right of those in authority to distinguish and punish cases of disorder was of the utmost importance to the upper classes of fifteenth-century England. As Chapter 4 shows, the legal authorities were especially eager to bring to court cases of alleged violence against the person, even if few guilty verdicts resulted.[6] Evidently the prestige of the law benefited merely from the courts being seen to be examining cases of violence. The agents of earthly authority—kings, knights, justices, and judges— were apparently expected to be constantly on the alert, ready to carry out godly violence, distinguishing the innocent from the guilty, protecting the helpless, and chastising the wicked. To be willing and able to perform this duty was to appear honourable and authoritative in fifteenth-century eyes. No wonder then that Sir John Cornewaill, a

---

[3] *PL* ii. 234.   [4] See Ch. 5.2.
[5] See Ch. 4 and Ch. 6.1.   [6] See Ch. 4, Table 4.1.

king's knight, felt himself compelled to challenge Sir Reginald Grey and his men for pre-eminence in the peace sessions of his local community.[7]

In short, right violence could be justified by the law, and was therefore dependent on it; but the law also gained authority from the use of public violence, and needed to be seen as the forum where violent actions were judged. Not surprisingly, then, the upper classes of fifteenth-century East Anglian society kept their honourable status, and maintained the distinctions of hierarchical order in their world, by the use of both chivalric courage and the law. Cornewaill and Grey, for instance, probably both arrived with armed retinues at the Silsoe sessions of 1437; but their precedence dispute was eventually fought out in the peace sessions and King's Bench in 1439. The citizens of Norwich, in their quarrel with the prior, employed both sophisticated legal techniques and a military procession through the streets of the town.

How does this understanding of the profoundly interlocked roles of violence and law in fifteenth-century East Anglian society affect the historiographical debates focusing on this period? Does it, for example, help us to judge which governments and kings were most, or least successful? In a direct sense, no. Yet an analysis of the essential role of violent action in sustaining good authority allows us to understand more fully the rhetoric used by fifteenth-century writers to praise or blame their kings. Lydgate, for example, at the end of his Troy Book, characterized Henry V as 'of Normaundie þe myȝti conquerour', who 'of knighthood shall so doon his peyne' that France and England would become one nation. The result of the king's prowess in war, however, would be that age of gold when 'cruel Mars shal no more manace | With his lokis furious and wood'. Here Lydgate attributes directly to Henry V the godlike power both to wage righteous war, and to bring about, by that means, true and lasting peace.[8] Similarly, the full damning force of the *English Chronicle*'s description of Henry VI—that 'he helde no householde ne meynteyned no warres'—is lost without an appreciation of the power of violence to justify authority.[9] Understanding the role of violence in the society does enable us better

---

[7] See Ch. 6.2.

[8] *Lydgate's Troy Book*, pt. 3, 869; see also Harriss (ed.), *Henry V*, intro., 20–3, for an analysis of this passage.

[9] *English Chronicle*, 79.

to assess which kings most closely approximated to the public image of authority in their day.

Similarly, the analysis of law and violence does not allow us to judge whether bastard feudalism typically produced more or less violence than any other form of social order. It does, however, lead to a fuller understanding of the forms and rituals of violence in that society, and the sort of social order produced by them. It is clear, for instance, that gentry violence rarely appeared in the courts. Few defendants in King's Bench, and probably even fewer in gaol deliveries, were of gentry status. This may lead us to be cautious in assessing the level of violence perpetrated by fifteenth-century gentlemen. Perhaps they were in fact more prone to assume the appearance of knighthood than to practise homicide or assault. We know that comparatively peaceful and law-abiding gentry, such as Sir Miles Stapilton of Norfolk, liked to picture themselves as the heroically bloodthirsty knights of chivalric romance.[10] The actual violence in their daily lives may thus have been more fictional that factual.

Yet it would, in any case, be surprising to find gentry violence subjected to legal scrutiny since in the social and political hierarchies of the day, the gentry were of that order of people authorized—indeed compelled—to use both right violence and the law in the defence of social order. To turn the law on their own forms of violence would be to set two complementary systems of authority at loggerheads. This undoubtedly meant that some gentry crimes of violence went unpunished. The Batemans apparently did kill John Broun, but theirs was not a crime that either the courts or their neighbours were eager to punish by anything worse than outlawry. On the other hand, the career of John Belsham suggests that the gentry community was unwilling to tolerate behaviour which openly defied the norms of just violence. Belsham's alleged crimes attacked, rather than sustained, legal forms and personnel. He practised what was seen to be unjust crimes of violence for his own ends; and apparently in consequence was isolated and shunned by his own community.[11]

To say that the gentry tended to practice violence with the tacit consent of the law (which they wholeheartedly supported) does not, of course, imply that their motives were purely altruistic. The fact that violent action could endow its perpetrators with prestige and authority

---

[10] *The Works of John Metham*, 77–8; see Ch. 3.
[11] See Ch. 5.3 and 5.4.

encouraged fifteenth-century gentry to acts of bravado in support of their own status. M. E. James is undoubtedly right to point out that the constant competition for honour among the gentry bred both overt and implicit violence.[12] Yet as we have seen in the Bedford disputes, and the Clopton/Eland quarrels, honour could also be satisfied by ritual legal exchanges, and by arbitration. Violence was only one element—albeit an important one—in the system of honour.[13]

The right use of violence, however, was certainly a vital factor in establishing each person's place in the social hierarchy. In theology, for instance, it effectively divided clergy from gentry. Clerics could not legitimately practise the violence which knights were enjoined to perform. Likewise the traditional medieval distinction between those who worked and those who fought was strongly reaffirmed in the society of fifteenth-century East Anglia, not least through the law-courts. Members of the labouring classes who stole goods, or servants who attacked their masters stood a fair chance of being tried and condemned to the gallows. By ordering such criminals to be hanged, the justices of gaol delivery simultaneously affirmed the wickedness of violence practised by the lower classes against their superiors, and the power of legal violence to wipe out this aberration, restoring true natural and social order.

As well as defining the orders of society, the practice of violence made plain the distinction between genders. Women were neatly placed in the subordinate position of being unable to wield the sanctions of just violence, or to gain status from the practice of chivalry. (Not for nothing was 'manly' a standard adjective for describing the heroes of the battlefield.)[14] Nor could women judge or execute by law. They were thus debarred from participating in two of the great legitimating systems of the fifteenth century. As a corollary, their place in the moral hierarchy of violence was low; men who beat their wives, according to fifteenth-century views, merely affirmed natural and normal order, whereas wives who attacked their husbands were seen as unnatural traitors against their true lords.

Indeed, the violence–law hierarchy was clearly internalized by fifteenth-century people. It differentiated even the miracles which

---

[12] M. E. James, *English Politics and the Concept of Honour, 1485–1642* (Past and Present Society Supplement, 3; Oxford, 1978), esp. 1.

[13] See Ch. 6.2 and Ch. 5.5.

[14] See Ch. 3, n.9.

late-medieval English people claimed to receive. Finucane notes, for example, that upper-class men reported many more miraculous cures of deliberately inflicted wounds than did lower-class men, or women. Presumably their status and self-image would suffer were they to claim the cure merely of a disease.[15] If this is so, then to understand the actions of the magnates and retainers engaged in bastard feudalism, it is essential that we understand their approach to the practices of right violence.

Finally, we must ask what effect this examination of violence and social order has on the question of the causes of the Wars of the Roses. One immediate benefit of this study is that it enables us to pose questions on the subject more precisely.

It is clear from the start that we can no longer suppose that *any* form of violence may be taken as evidence of a breakdown in governing order. In the fifteenth century, violence could either sustain or undermine authority, depending on how it was exercised. It may well be true both that in the period 1422–42, East Anglians as a whole practised violence which affirmed social order, and that in the 1450s (as Storey, Griffiths, and Payling argue) the violent actions of magnates and their retainers helped to disrupt civil society and bring down the Lancastrian dynasty.[16] Certainly, the intervention of the earl of Suffolk in the affairs of Norwich, 1442–3, was anything but conciliatory. It might well be argued that this supports the case that magnate intervention in provincial affairs caused violent disturbances. But three points must be noted here. First, whatever disorder arose in Norwich in 1443 did not ultimately prejudice the king's rights. On the contrary the immediate effect was to place the city in the king's hand. Secondly, the trouble arose not because Suffolk supported armed retainers within the city, but because his attempt at arbitration in 1442 was clearly partisan and ill-conceived. Thirdly, magnate intervention in the provinces did not of itself necessarily lead to lawlessness and

---

[15] R. Finucane, *Miracles and Pilgrims* (London, 1977), 148–50. Finucane also suggests that the difference may have been produced by the fact that deliberately inflicted wounds were a sort of 'occupational hazard' of the knightly classes. I find this argument less convincing than his suggestions as to the role of honour in the construction of these accounts, since it seems to ignore the fact that many deliberate wounds were inflicted on the poorer classes, with humble farming implements, see above, pp. 19–20.

[16] Storey, *End of the House of Lancaster*; R. A. Griffiths, 'Local Rivalries and National Politics: The Percies, the Nevilles and the Duke of Exeter, 1452–1455', *Speculum*, 43 (1968), 589–632; Payling, 'The Ampthill Dispute', 881–907.

disorder. In contrast to Suffolk's award, Sir Thomas Erpingham's arbitration in Norwich in 1415 apparently produced, for some years at least, harmony and stability.[17] Similarly, the duke of Norfolk was apparently prepared to shield Belsham from the more drastic consequences of his violent acts; yet he may also have used his authority to prevent Belsham from continuing his career of crime.[18]

In short, in East Anglia in the 1420s and 1430s, the systems of violence, law, and authority were, it seems, finely balanced. The gentry communities in general maintained a sense of unity, a tacit agreement as to the ground rules of disputes, and an unwillingness to allow truly disruptive violence to occur, or to go unpunished. The studies of Griffiths and Payling would suggest that in other areas of England in the 1450s and 1460s this consensus broke down; acts of violence came to divide, not unite, the English upper classes, and to undermine, rather than support, governmental authority. This should lead us to focus more closely on these vital years, and on to the analysis of the changing roles and functions of violence and the law in English society at that time. The present study may form a basis for this further analysis; but only after it has been undertaken will we be able to assess the true role of gentry violence in bringing about the civil war.

Was East Anglia a violent society in the period 1422–42? In some senses, probably not. The actual level of illegal violence may not have been high. The knights and gentry may have been more warlike in appearance than in fact. Even legal executions, though they were a constant feature of court practice, rarely took place in great numbers. Yet in other ways, fifteenth-century East Anglian society was entrenched in, and founded on, violence. The beliefs of fifteenth-century people about violence ruled and ordered their lives. God used and suffered violence; for humans, the judicious exercise of violence not only created an image of God, but justified authority, displayed hierarchy, maintained status, transformed chaos into order, and separated humans into their appointed roles. Violence, in short, was a language of social order; and so effectively was it used that it bars our comprehension of some forms of what we would now call violence. The chastisement of women and servants, for instance, was so normal in fifteenth-century East Anglia that it was probably rarely recorded. From the historian's point of view, this means that we may never be

---

[17] See Ch. 6.1.   [18] See Ch. 5.4.

able to recover the full story of what was perhaps the commonest form of social violence.

What East Anglians in this period reprobated was not violence as such, but misrule—indiscriminate violence, outside the bounds of law, such as that exercised by women against men, or by the powerless against their rulers. The other sort of violence—God's judgement against sinners, the law's execution on criminals, the knight's campaign against the unjust, the master's discipline of his servant, or the husband's of his wife—was in fifteenth-century eyes not reprehensible chaos, but the normal upholder of secure, lawful, hierarchical, godly, order.

APPENDIX I

The Method of Analysing King's Bench Records by Computer

All my information from the plea rolls of the King's Bench was first recorded on cards, filed by surname of the plaintiff (or, for cases in the Rex section, under 'Rex'). For each case I aimed to record:

1. Name(s) of the plaintiff(s) and defendant(s) with status/occupation and place of residence where given.
2. Names of attorneys, where given.
3. Details of the charge, and date of the alleged crime.
4. Details of the origins of the case (e.g. peace sessions, by appeal, and so on).
5. County of origin.
6. Weapons alleged to have been used.
7. Stages through which the case passed while in court; including whether the defendant(s) ever appeared, and if so after what process; what pleas were entered; whether a verdict was reached and if so, what; whether the defendant was bailed or mainprized, and by whom; amounts of any fines or damages paid.

In practice, however, not many cases entered in the rolls included all this information. Relatively few reached a verdict; and the diplomatic practice of the King's Bench seems to have been to record all suits initially as cases of trespass (with no allegation of the use of force) for which the defendant was to be arrested. If, as usually happened, the sheriff failed to make an arrest, the same case would appear as a trespass *vi et armis*, and the exigents would be recorded. Only if the defendant actually appeared would further details such as the alleged date of the crime, and the weapons used, be given.

The card file proved an insufficiently sophisticated way of coping with the bulk of this material and the consequent difficulty of cross-referencing, and finding defendants who appeared in more than one case; so I decided to supplement it by putting a coded form of the data into a computer file, and extracting the necessary information using programs I had written in SPIT-BOL. This language was particularly suitable because of the facility with which it recognises and sorts names.

The data was coded into lines of 55–80 characters, divided into eighteen fields, thus:

Line	1182	A	Z	999	088	H	CB		Z		089	1	M	oo	o	M	30	S	DOE,JOHN*	ROE,JOHN
Field	1	2	3	4	5	6		7		8	9	10	11	12	13	14	15	16	17	18

The fields represented:

1. Identification number of the case.
2. County of origin (A = Norfolk, B = Suffolk, and so on)
3. How the case came to court.[1]
4. The law term in which the crime was said to have been committed, numbered from 001 (Hilary 1415) to 112 (Michaelmas 1442). Any crimes alleged to have been committed before 1415 were labelled 000; where no date of crime was given, field 4 contained 999.
5. The law term in which the case first appeared in court, numbered from 029 (Hilary 1422) to 132 (Michaelmas 1447).
6. The furthest stage in the legal process reached in the case.
7. The charges alleged (up to eight in any one case).
8. The weapons alleged (up to seven in any one case).
9. The law term in which the case last appeared in King's Bench, numbered as in field 5. Where the plea roll recorded that the case reached a conclusion after Michaelmas 1447, field 9 contained 150.
10. Whether the plaintiff appeared by attorney (1 = yes, 0 = no). This information was not used, since it appeared that the plaintiffs' attorneys, rather than the defendants', were selectively recorded.
11. The sex of the plaintiff.
12. The status/occupation of the plaintiff.
13. Whether the defendant appeared by attorney (see field 10).
14. The sex of the defendant.
15. The status/occupation of the defendant.
16. The verdict given in the case (including 'none known').
17. The plaintiff's name (or Rex, for cases in the Rex section).
18. The defendant's name.

In cases which had more than one defendant or plaintiff the line was repeated (*mutatis mutandis*, for example in fields 11–15) until all names had been recorded.

The decision to record the alleged dates of crimes by law terms requires some justification. Since the dates are given in the rolls by day, month, and year, this method is less precise than need be, and involved backdating some crimes which allegedly occurred between two law terms. On the other hand,

---

[1] Features recorded in fields 2, 3, 6, 7, 8, and 16 can be seen in Tables 2.1, 2.2, and 2.3.

it saved space, and allowed the date of the crime to be compared easily with the dates of the first and last appearance of the case in King's Bench.

In field 7, again to save space, I combined in one feature (trespass) a number of charges, such as breaking and entering, depasturing, and illegally ploughing someone else's land, or felling woodland. None of these necessarily involve the use of violence, whatever the charges may say, and all suggest damage to property. They are thus distinct both from violence, threatened or actual, against the person, and from the actual theft of goods.

Six programs were written to run on the material, of which one, DATA-PROG, acted as a master program to pick out of the main file (KB27) material for other programs to work on. DATAPROG examined a particular field in each line of the file KB27 to determine whether it contained certain characters. If it did, the whole line was put into a second, smaller, file. The field examined and the characters searched for could be altered every time the program was run. For instance, the computer could be ordered to check field 17 in each line for 'Rex', and to output all 'Rex' lines, thus producing a file containing only cases from the Rex side of King's Bench. Or it could be ordered to find those lines where 12 appeared in field 15, thus producing a file of cases where clerics were the defendants; and so on. By extension, this program could be used to produce cross-referenced files; to pick out, say, all the alleged murders that came from Bedford.

CASEPROG could be run on the main file or on any file produced by DATAPROG. It identified each new case (however many lines it might occupy) by its number, and classified and counted the features of fields 2, 3, 6, 16, 7, and 8. The results from the run on KB27 can be seen in Tables 2.1, 2.2, and 2.3. Run on smaller files produced by DATAPROG, this program produced cross-referencing information, such as how many cases originating in the peace sessions came from Norfolk, or in how many cases where the defendant was of gentry status was a verdict reached. The drawback was that it dealt with only the first line in any case; variants in fields 6 to 8 and 11 to 16 in succeeding lines would not be recorded, though they would, of course, appear in any file where DATAPROG had been made to pick them out. Thus there may be slight discrepancies between the numbers of some features appearing on different sets of results.

TIMEPROG identified each case; picked out fields 4, 5, and 9; subtracted 5 from 9 (giving the number of terms the case stayed in court); 4 from 5 (the number of terms between an alleged crime and the court appearance), and 4 from 9 (to give the total number of terms between the alleged crime and last court appearance). The results of these calculations, condensed into table form, can be seen in Table 2.4. Where field 4 contained 999, no calculation was carried out, which accounts for the smaller number of cases in the second and third columns. TIMEPROG too could be run on any file produced by DATAPROG. However, this process contained some inaccuracies inseparable from the information and the method of recording it. Where cases first appeared in the rolls as simple trespass, with no mention of force and arms, I would have no reason to note them down; which means that the time between any case's first and last court appearance may be artifically shortened, and the time between the alleged date of the crime and the case's first appearance may be lengthened. This error is partly compounded by my backdating of crimes which occurred in between two law terms.

ADDPROG identified the different names in fields 17 and 18 in all lines of each case, and classified and counted their recorded status/occupation. Its output file for the run on KB27 can be seen in Table 2.5. ADDPROG was also run on files produced by DATAPROG; but where DATAPROG was selecting for (say) a particular name or status, it would in many instances pick out only one line of a case consisting of several, and the results of ADDPROG would therefore not include all the people involved in the cases on the file.

PERSPROG and NAMEPROG were run only on KB27. PERSPROG identified the different names in each case; counted the number of times any one name (that is, surname with Christian name) occurred in the file, and printed, as its output, a list of names which occurred twice or more, together with the numbers of the cases in which they occurred, and (where they were defendants) the names of the plaintiffs. This was intended to pick out multiple users of, and recurring defendants in, King's Bench. There were, however, two drawbacks to the program. One was that the computer had no way of distinguishing between two people of the same name. Sorting through the output file and correlating information from the file cards, such as places of residence, still left room for doubt. In many cases, the status/occupation of the plaintiff was not given, so plaintiffs were harder to identify than defendants. It may be, too, that the recording of status/occupation was not consistent, or that two places of residence for one name merely indicates that the person had moved. Also, the fifteenth-century habit of naming sons after their father may have resulted in many pairs of people who had the same name, lived in the same town, and (possibly) followed the same trade. Unless one of them was identified as 'senior' or 'junior', this may lead to a conflation of identities. In short, the data has embedded tendencies to distort the numbers both upwards and downwards; and in view of this, I am reluctant to speak of any exact number of people appearing in King's Bench at this period.

Secondly, PERSPROG did not count together variant spellings of the same name (indeed, with some fifteenth-century names, it is not always easy to tell what is a variant and what is a distinct name). I have tried in my own notetaking to use one fifteenth-century spelling of a name consistently (thus 'Caundyssh' rather than 'Caundissh' or 'Cavendyssh'; 'Tuddenham' rather than 'Tudenham' or 'Todenham'); but this is no very reliable defence against a multitude of variant names in a collection of otherwise indistinguishable people.

I therefore ran NAMEPROG on the KB27 file. This program picked out fields 17 and 18, split them into their component surnames and Christian names, and listed all the separate names in alphabetical order, with a count of how many times they appeared. It is thus possible to go through the list and pick out names so similar in fifteenth-century spelling or pronunciation that they seem likely to be variants of one name; and then pick possible variants out of KB27 using DATAPROG.

Clearly, in some respects putting the material onto computer involved impoverishing and simplifying the information to hand. The computer files do not show all the stages through which a case passed, nor what pleas were entered, nor what mainpernors appeared; and they compound various dates and charges. But the gain in efficiency in compiling figures and sorting information seems to me to compensate amply for the shortcomings of the system.

APPENDIX II

Brief Biographies of Prominent Participants in the Norwich and Bedford 'Riots'

1. *Norwich*

Key to symbols:

A Named as certifier or victim of attack in the certification of 17 May 1437.
B Named as rioter in the certification of 17 May 1437.
C Indicted as rioter in 1443 (KB 27 728 Rmm 24–25).

Note: Sources appear in brackets after each biography.

WILLIAM ASSHEWELL, MERCHANT, MANCROFT WARD, BC

Sheriff of Norwich 1431 in mayoralty of Thomas Ingham, burgess in parliament five times 1433–55, mayor 1441 and 1448. April 1437 mainprized Robert Suker in security of peace towards John Heydon. June 1437 appeared before privy council. July 1443 granted pardon for his part in the riots. Member of St George's guild, 1452: will proved 10 March 1457, including bequests of over £26 in ready money.

(B. Cozens-Hardy and E. A. Kent, *The Mayors of Norwich, 1403–1835* (Norwich, 1938), hereinafter referred to as *Norwich Mayors*; KB 27 711 Rm 17ᵈ, *POPC* v. 33; KB 27 729 Rm 28ᵈ; N & NRO wills, Brosyard, fos. 78–9, M. Grace (ed.), *Records of the Gild of St George in Norwich 1389–1547* (Norfolk Record Society, 9; 1937), 39.)

PETER BRASIER, CONESFORD AND MANCROFT WARDS, A

Attended city assembly of 5 February 1414; sheriff 1424 in mayoralty of Robert Baxter, died before 1457 (widow's will made).

(W. Hudson and J. C. Tingey (eds.), *The Records of the City of Norwich* (2 vols; Norwich, 1906 and 1910), i. 112 and 273 (hereinafter referred to as *Norwich Records*); N & NRO wills, Brosyard, fos. 58–9.)

RICHARD BRASIER, GOLDSMITH, CONESFORD AND MANCROFT WARDS, A

Justice of the peace for Norwich 1421, sheriff 1436 in mayoralty of Robert Chapeleyn, mayor 1456 and 1463. Said to have been instrumental in reinstating Wetherby's associate, John Hauke, 1436. Chancery petition against him sometime 1407–57 over misuse of position as feoffee. Will dated 31 August 1475, proved 2 July 1482.

(*Norwich Records*, ii. 276; *Norwich Mayors*; N & NRO case 9, shelf c; C 1 17/22; N & NRO wills, A. Caston, fos. 122–3.)

EDMUND BRETAYN/FULLER, DRAPER, WYMER WARD, BC

Elected 1421 to oversee repair of walls in Wymer, 1428 constable for Wymer, 1435 sheriff in mayoralty of Robert Toppes. Chosen 1426 to treat with prior over Cringleford inquisition. April 1437 mainpernor for Robert Suker in security of peace towards John Heydon. Will proved 6 March 1446.

(N & NRO case 8, shelf d and case 17, shelf b, Book of Pleas, fo. xlii^d; KB 27 711 Rm 17^d; N & NRO wills, Wylbey, 136.)

JOHN CAUMBRIGGE, MERCER, WYMER WARD, BC

Common councillor 1414 for Wymer, sheriff 1418 in mayoralty of William Appleyard, mayor 1430 and 1437 (won disputed election, was deposed, and reinstated). June 1437 appeared before privy council. Will proved 1442. Made loan to the king, 1430, with Thomas Ingham and Richard Monesle, of £172. 16s.

(*Norwich Records*, i. 273 and 276; *Norwich Mayors*, 22; N & NRO case 16, shelf a, Court book, fo. 3^r; *CPR, 1429–36*, 61; *POPC* v. 33; N & NRO wills, Doke, fos. 192–5.)

ROBERT CHAPELEYN, MERCER, WARD-OVER-THE-WATER, A

Attended city assembly 5 February 1414; sheriff 1423 in mayoralty of Walter Daniel, burgess in parliament 1430, mayor 1436, collector of the fifteenth 1430. On jury in Heydon/Toppes case.

(*Norwich Records*, i. 274; *Norwich Mayors*; N & NRO case 16, shelf d, fo. 3 and case 7, shelf i; KB 27 715 m 62^r.)

JOHN FOLCARD, SPICER, CONESFORD WARD, BC

First mentioned in assembly rolls October 1420; 1423 constable for Conesford, 1436 claverer of the city, alderman by 1440. Will proved 15 March 1464, leaving bequests of over £6 in ready money.

(N & NRO case 8, shelf d and case 16, shelf d; *Norwich Records*, i. 279; N & NRO wills, Brosyard, fos. 350–1.)

WALTER GEFFEREY, SCRIVENER/CHOPCHURCH/CLERK/
GENTLEMAN, CONESFORD WARD, C

Expelled from St George's guild 1436, but appears to have been a member 1452–70. Named as security for Toppes's fine in the Heydon/Toppes case. Will proved 1476.

(Grace (ed.), *Records of the Gild of St George*, 39 and 46–65; KB 27 720 fines m r; N & NRO wills, Gelour, fos. 128–9.)

JOHN GODDES, GOLDSMITH, WYMER WARD, BC

Auditor of the city, 1436. Witnessed quitclaim to Thomas Wetherby and others, 1428.

(N & NRO case 16, shelf d; *CCLR, 1429–35*, 63.)

JOHN GERARD, BUTCHER, WYMER WARD, BC

Sheriff 1422 in mayoralty of John Mannyng; burgess in parliament six times 1423–46, mayor 1434, said to have been commons' choice for mayor in 1433. Appointed to treat with Carrow priory, 1436. Appeared before privy council June 1437.

(*Norwich Mayors*; N & NRO case 9, shelf c and case 16, shelf d, fo. 4^d; *POPC* v. 33.)

WILLIAM GREY, MERCER, WARD-OVER-THE-WATER, A

Attended assembly of 5 February 1414, sheriff 1424 in mayoralty of Robert Baxter, unsuccessful mayoral candidate in 1433, supported by Wetherby. Collector of fifteenth 1430, assessed as owning land worth £5 p.a. in Ward-over-the-Water in 1431. July 1437 ordered to leave Norwich by the privy council. Will proved 1449.

(*Norwich Records*, i. 174 and 112; N & NRO case 9, shelf d and case 7, shelf i; also case 16, shelf d, fo. 2^r and case 17, shelf b, Liber Albus, fo. 179^d; *POPC* v. 45; N & NRO wills, Aleyn, fos. 26–7.)

JOHN HAUKE, CONESFORD

First appears in assembly rolls 1421. Acts as prior's attorney in assize of freshforce in guild-hall in 1429, common clerk 1431. Active in treaties with prior over Cringleford dispute in 1426–9. Removed from offices 1433. Petition in the period 1432–43 against him and John Belhaugh over misuse of feoffee's position.

(N & NRO case 8, shelf d, case 17, shelf b, Book of Pleas, fo. lxxx^d, case 7, shelf d, case 9, shelf c; C 1 10/144.)

WILLIAM HEMPSTEDE, MERCER, WYMER WARD, BC

Sheriff 1433 in mayoralty of Richard Purdaunce, mayor 1442 and 1447. Burgess in parliament 1449. June 1437 appeared before privy council. Defendant with Robert Toppes in suit by Heydon. Will dated 1474-5.

(*Norwich Mayors*; *POPC* v. 33; KB 27 715 m 62[r] and 720 fines m 1[r].)

JOHN HOGEKYNS, WYMER WARD, AC

Sheriff 1423 in mayoralty of Walter Daniel, mentioned as alderman 1424.

(*Norwich Records*, i. 112.)

THOMAS INGHAM, MERCER, WYMER WARD, A

Freeman of the city 1401-2, treasurer 1417-18, sheriff 1420 in mayoralty of Richard Purdaunce, burgess in parliament 1427-9 and 1444, mayor 1425 and 1431. Feoffee of Thomas Tuddenham. Sold land to the prior of Norwich, 1440. Said to own land in Wymer worth £6 p.a. in 1431, and with John Caumbrigge and Richard Monesle loaned £172. 16s. to the king in 1430. Last known alive October 1457.

(*Norwich Mayors*; *CCLR, 1441-7*, 22; KB 27 728 Rm 28[r]; N & NRO case 17, shelf b, Liber Albus, fo. 179[d], *CPR, 1429-36*, 61; Grace (ed.), *Records of the Gild of St George*, 54.)

BENEDICT JOLY, CHANDLER, MANCROFT WARD, BC

First appears in assembly rolls 1420; 1436 petitioned against the reinstatement of John Hauke *et al.* Member of jury presenting against servants of the prior in the guild-hall, 1441. Member of St George's guild at least 1429-58.

(N & NRO case 8, shelf d, case 9, shelf c, case 8, shelf a and case 8, shelf e; Grace (ed.), *Records of the Gild of St George*, 56.)

RICHARD MONESLE, MERCER, WYMER WARD, A

Sheriff 1415 in mayoralty of John Mannyng; burgess in parliament five times 1422-33, mayor 1428. With John Caumbrigge and Thomas Ingham, lent £172. 16s. to the king in 1430. Petitioned against William Asshewell in the period 1405-24 over case of debt. Supported claims of John Hauke in 1437.

(*Norwich Mayors*; *CPR, 1429-36*, 61; C 1 5/189; N & NRO case 9, shelf c.)

RICHARD PURDAUNCE, MERCER

Bailiff 1403, sheriff 1405, burgess in parliament 1414, mayor 1420 and 1433 (winning disputed election). Died 25 April 1436.

(*Norwich Mayors*; N & NRO case 9, shelf c.)

GEOFFREY QUYNCY, WARD-OVER-THE-WATER, A

Constable 1423, member of St George's guild at least 1436–52. Petitioned against the sheriffs, 1433, for unlawful imprisonment. Mainpernor, 1437, for Thomas Wetherby in bond of peace towards Henry Kyng. Will proved 30 June 1461, with bequests of over £1 in ready money.

(*Norwich Records*, i. 279; Grace (ed.), *Records of the Gild of St George*, 39 and 46; C 1 75/71; KB 27 726 Rm 35ʳ; N & NRO wills, Brosyard, fo. 240.)

ROBERT SUKER, SOUTER, C

April 1437, made security of peace towards John Heydon (mainpernors, William Asshewell and Edmund Bretayn). Said to have escorted Gladman in procession in 1443. Died between 1465 (when mentioned in Chancery petition) and 1483 (date of widow's will).

(KB 27 711 Rm 17ᵈ; C 1 37/41; N & NRO wills, A. Caston, fo. 181.)

ROBERT TOPPES, MERCER, MANCROFT WARD, BC

Freeman of the city 1422, sheriff 1430 in mayoralty of John Caumbrigge, burgess in parliament 1436, 1444, and 1448, mayor 1435, 1440, 1452, 1458. June 1437, appeared before privy council, July 1437 exiled to Bristol, 1438–40 sued by John Heydon for assault. July 1443 granted pardon for his part in the riots. Alderman of the St George's guild, 1452–3. Will proved 1467.

(N & NRO case 8, shelf d; *Norwich Mayors*; *POPC* v. 33 and 45; KB 27 715 m 62ʳ and 720 fines m r; Grace (ed.), *Records of the Gild of St George*, 47; N & NRO wills, Jekkys, fos. 97–9.)

THOMAS WETHERBY, MERCER, CONESFORD WARD, A

First known adult 1413, sheriff 1425 in mayoralty of Thomas Ingham, burgess in parliament 1429 and 1431, mayor 1427 and 1432. April 1437 ordered to appear before privy council; July 1437 exiled from Norwich. April 1437 gave security of peace towards Henry Kyng, mainpernors include Geoffrey Quyncy. Prominent in treating with the priory 1426–9. Will proved 1445.

(W. J. Blake, 'Thomas Wetherby', *Norfolk Archaeology*, 32 (1961), 60–72; *Norwich Mayors*; *POPC* v. 15 and 45; KB 27 726 Rm 35ʳ; N & NRO case 7, shelf d.)

2. *Bedford*

Key to symbols:

A Named on Grey's side in 1437.
B Named on Grey's side in 1439.

C Named on Cornewaill's side in 1437.
D Named on Cornewaill's side in 1439.

JOHN BROUGHTON OF TODDINGTON, A

Born probably 1407, sheriff of Bedford and Buckingham 1435 and 1459, justice of the peace 1439 to 1479. John Enderby conveyed a mill of Stratton manor, Biggleswade, to him, 1436. Said to be one of Grey's council, 1437. Will proved 14 August 1489.

(M. McGregor (ed.), *Bedfordshire Wills proved in the Prerogative Court of Canterbury, 1383–1548* (Publications of the Bedfordshire Historical Record Society, 58; 1979), 29–34; *VCH Bedfordshire*, ii. 212; *POPC* v. 37.)

JOHN ENDERBY OF STRATTON IN BIGGLESWADE, GENTLEMAN, AB

First known adult 1405, member of parliament 1414, 1419, 1422, 1423–4, 1426, 1427–8, 1429–30, 1431, 1435, 1442, 1445–6. Attestor on indentures of return at almost every Bedfordshire election 1417–32, justice of the peace 1424–37, loans commissioner 1430 and 1431. Acting as counsel to Grey by 12 March 1413. Acted as Grey's attorney in transactions with St Albans, 1431–33. Received recognizance from Henry Percy of Northumberland to Edmund Grey of Ruthyn February 1441. Grant for repayment of £20 loan to the king, 1435.

(*CCLR, 1402–5*, 522; J. S. Roskell, *The Commons in the Parliament of 1422* (Manchester, 1954), 126–7; *CPR, 1429–36*, 51, 125, and 467; *CCLR, 1409–13*, 434, *1435–41*, 466–7.)

HENRY ETWELL OF PUTNOE, GENTLEMAN, B

First known adult 1431. May 1437, received quitclaim of Yorkshire lands from Thomas Hasilden. Named on two Bedfordshire peace commissions in 1437. Alive after 1461.

(*CCLR, 1429–35*, 132 and *1435–41*, 120; C 1 27/312.)

JOHN FITZ OF WESTHAY, GENTLEMAN, AB

Appears as mainpernor and witness, June 1425 (with Thomas Kempston) and 1429 (with John Enderby). Commissioned to determine who should pay parliamentary grant, 1431. Justice of the peace 1435–7, last known alive in October 1447, witnessing charter to John Wenlok.

(*CCLR, 1422–9*, 207 and 465; *CPR, 1429–36*, 137; *CCLR, 1447–54*, 20.)

JAMES FYNAUNCE OF HUSBORNE CRAWLEY, YEOMAN, D

Married Agnes, daughter of Nicholas Ravenhull of Stagsden (also indicted with Cornewaill in 1439). Cornewaill's will gave him 20 marks and custody of his bastard son Thomas. Adult 1434, when indicted of homicide, and acquitted. Died before July 1458 (mention of his widow).

(H. Jenkinson and G. H. Fowler (eds.), 'Some Bedfordshire Wills at Lambeth and Lincoln', *Publications of the Bedfordshire Historical Record Society*, 14 (1931), 108–9; *VCH Bedfordshire*, iii. 97; JUST 3 220/1, m (15) S4; *CCLR, 1454–61*, 291.)

JOHN GREY OF RUTHYN, KNIGHT

Son and heir apparent of Reginald Grey until his death in 1440. Married Constance Holland, sister of the earl of Huntingdon, before 1413, held land in Norfolk of the duke of Bedford. Fought at Agincourt, deputy of Ireland 1427–8, peace commissioner for Bedford 1437–40.

(*DNB* entry for Reginald Grey; *IPM* iv. 172; *CCLR, 1409–13*, 434.)

THOMAS KEMPSTON OF BEDFORD, ESQUIRE, D

Lawyer, first known adult 1421, mayor of Bedford 1427, 1440, 1446, 1447, 1448, and 1457, member of parliament 1421, 1422, 1429, 1431, 1432, 1433, 1435, 1437, 1442, 1450. Mainpernor, 1425, for Thomas Pekke with John Fitz and others, feoffee 1440 of Thomas Rufford with John Enderby and others. Will proved 19 March 1458.

(McGregor (ed.), *Bedfordshire Wills*, 18–19; *CCLR, 1422–9*, 207 and *1435–41*, 319.)

WILLIAM LUDDESOP OF ODELL, ESQUIRE, CD

Adult 1415; at Agincourt with Thomas Wenlok. Member of parliament 1427, justice of peace 1435–55, loans commissioner 1436. Involved in Cornewaill's transactions for the release of the earl of Huntingdon, 1426, and feoffee of Cornewaill 1439. Mainpernor of Thomas Kempston, 1428.

(J. Godber, *History of Bedfordshire 1066–1888* (Bedfordshire County Council; Bedford, 1969), 138; *CPR, 1429–36*, 529 and *1436–41*, 286; A. H. Thomas (ed.), *Calendar of Plea and Memoranda Rolls preserved among the Archives of the Corporation of the City of London at the Guildhall, A.D. 1323–1482* (6 vols.; Cambridge, 1926–61), iv. 183–4; KB 27 668 Rm 19ʳ.)

WILLIAM PEKKE OF COPLE, CD

Adult 1434, when required to take oath against maintaining peace-breakers. Said to have counselled Cornewaill in 1437 to hold sessions at Silsoe. Member of parliament 1439–40, and 1449, justice of the peace 1437–76, witnessed the Beauchamp/Cornewaill quitclaim, 1441.

(*CPR, 1429–36*, 374; *POPC* v. 36; *CCLR, 1435–1441*, 431–2.)

THOMAS WAUTON OF EATON SOCON, KNIGHT, AB

Member of parliament, Huntingdon, 1397–1401, 1407, 1414, 1420, 1427, and for Bedford 1413, 1414, 1419, 1425 (speaker), and 1432. Sheriff of Bedford and Buckingham 1415–16, 1422–3, 1428–9, 1432–3. Justice of the peace, Bedford, 1422–43, and other commissions, e.g. loans commission 1434, 1436, and 1440. Feoffee of Sir John Tiptoft.

(Roskell, *Commons 1422*, 233–5; *CPR, 1429–36*, 354 and 529, and *1436–41*, 505.)

APPENDIX III

Days Worked by East Anglian Peace Commissioners

TABLE A3.1. *Days worked by Norfolk commissioners*

Names	1422–6	1427–31	1432–6	1437–42	Total
John Clyfton			—/1/—/	2/1/—/	3
John Cottesmore		1/—/—/	1/—/—/		2
Thomas Derham*	4/—/21/	12/15[a]/18[b]/	—/—/2/		41
Thomas Erpingham		1/—/—/			1
Simon Felbrigge				1/—/—/	1
John Fray		2/—/—/		1/—/—/	3
William Goderede*		4/6/—/	8/8/6/	11/13/—/	27
Henry Inglose		1/—/4/			4
William Paston*	2/—/21/	15/21/18/	9/10/8/	20/14/—/	72
Thomas Tuddenham*			2/8/—/	10/12/—/	20
William Westbury		1/—/—/			1
John Wodehous		1/—/—/			1
William Yelverton*		3/5/—/	7/6/5/	16/11/—/	28

Total: 13 out of a possible fifty commissioners

Note: Where accounts of payments of justices of the peace survive in Pipe Rolls or sheriff's records, I have collated them with the data from the King's Bench and goal delivery records. None of these sources is complete, which I hope accounts for the great discrepancies between the three sets of figures. Because of this, I have used whichever set of figures is the highest when computing the total of days worked for any one commissioner. The resulting totals are still almost certainly too low; not only is it likely that there were sessions of which all record is lost, but it is possible that in any five-year period, the sheriff's accounts complement rather than duplicate the court records. However, they are the best figures available, and are useful in comparing the careers of individual gentry justices, since there is little reason to suppose that any individuals were selectively represented in the records. Justices who sat frequently are marked with an asterisk. The three sets of figures for each justice for each five-year period are set out thus: (days worked from court records) (days worked from sheriff's accounts) (days worked from Pipe Rolls).

So Thomas Derham, 1427–31, sat on 12 days according to the court records; on 15 days according to sheriff's accounts; and on 18 days according to the Pipe Rolls accounts.

[a] Figures from sheriff's accounts (E 101 572/32).
[b] Figures from Pipe Rolls accounts (E 372 270, 271, 272, 273, 275, and 279).

TABLE A3.2. *Days worked by Suffolk commissioners*

Names	1422–6	1427–31	1432–6	1437–42	Total
William Babyngton	1/—/—/	2/—/—/			3
Thomas Bernard				—/4/—/	4
Andrew Botiller*	4/—/4/	12/11ᵃ/20ᵇ/			24
Robert Caundyssh*	16/—/36/	35/20/33/	11/4/—/	11/12/4/	94
John Cottesmore	1/—/—/		4/—/—/	2/—/—/	7
Robert Crane*			9/8/—/	45/25/8/	54
Gilbert Debenham				2/1/—/	2
Duke of Exeter	1/—/—/				1
John Fray			4/—/—/	2/—/—/	6
Thomas Fulthorpe*			4/3/—/	7/—/3/	11
William Goderede	4/—/1/	1/—/—/			5
John Harleston				4/2/—/	4
Thomas Higham				5/3/—/	5
J. Heveningham I*	2/—/11/				11
J. Heveningham II				4/5/—/	5
John Howard	2/3/2/	—/—/4/			7
John Lancastre	2/—/3/				3
John Mannyng*	9/—/15/				15
Duke of Norfolk				1/—/—/	1
William Phelipp	1/—/3/	1/—/—/			4
Reginald Rous*				14/9/—/	14
Miles Stapilton				2/4/—/	4
William Wolf*	2/—/19/	14/8/19/	9/2/—/	13/10/2/	60
Robert Wingfield			2/—/—/		2

Total: 24 out of a possible 49 commissioners

ᵃ Figures from sheriff's accounts (E 101 575/33).
ᵇ Figures from Pipe Rolls accounts (E 372 270, 272, 274, 277, and 283).

TABLE A3.3. *Days worked by Cambridge commissioners*

Names	1422–6	1427–31	1432–6	1437–42	Total
W. Alyngton I*	2/10ᵃ/	2/12/			22
W. Alyngton II				2/—/	2
John Ansty			3/12/	6/—/	18
William Asenhull*	1/8/	5/12/			20
John Burgoyne*	7/25/	14/30/	5/14/		69
Thomas Burgoyne				2/—/	2
Laurence Cheyne*	1/18/	6/19/	1/4/	9/—/	50
William Cotton				4/—/	4
Walter de la Pole	—/6/	3/4/			10
Richard Forster			2/4/	8/—/	12
William Fulburne*	7/26/	14/30/	6/20/		76
John Fray		1/—/			1
William Goderede	7/18/				18
Gilbert Haltoft				4/—/	4
Nicholas Hywyssh	1/—/				1
John Prysot				8/—/	8
John Tiptoft	1/2/	1/—/			3

Total: 17 out of a possible 34 commissioners

ᵃ Figures from Pipe Rolls accounts (E 372 270, 271, 273, 275, 276, 278, and 281).

TABLE A3.4. *Days worked by Huntingdon commissioners*

Names	1422–6	1427–31	1432–6	1437–42	Total
William Babyngton	—/1/				1
John Bekeswell		4/6ª/	1/—/		7
Thomas Bevyle*	1/22/	6/14/	6/2/		42
Everard Dygby				4/—/	4
John Eyr				10/—/	10
Henry Hethe*	7/19/	10/15/	16/2/		50
Roger Hunte*	7/21/	9/6/	3/—/	1/—/	34
Roger Louthe*	6/16/	6/9/	5/—/		30
Robert Stonham				6/—/	6
Nicholas Styuecle*	—/12/	7/10/	6/2/	6/—/	34
Walter Taillard*		1/—/	5/2/	10/—/	16
William Wauton				3/—/	3
Thomas Wesenham				4/—/	4

Total: 13 out of a possible 30 commissioners

ª Figures from Pipe Rolls accounts (E 372 272, 275, 276, and 281).

TABLE A3.5. *Days worked by Bedford commissioners*

Names	1422–6	1427–31	1432–6	1437–42	Total
William Beauchamp				7/—/—/	7
William Boson	3/—/—/				3
Giles Brigge				2/2/—/	2
John Broughton				8/9/—/	9
Henry Brounflete				2/—/—/	2
Thomas Brounflete	1/—/—/	8/—/—/			9
John Cokayn	2/—/—/	3/—/—/			5
Richard Colfox	1/—/—/				1
John Cornewaill*	2/—/—/	13/—/—/	5/—/—/	8/—/—/	28
John Cottesmore				1/—/—/	1
John Enderby*	2/—/—/	16/15/—/	4/12^a/12^b/	4/6/—/	36
Henry Etwell				4/6/—/	6
John Fitz*			1/7/7/	4/16/—/	23
John Fortescu				1/—/—/	1
John Fray				3/—/—/	3
Henry Godfrey				5/10/—/	10
John Goldyngton^c	1/—/—/				1
Edmund Grey				4/—/—/	4
John Grey				4/—/—/	4
Reginald Grey*	2/—/—/	13/—/—/	4/—/—/	7/—/—/	26
Hugh Hasilden*	5/—/—/	15/19/—/	6/—/—/		30
Walter Hungerford	1/—/—/				1
Roger Hunte				4/5/—/	5
Earl of Huntingdon		8/—/—/		4/—/—/	12
John Launcelyn	3/—/—/				3
Bishop of Lincoln				1/—/—/	1
William Luddesop*		1/1/—/	7/10/10/	10/23/—/	34
T. Manningham*	2/—/—/	14/7/—/	4/14/14	9/8/—/	39
Duke of Norfolk		8/—/—/			8
William Pekke				8/7/—/	8
Earl of Suffolk				1/—/—/	1
Thomas Wauton*	1/—/—/		5/11/11	5/—/—/	17

Total: 32 out of a possible 33 commissioners

^{a} Figures from sheriff's accounts (E 101 550/42).
^{b} Figures from Pipe Roll accounts (E 372 282).
^{c} Not named on any known peace commission in Bedford.

TABLE A3.6. *Days worked by Buckingham commissioners*

Names	1422–6	1427–31	1432–6	1437–42	Total
John Barton I			2/5/—/		5
John Barton II*	7/—/—/	9/4/—/	—/4/—/		20
E. Brudenell I	4/—/1/				4
E. Brudenell II				1/1/—/	1
Archbishop of Canterbury				1/—/—/	1
Sir John Cheyne	6/—/—/	3/—/—/			9
John Cheyne, esq	3/—/—/				3
William Cheyne	1/—/1/				1
John Ewardby			1/—/3/	4/2/—/	7
Richard Forde	1/—/—/				1
William Foweler				2/6/—/	6
Edmund Grey				2/—/—/	2
Reginald Grey*	3/—/—/	6/—/—/	2/—/—/	6/—/—/	17
John Gyffard	5/—/—/				5
Edmund Hampden				4/1/—/	4
John Hampden I*	2/—/—/	2/2/—/	5/10ᵃ/7ᵇ/	8/7/—/	22
John Hampden II*			3/10/10/	9/15/—/	25
Walter Hungerford	1/—/—/			1/—/—/	2
Bishop of Lincoln				1/—/—/	1
George Longevyle*			1/—/3/	11/10/—/	14
Robert Manfield				4/3/—/	4
William Massy	2/—/—/				2
William Molyns	2/—/—/				2
Robert Olney				—/2/—/	2
Thomas Rokes*			6/13/10/	9/7/—/	22
Thomas Sakevyle*			1/—/1/	9/2/—/	10
Andrew Sperlyng*		3/5/—/	7/23/14/	3/3/3/	31
Edmund Rede				1/3/—/	3
Thomas Stokes*		2/2/—/	5/8/7/	6/1/—/	16
Thomas Syngelton				8/4/—/	8
Earl of Warwick				1/—/—/	1
William Whaplode*	2/—/2/	7/2/—/	3/7/5/	9/4/—/	25
Bishop of Winchester				1/—/—/	1
Richard Wyot	3/—/—/	3/2/—/	—/1/—/		7

Total: 34 out of a possible 35 commissioners

ᵃ Figures from sheriff's accounts (E101 550/42).
ᵇ Figures from Pipe Roll accounts (E 372 270, 282, and 283).

BIBLIOGRAPHY OF MANUSCRIPTS AND WORKS CITED

1. *Manuscript Sources*

Bedford Record Office
BW 1248, 1250, and 1253 (Bury Hatley records).

British Library
Egerton Roll 8779 (accounts of the duchess of Suffolk).
Harleian Manuscripts   2900
                   1178

Norfolk and Norwich Record Office

case 7, shelf d	Rolls of account.
case 8, shelf a	Presentments in the guild-hall, 1439–41.
case 8, shelf d	Rolls of the city assembly.
case 8, shelf e	Rolls of surveyors accounts of the Guild of St George.
case 9, shelf c	Documents relating to Wetherby's disputes
case 9, shelf d	with the city, 1433–46.
case 16, shelf a	Court book.
case 16, shelf d	Book of proceedings of the municipal assembly.
case 17, shelf b	Book of pleas.
DCN 79/1–9	Holmstrete Leet and Fair Court Rolls, 1429–41.
Wills	
YC/4	Yarmouth court records.

Public Record Office

C 1	Chancery petitions.
C 44, C 241,	Chancery miscellanea.
C 244,	
C 260	
CP 40, 703	Plea rolls, Common Pleas, Michaelmas 1436.
CP 40, 712	Plea rolls, Common Pleas, Hilary 1439.
E 28, 59, 62,	Council records.
71	
E 101, 550/42,	Sheriff's accounts.
572/32,	
575/33	

E 129, 240/ 268		Taxation returns, Cambridge and Huntingdon, 1436.
E 175, File 4		Petition to the king.
E 372, nos. 270–9 and 281–3		Pipe Rolls.
JUST 1, 1533, 1535, 1539, 1541, 1543, 1545		Assize records, East Anglia, 1421–41.

	Rolls	Files	East Anglian gaol deliveries, 1422–41.[1]
JUST 3,	200	218/6	
	201	219/1	
	204	219/2	
	206	219/3	
	207	219/5	
	209	220/1	
	210	220/2	
	212	220/3	

JUST 3, 50/ 12, 50/13, 50/14	Rolls and files of Norwich gaol deliveries, 1427–30.
JUST 3, 65/6, 65/7	Rolls and files of Ipswich gaol deliveries, 1434–9.
JUST 3, 7/4, 8/10, 8/11, 8/12, 8/13, 8/14, 8/15, 8/17	Rolls and files of Cambridge gaol deliveries, 1422–41.
JUST 3, 2/8	Roll and file of Bedford gaol delivery, 1426.
KB 9	Ancient Indictments.
KB 27, nos. 643–746	Plea rolls, Hilary 1422 to Michaelmas 1447, excluding 679, which was under repair.
PCC Wills	
SC2, 171/53, 192/75, 192/79, 194	Court rolls.
SC8	Ancient Petitions.

Trinity College, Cambridge, Wren Library
BI Dc 12, 15, 16, 17, and 24 (Barrington records).

---

[1] Each roll corresponds to the file on the same line; so JUST 3,200 e.g. contains, in enrolled form, the cases dealt with in the files of JUST 3, 218/6.

2. *Published and Calendared Documents*

BATESON, M. (ed.), *Borough Customs* (2 vols.; Selden Society, 18 and 21; 1904 and 1906).

The Boke of Justices of the Peas (n.p., 1506; repr. London Professional Books Ltd.: London, 1972).

The Brut, pt. 2, ed. F. W. Brie (EETS, 136; 1908).

Calendarium Inquisitionum post mortem sive excaetarum, iii and iv (London, 1821 and 1828).

Calendar of Close Rolls (HMSO, 1892–).

Calendar of Patent Rolls (HMSO, 1904–).

The Cely Letters 1472–1488, ed. A. HANHAM (EETS, 273; 1975).

The Chronicle of John Hardyng, ed. H. Ellis (London, 1812).

Dives and Pauper, i/1 and 2, ed. P. H. Barnum (EETS, 275; 1976 and 280; 1980).

An English Chronicle of the Reigns of Richard II, Henry IV, Henry V, and Henry VI, (1377–1461), ed. J. S. Davies (Camden Society, OS 64; 1855).

Feudal Aids (6 vols.; HMSO, 1899–1920).

Four English Political Tracts of the Later Middle Ages, ed. J.-P. GENET (Camden Society, 4th series, 18; 1977).

GASCOIGNE, THOMAS, *Loci e libro veritatum*, ed. J. E. Thorold Rogers (Oxford, 1881).

GRACE, M. (ed.), *Records of the Gild of St George in Norwich 1389–1547* (Norfolk Record Society, 9; 1937).

The Great Chronicle of London, ed. A. H. Thomas and I. D. Thornley (London, 1938).

HALE, M., *Historia Placitorum Coronae* (2 vols.; London, 1736; repr. London Professional Books Ltd.: London, 1971).

The Historical Collections of a Citizen of London, ed. J. GAIRDNER (Camden Society, NS 17; 1876).

Heresy Trials in the Diocese of Norwich, 1428–31, ed. N. TANNER (Camden Society, 4th series, 20; 1977).

Historie of the Arrivall of Edward IV, ed. J. Bruce (Camden Society, OS 1; 1838).

HUDSON, W. and TINGEY, J. C. (eds.), *The Records of the City of Norwich* (2 vols; Norwich, 1906 and 1910).

JENKINSON, H. and FOWLER, G. H. (eds.), 'Some Bedfordshire Wills at Lambeth and Lincoln', *Publications of the Bedfordshire Historical Record Society*, 14 (1931), 79–131.

JOHNSON, G. (ed.), 'Extract from the Books of the Corporation of Norwich relative to . . . Gladman's Insurrection', *Norfolk and Norwich Archaeological Society*, 1 (1847), 294–9.

KEMPE, M., *The Book of Margery Kempe*, ed. S. B. Meech and H. E. Allen (EETS, 212; 1940).

KIMBALL, E. (ed.), *The Shropshire Peace Roll, 1400–1414* (Shrewsbury, 1959).

—— *Sessions of the Peace for Bedfordshire, 1355–1359 and 1363–1364* (London, 1969).

KINGSFORD, C. L. (ed.), *Chronicles of London* (Oxford, 1905).

Laud Troy Book, ed. J. E. Wulfing (EETS, 121–2; 1902).

Lay Folks' Catechism, ed. T. F. Simmons and H. E. Nolloth (EETS, 118; 1901).

LEADAM, I. S., and BALDWIN, J. F. (eds.), *Select Cases before the King's Council, 1243–1482* (Selden Society, 35; 1918).

List of Sheriffs for England and Wales from the Earliest Times to A.D. 1831, (PRO Lists and Indexes, 9; 1898).

LYDGATE, JOHN, *The Minor Poems of John Lydgate*, pt. 2, ed. H. N. Mac-Cracken (EETS, 192; 1934).

—— *Lydgate's Troy Book*, pt. 1, ed. H. Bergen (EETS, ES 97; 1906).

MCGREGOR, M. (ed.), *Bedfordshire Wills proved in the Prerogative Court of Canterbury, 1383–1548* (Publications of the Bedfordshire Historical Record Society, 58; 1979).

The Macro Plays, ed. M. ECCLES (EETS, 262; 1969).

Manners and Meals in Olden Times, ed. F. J. FURNIVAL (EETS, 32; 1868).

Medieval English Lyrics, ed. R. T. DAVIES, Faber edn. (London, 1963).

METHAM, J., *The Works of John Metham*, ed. H. Craig (EETS, 132; 1916).

MYRC, J., *Festial*, pt. 1, ed. T. Erbe (EETS, ES 96; 1905).

—— *Instructions for Parish Priests*, ed. E. Peacock (EETS, 31; 1868).

NEILSON, N. (ed.), *Year Books of Edward IV: 10 Edward IV and 49 Henry VI* (Selden Society, 47; 1930).

Paston Letters and Papers of the Fifteenth Century, ed. N. Davis (2 vols; Oxford, 1971 and 1976).

Proceedings and Ordinances of the Privy Council of England (1386–1542), ed. Sir N. H. Nicolas (7 vols.; Record Commission: London, 1834–7).

Rotuli Parliamentorum: ut et petitiones et placita in parliamento (6 vols.; n.p., 1832).

RYE, W. (ed.), *A Calendar of the Feet of Fines for Suffolk* (Suffolk Institute of Archaeology; Ipswich, 1900).

SMITH, L. T. (ed.), *A Commonplace Book of the Fifteenth Century* (London, 1886).

St. Germain's Doctor and Student, ed. T. F. PLUCKNETT and J. L. BARTON (Selden Society, 1974).

The Stonor Letters and Papers, 1290–1483, ed. C. L. Kingsford (Camden Society, 3rd series, 29 and 30; 1919).

THOMAS, A. H. (ed.), *Calendar of Plea and Memoranda Rolls preserved among the Archives of the Corporation of the City of London at the Guildhall, A.D. 1323–1482* (6 vols.; Cambridge, 1926–61).

Treatises on Precedence and Courtesy, English and Foreign, ed. F. J. Furnivall (EETS, ES 8; 1869).

The Wakefield Pageants, ed. A. C. CAWLEY (Manchester, 1958).

WHITING, B. J. *Proverbs, Sentences and Proverbial Phrases from English writings, mainly before 1500* (Cambridge, Mass., 1968).

WORCESTER, W., *Itineraries*, ed. J. H. Harvey (Oxford, 1969).

3. Published Secondary Sources

AVERY, M., 'The History of the Equitable Jurisdiction of Chancery before 1460', *BIHR* 42 (1969), 129–44.

BAKER, J. H., *An Introduction to English Legal History* (London, 1971).

—— (ed.), *Legal Records and the Historian* (London, 1978).

BASSETT, M., *Knights of the Shire for Bedfordshire during the Middle Ages*, (Publications of the Bedfordshire Historical Record Society, 29; 1949).

BELLAMY, J. G., 'The Coterel Gang: An Anatomy of a Band of Fourteenth-Century Criminals', *English Historical Review*, 79, (1964), 698–717.

—— *Criminal Law and Society in Late Medieval and Tudor England* (Gloucester, 1984).

—— *Crime and Public Order in England in the Later Middle Ages* (London, 1973).

—— *Bastard Feudalism and the Law* (London, 1989).

BENNETT, J. W., 'The Medieval Loveday', *Speculum*, 33 (1958), 351–70.

BENNETT, M., *Community, Class and Careerism* (Cambridge, 1983).

BLAKE, W. J., 'Thomas Wetherby', *Norfolk Archaeology*, 32 (1961), 60–72.

BLATCHER, M., *The Court of King's Bench, 1450–1550* (London, 1978).

BLOMEFIELD, F., *An Essay towards a Topographical History of the County of Norfolk* (11 vols.; London, 1805–10).

CARPENTER, C., 'Sir Thomas Malory and Fifteenth-Century Local Politics', *BIHR* 53 (1980), 31–43.

—— 'Law, Justice and Landowners in Late Medieval England', *Law and History Review*, 1 (1983), 205–37.

CLANCHY, M. T., 'Law, Government and Society in Medieval England', *History*, 59 (1974), 73–8.

CLARK, P., and SLACK, P. (eds.), *Crisis and Order in English Towns 1500–1700* (London, 1972).

COCKBURN, J. S., *A History of English Assizes 1558–1714* (Cambridge, 1972).

—— 'Early Modern Assize Records as Historical Evidence', *Journal of the Society of Archivists*, 5 (1975), 215–31.

—— (ed.), *Crime in England 1550–1800* (London, 1977).

COPINGER, W. A., *The Manors of Suffolk* (7 vols.; London and Manchester, 1905–11).

COZENS-HARDY, B., and KENT, E. A., *The Mayors of Norwich, 1403–1835* (Norwich, 1938).

CULLUM, Sir J., *History of Hawsted and Hardwick*, 1st edn. (London, 1784).

DAVIS, N. Z., 'The Rites of Violence: Religious Riot in Sixteenth-Century France', *Past and Present*, 59 (1973), 51–91.

DUBY, G., *The Three Orders: Feudal Society Imagined*, tr. A. Goldhammer (Chicago, 1980).

DUNHAM, W. H., *Lord Hastings' Indentured Retainers 1461–1483* (New Haven, Conn., 1955).

FLOUD, R., *An Introduction to Quantitative Methods for Historians*, 2nd edn. (London, 1979).

FOUCAULT, M., *Discipline and Punish: The Birth of the Prison*, tr. A. Sheridan (Harmondsworth, 1979).

GABEL, L. C., *Benefit of Clergy in England in the Later Middle Ages* (Northampton, Mass., 1929).

GEERTZ, C., *The Interpretation of Cultures* (London, 1975).

GEREMEK, B., *The Margins of Society in Late Medieval Paris*, tr. J. Birrell (Cambridge, 1987).

GIVEN, J. B., *Society and Homicide in Thirteenth-Century England* (Stanford, Calif., 1977).

GODBER, J., *History of Bedfordshire 1066–1888* (Bedfordshire County Council; Bedford, 1969).

GOODMAN, A., *A History of England from Edward II to James I* (London, 1977).

GREEN, T. A., 'Societal Concepts of Criminal Liability for Homicide in Medieval England', *Speculum*, 47 (1972), 669–94.

—— 'The Jury and the English Law of Homicide, 1200–1600', *Michigan Law Review*, 74 (1976), 413–99.

GRIFFITHS, R. A., 'Local Rivalries and National Policies: The Percies, the Nevilles and the Duke of Exeter, 1452–1455', *Speculum*, 43 (1968), 589–632.

—— *The Reign of King Henry VI* (London, 1981).

—— (ed.), *Patronage, the Crown and the Provinces in Later Medieval England* (Gloucester, 1981).

GUY, J. A., and BEALE, H. G. (eds.), *Law and Social Change in British History* (London, 1984).

HAINES, K., 'Attitudes and Impediments to Pacificism in Medieval Europe', *Journal of Medieval History*, 7 (1981), 369–88.

HAMIL, F. C., 'The King's Approvers: A Chapter in the History of English Criminal Law', *Speculum*, 11 (1936), 238–58.

HAMMER, C. I., 'Patterns of Homicide in a Medieval University Town: Fourteenth-Century Oxford', *Past and Present*, 78 (1978), 3–23.

HANAWALT, B. A., 'Fur Collar Crime: The Pattern of Crime among the Fourteenth-Century English Nobility', *Journal of Social History*, 8 (1974–5), 1–17.

—— 'Violent Death in Fourteenth and Early Fifteenth-Century England', *Comparative Studies in Society and History*, 18 (1976), 297–320.

—— *Crime and Conflict in English Communities, 1300–1348* (Cambridge, Mass., 1979).

HARDING, A., *The Law Courts of Medieval England* (London, 1973).

HARRE, R., and SECORD, P., *The Explanation of Social Behaviour* (Oxford, 1972).

HARRISS, G. L. (ed.), *Henry V: The Practice of Kingship* (Oxford, 1985).

HASSELL SMITH, A., *County and Court: Government and Politics in Norfolk 1558–1603* (Oxford, 1974).

HASTINGS, M., *The Court of Common Pleas in Fifteenth-century England* (New York, 1947).

HAWARD, W. I., 'Gilbert Debenham: A Medieval Rascal in Real Life', *History*, NS 13 (1929), 300–14.

HOLDSWORTH, Sir W., *A History of English Law* (16 vols.; London, 1903–66).

HOLT, J. C., *Robin Hood* (London, 1982).

HUNNISETT, R. F., 'The Medieval Coroners' Rolls', *American Journal of Legal History*, 3 (1959), 95–124, 205–21, 324–59, and 383.

—— 'Pleas of the Crown and the Coroner', *BIHR* 32 (1959), 117–37.

—— *The Medieval Coroner* (Cambridge, 1961).

—— and POST, J. B. (eds.), *Medieval Legal Records Edited in Memory of C. A. F. Meekings* (London, 1978).

HURNARD, N., *The King's Pardon for Homicide before A.D. 1307* (Oxford, 1969).

IVES, E. W., *The Common Lawyers of Pre-Reformation England; Thomas Kebell: A Case Study* (Cambridge, 1983).

—— and MANCHESTER, A. H. (eds.), *Law, Litigants and the Legal Profession* (London, 1983).

JAMES, M. E., *English Politics and the Concept of Honour, 1485–1642* (Past and Present Society Supplement, 3; Oxford, 1978).

JEFFS, R., 'The Poynings-Percy Dispute: An Example of the Interplay of Open Strife and Legal Action in the Fifteenth Century', *BIHR* 34 (1961), 148–64.

KAEUPER, R. W., 'Law and Order in Fourteenth-Century England: The Evidence of Special Commissions of Oyer and Terminer', *Speculum*, 54 (1979), 734–84.

—— *War, Justice and Public Order: England and France in the Later Middle Ages* (Oxford, 1988).

KAYE, J., 'The Early History of Murder and Manslaughter', *Law Quarterly Review*, 83 (1967), 365–95 and 569–601.

KEEN, M., *Chivalry* (New Haven, Conn., 1984).

KELLUM, B. A., 'Infanticide in England in the Later Middle Ages', *History of Childhood Quarterly*, 1 (1974), 367–88.

LADURIE, E. LE ROY, *Carnival in Romans*, tr. M. Feeney, Penguin edn. (Harmondsworth, 1981).

LE GOFF, J., *Time, Work and Culture in the Middle Ages*, tr. A. Goldhammer (Chicago, 1980).

LOBEL, M. D., *The Borough of Bury St Edmunds* (Oxford, 1935).

MCFARLANE, K. B., *The Nobility of Later Medieval England* (Oxford, 1973).

—— *England in the Fifteenth Century: Collected Essays* (London, 1981).

MCLANE, B., 'A Case Study of Violence and Litigation in the Early Fourteenth Century: The Disputes of Robert Godsfield of Sutton-Le-Marsh', *Nottingham Medieval Studies*, 28 (1984), 22–44.

MADDERN, P., 'Honour among the Pastons: Gender and Integrity in Fifteenth-Century English Provincial Society', *Journal of Medieval History*, 14 (1988), 357–71.

MAITLAND, F. W., *Selected Historical Essays of F. W. Maitland*, intro. H. Cam (Cambridge, 1957).

MARSH, P., ROSSER, E., and HARRE, R., *The Rules of Disorder* (London, 1978).

MARTINES, L. (ed.), *Violence and Civil Disorder in Italian Cities, 1200–1500* (Los Angeles, 1972).

MORGAN, P., *War and Society in Medieval Cheshire 1277–1403* (Manchester, for the Chetham Society, 1987).

ORME, N., *Education and Society in Medieval and Renaissance England* (London, 1989).

PARKER, W., *The History of Long Melford* (London, 1873).

PAYLING, S. J., 'Inheritance and Local Politics in the Later Middle Ages: The Case of Ralph, Lord Cromwell, and the Heriz Inheritance', *Nottingham Medieval Studies*, 30 (1986), 67–95.

—— 'The Ampthill Dispute: A Study in Aristocratic Lawlessness and the Breakdown of Lancastrian Government', *English Historical Review*, 104 (1989), 881–907.

PHYTHIAN-ADAMS, C., *Desolation of a City: Coventry and the Urban Crisis of the Late Middle Ages* (Cambridge, 1979).

PITT-RIVERS, J., 'Honour and Social Status', in J. G. Peristiany (ed.), *Honour and Shame: The Values of Mediterranean Society* (London, 1965).

POLLARD, A. J., *John Talbot and the War in France 1427–1453* (London, 1983).

POLLARD, T. (ed.), *Property and Politics: Essays in Later Medieval English History* (Gloucester, 1984).

POST, J. B., 'Some Limitations of Medieval Peace Rolls', *Journal of the Society of Archivists*, 4 (1973), 633–9.

—— 'Sir Thomas West and the Statue of Rapes, 1382', *BIHR* 53 (1980), 24–30.

POWELL, E., 'Arbitration and the Law in the Late Middle Ages', *Transactions of the Royal Historical Society*, 5th series, 33 (1983), 49–67.

—— 'Settlement of Disputes by Arbitration in Fifteenth-Century England', *Law and History Review*, 2 (1984), 21–43.

PUGH, R. B., 'Some Reflections of a Medieval Criminologist', *Proceedings of the British Academy*, 59 (1973), 83–103.

PUTNAM, B. H. (ed.), *Proceedings before the Justices of the Peace in the Fourteenth and Fifteenth Century* (London, 1938).

—— *Early Treatises on the Practice of the Justices of the Peace in the Fifteenth and Sixteenth Centuries* (Oxford Studies in Social and Legal History, 7; 1924).

REEVES, A. C., *Lancastrian Englishmen* (Washington, DC, 1981).

RICHMOND, C., *John Hopton, a Fifteenth-Century Suffolk Gentleman* (Cambridge, 1981).

—— 'The Expenses of Thomas Playter of Sotterley, 1459–1460', *Proceedings of the Suffolk Institute of Archaeology and History*, 35 (1981), 41–51.

ROSENTHAL, J., 'Feuds and Private Peace-Making: A Fifteenth-Century Example', *Nottingham Medieval Studies*, 14 (1970), 84–90.

—— and RICHMOND, C. (eds.), *People, Politics and Community in the Later Middle Ages* (Gloucester, 1987).

ROSKELL, J. S., *The Commons in the Parliament of 1422* (Manchester, 1954).

—— *Parliament and Politics in Late Medieval England* (2 vols.; London, 1981).

ROSS, C. (ed.), *Patronage, Pedigree and Power in Later Medieval England* (Gloucester, 1979).

RUGGIERO, G., *Violence in Early Renaissance Venice* (New Brunswick, NJ, 1980).

RUSSELL, F. H., *The Just War in the Middle Ages* (Cambridge, 1975).

SAUL, N., *Knights and Esquires: The Gloucestershire Gentry in the Fourteenth Century* (Oxford, 1981).

—— *Scenes from Provincial Life: Knightly Families in Sussex 1280–1400* (Oxford, 1986).

SHARPE, J. A., 'Domestic Homicide in Early Modern England', *Historical Journal*, 24 (1981), 29–48.

—— 'The History of Violence in England: Some Observations', *Past and Present*, 108 (1985), 206–15.

SHAW, J., 'Corporeal and Spiritual Homicide, the Sin of Wrath and the "Parson's Tale"', *Traditio*, 38 (1982), 281–300.

SILLEM, R., 'Commissions of the Peace, 1380–1485', *BIHR* 10 (1932–3), 81–104.

SKOLNICK, J. H., 'Interpreting Violence', *Journal of Interdisciplinary History*, 3:1 (1972), 177–85.

STONES, E. L. G., 'The Folvilles of Ashby-Folville, Leicestershire, and their Associates in Crime, 1326–1347', *Transactions of the Royal Historical Society*, 5th series, 7 (1957), 117–36.

STOREY, R. L., *The End of the House of Lancaster* (London, 1966).

—— 'Lincolnshire and the Wars of the Roses', *Nottingham Medieval Studies*, 14 (1970), 64–83.

TANNER, N., *The Church in Late Medieval Norwich, 1370–1532* (Toronto, 1984).

TREXLER, R., *Public Life in Renaissance Florence* (New York, 1980).

—— (ed.), *Persons in Groups* (New York, 1985).

The Victoria History of the Counties of England:
   Bedfordshire, ii and iii (1908 and 1912); *Buckinghamshire*, ii, iii, and iv (1908, 1925, 1927); *Cambridgeshire*, iv, v, vi, and viii (1953, 1973, 1978, and 1982); *Huntingdonshire*, ii and iii (1932 and 1936).
VIRGOE, R., 'The Murder of Edmund Clippesby', *Norfolk Archaeology*, 35 (1972), 302–7.
—— 'Three Suffolk Parliamentary Elections of the Mid-Fifteenth Century', *BIHR* 39 (1966), 185–96.
—— 'The Murder of James Andrew: Suffolk Faction in the 1430s', *Proceedings of the Suffolk Institute of Archaeology*, 34 (1980), 263–8.
—— 'The Cambridgeshire Election of 1439', *BIHR* 46 (1973), 95–101.
WALKER, S. S., 'Convicted Ravishers: Statutory Strictures and Actual Practice in Thirteenth and Fourteenth Century England', *Journal of Medieval History*, 13 (1987), 237–50.
WRIGHT, S., *The Derbyshire Gentry in the Fifteenth Century* (Derbyshire Record Society, 8; 1983).

4. *Unpublished Theses*

ARCHER, R., 'The Mowbrays, Earls of Nottingham and Dukes of Norfolk, to 1432', D.Phil. thesis (Oxford, 1984).
AVRUTICK, J., 'Commissions of Oyer and Terminer in Fifteenth-century England', M. Phil. thesis (London, 1967).
CARPENTER, M. C., 'Political Society in Warwickshire, *c.*1401–1472', Ph.D thesis (Cambridge, 1976).
ENDELMAN, S. J. B., 'Patronage and Power: A Social Study of the Justice of the Peace in Late Medieval Essex', Ph.D thesis (Brown University, 1977).
GOLLANCZ, M., 'The System of Gaol Delivery as Illustrated in the Extant Gaol Delivery Rolls of the Fifteenth Century', MA thesis (London, 1936).
POST, J. B., 'Criminals and the Law in the Reign of Richard II with Special Reference to Hampshire', D.Phil thesis (Oxford, 1976).
POWELL, E., 'Public Order and Law-Enforcement in Shropshire and Staffordshire in the Early Fifteenth Century', D.Phil thesis (Oxford, 1979).
SMITH, A. R., 'Aspects of the Career of Sir John Fastolf (1380–1459)', D.Phil thesis (Oxford, 1982).

Index

KING ALFRED'S COLLEGE
LIBRARY